IRELAND IN THE MEDIEVAL WORLD

Ireland in the medieval world, AD400–1000

Landscape, kingship and religion

EDEL BHREATHNACH

FOUR COURTS PRESS

Typeset in 10 pt on 13.5pt Sabon by
Carrigboy Typesetting Services for
FOUR COURTS PRESS LTD
7 Malpas Street, Dublin 8, Ireland
www.fourcourtspress.ie
and in North America for
FOUR COURTS PRESS
c/o ISBS, 920 NE 58th Avenue, Suite 300, Portland, OR 97213.

A catalogue record for this title is available
from the British Library.

ISBN 978–1–84682–341–1 hbk
ISBN 978–1–84682–342–8 pbk

SPECIAL ACKNOWLEDGMENT

This publication has been made possible by financial assistance from the
Marc Fitch Fund for Research and Publication (established by Marcus
Felix Brudenell Fitch CBE DLitt HonFBA FSA in 1956).

MARC FITCH FUND

Printed in England
by CPI Antony Rowe, Chippenham, Wilts.

Contents

Illustrations

PLATES
(between p. 178 and p. 179)

Abbreviations

AFM	*Annala Rioghachta Éireann. Annals of the Kingdom of Ireland by the Four Masters from the earliest period to the year 1616*, ed. John O'Donovan (7 vols, Dublin, 1848–51; repr. Dublin, 1990)
AI	*Annals of Inisfallen*, ed. Seán Mac Airt (Dublin, 1951)
AL	*Ancient Laws of Ireland* (6 vols, Dublin, 1826–1901)
ATig.	'The Annals of Tigernach', ed. Whitley Stokes, *Revue celtique*, 16 (1895), 374–419; 17 (1896), 6–33, 119–263, 337–420; 18 (1897), 9–59, 150–97, 267–303, 374–91 (repr. 1993, Felinfach, 2 vols)
AU	*The Annals of Ulster (to AD1131)*, ed. Seán Mac Airt and Gearóid Mac Niocaill (Dublin, 1983)
Byrne, *IKHK*	Francis John Byrne, *Irish kings and high-kings* (London, 1973; repr. 2001)
CCH	H. Wasserschleben (ed.), *Die irische kanonensammlung* (Leipzig, 1885)
CG	D.A. Binchy (ed.), *Críth Gablach* (Dublin, 1970)
CGH	M.A. O'Brien, *Corpus genealogiarum Hiberniae* (Dublin, 1962; repr. 1971)
Charles-Edwards, ECI	T.M. Charles-Edwards, *Early Christian Ireland* (Cambridge, 2000)
Charles-Edwards, EIWK	T.M. Charles-Edwards, *Early Irish and Welsh kinship* (Oxford, 1993)
CIH	D.A. Binchy, *Corpus iuris Hiberniae: ad fidem codicum manuscriptorum* (6 vols, Dublin, 1978)
CIIC	R.A.S. Macalister, *Corpus inscriptionum insularum Hiberniae* (2 vols, Dublin, 1945–9)
Confessio	St Patrick's *Confessio* Hypertext Stack Project (www.confessio.ie)
DIL	*Dictionary of the Irish language* (www.dil.ie)
FAIre.	*Fragmentary annals of Ireland*, ed. J.N. Radner (Dublin, 1978)
FFÉ	*Foras feasa ar Éirinn le Seathrún Céitinn DD: The history of Ireland by Geoffrey Keating DD*, ed. David Comyn, Patrick S. Dinneen and David Nutt (4 vols, London, 1902–14)

HE	*Bede: Ecclesiastical history of the English people, with Bede's letter to Egbert and Cuthbert's letter on the death of Bede* (trans. Leo Sherley-Price; rev. R.E. Latham; new intr. and notes D.H. Farmer (London, 1990))
Heist, *VSH*	W.W. Heist (ed.), *Vitae sanctorum Hiberniae ex codice olim Salmanticensi nunc Bruxellensi* (Brussels, 1965)
JIA	*Journal of Irish Archaeology*
JRSAI	*Journal of the Royal Society of Antiquaries of Ireland*
Kelly, *EIF*	Fergus Kelly, *Early Irish farming* (Dublin, 1997)
Kelly, *GEIL*	Fergus Kelly, *A guide to early Irish law* (Dublin, 1988)
Kenney, *Sources*	J.F. Kenney, *The sources for the early history of Ireland: ecclesiastical. An introduction and guide* (New York, 1929; repr. Dublin, 1995)
Ní Bhrolcháin, *EIL*	Muireann Ní Bhrolcháin, *An introduction to early Irish literature* (Dublin, 2009)
NIEA	Northern Ireland Environment Agency
Ó Riain, *CGSH*	Pádraig Ó Riain, *Corpus genealogiarum sanctorum Hiberniae* (Dublin, 1985)
Ó Riain, *DIS*	Pádraig Ó Riain, *Dictionary of Irish saints* (Dublin, 2011)
PHCC	*Proceedings of the Harvard Celtic Colloquium*
Plummer, *Bethada*	Charles Plummer (ed. and trans.), *Bethada náem nÉrenn: Lives of Irish saints* (2 vols, Oxford, 1922)
Plummer, *VSH*	Charles Plummer (ed.), *Vitae sanctorum Hiberniae* (2 vols, Oxford, 1922)
PMLA	*Proceedings of the Modern Language Association of America*
PRIA	*Proceedings of the Royal Irish Academy*
PSAS	*Proceedings of the Society of Antiquaries of Scotland*
SMR	Sites and Monuments Record, National Monuments Service, Ireland
UJA	*Ulster Journal of Archaeology*
VPrima	Sean Connolly, '*Vita Prima Sanctae Brigitae*: background and historical value', *JRSAI*, 119 (1989), 5–49
VSC	A.O. Anderson and M.O. Anderson (eds and trans.), *Adomnan's Life of Columba* (London, 1961; rev. ed. Oxford, 1991)

Acknowledgments

This book marks the completion of a journey that began when my mother introduced me to Canon John O'Hanlon's monumental Lives of the Irish Saints, which, to the amusement of my siblings, I often leafed through on wet winter evenings. To my parents, Meabh and Fionnbharra Breathnach, and those same siblings, Áine, Colm and Bríd, I owe a debt of gratitude for their enthusiasm and forebearance.

My knowledge of early Irish history resulted from the profound scholarship of my teachers, Charles Doherty, Professors Francis John Byrne, Marie Therese Flanagan and Thomas Charles-Edwards. They taught me how to read and interpret the sources and to grasp the complexity of early Irish society in all its facets. I have worked closely with Dr Elizabeth O'Brien on the Heritage Council INSTAR-funded 'Mapping Death' project and have benefitted hugely from our collaboration. This book took a very different route as I encountered the remains of real people and began to consider the reality of their lives from the burial record as well as from the written sources. I also owe much to Conor Newman, Joe Fenwick, Claire Cotter and Dr Muireann Ní Bhrolcháin for many inspiring discussions over the years.

I am grateful to the Benedictine monks of Glenstal Abbey, Co. Limerick, for their hospitality and permission to use their wonderful library. Dr Colmán Ó Clabaigh OSB not only read a draft of the book but guided me through the complexities of medieval liturgy and monasticism. His advice combined with the experience of visiting Glenstal enabled me to read the early ecclesiastical sources from a different perspective. I am also very grateful to Dr Rachel Moss who not only provided me with some of her splendid images but also shared many coffees with me as we both worked on our respective projects! I also wish to thank Tony Roche, National Monuments Service, Dublin, for supplying me with excellent images of various sites. Dr Michael Potterton, Four Courts Press, assisted me through the editorial process with his customary efficient skill and ever-present courtesy. I would like to thank two anonymous readers who read an earlier draft of the text for Four Courts Press and who made many detailed comments and suggestions, which improved it greatly. I am grateful to Christopher Catling and the Marc Fitch Fund for their generous financial support of this publication.

I owe my greatest debt to Raghnall, Sorcha and Muiris Ó Floinn. Raghnall's knowledge of medieval Ireland is immeasurable and our conversations over the past twenty-five years could fill many books. Travelling with him throughout Ireland has been a constant adventure as a monument or a place name triggered a memory of an object and the circumstances of its discovery. Sorcha and Muiris (who compiled the index) have begun their own scholarly journeys in other fields and, in doing so, are forever challenging their mother's learning. To them and to all young scholars willing to read this book, I offer it in the hope that it will inspire them to explore the fascinating culture and history of early medieval Ireland.

Ballingowan, Co. Waterford
1 August 2013

The tradition of writing history in medieval Ireland

The Irish claim unique characteristics for themselves as dreamers, poets, storytellers and writers. We believe this construct and we have convinced most of the world of its veracity. And yet we rarely question it: have other peoples and cultures not produced equally important and numerous artists and wordsmiths? Are these qualities not the essence of humanity itself: a community devoid of dreamers, poets, storytellers and writers can hardly express itself nor progress without such creative activity. Is this claim, therefore, a fiction? In reality it is, but from the earliest period of Irish history we have portrayed ourselves as unique and as an axis on which the world revolves. Columbanus, the sixth-century Irish monk who travelled from the north-east of Ireland through the Frankish and Lombardic kingdoms as far as Bobbio in northern Italy, when addressing Pope Gregory the Great in AD600 in eloquent Latin, betrays an Irish trait that recurs throughout history, that of false modesty combined with an exaggerated confidence. The letter arose from Columbanus' dispute with Frankish bishops about the date of Easter, a controversy that caused much conflict throughout Christendom in the sixth and seventh centuries. Columbanus opens his letter to Gregory with the following ostentatious flourish, which draws on Latin rhetorical style and biblical allusion:[1]

> It is my desire, Holy Father, (let it not be extravagant in your sight) to ask about Easter, in accordance with that canticle, *Ask thy father and he will show thee, thy elders and they will tell thee.*
>
> For although, considering my insignificance, when my poverty writes to your distinction, I might be branded with that unusual remark of a certain philosopher, which he is said once to have made at the sight of a painted harlot, *I do not admire the art, but I admire the cheek*; yet trusting in the faith of your evangelical humility I dare to write to you, and subjoin the matter of my grief. For there is no pride in writing when necessity demands a letter, though it be addressed to one's superiors.

Although Columbanus had left Ireland, and had no wish to return, he resorted to the historical erudition of his compatriots to support his own position on the Easter controversy:[2]

> For you must know that Victorius [author of the Paschal cycle accepted in fifth-century Gaul] has not been accepted by our teachers, by the ancient Irish philosophers and by the mathematicians most skilled in reckoning chronology, but has earned ridicule or indulgence rather than authority.

Recourse to history, myth and tradition has always been a critical element of the Irish construct of their place in the known world and the world's view of them. History, myth and tradition were often interwoven and defined by the native term *senchas*. In Modern Irish, *seanchas* is used to describe storytelling, tradition and folklore, but in its earlier articulation *senchas* encompassed the collective consciousness of the Irish as expressed by their historians.[3] Historians, who were an esteemed class in medieval Ireland, were *senchaide* (Modern Irish 'storytellers'), the custodians of *senchas*.[4] *Stair*, a word borrowed from Latin *historia* and used in Modern Irish as the term for 'the science of history', was rarely employed in medieval Ireland. Nevertheless, universal forms of recording history were also employed by the *senchaide*. Annals or chronicles, for example, were compiled from the sixth century and probably originated in major churches such as Armagh, Iona, Kildare and Clonmacnoise with the noting of Easter cycles, saints' feastdays and the deaths of important religious and secular figures.[5] The apex of the tradition of compiling Irish chronicles came with the production in the early seventeenth century of the Annals of the Four Masters, an immense task that drew on an array of medieval sources and for the first time created a 'national' chronicle. This enterprise was a response to early modern English and Continental histories, which were part of the formation of nation states. And yet through its compilers, the Franciscan lay-brother Mícheál Ó Cléirigh and his collaborators, who all belonged to hereditary families, learned in *senchas*, the Annals of the Four Masters fitted in well with traditional history writing in Ireland. In the preface to his patron Fearghal Ó Gadhra, an MP from Co. Sligo, written in 1636, Ó Cléirigh revealed an approach to history that was deeply imbued in the medieval *senchas* tradition:[6]

> It is a thing general and plain throughout the whole world, in every place where nobility or honour has prevailed in each successive period, that nothing is more glorious or more honourable (for many reasons) than to bring to light the knowledge of antiquity of ancient authors and a

knowledge of the chieftains and nobles that existed in preceding times, in order that each successive generation might possess knowledge and information as to how their ancestors spent their time and life, how long they were successively in the lordship of their countries, in dignity or in honour, and what sort of death they met.

Here Ó Cléirigh draws attention to the Irish fixation with noble ancestry, with heroic deeds and with the craft of history itself. This fixation ensured that from the beginning of literacy in Ireland, at least from the sixth century onwards, material was constantly being written and copied, even when the language was not always fully intelligible to the copyist or compiler. Contrary to the widespread popular perception, therefore, the legacy of Ó Cléirigh and that of the many hereditary families learned in history, was not confined to an oral tradition but was a written tradition that resulted in the survival of hundreds of medieval Irish texts to the present day. Ó Cléirigh's contemporary, the scholarly priest-historian Geoffrey Keating, wrote his own monumental history of Ireland, *Foras feasa ar Éirinn*, refuting the views of the Irish as depicted by 'foreign' historians from the classical historian Strabo to the twelfth-century Welsh prelate Giraldus Cambrensis and the sixteenth-century Dubliner Richard Stanihurst. Keating boasted that the Irish historical record (*seanchas Éireann*) was authoritative because of its antiquity and the number of historians who had preserved ancient records under the scrutiny of both clergy and nobility, 'wherefore I think that it is more fitting to rely on the history of Ireland than on the history of any other country in Europe'.[7]

Whatever about the reliability of *senchas* as an accurate record of Ireland's history and the settlement of people on the island, its reach was comprehensive. Senchas embraced different branches, *scélshenchas* 'the lore of stories', *laídshenchas* 'the lore of poetry', *náemshenchas* 'the lore of saints' and *dindshenchas* 'the lore of places'. Part of the tradition was also linked to law (*recht, fénechas*) and to genealogy (*cráeb choibnesa* 'a branch of blood relationship') and in practical terms *senchas* was often essential to the legal rights to land and inheritance. The collective memory of elders, which may have depended on an oral tradition, and of the *senchaide* 'historian', which was mainly written, concerning landholdings, boundaries and legal disputes, constituted part of early legal court proceedings. The historian or elder sat in the side court (*táebairecht*) 'because it is on the lore [*senchas*] of the custodians of tradition and the clarification of the custodians of tradition that the court relies'.[8]

Senchas was not confined to the local or the familial. The Irish learned class emerged in the seventh century, asserting a sense of a united ethnicity among the island's people even if in reality power was very fragmented. They constructed a centralizing authority around the kingship of Tara, a kingship that had been sacral and exceptional in prehistory. The regnal list of those recognized officially as kings of Tara provided a chronological framework for Irish history and prehistory. Even if a heroic king such as Cormac mac Airt never existed, his supposed reign as king of Tara was one of the important ages of the pre-Christian era. This was followed by a shadowy era that was suspended between a mythical and an historical world. This was the period of the ancestors of many later powerful dynasties. Such was the case with Niall Noígiallach ('Niall of the Nine Hostages'), the ancestor of the Uí Néill dynasty who, with few exceptions, held the kingship of Tara in their grip from the seventh to the late tenth century. Numerous dynasties claimed descent from Niall, but these assertions in many instances were fabricated. Niall, if he ever existed, lived in the early fifth century, a period that is bereft of written documentation that would corroborate the events of his reign. Nevertheless, a constant theme relating to the reigns of these dubious kings associated them with military expeditions to Britain and further afield, and also with taking British wives. Of Labraid Loingsech, the reputed ancestor of the Laigin (Leinstermen), a genealogical poem possibly composed in the seventh century proclaimed:[9]

> He fettered Gaulish hostages as far as the five peaks of the Alps; scores of fierce lords, of armoured legions, go into hiding.

Of Conall Corc, the reputed ancestor of major dynasties in Munster, a similarly early text tells of how[10]

> he was sent to Britain (Alba) to the king of the Pictish people to be put to death, and information to his detriment was written on the shield in covert ogam which no one understood except Crimthann [the king of Ireland] and the king of the Pictish people. When the daughter of the king of Britain was given to Corc, druidical incantations were put upon him so that for seven years he should forget Ireland … They intended to give him the kingship of Britain if he would forget Ireland.

While these tales may not be factual, they tie in with the testimony of the British missionary Patrick and the later British cleric Gildas and with other evidence that Britain was subject to constant raids from the west and north by the Irish (*Scotti*) and the Picts. Expeditions were undoubtedly led by Irish kings or adventurers who were familiar with western Britain, and who sought to be part of the culture of *romanitas* 'romanization'. They may even have served in the

Roman army in far-flung places in the empire.[11] While regarded by the outside world, including St Patrick, as inhabiting the ends of the earth,[12] the Irish themselves constantly turned this around and, as with Columbanus, proclaimed that their island was a focal point on earth.

The foremost version of the Irish national origin legend, and one that framed most histories of Ireland to the twentieth century, was the *Lebar Gabála* 'Book of Invasions'. Even to the present time, popular histories retain the *Lebar Gabála* narrative of the original settlers on the island, be they the sons of Milesius from Spain, the Fir Bolg or the Túatha Dé Danann. This eleventh-century narrative in Middle Irish has been best defined by John Carey as[13]

> Bringing together a heterogeneous body of legends and speculations regarding the ancient history of the country and the origin of its people, and fitting them into a single comprehensive framework, *Lebar Gabála* provided a narrative extending from the creation of the world to the coming of Christianity, and beyond – a national myth which sought to put Ireland on the same footing as Israel and Rome.

The construction of the Irish national origin-legend, which ultimately became *Lebar Gabála*, had its beginnings as far back as the seventh century and consisted of an amalgam of material from classical and Christian sources, and most especially from the Book of Genesis and early Christian historiography including the Chronicle of Eusebius (d. 379), the 'History against the Pagans' of Paul Orosius (d. 417) and the encylopedic *Etymologiae* and 'History of the kings of the Goths, Vandals and Suebi' of Isidore of Seville (d. 636).[14] These universal histories offered a Christian biblical historiography to the Irish into which they fitted themselves and their origins. But this historiography was not complete without the addition of their own traditions, which were deeply rooted in vernacular literature and oral tradition. Various ninth-century texts, the poem *Can a mbunadas na nGaedel* 'What is the origin of the Irish'[15] attributed to Máel Muru Othna (Fahan, Co. Donegal), who died in 887, the *Historia Brittonum* 'History of the Britons', which was probably compiled in north Britain, and the prose tract *Scél Tuain Meic Chairill* 'The tale of Tuan mac Cairell' present us with direct testimony for the early creation of the Irish origin legend. Their concerns with their sources were not identical and this led to the invention of different versions of the legend. In his poem, Máel Muru claimed that the Irish descended from Japhet son of Noah, and in particular from a Scythian man learned in the languages of the world, Fénius Farsaid, whose son Nel begot a son with the Egyptian princess Scota. Their son Gáedal Glas and his descendants wandered through the known world until they came to Spain, and from there the sons of Míl Espáine set forth and ultimately settled and populated the island. Máel Muru tried to impress his audience with his learning:[16]

> Fully have we made our chronicle
> Who will criticise it?
> It has its middle, and its beginning,
> And its end.

> Sufficiently have we followed their true history,
> Much more do we know.
> The race of Bregon, as it is handed down,
> From whence is their origin.

Despite his attempts to impress with his pseudo-classical and biblical allusions, however, his finest scholarship is derived from his native learning and in it he finds contradictions with the foreign stories. On their arrival in Ireland, the sons of Míl Espáine were confronted by an array of enemies, portrayed by the poet as human but in reality recognizable as the pantheon of the otherworldly Túatha Dé Danann and other deities. One ancestor is Donn of Tech Duinn 'the house of Donn', an undersea kingdom of the dead:[17]

> This was his great testament
> To his numerous children,
> 'To me, to my house, come ye all
> After your deaths'

The newcomers made an alliance with the Túatha Dé Danann, who, in return for half of all the land, allowed them to take their women. It is difficult to believe that Máel Muru, a learned man associated with the church of Fahan, Co. Donegal, was unaware of the implication of this alliance, namely, that the Irish were descended from deities: to the contrary, he lists all the important peoples of Ireland and their ancestors, often using mythological allusions to describe them:[18]

> Blackness, darkness, dimness, greyness,
> The Fothads, the plunderers,
> Aendia, Trennia,
> Coennia of chariots.

The wonderful tale of Túan son of Cairell elegantly draws together native *senchas* lore about the origins of the Irish and the version developed in a

Christian milieu.[19] Tuán lived in a hermitage in Ulaid (the north-east of Ireland) where he was visited by Finnia of Mag Bile (Movilla, Co. Down), one of the fathers of Irish monasticism. This encounter typifies a topos that recurs in early Irish literature in which a prominent saint meets someone from another age who narrates the history of Ireland's races and landscape to him. Time is suspended as the history is related and the audience is in an otherworld oblivious of their own human need for food and drink:[20]

> Finnia asked him for tidings of Ireland, all that had happened since the time of Parthalón son of Agnoman. Finnia said that they would not taste food until (he told) them. Tuán said to Finnia. 'Let me not be constrained on that account. We had rather contemplate the word of God, which you may relate to us'. 'Nevertheless', said Finnia, 'you must tell us your own adventures, and the history of Ireland'.

In this passage, we get a glimpse of how so much native tradition percolated through a Christian culture: time could be put aside for *senchas* as well as for the word of God. Tuán explains that he was the sole survivor from among the first settlers, who had come from Greece, and who had perished in a plague. He survived the different ages of Ireland's pre-Christian history through the power of shape-shifting. He took the shapes of a wild stag, a wild boar, a hawk and a salmon. He was caught by fishermen and eaten by the wife of Cairell, a king of the north-east. She was impregnated and gave birth to Tuán:[21]

> I remember then how speech came to me as to every infant, and I found out everything that was done in Ireland, and I was a prophet, and a name was given to me, that is, Tuán son of Cairell. Then Patrick came with the Faith. I was very old then, and I was baptized, and of my own accord I accepted belief in the King of All, with his creatures.

As with Máel Muru Othna, the author of Tuán's story had to deal with those otherworld creatures that still frequented the landscape and hovered in the recesses of people's lives. Of the Túatha Dé Danann, Tuán feigned ignorance of them:[22]

> Beothecht son of Iordanen took this island from the people that were in it. Of them are the Gáilióin, and the Túatha Dé and Andé, whose origin the men of learning do not know; but they thought it likely that they are some of the exiles who came to them from Heaven.

There could be no better articulation of the dynamics of history-making in medieval Ireland than the story of Tuán mac Cairell, in which oral memory and the written word, native traditions and biblical and classical learning were interwoven. A Christian Latin culture was availed of by the custodians of a deep-rooted vernacular culture to produce a collection of texts that is among the most significant and varied to emanate from early Western Christendom.

CHAPTER I

The landscapes of early medieval Ireland

One of the most beautifully crafted early Irish tales, *Aislinge Óenguso* 'The dream of Óengus', ends with the charming image of the deity Óengus son of the Dagda and the river goddess Bóand uniting with his otherworldly lover Caer Ibormeith from Síd Úamain in Connacht:[1]

> *Téiti cucci. Fo-ceird-sium dí láim forrae. Con-tuilet i n-deilb dá géise co timchellsat a l-loch fo thrí conná bed ní bad meth n-enech dó-som. To-comlat ass i n-deilb dá én find co m-batar ocin Bruig Maicc in Óicc, ocus chechnatar cocetal cíuil co corastar inna dóini i súan trí láa ocus teora n-aidche. Anais laiss ind ingen íar sin.*

> She went to him. He cast his arms about her. They fell asleep in the form of two swans, and went around the lake three times so that his promise might not be broken. They went away in the form of two white birds till they came to Brug maic ind Óic, and sang a choral song so that it put the people to sleep for three days and three nights. The girl stayed with him after that.

This tale, probably written in the eighth century, is one of the many literary compositions of the period that fashioned a great vernacular literary tradition out of old and declining beliefs, new moral tales and a countryside alive with heroic, mythical and holy memories. In his quest to find Caer Ibormeith, Óengus searched some of the main *sída* ('otherworldly mounds') of Ireland and, once united with her, brought her to his own residence at Brug maic ind Óic, the great Neolithic passage tomb at Newgrange, Co. Meath. By the eighth century, four hundred years had passed since another group of people had left a considerable deposit of valuable votive offerings, including jewellery and late Roman gold military medallions, around the entrance to the same tomb.[2] Much had changed in Ireland between the mid-fourth and the eighth century: the earlier people had celebrated some form of ritual that had the great tomb as its focus, while the later author conceived of the same mound as the residence of the ancient gods, even if he did not worship them. Yet the place evoked a response from people of different times, as did so many other features, man-made and natural, throughout the island. Even if it is not possible for us to envision an early medieval landscape through the lens of the modern landscape, the great mass of historical, literary, topographical and archaeological evidence provides us with a portal into the surroundings occupied by the people of early Ireland. And theirs was not a one-dimensional landscape; they viewed their environment through many lenses. For them, there existed a natural environment that had to be worked to survive, that had to be encountered when travelling or migrating; a real landscape that they themselves had created and that was dotted with boundaries, settlements, roads and field systems; a sacred landscape that contained the monuments of their ancestors, graves and cemeteries, sacred springs and holy wells, churches and crosses; a ceremonial landscape in which their kings were inaugurated and public events took place; and a heroic or military landscape in which battles were fought and violent conflict erupted. This myriad of landscapes and their populations gave soul to early medieval Ireland.

The natural environment

A commentary on the early Irish law of neighbourhood, *Bretha Comaithchesa*, lists various landmarks that might mark a boundary: a rock (*ailblá*), a ditch (*cladblá*), a tree (*fidblá*), water (*linnblá*), a plain (*clárblá*), a marsh (*nóesblá*), or a road or lane (*blá réime*). It even lists *rodarcblá*, which loosely equates to the modern idiom 'as far as the eye can see', although probably the breadth of the eye's view was defined by prominent natural features in the landscape.[3] So, what did the early medieval eye see when it scanned its surroundings? In her masterly study of the landscape of place-names in Britain south of the Forth–Clyde line, Margaret Gelling produced an exceptionally vibrant account of Britain's early landscape based on Celtic, English and Norse place-names.[4] She drew together place-name elements, natural features and settlement imprints and brought many natural features to life: rivers, springs, ponds and lakes; marshes, moors and floodplains; roads and trackways, river crossings and landing places; valleys, hollows and remote places; hills, slopes and ridges; woods and clearings; ploughlands, meadows and pastures. How much more dynamic would the portrayal of early Ireland become if Gelling's pioneering study were replicated using Irish sources? One starting point would be the corpus of early Irish genealogies. Unlike sagas and saints' Lives, which, although colourful, can be impressionistic, the genealogies are often closer to an authentic reality, especially as they deal with power and the legitimacy of a kindred's authority over land. The common place-name elements that occur in the genealogies are not unexpected: meadows (*achad, cluain*), heights of various types (*ard, bendchor, brí, cend, cnocc, cruach(an), druim, leittir, mullach, óchtar, sliab, tulach*), river crossings (*áth, drochet*), roads (*belach, cóelbóthar*), trees (*bile, coill, daire, fid, ros*), ridges (*eiscer*), recesses (*cúl*), watery places (*enach, ess, gabur, glais, imlech, loch, muir*) and valleys (*glenn, lethglenn*).[5] These and other similar terms are often part of the names of Irish kindreds, and the genealogies demonstrate clearly that attaching the names of natural features to people anchored them in particular localities and defined the territorial relationships between them. Some held lands by lakes: the Éoganacht Locha Léin's core kingdom was located around Lough Leane in Killarney, Co. Kerry. Rivers and even streams were barriers and boundaries, and kingdoms were frequently defined by them: the River Liffey was a key geographical determinant in north Leinster, with Airther Life (the eastern reaches of the river) defining various peoples such as the Fothairt Airthir Liphi. Áth Cliath, later to be incorporated into the Viking settlement of Dublin, was a vital crossing over the Liffey mentioned in Adomnán's late seventh-century Life of Columba, and it defined a border for the region between the Liffey and River Delvin (Ailbine).[6] The proliferation of place-names with the element *mag* 'plain' (Latin *campus*) is a well-known phenomenon. This simply indicates that fertile regions were much contested territories and hence Mag Feimin (the plain between Cashel and Clonmel, Co. Tipperary) and Mag Breg (that region between the rivers Delvin and Liffey), in which Cashel and Tara were located respectively, were the most disputed territories in Ireland. Occasionally, the genealogies define the extents of kingdoms with reference to natural features and, in certain cases, they give the clear impression that mental maps of the landscape existed and were transposed onto the political landscape. Ireland was made up of a very complex tapestry that consisted of many layers of kindreds claiming ownership of lands. Short topographical notes incorporated into the genealogies amount to informal charters reflecting land ownership at particular periods. These notes range from general extents (as in **a**) to more precise and detailed local definitions (as in **b**):[7]

(a) The land of Éile extending east and south of the Shannon. The land of Uaithne extending west and north of the Shannon to Lough Derg [on the Shannon].

(b) [Fothairt] Danbarr mac Déin from whom are descended the Uí Danbairr from Cend Chláir [Grangeclare, Co. Kildare] to *Scuinnitin* and from *Dubátha* to Ráith nAirbe [?Rathnarrow, Co. Westmeath] and from these descendants of Danbarr are the Uí Bánáin from Móen [Moone, Co. Kildare], Uí Marggáin and Uí Diamráin and Uí Báetáin beside Maistiu [Mullaghmast, Co. Kildare].

While hagiography, poetry and sagas are often impressionistic, they must reflect the environment known to their authors and often colourfully express either the beauty of the countryside or its harsh reality. An episode in the Latin Life of Colmán Elo (Lynally, Co. Offaly) tells of how a certain Becanus filled his cart with fine foodstuffs for the saint and his monks and yoked his oxen to bring his gift to Lynally. But to complete his journey he needed the saint's intervention as the road between his house and Lynally was wooded and hilly (*sed siluatica et implana erat via inter villam eius et Lann Elo, monasterium sancti Colmani*).[8] Lynally was located in a fertile corridor surrounded by large expanses of bog and woodland, and even though it was on a primary communication axis in the midlands, access to it through these wet and wooded fastnesses was probably difficult.

Although highly exaggerated – as they were undoubtedly read to entertain or written to illustrate their authors' mastery of the vernacular – early Irish sagas often excel in vibrant descriptions of the landscape. The great hero of the Ulster sagas, Cú Chulainn, was a master at directing his comrades through the countryside. In this episode from *Mesca Ulad* ('The intoxication of the Ulstermen'), the hero guides the Ulstermen deep into the southwest and into the Shannon region around modern Limerick city:[9]

> Cú Chulainn went to Druim Collchaille, which is called Áne Cliach. 'Say, dear kinsman Lóeg, do you know what territory we are in?' 'No, truly, I do not'. 'Truly, I do know', Cú Chulainn said. 'Cenn Abrat in Slíab Caín is this to the south. Sléibti Éblinni is this on the north-east. The distant huge bright water that you see is the Pool of Limerick'.

Here, Cú Chulainn is pointing out the natural features in the vicinity of Áne Cliach, the area around Knockainy, Co. Limerick, an area rich in archaeological monuments.[10] Looking from *Druim Collchaille* ('The ridge of the hazel wood'), he could see the Ballyhoura Mountains and Slieve Reagh (Sliab Caín), Cos Cork and Limerick, to the south and the Slieve Phelim Mountains (Sléibti Éblinni), Co. Limerick, to the north-east. Just north was 'the Pool of Limerick' (*Linn Luimnig*) on the River Shannon and what at the time could be distinguished as the opening of the river into its great estuary as it flows into the Atlantic. As in so many of the descriptions and directions of the sagas, Cú Chulainn's mental map is dependent mainly on natural features: hills, woods, mountains, rivers and the sea. Not that settlements were unknown to the heroes or their authors – as in the following section Cú Chulainn, when asked by his king Conchobar mac Nessa where the troop should set up camp, he wisely suggested *Óenach Senluachair* ('the assembly place of Senluachair') as it was winter 'and this rough wintry season is no season of tribal assembly (*óenach*)'.[11] Cú Chulainn's advice demonstrates the common phenomenon of the reuse of existing monuments by different generations for the same or new purposes, a phenomenon well-documented in the archaeological record.

Ireland is an island and the sea was a powerful force in reality and in the Irish imagination. The ancestors of all inhabitants on the island had at one stage crossed the sea to settle there, all visitors had to make that journey and anyone wishing to leave had to face the perils of a sea crossing. Ireland's perceived isolation and distance from the rest of the world pervades many accounts from classical authors to the medieval English historian Bede. Strabo, the Greeek geographer who lived in the first century AD, related that the farthest sea voyage from Celtica to the north was reputedly to Ierne [Ireland], which was beyond Britain and was barely habitable because it was so cold.[12] Bede was one of the first authors to introduce the idea that snakes could not survive on the island, 'for although often brought over from Britain, as soon as the ship nears land, they breathe the scent of the air, and die'.[13] Bede also presented the classical mental map of Ireland's position in the known world:[14]

> Ireland is the largest island after Britain, and lies to the west of it. It is shorter than Britain to the north, but extends far beyond it to the south towards the northern coasts of Spain, although a wide sea separates them.

The sea could be powerful, and tragic consequences awaited many who took to it, an experience known universally to people dependent on coastal living and seafaring. A poignant verse in the Annals of Ulster, which captures man's helplessness against the sea, laments the drowning in 622 of Conaing son of Áedán mac Gabráin, king of the Dál Riata (in western Scotland):

> *Tonna móra mórglanna, grïan roda-toigsetar, fri curach flescach fann for conaing con-coirsetar*

> The waves of the sea great and clear [and] the sands have covered them; against a frail wattled curach [small rowing boat made of hides] they have combined to destroy Conaing.

Coastal erosion and changes in coastal formations could upset a community's life and were associated with other natural and wonderous phenomena. In 804, the same chronicle (*AU*) records that 'violent thunder, accompanied by wind and fire, on the night before St Patrick's Day' killed many people in Corcu Baiscinn (a kingdom in Co. Clare) 'and the sea divided the island of Fita (possibly Mutton Island, baronies of Kilmurry/Ibrackan, Co. Clare) into three parts, and covered the land of Fita with sand, that is as much land as would support twelve cows'.

The sea, however, was an essential economic resource and not the barrier that isolated Ireland, as portrayed by classical and modern authors alike. It opened the island up to trading with the world and made it part of a network of international sea routes.[15] The earliest image of Ireland, based on the information gathered by the second-century Egyptian geographer Ptolemy, clearly demonstrates that the island's coastline and main riverine estuaries were known to ancient navigators and traders, and that the coasts and rivers were not only the conduits of trade but also of external influences.[16] With trade came power and hence kings and kindreds who controlled coastal and estuarine regions were powerful and wealthy. This potential is expressed as a metaphor for the success of the mythical heroic king Conaire Mór's reign in the early Irish saga *Togail Bruidne Da Derga*:[17]

> Now there was in his reign great bounties, namely, seven ships in every June of every year arriving at Inber Colptha [the Boyne Estuary] ... and plenty [of fish] in [the rivers] Bush and Boyne in the June of each year.

The few surviving fragments and commentary of the law *Muirbretha* 'sea judgments' lay out how this royal control of harbours and estuaries operated.[18] The repeated mention of the distance of 'nine waves' offshore as subject to law – in Jonathan Wooding's estimation in his study of the sea and shipping lanes around Ireland – 'constituted, if not "territorial" waters, at least a statutory limit to jurisdiction'.[19] If a king's territory was coastal, he had a right to revenue from ships and boats (*long 7 barc*) and to the contents of shipwrecks. A substantial amount of this revenue or bounty had to be shared with his own church, with the provincial king and, at times, presumably if he was willing to declare his income, with the king of Ireland.[20] A king was also entitled to part of the sea-catch and specifically to salmon, seals and porpoises. An interesting detail in the fragmentary *Muirbretha* is the reference to *fir puirt*, possibly the men who collected the king's levies, who were also included in a share of the sea's bounty. Though brief and patchy, the text nevertheless sketches an organized control of the coast and the distribution patterns of sea-trade and fisheries. The existence of a companion law to *Muirbretha*, *Cáin Inbir* ('the law of the estuary'), which does not survive, underscores the economic significance of estuarine fisheries and the need to regulate ownership of these, and especially those with lucrative stocks of eel, mackerel and salmon. Complex fishtraps, artificial barriers of stone or wood used to divert fish into an opening where they could be trapped in nets or baskets, have been discovered in Ireland along the River Fergus Estuary, Co. Clare, the Shannon Estuary and most spectacularly in Strangford Lough, Co. Down.[21] Radiocarbon dates fix some of the wooden posts from these extensive excavations and surveys to periods between the fifth and fourteenth centuries and investigations have uncovered a constant process of repair involving the use of thousands of ash, hazel and oak poles and rods. The Strangford fisheries were developed by monastic communities, not only the late medieval Cistercian community of Grey Abbey, but most likely by the early monastery of Nendrum, on Strangford Lough. That the lough was vital to the economic life of Nendrum is clearly illustrated by the discovery of a series of seventh- and eighth-century mills powered by tidal water close to the monastery (pls 4, 5).[22] These mills would have provided much flour for bread, and while it is assumed that this bread would have been baked for the monastic community and its dependents, it is likely that surpluses would have been traded in exchange for other useful products.

The vastness of the water beyond Ireland could only have caused a sense of awe, not alone to inhabitants of the island's coasts but also to all those who sailed the western seas. In biblical and Christian terms, this was the ocean, the abyss and the edge of the earth where the struggle between God and evil was continuous and this view of the world also located Ireland at the very ends of the earth. Once this most westerly of islands had been Christianized, St Patrick imagined that the gospel message had been preached through the whole earth, 'from the rising of the sun to its setting'.[23] The awe of the sea is best expressed in the early Irish voyage tales, one of which, the voyage of St Brendan the Navigator, became a renowned text in the medieval world. Brendan's voyage and those of others such as the imaginary tale of Máel Dúin and his companions who sailed off the west coast into the 'great limitless ocean' (*isin n-ocian mór nemforcendach*),[24] were confronted with many islands inhabited by fantastic animals such as giant ants or chaste women who refused to make love to them or hermits with beards that covered their nakedness. These tales transmitted moral messages to their audiences, but they were imbued with knowledge of sailing and the dangers encountered at sea. At the end of Máel Dúin's voyage, the crew recognized that they were nearing Ireland when they spotted a large bird that was familiar to them:[25]

> Now after they had gone thence they come to an island with abundant cattle, and with oxen and kine and sheep. There were no houses nor forts therein, and so they eat the flesh of the sheep. Then said some of them seeing a large falcon there: 'The falcon is like the falcons of Ireland!' 'That is true indeed', say some of the others. 'Watch it', saith Mael Duin, 'and see how the bird will go from us'. They saw that it flew from them to the southeast. So they rowed after the bird, in the direction in which it had gone from them. They rowed that day till vespers. At nightfall they sight

land like the land of Ireland. They row towards it. They find a small island and it was from this very island that the wind had borne them into the ocean when they first went to sea.

Hence the bird led them home to Ireland – a phenomenon known by fishermen and sailors the world over, including the biblical story of Noah and the Flood. And they reached land, not the mainland but an island with a fort in which the inhabitants just happened to be wondering about Máel Dúin's fate as he had disappeared so long ago. When he and his men entered the fort their return caused much astonishment to its residents. Máel Dúin's landing on an inhabited island off the Irish coast reflects reality as all around the coast there were islands that were heavily settled and busy since prehistoric times. Our modern view of these islands associates them with remoteness and isolation where monks eked out an existence with little between them and God but wild birds, the sea, rain and gales. While there was a certain element of such an existence and withdrawal from the world, as there was on the mainland, islands were important strategic stopping points for navigation and for gaining a foothold in a territory. Iona and the Aran Islands are classic examples of islands that were at the centre of seafaring communications, and the excavations at the great stone fort of Dún Aonghasa on Aran confirmed that this apparently remote island was a centre of activity from the late Bronze Age to the late medieval period. Late Bronze Age clay moulds for the casting of swords, knives, socketed axeheads and other objects were discovered within the fort's enclosure, and these may have been made either for export to the mainland or for elaborate votive offerings. Likewise, during the early medieval period, these were vibrant places, as is clear from the density of churches and stone forts scattered through the three islands.[26] Of course, as highly experienced seafarers, the Vikings knew the value of gaining a foothold on islands and using them as springboards to move onto the mainland. The list of their first raids around the coast off western Scotland and Ireland is indicative of this tactic: from their first appearance (at least in annalistic records) on Skye and Rathlin Island (795), they moved to Inis Pátraic (St Patrick's Island off the east coast; 798), Iona (802, 806), Inismurray (807) and Skellig (824). By 808, they were battling with coastal communities such as the people of Umall, the territory around Clew Bay, Co. Mayo, and of Conmaicne, a people scattered throughout the west but in this instance probably the Conmaicne Mara, whose name survives in the place-name Connemara. By the 820s, they had gained a foothold on the mainland and carved out spaces for themselves along the coast, usually in busy and populated locations such as the monasteries of Bangor, Downpatrick and Movilla.

The Irish were moulded by their natural surroundings, which, despite the relatively small size of the island, had deeply contrasting environments, between mountainous regions and flatlands, rugged coastal regions and fertile river flood plains. This striking diversity generated particular responses from those settled in the various regions, and in no more distinctive way than in the types of settlements that were constructed thoughout the countryside.

The settled landscape: rural

Archaeology, laws and place-names together produce a tapestry revealing how humans controlled the medieval Irish landscape. Throughout the country, there are place-names that denote the existence of early homesteads (*dún, faithche, fossad, lios, ráith, tech*), defended residences (*brug, daingen, caisel, durlas*), cultivation and field systems (*aball, achad, cluain, gort, muine*), forests and trees (*coill, doire, ros*), communications networks (*áth, belach, ród, tóchar*) and industry (*muilenn*). Many of these place-names still exist. The name Rathmore 'the large fort' is found throughout Ireland, while Thurles, Co. Tipperary, originates from *Daur Lis* 'the oaken fort', Bruree, Co. Limerick, from *Brug Ríg* 'the king's fort', and Derry from *doire* 'an oak wood'. A journey through the Irish landscape, be it through a rural or a modern urban or semi-urban landscape, can often conjure up from place-name evidence alone a fairly accurate image of a busy medieval world. In recent decades, Ireland has been subject to an inordinate – and often unsustainable – degree of infrastructural and property construction, which has resulted in the disturbance of large swathes of the landscape. Road-takes following the lines of motorways have sliced through town and countryside, and archaeological investigations have preceded the road construction. While such investigations differ from research archaeology in that they are indiscriminate in their choice of site or research questions and are dictated by engineering and planning considerations, their very randomness from an archaeological and historical perspective has enabled us to gain some sort of overview of the landscape across the country during different eras.[27] Remarkable patterns have emerged with regard to early medieval settlement. The countryside was a busy place and was fairly densely populated in certain areas. Settlements consisted of houses, some single, others in clusters, enclosed by ditches and earthen banks that offered varying degrees of defence to their inhabitants (fig. 2). There were many other earthen enclosures without dwellings, which had different purposes, some for containing livestock and probably others for communal activities. The most common industrial activities were metalworking – mainly domestic, although occasionally sophisticated craftworking occurs –

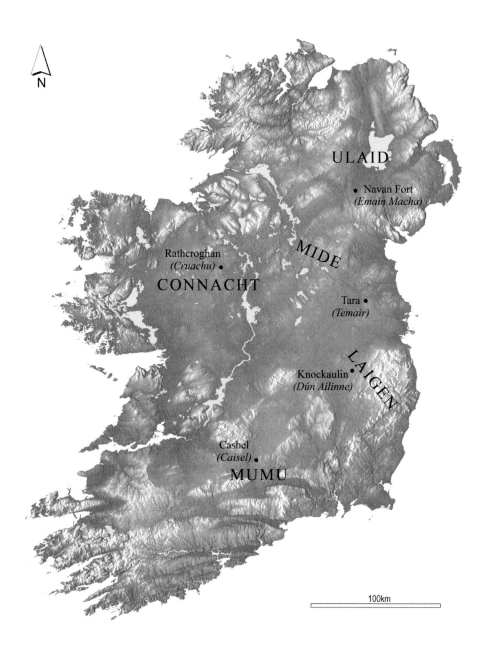

1 Map of Ireland showing the traditional provinces and the early provincial capitals.
Map prepared by Robert Shaw; © Discovery Programme, Dublin.

corn-drying and milling, woodworking, bone-working, weaving, hunting and butchery. Kilns and milling complexes were common, as were furnaces, which, due to the risk of fire, were often sensibly located at a distance from habitations. They were frequently located close to familial cemeteries. A complex at Twomileborris, Co. Tipperary (fig. 3), built on a ridge over the River Suir presents a textbook template for an early medieval Irish settlement, and fits well with descriptions in the laws. It consisted of three elements: an oval enclosure edged by large posts, a ringfort defined by a circular ditch, and a large rectangular enclosure that surrounded the earlier enclosures entirely. Inside the ringfort's circular ditch were four round houses identified by post-holes, curvilinear wall-slots and drainage gullies. There was a north-east-facing entrance in the circular ditch. The material culture was typical of such a farmstead and included iron knives, a glass bead, a fragmentary bone comb, bone pins, a fragment of a rotary quern, a stone gaming board and metallurgical waste. Although it is difficult to date many of these objects, they reflect the everyday life of people working arable land, cooking and baking, dealing with the hygiene of daily life, and entertaining themselves. In a nearby enclosed settlement defended with a substantial ditch that included a complex entrance and an internal palisade, there was a cemetery containing twenty burials. While it is not clear that the burials were contemporary with the ringfort settlement, as they probably date to the fifth or sixth centuries, they are indicative of a pattern now emerging throughout the countryside of settlements with associated familial cemeteries and a range of industrial activities including milling, metal- and woodworking and butchery.

Exploration of the evidence of place-names, topography and archaeology of a specific area can be very productive in attempting to reconstruct a medieval landscape.[28] In a study of the barony of Decies-without-Drum, Co. Waterford, for example, townlands with the place-name element *Curragh* (*currach* 'a marsh, fen') contain a maximum of two ringforts and most often they are located on high ground. The place-name elements *Faha* (*faithche* 'a green, infield near a dwelling'), *Garran* (*garrán* 'a grove'), as well as the common and widespread *Rath* (*ráith* 'an earthen rampart') and *Lis* (*les* 'a farmstead'), also normally signify the existence of ringforts. At the other end of the country, place-names around Lough Neagh retain the profile of an almost vanished lakeside wooded landscape.[29] The barony of Massereene Upper, Co. Antrim, an area lying between the lakeshore and the Belfast hills, is known as Killultagh (*An Choill Ultach* 'the Ulster wood'), and although most of these woods have long disappeared, the concentration of place-names consisting of tree and wood elements attest to their historical existence. *Derry* (*doire* 'an oak wood') is particularly prevalent.[30] Oak was not the only tree to grow in these woods; place-names such as Ballytromery, Co. Antrim (*Baile Tromraí* 'townland of the place of the elder trees'), and

2 Knockadrina, Co. Kilkenny: a habitation on the southern slopes of a hill was divided into three distinct zones of occupation, possibly reflecting the various functions of the settlement – agriculture, industry and habitation. It was enclosed by a ditch and had a cobbled causeway at its entrance. Occupation evidence dated the site to a period between AD650 and 890. © National Roads Authority.

Ballyshanaghill, Co. Antrim (*Baile Seaneochaille* 'townland of the old yew wood'), testify to the growth of other species such as elder, yew, holly and hazel. The element *eochaill* 'yew wood', as in Youghal, Cos Cork and Tipperary, and Oghil(l), Cos Galway, Leitrim, Longford, Monaghan and Sligo, suggests that at some period these places were dominated by yew trees. In her description of the Irish landscape in late prehistory, Valerie Hall outlines the transition from the abandonment of earlier clearances to their rapid replacement by new woodland. The most common trees growing in Ireland were hazel, holly, birch alder and willow. Yew predominated in the newly expanded woodlands in the west.[31] The harnessing of woodlands and their products – timbers, rods, firewood and nuts – was a necessary part of the economy and it can be deduced from the laws and tales, along with archaeological evidence, that exploitation of woodland and coppicing was a valuable enterprise.[32] Most buildings throughout the country were wooden, as were field fences and roads over bogs and wetlands, domestic utensils and vessels, and weapons and carts. Trees supplied acorns and apples to

3 Twomileborris, Co. Tipperary: this settlement complex is characteristic of the long
horizon of settlement often uncovered in the Irish landscape. Excavations on the line
of a motorway uncovered a Bronze Age settlement and an early medieval farmstead
(ringfort). The late medieval tower house and adjacent cemetery – which might
originally have replaced an earlier cemetery associated with the ringfort – are further
common components of the settled landscape. © National Roads Authority.

fatten pigs, and hazelnuts had a variety of uses. It was thus necessary to regulate
the harvesting of wood between neighbours. The law on neighbourhood and
farming, *Bretha Comaithchesa*, arranged trees and shrubs in four classes
according to their economic value: *airig fedo* 'nobles of the wood' (e.g. oak),
aithig fhedo 'commoners of the wood' (e.g. alder), *fodla fedo* 'lower divisions of
the wood' (e.g. blackthorn) and *losa fedo* 'bushes of the wood' (e.g. bracken).[33]
Fines could be imposed for damaging a neighbour's trees or copse, and a client
might be expected to provide his lord with wood or rods as an annual rent.

The dominance of ringforts in the early medieval Irish landscape and the
survival of up to fifty thousand sites offers an indispensable view of settlement
and agri-economic patterns for the period.[34] While the predominant description
of the settlement pattern is that of dispersed farmsteads, increasing archaeological evidence points to areas of dense population and the apparent regulation
of spatial planning between settlements and also generational renewal – or

sometimes abandonment – of these farmsteads through the medieval period. All physical, legal and historical evidence as well as the themes of sagas confirm that rearing cattle and dairying were the primary agricultural activities and the basis of wealth until the eighth century. There are numerous references to large-scale cattle raids in the annals, even at a provincial level, as demonstrated by the *bórama* 'cattle-tribute' levied by the northern and midland Uí Néill kings of Tara on the Leinstermen. The impetus for the great heroic epic *Táin Bó Cuailnge* 'The Cattle Raid of Cooley' was the jealousy between Medb, queen of Connacht, and a reflex of the sovereignty goddess, and Conchobar mac Nessa, the equally otherworldly king of Ulaid, over the superiority of their respective bulls. In a coinless society, cows and slave-girls were regarded as units of value and wealth, and, therefore, the acquisition of cattle was often a measure of one's wealth. Other less valuable animals, mainly sheep, pigs and horses, were also counted as sources of wealth. In an assessment of changes in settlement and agri-economic patterns around the eighth century, Finbar McCormick has proposed that the Irish economy moved from being singularly based on cows and dairying and diversified into great concentration on other domesticated animals, and even more so on arable farming.[35] Thus, the defended 'flat' ringfort with its bank and ditch, which were needed to protect cattle from raiding parties, gave way to less defensive raised or platform ringforts and also to later unenclosed settlements with associated underground or sunken stone-built passageways known as 'souterrains'. These latter monuments are also found throughout the countryside, normally attached to some form of settlement, and it is believed that they were used mainly for the protection of the inhabitants or for storage, and may have replaced the defensive role of the ringfort's bank and ditch.[36] These developments have been recorded in large-scale excavations such as those of Deer Park Farms, where the settlement began as one enclosed by a ring-ditch dating to the seventh century and was later transformed into a raised rath. Cows and dairying were the basis of its early economy, but this may have changed in the mid-eighth century, although the site's acidic soil conditions did not allow for a full evaluation of that later phase.[37] The increased number of horizontal mills in the late eighth and early ninth centuries reflected the change to large-scale grain production and the development of a sophisticated trade in cereal products.[38] As noted previously in the context of the Nendrum tidal mill, this tendency may have started in the seventh century and could have been a consequence of the communal structure of monastic settlements. Indeed, horizontal mills and milling complexes dating to between the mid-eighth and tenth century and excavated at Clonlea, Co. Clare, Kilbegley, Co. Galway, and Templescoby, Co. Wexford, suggest, from their proximity to ecclesiastical sites, that the church may have retained rights to grain production and larger milling complexes. As churches were part of a closely connected settled landscape and were often one element in the landscape of the kindred, however, this apparent pattern may simply reflect the contribution of a church to its community and its ruling kindred, with which it was intimately connected.

Given Ireland's climate and geomorphological formation, wetlands made up a considerable part of the landscape, manifested in bogs, marshes and lakes. Substantial prehistoric timber trackways have been found in places such as Corlea Bog (trackway dated to *c.*148BC), Co. Longford, while a complex network of lesser wooden and brushwood roads and pathways constructed well into the medieval period has been found in many other Irish bogs.[39] The onerous task of building such trackways is colourfully reflected in the saga *Tochmarc nÉtaíne* 'The Wooing of Étaín', in which Eochaid Airem, king of Tara, imposed four great burdens on the otherworldly Midir, who was seeking to woo the king's beautiful wife Étaín back to the otherworld from whence she had come. The tasks were to clear stones from Mide, to lay rushes across Tethba, to build a causeway across the bog of the Lámraige (*Móin Lámraige*) and to clear a wood across Bréifne. No one had trodden the bog of the Lámraige before. The tale continues:[40]

> Then Eochaid commanded his steward (*rechtaire*) to watch the effort they put forth in making the causeway (*tóchar*). The steward went into the bog. It seemed to him as though all the men in the world from sunrise to sunset had come to the bog. They all made one mound (*óendumae*) of their clothes, and Midir went up on that mound. Into the bottom of the causeway they kept putting a forest with its trunks and its roots, Midir standing and urging on the host on every side … After that, clay and gravel and stones (*úir 7 grian 7 clocha*) are placed upon the bog … There had been no better causeway in the world, had not a watch been set on them. Defects (?*lochtai*) were left in it then …

Whatever the defects were, they were not immediately visible to Eochaid's steward, who returned to his king to report that 'there was not on the ridge of the world a magic power that surpassed it'.[41]

Bogland, marsh and land covered with bracken, heather or rushes were classified as various degrees of rough land (*ainmín, antrenn, andomain*) and were obviously less valuable than arable land.[42] Nevertheless, such lands were not uncultivated or uninhabited, and this is particularly evident from the common place-name, especially in the midlands, containing the element *cluain* (*Clon-*) 'a damp pasture'. Many of these places were small elevated islands of grazing land in bogs, and quite a few appear to have been the location of churches or on church lands. Clonfad, Co. Westmeath (*Cluain Fota* 'the long meadow'), a church reputed to have been founded in the sixth century by Bishop Etchén, was built on a hill overlooking low-lying marshland that extended to Lough Ennell. Excavations revealed that, far from being an isolated location, Clonfad was encircled by three large enclosing ditches. This was a busy place between the sixth and tenth centuries and the excavations there yielded one of the largest assemblages of evidence for metalworking in Ireland to date, including indications of hand-bell production.[43] Nor was Clonfad isolated from an important centre of royal power. The midlands, as well as the north and west of Ireland, are densely dotted with lakes of all sizes. These lakes were an important part of the settlement landscape and were inhabited either along their shores or on natural and man-made islands known as crannogs (*crannóc* 'wooden lake-dwelling'). Midland lakes such as Lough Ennell, Lough Derravaragh and Lough Kinale were used from prehistory as habitations, hermitages, defensive bolt-holes and fishing and industrial platforms. Although crannogs are normally identified with the highest stratum in society and with a wealthy culture, mainly as a result of rich and spectacular excavations – as those undertaken at Lagore, Ballinderry and Lough Gara – lakes probably attracted all sections of society and were also deeply embedded in the Irish consciousness. Crannogs varied in size and were usually built with layers of stone boulders, cobbles, branches and timbers, lake-marl and organic debris.[44] Lough Derravaragh, Co. Westmeath, for example, was a densely settled landscape in the early medieval period, with sizeable clusters of ringforts on ridges above the lake, clusters of crannogs, and platforms on the lakeshore or in the water near the shore. Coolure Demesne at the north-east end of Lough Derravaragh is one such cluster that provides an insight into the archetypal early Irish lacustrine community: a large well-defended crannog with an equally large raised ringfort close to it on dry land, and smaller crannog platforms and islets surrounding it in a little bay. Aidan O'Sullivan has commented that

> the presence of the smaller lakeshore crannogs may suggest that both high-status and low-status sites clustered together there [Coolure Demesne], representing the dwellings of a community who resided around their lord or gathered for public assemblies, hosting, feastings or other activities associated with kingship.[45]

This community was in reality a form of nucleated settlement that many commentators on medieval Ireland are reluctant to categorize as such, preferring to describe the island's settlement patterns as dispersed and haphazard. This was hardly likely, given the complex and detailed structure of the kindreds and of the systems of clientship, free and unfree, described in early Irish laws.[46]

Further to the west, there were changes in the landscape, parts of which were probably less densely populated regions and somewhat isolated. However, the evidence of archaeology and written sources suggest that other regions were very busy. For example, some of the greatest concentrations of earthen ringforts and their stone equivalents (cashels) occur in areas such as north Sligo, east Galway and the Burren in north Clare, all of which were fertile regions that were intensively worked and produced commodities such as calves and wool for eastern and southern regions. What now seems to be an isolated site could have been at the heart of a well-structured community, as in the case of the stone fort of Cahercommaun, Co. Clare, which is likely to have been a king's residence – probably controlled by a branch of the Uí Fhidgenti dynasty, whose power stretched from west Limerick to the Aran Islands during the seventh and eighth centuries. Cahercommaun (pl. 2) is sited overlooking a narrow sheer gorge on an extensive plateau in the Burren and, despite its apparent isolation, it was on a natural routeway in lands that were especially fertile for the winter grazing of cattle. Nearby is Caisleán Gearr, another spectacular stone fort that protects the entrance to the gorge, and over twenty cashels, enclosures, prehistoric burial monuments and other remains have been identified on the limestone plateau.[47] Nevertheless, there must have been wildernesses and sparsely populated areas in mountainous regions and in wetlands. In his seventh-century depiction of Patrick's visitation to the west of Ireland, Bishop Tírechán, a native of Connacht himself, repeatedly uses *desertum* 'waste land' to describe parts of modern Co. Mayo,[48] and in particular the kingdom of Cíarraige Airni around the northern shores of Mannin Lake, where 'there is no shortage of poor, boggy land'.[49] Woods and mountains were the main areas of wilderness, as the Triads of Ireland identify Fid Mór ('the Great Wood') in Cuailnge, Fid Déicsin ('the Spy Wood') in Tuirtri and Fid Mothar ('the Wood of Moher') in Connacht as the three deserted places of Ireland.[50] And, of course, a literature grew out of the existence of these wild places, which related mainly to Finn mac Cumaill and his *féinnidi* 'warriors', who spent their time hunting and living in these regions. Finn himself was reared in the woodlands of Sliab Bladma (Slieve Bloom Mountains):[51]

> Then Bodbmall and the Gray One went with the boy into the woodlands of Sliab Bladma. The boy was reared there in secret … Those two *banfhéinnidi* [female *féinnidi*] reared him for a long time in that way.
>
> At the end of six years, his mother came to get tidings of her son; for she had been told that he was in that place, and she feared for him because of the sons of Morna. At all events, she went from one wilderness into another until she came into the woodlands of Sliab Bladma. She found the *fian*-hut, and the boy sleeping in it.

While this tale is fiction, it supposes that people sought refuge in the wilderness, whether they were dispossessed or had got on the wrong side of the law. It was also a place hidden from the rest of 'normal' society to which various groups could retreat, and these groups varied from holy people seeking God to young men being put through their paces as part of initiation rites.

The settled landscape: urban and semi-rural

Ireland's profile of settlement and urban centres differs from much of Western Europe and parts of Britain, insofar as cities – in the classical Roman sense of the term – did not develop there. The absence of such urban centres has led to intense scholarly debates regarding the nature of urbanization in Ireland before the growth of Viking towns in the tenth century. In a series of challenging papers written in the 1980s, Charles Doherty argued for the existence of 'monastic towns', on the basis that commerce took place in some of the larger ecclesiastical settlements, that they had greater concentrations of population than elsewhere, and that these populations belonged to different classes and were engaged in different activites. He supported his hypothesis from an archaeological and urban planning perspective by arguing that these places were not just ecclesiastical centres consisting of a church, a cemetery and the houses and other necessary buildings used to service a 'monastic' community. They also functioned as royal centres and included royal residences as well as 'urban' features such as dedicated quarters, streets and non-'monastic' houses.[52] The concept of a 'monastic town' was advanced from an archaeological perspective by John Bradley, who suggested that a settlement might be recognized as such if it fulfilled a number of criteria, namely, settlement complexity, the presence of domestic houses and workshops, evidence for streets and rows of buildings, for trade, markets and fairs, for enclosure and for defence, and, finally, evidence that the settlement was a political centre. He concluded, for example, that the ecclesiastical settlement of Clonmacnoise, Co. Offaly, fulfilled these criteria. He argued further, that as other sites including Kells, Co. Meath, and Tuam, Co. Galway, followed broadly similar plans, and

> since it is too much of a coincidence to find that monastic towns in quite disparate parts of Ireland had much the same plan, it suggests that the concept of an ideal monastic town plan existed in the minds of the authorities responsible for its layout.[53]

Not all scholars have agreed with the concept of the 'monastic town' and the common plan of an ecclesiastical settlement, which was distinct from secular settlements. Cathy Swift countered this model by examining the use of certain architectural and habitation terms used in Hiberno-Latin and vernacular Irish texts. These include *tabernaculum, civitas, porta, atrium, platea* and *faithche*. She concluded that ecclesiastical settlements were organized on the same basis as secular settlements and could consist of a central focus – a church or a royal residence – surrounded by an ill-defined area in which one might find agricultural buildings, domestic animals and fields of crops, trees, grass, pools of water, houses of clerics and warriors, who lived in scattered, not clustered houses. These settlements could function as arenas for public assemblies, including the conducting of judicial courts at the *porta tabernaculi* 'the gateway of the church' in an ecclesiastical site.[54] The lower classes lived at a remove from the central focus and could only enter on certain occasions, either as pilgrims or to celebrate saints' feastdays, or public assemblies.

This debate highlights some fundamental issues concerning the origins and manifestation of urbanization in early Ireland. As with so many aspects in its history, the Irish evidence is not placed in its proper context, either in scale or intent. Irish settlements are viewed against the familiar urban models of Western Christendom, and the Mediterranean and even into the Middle East. At the heart of Doherty's argument is the universal idea of the concept of 'a city of God', or celestial city, and not necessarily something comparable to a Roman municipality with its particular features. If there is any valid comparison, it is with the early stages of many Roman urban centres that formed around a temple, or with the reconfiguration of Rome itself, when its landscape was Christianized by influential figures such as Pope Gregory the Great in the late sixth century. Indeed, it is clear from early ecclesiastical literature and borrowings into the Irish language, including the use of the word *rúam* from *Roma*, meaning 'a church, cemetery', and constant mention of Jerusalem as the ideal city, that the Irish did have a sense of urbanization. Where Ireland differed from parts, though not all, of Britain, and the Continent, was in scale and the materials used for construction. Concentrations of population were on a smaller scale, the economy and trading were not as intensive, and with the exception of the west, stone was rarely used in construction. If the debate changed direction from definitions based on classical and medieval urbanization to a more universal and anthropological approach, then the evidence for pre- and non-Viking Irish urbanization would make more sense. Aidan Southall's more expansive definition of 'the city' in world history, albeit informed by a certain modern political perspective, opens a new vista on the issue:[55]

> All these cities [throughout history], from the smallest to the largest, the earliest to the latest, have been the greatest points of concentration and

of increasing density in their time and space: a concentration of women and men and their social relationships; of shelter, buildings and physical plants; of productive resources, goods and services, consumption and exchange activities; of wealth, power and energy; of information, communication and knowledge, intellectual training and even thought; of religion, ritual, and ceremonial, of creative, aesthetic sensibility and innovative stimuli, all necessarily correlated with parallel processes of the division of labour, role differentiation and general specialization involving increasing inequality and growth in coordination and hierarchy, aimed at increasing efficiency and reduction of friction.

A city could and often did develop around a religious centre – a temple, a shrine, a sanctuary – that, in turn, attracted pilgrims, ceremonies and usually led to the creation of a religio-political hierarchy. There is no difficulty in identifying such places in Ireland: the prehistoric royal ceremonial sanctuary at Tara was a public arena, as evidenced by the scale of the monuments on the hill and in the surrounding countryside. It may not have functioned as a permanent residence for many people, or as a trading centre, but undoubtedly when royal assemblies were held there it was not only a 'city of god(s)', but was also bustling with activities ranging from horse-racing to religious rituals. A settlement such as the church of Armagh consisted of even more elements of recognizable urbanization: it was 'a city of God' with a greater population density than its hinterland; it attracted both religious and secular power brokers and was a centre of major rituals including pilgrimage. There was also a spatial differentiation between those in authority and their guests, the eremitical monastic community, and the various grades of people who serviced the settlement. Given the size of Armagh, this spatial differentiation may not have been considerable and may have been based as much on practical considerations such as keeping metalworking and other industrial areas with their attendant fires and furnaces away from residential quarters. The annals record many instances of conflagration at Armagh (for example, 672, 690, 775, 840, 916), not all due to raids but 'through carelessness', as explained by the Annals of Ulster in recording the burning of many houses in the close (*i rraith*) of Armagh in 912. As the records become more detailed, and presumably the settlement grew in power and size, especially from the mid-ninth century, there is a greater sense of the existence of Southall's increasing density in time and space in Armagh. The abbot had his own house, one or more stone oratories were built, as was a king's residence, and it had its own market. In 921, the Vikings of Dublin invaded Armagh on 10 November, the feast of St Martin (Martinmas), which was the traditional end to a period of fasting and the time to prepare food, especially meat, for winter. Martinmas was

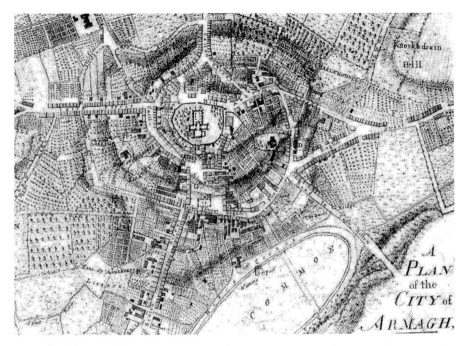

4 Armagh city plan, 1766: this sketch of the ecclesiastical city of Armagh demonstrates how the urban layout was determined by the early monastic settlement with its churches and enclosures. © Collection of Armagh City Museum.

celebrated with feasting and was often associated with a market or fair. No doubt the Vikings knew that Armagh on such a feastday would be replete with people and food, thus offering them a good source for supplies and potential slaves. One of the most significant aspects of the urban nature of Armagh is that it was perceived in the *Liber Angeli*, a composite seventh-century foundation charter, as an urbs and an archiepiscopal see (*receptio archiespiscopi heredis cathedrae maea urbis*).[56] Those who were involved in composing this charter were constructing in their own minds an *urbs* parallel to Rome or Tours, albeit on a smaller scale and without a comparable economic and power base.[57] Despite their grandiose notions, however, Armagh was still an *urbs in rure*, an entity completely dependent on its rural hinterland. In this hinterland were many farmsteads – ringforts and cashels – built on glacial heights known as drumlins, and evenly spaced. Given the number of surviving sites, it is estimated that the landscape was under intense pressure from agricultural activity.[58] This *urbs in rure* model was not exceptional, as John Blair has posited that in England minsters were often pre-urban nuclei that later developed into planned towns. Their static presence in the landscape attracted wealth and the powerful in society as well as pilgrims, all of which brought about the creation of structured settlements. He cites the case of Cookham in Berkshire, noted in Domesday Book as a royal manor in a small town, which developed originally as a settlement around a major eighth-century minster 'fit to be described as an *urbs*, at the centre of its own huge estate'. The minster declined in significance, whereas the royal palace became the focus of the urban settlement.[59] In Armagh's case, it became a small town dominated by its ecclesiastical function, and to this day its street pattern reflects elements of its earliest plan (fig. 4).

From late antique trading hubs to Viking coastal towns

The existence along the Irish coast of trading hubs that were part of a wider economic network is comparable to similar posts in Britain and elsewhere.[60] To a certain extent, some of these coastal gateways functioned like English *wics* of the late seventh and eighth centuries, although they were smaller, developed somewhat earlier and, so far, show no signs of organized spatial planning. Nevertheless, they were the starting points for a regional distribution system controlled by local and regional elites and they provided inland noble communities with goods including wine, olive oil, imported pottery and glass. The English wic Hamwic, now part of modern Southampton, showed 'high-status trade links with the Continent in terms of large quantities of Frankish and German pottery and glass'.[61] The Irish Sea bound together communities in its coastal regions rather than separating them. Yet, despite the art historical and historical evidence for strong links between Ireland and Britain in the pre-Viking era, the extent of surviving post-seventh-century imports in Ireland is modest. These are confined to a handful of Anglo-Saxon coins and objects that could have been deposited in Ireland as parts of Viking hoards.[62] There are slight hints in early texts, such as the late ninth-/early tenth-century 'Cormac's Glossary', that concepts of a monetary economy in Ireland were based on a familiarity with Anglo-Saxon coins, with borrowings such as *puingcne, penning* and *affaing* used to denote monetary units.[63] There is no denying, however, that trading links seem to have been insignificant and that coastal urbanization was not yet a phenomenon in Ireland. When and how did this pattern change and was Ireland out of step with the rest of Europe in the development of major towns from the tenth century onwards? The traditional narrative normally links the development of coastal towns – Dublin, Limerick and Waterford – with international trade routes opened up by the Vikings and regards Ireland as lagging behind England, Scandinavia and the Continent. This paradigm needs to be approached differently. As David Griffiths observed, 'how can a step-change in broad-based economic and social behavior across a diverse maritime region be attributed exclusively to the activities of a new, even if fairly vigorous, ethnic minority [the Vikings]?'[64] Griffiths suggested that the beginnings of a true commercial economy and urbanization in the Irish Sea province were 'a knock-on effect of the powerful changes and innovations going on within Anglo-Saxon England, and on the Continent'.[65] Powerful changes happened in Ireland in the ninth century too, which had much to do with the arrival of the Vikings, but also with changes in royal authority and administration and with the rise of a relatively small number of very wealthy and powerful churches.

Dublin provides one of the best examples of the development of urbanization in Europe from the tenth century onwards. Its growth into a major coastal trading town is not only explained by the arrival of the Vikings and their colonization of the mouth of the River Liffey and its environs. In assessing the origins of Dublin as a town, other dynamics feed into its economic and spatial expansion. Prior to the coming of the Vikings, this location at the mouth of the river had been a strategic crossing-point between two powerful and wealthy kingdoms, Brega to the north and Cualu to the south. Since prehistory, both kingdoms were probably those most receptive to external influences and had along their coasts some of the most important trading posts or gateway communities in Ireland: Dalkey Island, the Liffey Estuary, Lambay and the Boyne Estuary. The ceremonial complex of Tara lay in Brega, and the kingdom was the most contested territory among Irish provincial kings. Whoever had Brega in his grasp might also be able to claim the title of king of Tara. As for Cualu (south Dublin/north Wicklow), this kingdom appears to have functioned similarly for the provincial kings of Leinster: if they were unable to claim the 'ale of Cualu' (*coirm Cualann*), a metaphor for the kingship of Leinster, their authority over Leinster was insecure. Such was the importance of Cualu in the early eighth century that when its king Cellach Cualann (d. 715) seized the kingship of Leinster, he extended his considerable influence northwards into Brega. The borders between both territories at Áth Cliath, the crossing point over the River Liffey at Dublin, were a contested zone, as noted under *AU* 770, when the Leinster dynasty, the Uí Théig, were slaughtered there by the Ciannachta, the people of a sub-kingdom of Brega. This was somewhat of a pyrrhic victory, as a number of Ciannachta were drowned in the full tide on their return home – presumably crossing the Liffey. An important routeway, Slige Chualann, ran from Cualu to Tara and is likely to have crossed the river at a point where the town ultimately developed. Early churches were located along the river, including an ecclesiastical settlement at Duiblinn (overlooking the 'Black Pool', the confluence of the tributary River Poddle and the Liffey) and Cell Maignenn (Kilmainham). It is clear, therefore, that the Vikings landed their ships and erected their ships' encampment (*longphort*) in a place already busy by the early ninth century.

The beginnings of Viking Dublin in the mid- to late ninth century were far from an urban conglomeration. *AU* 841 records the establishment of the *longphoirt* of Dublin and Linn Dúachaill (Annagassan, Co. Louth), another estuarine site further up the east coast, which lay close to an ecclesiastical settlement. The annals claim that these encampments were used as bases from which the Vikings organized attacks well into the midlands. These first generations of newcomers maintained their own customs, especially in regard to warrior burials. Unlike the Irish, who were rarely buried with any significant grave goods, Vikings buried in Dublin were often accompanied by objects fitting with the individual's gender, occupation and status. For example, single warrior burials – likely to be those of the first generation – have turned up around Dublin since the nineteenth century.[66] In a recent important excavation in South Great George's Street/Ship Street Great, a young man aged between 17 and 20 was found buried with a finger ring, a silver ring, a decorated bead and a fragment of corroded iron around his neck. He also was buried with his pattern-welded sword.[67] While weapons dominate the Dublin Viking burial culture, occasionally other crafts and activites are reflected in grave goods: a single tongs, three hammers and pincers discovered in the large cemetery of Kilmainham/Islandbridge probably came from a smith's grave. Although much fewer, female burials occur in Dublin and are often adorned by oval brooches and weaving equipment such as spindle-whorls, a needle case, a linen-smoother and a whalebone plaque.[68] A fine example of a female grave was the ninth-century burial discovered close to St Canice's church in Finglas. A gold and silver oval brooch was placed above the woman's left hand and small fragments of textile were still attached to the brooch. A single post-hole may indicate that a wooden post marked her grave. A notable aspect of early Viking settlement and burial appears to be their proximity to or even position within the precincts of early churches. This is a phenomenon replicated elsewhere, most especially at Repton in Derbyshire, which had a similar topography to Dublin: a prominent position overlooking the confluence of two rivers.[69] And while the native Irish population may have been somewhat overwhelmed by this intrusion on their soil, and especially by the scale of Viking ships and their weaponry, other aspects of the lifestyle of the newcomers were not unlike their own. Familial cemeteries with no associated church or on the outer margins of church precincts were a common feature in the Irish landscape. The Irish had only begun to bury in or close to churches since the eighth century, and some had continued old customs in any case. The earliest Viking settlement in Dublin, as suggested by Linzi Simpson, following on the South Great George's Street excavations, was located to the east of the later planned town and overlooked the *duiblinn* 'black pool', the tidal pool at the confluence of the rivers Poddle and Liffey where their boats were moored. This was an enclosed and defended habitation that, on the evidence of the large volume of animal bones discovered on the site, was densely populated. Most notably, the essential form of the distinctive Viking-type Dublin house, which continued in use for a long period in the planned town, was recognizable in one early building: the roof was supported by large load-bearing supports, flanking the main central aisle, with a hearth at one end and a substantial stone floor.[70]

What changed Dublin from a series of scattered settlements and cemeteries around the Liffey, with a defended focus overlooking the confluence of the rivers Liffey and Poddle, to a planned town and a hub in an international trading centre? Various factors contributed to Dublin's expansion and urban development similar to urbanization in Britain and Europe. Locally, in 902, the kings of Leinster and Brega, the Irish power brokers in the environs of Dublin, attacked the settlement and expelled its dynasty, the descendants of the early Viking leader named Ívarr (d. 873) and its military elite.[71] Archaeology suggests that the settlement was not wiped out and that it continued to exist, most likely under the authority of Irish kings. Dublin's exiled elite went to France, to Chester and York in Britain, and most particularly to the Hebrides in Scotland, from where they launched attacks on the northern kingdoms of Cenél Conaill and Cenél nEógain. The dynasty of Ívarr, in the guise of his grandsons Røgnvaldr, Ívarr, Sigtryggr and Guðrøðr, embarked on a campaign in 914 to re-establish themselves in Ireland, and by 919 they had succeeded in doing so in Dublin and Waterford. For Dublin, this dynasty's connections to the outer world must have triggered the greater urbanization and internationalization of the riverine settlement. Dublin became the primary international trading gateway into Ireland from the tenth century onwards, and in attaining this status it acted as a gateway for the many regional hubs within Ireland and around the Irish Sea. The dynasty of Ívarr saw off opposition from a rival Viking dynasty based in the southwestern region at Limerick in a fiercely fought war waged in the 920s and 930s that also involved native Irish kings. As the town's wealth and the power of its dynasty became apparent, these same Irish kings became increasingly keen to rule it and the other embryonic Viking towns of Limerick and Waterford, and to benefit from their prosperity.

An obvious indicator of Viking influence on the Irish economy, and the changing patterns of trading activity on the island, is reflected in the large number of Scandinavian or Hiberno-Scandinavian silver hoards dated to the ninth to eleventh centuries found in Ireland.[72] These consist of coinless hoards, mixed hoards and coin-only hoards and their find locations are predominately in the midlands and along the east coast. Mixed hoards made up of ornaments such as Hiberno-Scandinavian broad-band armrings (fig. 5), probably manu-

5 Hiberno-Norse silver armrings, AD850–950. Armrings are among the most important Viking artefacts found in Ireland, as they provide evidence for economic activity, craftsmanship and use of such objects in the exchange of gifts or payment. © National Museum of Ireland.

factured from silver from southern Scandinavia and the Baltic region, ingots and hack-silver, constitute the earliest type of hoards (c.850–950). This was a first attempt at introducing bullion, the equivalent of a nascent coin-based system, into a barter-based economy. The prevalence of weights and scales in graves and in the Dublin excavations in general signifies the existence of a system of measurements that governed exchange between the traders of Dublin and an interior regional hinterland. These exchanges no doubt were made for practical daily necessities such as foodstuffs – primarily cereals – and also for payment of tribute or ransom to Irish kings, or by the Irish to Viking leaders for services rendered or after a defeat at battle. In 964 (AU), for example, the church of Kildare was attacked by the Vikings and its clerics were captured, but they were ransomed by Niall úa Eruilb – probably a Hiberno-Norse leader – 'with his own silver Niall ransomed of them as many as would fill Brigit's great house and the oratory'. Silver must have been exchanged as part of the many alliances forged between the Vikings and Irish kings from the ninth century. This was the case with the northern king Áed Findliath, who attacked the midlands kingdom of Mide in 862 with the aid of the Vikings and Irish allies as part of his campaign to claim the kingship of Tara. All such contacts, belligerent or otherwise, necessitated a common notion of material values, and the surviving physical evidence of this lies in hoards and instruments of metal and monetary measurement.

The shift to mixed hoards of bullion and coins and then to coins only by the tenth century offers further evidence for the urbanization and internationalization of Dublin and for increasing external influences in the town. Arabic Kufic coins were used as bullion in the Viking world and were sourced in large quantities ultimately back to Russia and from there through the Baltic and Gotland to Britain and Ireland.[73] Hence, Dublin became one of relatively few nodal centres of long-distance trade in early Viking Age northern Europe, and having established itself as such, followed the model of similar centres and began to develop as a town. An essential component of these nodal centres and their trading patterns was not alone an economic network but also close social ties and the creation of 'a small world phenomenon'.[74] The Irish Sea between Britain and Ireland was, for Dublin, Chester and York, a 'small world' in which family and dynastic connections were so tightly knit that, for the elite at least, it operated as one economic and social, if politically complicated, region. Among the descendants of Ívarr between the 920s and 950s, three generations produced kings of Dublin and York: Røgnvaldr (d. 921), Sigtryggr (d. 927), Óláfr (d. 941) and Óláfr (d. 980). The dynasty did not hold a secure grip on either kingship or region, as they were often threatened by internal rivalries and their constantly changing relations with English, Irish, Scottish and Welsh kings.[75] Nevertheless, they controlled the sea with their superior fleets and knowledge of the coasts. This is powerfully expressed in the ship-related borrowings from Old Norse into Middle Irish: *birling* (*byrðing* 'a cargo-ship'), *carb* (*karfi* 'an inland ship'), *ciúil* (*kjóll* 'big ship') and *laídeng* (*leitangr* 'people of a war fleet, ship').[76] Ninth- and early tenth-century mixed and coin hoards also reflect this 'small world phenomenon', as they include Anglo-Saxon, Viking Northumbrian and Anglian, and Carolingian coins. Dublin was at the heart of the Irish component of the international 'small world' and it became increasingly the core of an all-island 'small world' that dominated not just economic activity but also political change.

One of Ireland's most important contributions to medieval studies, and sadly a contribution little recognized outside of the world of Viking scholarship, is the immense amount of material evidence of early medieval urban life unearthed from excavations in Dublin, Waterford, Limerick and to a lesser extent Cork and Wexford.[77] While the immediate models for the urbanization of Irish towns are undoubtedly found in contemporary trends in England, and especially in York, other forms of interaction with the Irish resulted in the distinctive development of Hiberno-Norse towns.[78] What was it like to live in tenth-century Dublin?[79] Domestically, people commonly lived in houses with low post-and-wattle walls incorporating materials such as brushwood and an insulating layer of cattle dung on the outside. Houses had doors at either end and a central stone-kerbed hearth. Floors were covered with wood-chips. On either side against the walls were raised benches and bedding areas, and all these structures were covered by a grassland sod and thatched roof supported by posts positioned well in from the side and end walls. These houses, classified by Patrick Wallace as Type 1 'Dublin building type par excellence',[80] consisted of an average floor area of about 40m². Outhouses, animal pens, yards, pathways, cesspits and dung heaps surrounded these houses. Houses and outhouses were frequently

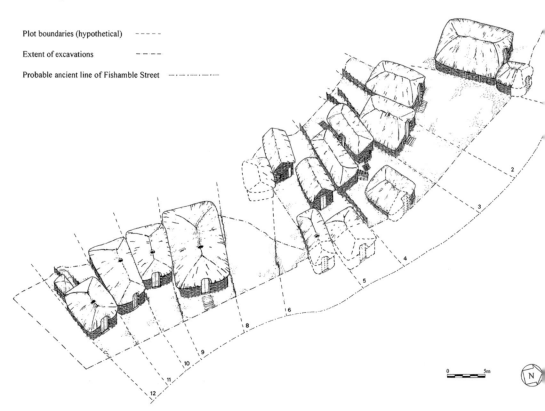

Plot boundaries (hypothetical)   ------

Extent of excavations   - - - -

Probable ancient line of Fishamble Street   —·—·—·—·—

6 Fishamble Street in Viking Dublin: the well laid out street is testimony to some form of urban planning in Dublin from the ninth century onwards. Thirteen levels of successive building phases were excavated at Fishamble Street, beginning with a house and outhouse in the ninth century and developing into a streetscape in the tenth and eleventh centuries. Like Armagh, this streetscape left an impression that survived to modern times. © P.F. Wallace/John Murray/National Museum of Ireland.

demolished or reorganized, but the dividing boundary fences that defined plot divisions remained constant over centuries. The plots on Fishamble Street, for example, remained unchanged throughout the tenth and eleventh centuries, and even left an imprint on the streetscape to modern times.[81] Thirteen levels of successive building phases were excavated at Fishamble Street, beginning with the first plot containing one house and outhouse built possibly in the ninth or tenth century, and developing at its height to a street comprising up to thirteen buildings of various sizes (fig. 6). Streets were paved with sand, gravel, estuarine clay, stones and seashells, or were boarded to cope with moist conditions and with weeds. In addition, drains and gullies helped to run off surface water, which, as might be expected in such a wet environment, often caused problems. Despite these conditions, in her description of Dublin's urban environment, Siobhán Geraghty estimates that the town was an 'urban heat island' with a higher ground temperature than in the surrounding countryside due to the heat emanating from domestic and industrial hearths, and fermenting organic accumulations.[82] Fishamble Street was less congested than other parts of the town such as High Street and Winetavern Street, which were made up of smaller buildings and lesser pathways leading down to the waterfront. Naturally, the dominant feature that shaped all major Hiberno-Norse towns was a waterfront located along a riverine estuary and a slope down to the river.

Much effort was put into defending Dublin from flooding and from hostile attacks. In the tenth century, a substantial embankment was constructed on a natural rising slope and was protected from erosion by a breakwater.[83] This embankment and another more solid defensive bank, which followed it c.1000, appear to have enclosed the whole town and to have also been designed to accommodate boats docking on the waterfront. The construction of successive defences, the enduring extent of plots and the layout of streets and pathways suggest that Dublin was subject to some form of civic planning. The increasing intervention by Irish kings in the affairs of Dublin, and other Hiberno-Norse towns, during the tenth century had two major repercussions: the towns needed to be more stoutly defended, and ultimately Hiberno-Norse kings became subject to Irish kings. The physical distress of the inhabitants of Dublin in 989, when the town was besieged by the powerful king of Tara, Máel Sechnaill mac Domnaill, is best explained by the universal phenomenon of besieged cities (ATig.):

> The Battle of Dublin gained over the Foreigners by Maelseachnaill son of Domhnall, wherein many were slain and the siege of their fortress afterwards for twenty nights, and during it they drank no water save brine. Wherefore they gave him his own award so long as he should be king, and an ounce of gold for every garden to be paid on every Christmas Eve for ever.

Six years later, in 995, Máel Sechnaill took away their royal regalia, Tomar's ring and Carlus' sword, in revenge for attacking his kingdom.

Excavations at Dublin have produced an inordinate amount of material evidence for all aspects of daily life in the town from the tenth century onwards, to the extent that it is possible to recreate the lives of various individuals from the elite warrior class of the earliest period to the craftsmen, merchants and women involved in metalworking, carpentery, long-distance trading and weaving of the tenth century and later. In the latter instance, a series of woollen and silk scarves, veils, bands and fitted caps offers tangible evidence for carding, weaving, sewing and dyeing techniques.[84] Silk was imported via Dublin's 'small world phenomenon' from centres such as Haithabu, Birka and Kaupang, linked to Novgorod and Kiev, to Byzantium and ultimately possibly to Baghdad.[85] Wool is likely to have come from a closer source, Dublin's rural hinterland known as *Dyflinarskiri*, that varied in its extent at different periods, but often stretched into Brega (modern Co. Meath), southwards into Cualu (south Co. Dublin/north Co. Wicklow) and westwards into Uí Dúnlaing kingdoms (modern Co. Kildare) as late as the twelfth century.[86] This hinterland supplied Dublin's ever-increasing urban population with foodstuffs and raw materials. The townsfolk had access to a relatively well-balanced diet of meat (primarily beef, but also mutton and pork), fish, cereals (wheat, barley and oats) for bread and porridge, peas and beans, fruits (apples and various berries), hazelnuts and honey.[87] Hides were brought into the town for its vibrant leather-making industry. In the mass of evidence uncovered in Dublin, fleeting glimpses of daily life often survive: these include efforts to keep the floors of the Fishamble Street houses clean and clear of food remains or the amber chips from a late tenth-century jeweller's workshop at the bottom of Fishamble Street.[88] No object, however, brings us closer to daily life than the wooden toy horse from Fishamble Street incised with a human face on each side.[89] Finds of this kind bring with them the human emotions felt by any child: the joy of receiving the toy and playing with it or the grief at its loss or being damaged.

Conclusion

A journey through early medieval Ireland could have been an adventure or a dangerous expedition, depending on where one travelled and who was encountered on the way. There might be a day when one barely met another human on a trackway over wetlands or mountains or along a pathway in dense woodlands. But the likelihood of going for long periods without meeting anyone was small. Parts of the island were fairly densely populated and one might come upon clusters of houses, most often defended, in which farming and other industrial activities were the mainstay of their economy. Larger settlements, royal or ecclesiastical, might be the locations of markets or other assemblies, conducted by kings and important churchmen. At the other extreme, people no doubt eked out a living in squalid conditions, often on the margins of society. These people rarely left either physical or historical traces behind, except perhaps fleetingly in tales as servants of the nobility or as lawless vagabonds and lunatics living outside the strictures of 'normal' communities. These people were the unheard and unseen in the landscape. Inevitably in a society in which violence was endemic, one would stumble upon charred houses or the evidence of killings due to battles or small-scale raids. Roads were wet and muddy, and even impassible, or may have barely existed as they trailed off into green pathways. In reality, this terrain was varied and often challenging, while in the imagination, the traveller was surrounded by hoards of benign and protective holy people and by dark and threatening powers.

CHAPTER 2

Kingdoms, kings and people

Early medieval Ireland was divided into a hierarchy of kingdoms from small local units to expansive provincial kingdoms. The boundaries of the smaller kingdoms remained relatively stable and were normally determined by natural physical features such as rivers, streams, bogs or high ground. This category of kingdom was a *túath* and its king the *rí túaithe*. Beyond the local kingdoms were larger *túatha*, regional and sub-regional kingdoms, and most importantly provincial kingdoms known as *cóiceda*.[1] Early Irish lawyers and traditional historians drew up a schematic division of the country that pervaded literature, chronicles and genealogies as late as the seventeenth century. The country was divided by them into two main divisions, Leth Moga (south) and Leth Cuinn (north). This division was effectively based on a line drawn across the midlands with the latter region generally being regarded as part of the northern half. The provinces were Laigen (east), Mumu (south), Connacht (west), Mide (midlands) and Ulaid (north). The boundaries of the provinces could vary depending on the strength of a provincial king or on the permanent alienation of part of one province to another. Each province, as indeed each kingdom, had a fixed core and this often centred on an old prehistoric capital. This old capital provided the provincial kingships with alternative titles: hence the king of Munster was also known as king of Caisel (Cashel, Co. Tipperary), of Connacht as king of Cruachu (Rathcroghan, Co. Roscommon), and the king of Mide as king of Uisnech (Usnagh, Co. Westmeath). A provincial king was classified in the laws as a *rí cóicid* 'king of a province' or a *rí ruirech* 'king of kings', that is an overking. In theory, the king of Tara took precedence over the provincial kings and was usually a provincial king himself.

The kingdom in medieval Western Europe has been defined as the ideal type of political unit and the king the ideal type of ruler. The kingdom was not merely a territory that happened to be ruled by a king, it comprised and corresponded to a 'people' (*gens, natio, populus*), which was assumed to be a natural, inherited community of tradition, custom, law and descent.[2] In Ireland, the terms *gens, natio, plebs, populus* to describe a 'people' were also used. Numerous analogous native terms identified the complex layers of kindred, community and kingdoms that constituted the *natio* of the Irish. Common terms used in Irish to denote kindred groups include *cenél*, *corcu* and *dál* and these are translated mainly into Latin as *gens*.[3] While Ireland did not encounter any major influx of people from prehistory to the Vikings and appeared culturally and linguistically homogenous, it is clear from place-name evidence and from the kindred names of various peoples that a British-speaking population had settled in the east.[4] Due to the fortunate survival of early sources, sufficient information is at hand to gain an impression of the identity of peoples settled in even the remotest part of the island.

Ptolemy's Geography

The earliest detailed record of the inhabitants of Ireland is found in the *Geography* written by the Egyptian astronomer and geographer Ptolemy (*c*.AD100–78). Ptolemy lists sixteen groups, six of which can be identified from later historical records and all of which lived in coastal regions.[5] This pattern, and the propensity of islands, promonteries and river estuaries noted in Ptolemy's work, was based on information brought back by seafarers and traders who were familiar with the Irish coast. The Uaithne (*Auteini*), for example, are located on the Shannon Estuary and their name survives in the modern barony of Owney (Uaithne) and Ara, Co. Tipperary. Ptolemy records two powerful and related people, the Ulaid (*Uoluntii*) and the Érainn (*Iverni*), in the north-east and south-west respectively, who dominated extensive parts of Ireland until the sixth century.[6] Heroes and pseudo-historic kings from among the Ulaid and the Érainn are among the major characters of early Irish literature. They include the heroes of the *Táin*, Cú Chulainn and Fergus mac Róich and the heroic kings of Tara, Conaire Mór and Lugaid mac Con. The Monaig (*Manapii*) and Corainn (*Coriondi*) were people who no longer occupied the areas in which Ptolemy located them, but appear elsewhere in medieval sources. The place-name Corainn survives in the modern barony of Corran, Co. Sligo, while the Monaig left their imprint in the place-name Fer Manach (Fermanagh). Although many of the peoples listed by Ptolemy cannot be identified, mainly due to corruption in the transmission of the names through the centuries, the survival of some people in the same place to the historic period points to relative stability on the island. Migration tales form part of early Irish literature, and no doubt migration happened in fact, but the disappearance of a people or a dynasty normally occurred as a result of being pushed into obscurity following a power struggle rather than complete extinction.

Ogam inscriptions

Ogam stones are distinct monuments scattered around the Irish countryside (fig. 7). They record hundreds of names written in Irish in an alphabet unique to that language. They also occur in Wales, Scotland, the Isle of Man and Cornwall. Scholars have dated the creation of the ogam alphabet, mainly on linguistic evidence, at least as far back as the fourth century. It would seem, however, that most ogam stones were inscribed in the fifth and sixth centuries.[7] The majority of ogam stones are distributed along the south and south-west coast, while smaller clusters are found in Cos Kilkenny, Meath, Mayo and Roscommon. Ogam inscriptions are of crucial importance in providing extensive evidence for the early development of the Irish language, for systems of kinship and for the dominant kindreds in parts of Ireland at the beginning of the historic period.[8] The kinship formulae found in ogam inscriptions consist mainly of personal names in relation to other personal names or occasionally to an ancestral descendant whose name is used to represent a people (*gens*). The formula most frequently used is X MAQQI Y 'X son of Y'. Other formulae include X MAQQI MUCOI Y 'X son of the people (*gens*) descended from Y', X MAQQI Y MUCOI Z 'X son of Y of the people of Z', and X AVI Y 'X grandson/descendant of Y'. The interpretation of both the inscriptions themselves, which are sometimes hard to decipher, and of how they might relate to historical kindreds has been a cause of lively scholarly debate. As with Ptolemy, they present a vital clue as to the prominent members of Irish society at various periods from *c*.400 to 600. They also link directly into the extensive genealogies that were recorded in writing from at least the seventh century, and survive in later medieval manuscripts.

Ogam inscriptions contribute not alone to the linguistic history of the Irish language, but are also historical sources in their own right. Some may be memorial stones, similar to commemorative monuments that are found throughout the Roman world. Others, however, had a legal function relating to boundaries and landholding, and probably acted as visible, physical declarations of land possession. An oft-cited example of ogam inscriptions linking with historical sources is that of the cluster of inscriptions in the barony of Corkaguiney, Co. Kerry, commemorating members of the Corcu Duibne who were undoubtedly the rulers of the area. Five of the inscriptions identify individuals as MAQQI MUCOI DOVVINIA[S] 'son of the people (*gens*) of Duibne'.[9] These ogams are in a district where they might be expected to occur and Corkaguiney itself retains an anglicized form of their name. There are other instances of similar names scattered in different parts of the country. This does not necessarily mean that they all belonged to the same group, and may indicate that various unrelated people adopted similar patronymics, especially in adhering

7 Ogham stone in Ardmore Cathedral, Co. Waterford: the ogham alphabet was devised for writing in the Irish language at least as early as the fifth century and is found inscribed on stones throughout Ireland, but especially along the south coast. This inscription reads Lugaid (*LUGUDECCAS*) descendant of Nia-Segemon (*NETA SEGAMONAS*) and is one of three stones in the region commemorating individuals of the same dynasty. Nia-Segemon is listed in early sources as a prehistoric king of Cashel. © Discovery Programme, Dublin/Dublin Institute for Advanced Studies.

to the names of deities. The inscriptions with the element LUGUNI (later Luigne) is an instructive example. It probably indicates that the people who adopted it regarded themselves as somehow descended from Lugnae, who appears in one saga as Lugnae Fer Trí, the fosterer of the heroic king Cormac mac Airt. In the medieval period, the Luigne lived in parts of north Co. Meath and in Co. Sligo (barony of Leyney). An Ogam inscription, COVAGNI MAQI MUCOI LUGUNI '(stone of) Cóemán son of the people (*gens*) of Luigne', is located in the churchyard of Castlekeeran, Co. Meath.[10] A stone commemorating a member of the Luigne here is unsurprising, as it fits well with the known historical kingdom of the eastern Luigne. An ogam inscription in Windgap, Co. Waterford, commemorates MODDAGN[I] MAQI GATTAGN[I] MUCOI LUGUNI '(stone of) Múadán son of Gáethán(?) of the people of Luigne'.[11] This individual may have been a member of the Dál Luigne, listed as a subject people in this region in the eighth-century Old Irish text 'The expulsion of the Déssi'. Interestingly, his name translates as 'Noble one (Múadán) son of Wise one (Gáethán)', which hints that the Dál

Luigne held a higher status prior to the eighth century. Finally, two inscriptions with the formula MAQ[I] LUGUNI were found in a souterrain in Knockshanawee, Co. Cork, and they may commemorate two brothers, the 'sons of Luigne'.[12] These inscriptions beg the question as to the origin of these men: were they from elsewhere in Ireland, or was this a common patronymic found throughout the country?

While most ogam inscriptions seem to commemorate individuals who may have been kings in their immediate regions, a few inscriptions, when associated with written genealogies, may have been erected to the memory of provincial kings or dynasties. Three stones in west Waterford, one each at Ardmore, Knockboy and Old Island, include the ancestral (*gens*) formula, MUCOI NETA SEGEMONAS, 'the people of Nia-Segamon'.[13] Nia-Segemon is listed in the historical sources as a prehistoric king of Cashel. His supposed grandson, Lugaid Luaigni, is also listed as a prehistoric king of Munster and of Ireland.[14] He may even be commemorated on the ogam stone in Ardmore that reads LUGUDECCAS MAQI[...MU]COI NETA-SEGAMONAS. It is possible that a dynasty claiming descent from these ancestral figures located in the lower fertile valley of the River Blackwater at one time claimed the provincial kingship of Cashel. That an inscription commemorating Lugaid descendant of Nia-Segamon is located in the early monastery of Ardmore might even suggest that this dynasty controlled the coast and the river and was instrumental in the adoption of Christianity in that region. This suggestion is supported by the locations of the other Nia-Segamon stones: the Knockboy stone is part of the fabric of a medieval church in the strategic pass of Sliab Cua (in the Knockmealdown Mountains), and the Old Island stone is located in a prehistoric henge on a significant coastal promontory. Holding such strategic locations might have enabled this dynasty to compete for the provincial kingship.

Annals and genealogies

Records of kings, kingdoms and dynasties extending reliably as far back as the late sixth century survive in the early layers of the medieval Irish annals and genealogies. Identifying genuinely early royal titles and designations for kingdoms can be difficult, as these were often subjected to revision with the rise or decline of dynasties. Nonetheless, a survey of the entries in the annals, especially the Annals of Ulster and the Annals of Tigernach, gives a fairly comprehensive idea of how kingdoms and kingships were defined. Their evidence populates the island with kingdoms of varying sizes, from small, local ones to the large provincial ones, with territories defined by natural features, and with people bound together by a variety of ancestral identities.

The different titles accorded to early Irish kings reflect how kingship was perceived and how a king might be viewed at one time, as ruling a geographical region, a people or a specific dynasty. The provincial kings of the east and west, the kings of Connacht and Laigen, were kings of a dominant people and all those subject to them. The Connachta consisted of those who regarded themselves as the descendants of Conn, normally identified as Conn Cétchathach 'Conn of the Hundred Battles'. They belonged to the dominant dynasties of Connacht, the Uí Ailello, Uí Briúin and Uí Fhiachrach. Subject to the descendants of Conn were once-powerful people such as the Cíarraige, and lesser people such as the Calraige, Partraige and many others.[15] The Laigin also consisted of four dominant dynasties, reputedly descended from different ancestors: Dál Níad Corb 'the descendants of Nia Corb', Dál Messin Corb 'the descendants of Mess Corb', Dál Cormaic 'the descendants of Cormac' and Dál Coirpri Araid 'the descendants of Coirpre Arad'. The origin of their collective name, Laigin, is obscure, but may be related somehow to Latin *legiones*.[16] There is evidence that until the sixth century, a king of the Laigin might have ruled a territory extending from the Shannon to north Wales, where the topographical name of the Lleyn Peninsula preserves their name. In the south of Ireland, Ptolemy's map places a tribal group, the Iverni, as dominant over much of the province of Mumu (Munster). The Iverni, or Érainn, their heroic kings and their descendants, feature in saga literature and the genealogies. Their doomed mythical king Conaire Mór was viewed as the ancestor of various peoples, including the Corcu Baiscinn and Corcu Duibne, settled along the western seaboard, and the Múscraige, who were dispersed around the southern province. The northern province of the Ulaid, which until the sixth century stretched as far as the Boyne, took its name from the Uoluntii, whose name appears in Ptolemy's *Geography*. The great prehistoric complex of Emain Macha (Navan Fort, Co. Armagh) was probably their capital. The Dál Fiatach, who ruled the north-east, were their descendants and were known as *fír Ulaid* 'true Ulstermen'. The king of Ulaid is occasionally accorded the title *rí in Chóicid* 'king of the Province' or *rí in Tuaiscirt* 'king of the North'. While this title was often used derogatively for kings of the Cruithin who seized the kingship from Dál Fiatach kings,[17] it also reveals a belief that this province was the true *cóiced* 'province', an ideal situation portrayed in early sagas such as *Táin Bó Cúailnge*.

Titles accorded to regional and local kings reflect an even more complex structure than that of the provincial kingships, with a myriad of designations used to describe the over-kings and subject kings of a territory. Titles also overlapped and changed at various periods. The system is best explained by examining the eastern and midland over-kingdom of Brega.

The kingdom of Brega (fig. 8)

The kingdom of Brega encompassed the modern counties of Meath, north Dublin and part of Louth, and was internally defined by rivers – the Liffey, Delvin, Inny, Boyne, Dee and Fane. Apart from its coastline, the Boyne was the most important natural feature in the landscape of Brega.[18] The name Brega originates from the plural of *brí* 'hill' and is a precise description of the kingdom's landscape, a region of low-lying hills. An over-kingship of Brega existed and this was variously held by kings of southern or northern Brega.[19] Subject to these over-kings were minor kings either belonging to their own kindreds or to unrelated subject peoples, whose kingships were often usurped by the dominant dynasties. Áed Sláine, the eponymous ancestor of Síl nÁedo Sláine ('the descendants of Áed Sláine'), king of Tara, was killed in 604, and following his death, his descendants fragmented into numerous dynasties whose bitter rivalry blighted this part of the country during the seventh and eighth centuries. A clear example of this fragmentation is illustrated by the activities of rival dynasties in southern Brega in the late ninth century. Tolarg, joint-king of southern Brega, died of old age in 888. Máel Sechnaill mac Néill, from a related but rival dynasty and accorded the title *lethrí deisceirt Breg* 'joint-king of southern Brega' was killed by a Viking in 870. Another king, Máel Augrai mac Congalaig, *rí Gabor* 'king of Gabor', probably a reference to the royal residence of Lagore, Co. Meath, was killed in 908 by Fogartach son of Tolarg. Tolarg's other son, Tigernach, described as 'eligible for the kingship of southern Brega' was slain in 887 by his own acquaintances (*a sociis suis*). This dissension in the southern sub-kingdom of Brega enabled another local king, Flannacán mac Cellaig (d. 896), to take advantage of this turmoil and to seize the over-kingship of Brega.

Brega was divided into lesser kingdoms, some of which continued to be ruled by dynasties that were not related to Síl nÁedo Sláine, and others that were usurped by the latter. Ciannachta Breg, for example, were a people whose rule extended over considerable lands in Brega until the eighth century, when the Síl nÁedo Sláine eroded their power considerably.[20] Flannacán mac Cellaig's dynasty, the Uí Chonaing, usurped the over-kingship of Ciannachta Breg at the beginning of the eighth century. Flann (d. 812) and Cummascach (d. 839) mac Congalaig adopted the title rex *Ciannachta* 'king of Ciannachta'. In doing so, they became the overlords of the kings of Ciannachta Breg, and also seized control of their territory north of the Boyne around Knowth.[21] Nonetheless, some of the earlier Ciannachta managed to hold onto lands and maintain a kingdom of their own, the kingdom of Fir Arda Ciannachta 'the men of Ard Ciannachta'. This coastal kingdom was roughly coterminous with the modern barony of Ferrard, Co. Louth. Their king, Cummascach mac Muiredaig, was

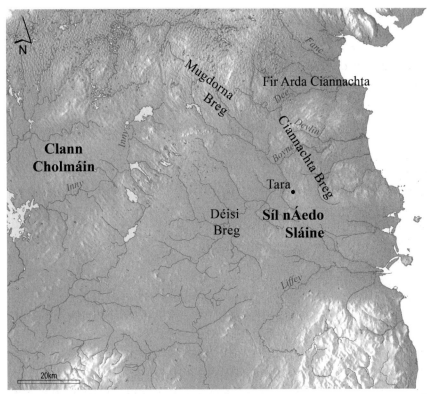

8 Map of the kingdom of Brega. This was the most sought after kingdom in Ireland, and kings vied with one another to attain the title of 'king of Tara'. Map prepared by Robert Shaw; © Discovery Programme, Dublin.

killed by the Ulaid in 896, the same year in which Flannacán mac Cellaig died at the hands of the Vikings.

There were other similar subject peoples and kingdoms in Brega.[22] The Mugdorna Breg held lands scattered throughout Brega. They had associations with the churches of Slane, Donaghmore and Kilbrew, Co. Meath. Ainfíth mac Mugróin, accorded the title *dux Mugdorna Breg* in 883 (*AU*), was the last king to hold the title, which either ceased to exist in the changing polity of ninth-century Brega, or was subsumed into an over-kingship of the Mugdorna. Less is known of the kingship of Déssi Breg 'the vassal people of Breg', who, as vassals, held lands throughout Brega, but maintained an important role in defending Tara. Three brothers, Daithgus (d. 732), Niallgus (d. 758) and Echtgus mac Buíth (d. 777), are the last to be referred to as kings of Déssi Breg until the eleventh century, when an intrusive dynasty seems to have usurped or revived the title.

This complex stratification of people, which defined them as belonging to kindreds, kingdoms and dynasties, is replicated throughout the country. Not all belonged to royal lineages. Most of the population were subject to kings and those at the lowest levels in society probably cared little as to their ancestry. They were on the margins due to unfortunate circumstances or to loss of power and lands in a society that was subject to a constant social movement towards the lowest in status and material possessions. Notions about specific ancestries and identities were defined by a privileged few – kings, their advisors, learned religious and learned guardians of *senchas*. To much of the rest of society, they were defined by bonds of clientship and kinship.

CONCEPTS OF KINGSHIP

The bond between a king and his people was one of the two fundamental bonds in early medieval Irish society. The bond of familial kinship, a more personal relationship, was the second pillar of society. Power was invested in kings. They ruled kingdoms. They competed with one another for territory. Their ability to rule was based on how effectively mutual obligations between them, their people, their clients and other kings were discharged. They administered justice and held public assemblies. They acted as patrons of poets, craftsmen and the church. Ireland was no different from other societies in which the king played a pivotal role in society. When the Irish encountered royal or imperial power elsewhere, be it in the late antique Roman world, in Anglo-Saxon England, in Carolingian Europe or in the Bible, they recognized both the obvious and the mysterious attributes that shrouded early kingship. Not only did they understand the institution, they spent considerable energy deliberating on it and in their efforts contributed to the shaping of medieval European kingship.

From prehistoric sacral kingship to kings 'ordained by God'

The deeds of kings permeate the extensive literature of early medieval Ireland. The importance of the institution of kingship and society's need for good royal governance resulted in the generation of a wide range of texts in which many facets of kingship were explored. These texts ranged from early forms of the *speculum principum* 'the mirror of princes', to secular law tracts, ecclesiastical canons, annals, saints' Lives and pseudo-historical texts and sagas. They were written in Irish and in Latin and some date to the seventh century, if not earlier. Certain texts adopt a theoretical and moralizing stance, often setting out the fundamental precepts of the ideal king: such is the nature of the discourse in the *speculum principum* texts, the canons and the saints' Lives. The legal rights and obligations of kings are detailed in the laws that encapsulate many of the concepts of the *speculum principum*. The annals chronicle the reigns of pre-Christian and Christian kings, concentrating mainly on battles and rivalry within kindreds and with other kings. Pseudo-historical texts and sagas narrate the heroic biographies of both historical and mythological kings, and like other texts often include an underlying debate about the nature of kingship and good governance.

A universal aspect of kingship combined political and religious powers: the king could be ruler and priest, an intermediary between heaven and earth, and in some civilizations, a deity in his own right, or a king subject to a great god.[23] Human and divine attributes could be blurred to the extent that scholars throughout the world have continually debated the nature of sacral kingship, and indeed its very existence.[24] Definitions of sacral kingship depended on a society's categorization of the divine, and more importantly on the beliefs of a society's elite. Divine or sacral kingships manifested themselves in various regions and societies at different times in their histories as necessitated by circumstances. A sacral kingship could emerge or acquire increasing ritual significance with the expansion of a dynasty or an empire. Elsewhere, as in ancient Egypt, sacral kingship was a constant. And the converse could occur with the decline of a divine or sacral kingship.[25] This general debate on kingship is particularly relevant to early medieval Irish kingship, and especially as to how a prehistoric, non-Christian institution was remoulded into to a medieval, Christian office. The extent to which older beliefs and rituals were lost or diminished is central to the discourse on Irish kingship, and the early texts present a valuable insight into the subject.

The earliest Irish text on royal governance is *Audacht Morainn* 'The Testament of Morann', advice given by the mythical judge Morann to a mythical king Feradach Finn Fechtnach.[26] This gnomic wisdom-text is based on known legal concepts and structures and may even be the composite product of a law school.[27] The essential vocabulary of medieval Irish kingship occurs throughout *Audacht Morainn* – *rí* 'a king', *túath* 'a people, tribe, kingdom, land unit', *flaith* 'rule(r)', *fír* 'true, just', *fírinne* 'truth', *fír flathemon* 'the justice of the ruler', *fó* 'good' and *gó/gáu* 'falsehood, injustice'. The king is not divine, but he is classified as a *fírfhlaith* 'a true lord', a *cíallfhlaith* 'a cunning ruler', a *tarbfhlaith* 'a bull ruler', or 'a ruler of occupation with hosts from outside' (*flaith congbále co slógaib díanechtair*). The last category refers to a king who seizes a kingdom other than his own. The fundamental divisions between kings involved the opposites of the good and bad king, and categories of acceptable rule, wise rule and righteous rule, which at times, especially in the case of the wise ruler, could involve occupation of territories or violence. All kings, except for the *tarbfhlaith*,

could aspire to becoming a *fírfhlaith*.[28] Feradach Finn Fechtnach himself was
just such an ideal king: he came from abroad to free Ireland from the oppressive
rule of vassal tribes. Morann, in his advice to Feradach, ends the text by
exhorting the young king to follow his advice. He claims that by doing so, his
words will bring him victory, and he can become a *fírfhlaith*. How was a king
classified as good or bad? *Audacht Morainn* concentrates on the good king, but
defines the *tarbfhlaith*, the bad ruler, in the following terms:[29]

> The bull ruler, then, is not a man worthy of love. He strikes [and] is struck,
> he injures [and] he is injured, he attacks and is attacked. Against him there
> is always clashing with horns. Harsh, unfortunate [is] the beginning of
> his reign, hateful, waning [is] its middle, [and it is] unstable, impermanent
> in the end. It is against his sons that [his] crimes will be heaped together,
> that faces will be raised, that hearts will be shut. 'Not welcome', says
> everyone to the sons of that king, 'the rule by your father was never good
> for us'.
>   The bull ruler strikes [and] is struck, wards off [and] is warded off,
> roots out [and] is rooted out, attacks [and] is attacked, pursuades [and] is
> pursued. Against him there is bellowing of horns (*is fris con bith-búirethar
> bennaib*).

This last phrase in describing a *tarbfhlaith* contrasts with the reaction to a
fírfhlaith 'for he whom the living do not glorify with blessings is not a true ruler'
(*ar ní fírfhlaith nad níamat bí bendachtnaib*).[30] What distinguishes the rule of a
fírfhlaith? This king is the ideal king. Fundamental to his rule is the concept of
fír flathemon, a universal concept of the 'Ruler's Truth'.[31] He is just and merciful,
and cares for his people. Through his justice, plagues are warded off, peace
reigns, enemies are kept away, the land and animals are fertile, fish are plentiful.
He is to respect 'old men in their seats of their ancestors' and to exalt judges
who know true legal precedents. He is to fulfil his obligations, not resort to
unnecessary violence, care for the weak and not be too interested in rich gifts. In
summary, 'Let him estimate the right and justice, truth and law, contract and
regulation of every just ruler towards all his clients' (*Ad-mestar cert 7 cóir, fír 7
dligeth, cumthus 7 córus cacha flatho fíre fria huili aicillni*).[32] It would not be
difficult to place these principles in any culture, be it ancient India, Mesopotamia,
Egypt, Rome or Carolingian Europe. And, whereas *Audacht Morainn* makes no
explicit reference to a Christian ethos, the phrase 'Let him estimate the creations
of the creator who made them as they were made' (*ad-mestar dúili dúilemon
tod[a]-rósat amal to-rrósata*)[33] suggests that the ideal king was not a deity but
was subject to one creator, likely by the seventh century to be the Christian god.

Ideas as expressed in *Audacht Morainn* are repeated in the seventh-century pseudo-Cyprian text of Irish origin, *De duodecim abusivis saeculi* 'On the twelve evils of the world', a text that influenced Anglo-Saxon and Carolingian medieval kingship to a great degree.[34] The *rex iniquus* 'unjust king' is compared to the *rex iustus* 'the just king', the latter retaining many characteristics of the *fírfhlaith* but with an overtly Christian disposition:[35]

> It is the justice of the king not to oppress anyone unjustly by force; to judge people without regard for the reputation of a person; to be the defender of strangers, orphans and widows; to prevent theft; to punish adultery; not to elevate the unjust; not to support the unchaste and minstrels; to destroy the godless; not to permit murderers and perjurers to live; to protect the churches and feed the poor with alms; to entrust the just with business of royal government; to have experienced, wise and prudent advisors; to pay no heed to the superstitious customs of magicians, soothsayers and sorceresses; to suppress rage; to defend the realm bravely and effectively against enemies and to trust God in all things.

From the beginning of the process of conversion of Irish society to Christianity, the clergy sought to influence kings and their families. Patrick gives witness to this strategy of conversion in his *Confessio*: 'Meanwhile I kept giving rewards to kings, besides which I kept giving a fee to their sons, who walk with me' (*Interim praemia dabam regibus praeter quod dabam mercedem filiis ipsorum qui mecum ambulant*).[36] Patrick, as an insightful missionary, was familiar with the centrality of customs of gift-giving in Irish society, and in this statement is explaining that his rewards to kings were essential to gain access to them, and that persuading their sons to follow him amounted to a form of fosterage. This activity, alien as it might be to some of his superiors, was necessary for the success of his mission. The extract quoted from *De duodecim abusivis saeculi* is essential to understanding how the church de-sacralized kingship in Ireland, and especially an exceptional kingship such as the kingship of Tara. Early Irish saints' Lives, especially the seventh-century Life of Patrick by Muirchú maccu Machtheni, and ecclesiastical synods, canons and penitentials either directly or obliquely dismantled the trappings of a sacral kingship, and, as so clearly depicted in the extract from *De duodecim abusivis saeculi*, replaced them with a Christian outlook on royal governance. Some elements of pre-Christian kingship were acceptable (justice, truth, peace, care of the weak), others had to be purged or subsumed cleverly into a new monotheistic religion where the division between human and divine depended on the figure of Christ. This transition can be traced in early genealogical and regnal vernacular poems such as *Móen óen*, a poem on Labraid Loingsech, ancestor of many dynasties in the east, and a figure in early sagas.[37] In this poem, he is called Móen 'the Dumb One'. As Carey observes, old gods and ancestral prehistoric – and presumably semi-divine – kings could be associated with biblical and Christian beliefs on human kingship. Old gods could be subject to the Christian God, who is the Supreme King – both human and divine:[38]

> Moen, alone since he was an infant:
> it was not the custom of a high-king.
> He smote kings, a splendid [spear-]cast,
> Labraid the grandson of Lorc ...
>
> ... The grandson of Loegaire Lorc
> was a gryphon attacking unknown lands,
> higher than men
> save the holy King of Heaven.
>
> Gold above the great bright sun,
> he gained the sovereignty over the world of men;
> [as] the one God to the gods
> is Moen son of Áine, the sole king.

In this poem, Labraid is the great king ruling the world of men, and his authority is compared to the one God who is superior to the pagan gods. A second poem quoted by Carey, *Lug scéith*, affirms this Christian polemic, and even more so as the subject is Lug, a god associated with the kingship of Tara:[39]

> Lug of a shield,
> a shining phantom:
> beneath the heavens there was not [anyone]
> who would be as great as the son of Áine.
>
> A mortal loftier than gods,
> a sturdy acorn,
> pure, with many branches,
> the grandson of Loegaire Lorc.

Here, the deity Lug appears to be one and the same as the great king Labraid, but Carey adduces that Labraid and Lug are subject to 'a mortal loftier than gods', namely Christ and ultimately, as in *Móen óen*, the Christian God. This poetry is a clever amalgam of pagan and Christian traditions about kingship, deities and the new Christian God. This new style of kingship is being shaped by the church,[40] and is 'a theology born of a Christian milieu ... but one in which it is still felt necessary to assert the claims of the Christian god against those of the divinities whose worship his cult was superseding'.[41]

The existence of this amalgam of two traditions offers a valuable approach through which the characteristics of pre-Christian Irish sacral kingship can be recognized with some degree of credibility. If pagan gods were a concern of early Irish Christian polemicists, they also focused their attention on other aspects of kingship that worried them: universal aspects of divine kingship that could undermine their omnipotent God and needed to be desacralized. In Egypt, for example, kingship was regarded as essential to the exercise of *maat* 'world order'[42] while Mayan rulers were the objects of royal cults in which they performed as deities, and in divine performances they demonstrated the ability 'to manifest the central axis of the cosmos'.[43] To assume this exceptional role, the king often performed a ritual marriage with a goddess and to uphold world order he had to adhere to certain prescriptions or taboos. How Irish texts known to have been composed in the seventh century deal with the attributes of sacral kingship is instructive in furthering an appreciation of the desacralization of the institution.

There has been a persistent debate in early Irish studies, particularly intense in the 1980s and 1990s, about the rationale of early vernacular and Latin sources, whether they are predominantly Christian and biblical in their inspiration or whether they can be relied upon to reflect elements of a native culture and polity that echoes back at least to the early centuries AD.[44]

One approach to understanding how kingship and its associated rituals were transformed with the final acceptance of Christianity in the seventh century is to trace how the land and its fertility as personified by a woman and the *banfheis*, a sacred marriage between the king and the goddess (the Irish reflex of the *hieros gamos*),[45] was revised and lessened in its potency.[46] There are many instances in Irish medieval literature of a union between a king and a woman who is the personification of sovereignty and sacral kingship.[47] The anecdotal text known as 'Conall Corc and the Corcu Luigde', which mainly dates to the seventh or eighth century, contains a passage on the late sixth-century king, Feidlimid mac Tigernaig, who reputedly attempted to become king of Munster by gaining entry to the provincial capital of Cashel. Feidlimid was barred from entering Cashel and from claiming the kingship:[48]

> Thus we have the proverb: 'Every descendant of Echu, though he may be king of all Munster, shall not go to Cashel'. That even applied to Feidlimid mac Tigernaig. He was king of Munster. He did not go to Cashel, but

Bodumbir [perhaps near Cahir, Co. Tipperary] was dug by him. So Cumman, the wife of Coirpre, made this quatrain after she had come to Feidlimid after Coirpre's death:[49]

> *Amra n-adamrae le nech*
> *iadad Caisil frim dá hech;*
> *amra n-adamrae leou*
> *iadad Caisil frim eochu*

Anyone would be greatly surprised
that my two horses were barred from Cashel;
they would be astonished to learn
of the shutting of Cashel against my two horses.

This passage embraces fundamental features of early Irish kingship. Feidlimid had to make a legal and ceremonial entry into the southern provincial capital, Cashel, to secure recognition of his claim to the kingship. He was required to follow a pre-ordained ceremony involving the procession of two horses through the entrance to Cashel. Failure to complete that ordeal meant that he could not claim to be king of Munster. In this instance, sovereignty is personified by Cumman, widow of Feidlimid's alleged predecessor Coirpre. As was often the case with historical royal widows who married their husbands' successors, Cumman came to Feidlimid, thus strengthening Feidlimid's claim to the kingship. It is Cumman who laments the barring of Cashel against Feidlimid and the horses were *her* horses.[50] This female and sexual aspect of kingship is apparent in one of the earliest king-lists of Tara, *Baile Chuinn Chétchathaig* 'The Frenzy of Conn of the Hundred Battles'.[51] Of the heroic king, Cormac mac Airt, the text claims 'he will be a glorious man upon her' (§4 *Bid án fer fuiri*), of the early historic king Coirpre mac Néill (possibly *fl.* 485–500) 'A glorious, noble bear upon her' (§13 *Art án féal fuiri*), and of Flann Asail mac Áedo (d. 714) 'Flann Asail will be upon her, glorious heir. He will betroth her by force of fists to hostages' (§31 *Bid fuiri Flann Asail, án orb. Arus-nena nertaib dorn do gíallaib*).

The long conversion process to Christianity necessitated that this primordial relationship between the land, as personified by a woman, and the king had to be altered to account for a new order. The *banfheis* or *hieros gamos* elevated the king to the status of sacral priest as well as ruler and successful warrior. The new relationship needed to be between the king and the Christian god, and the broker between human and divine was the church. The vocabulary of sacral kingship did not change in its terminology, but shifted in meaning and language: thus, as so clearly expressed in the Latin writings of Columbanus, the centre of the world (*caput mundi*), the king of kings (*rex regem*) and the 'supreme driver of the chariot' (*supremus ipse auriga currus illius*) were no longer to be found in Ireland, but were now equated with Rome and Christ through his representative on earth, the pope.[52] Irish kings began to be portrayed in biblical terms: in Muirchú's Life of St Patrick, the saint's opponent, Lóegaire mac Néill, king of Tara, is compared to Nebuchadanezzer of Babylon.[53] By the late seventh century, a senior cleric such as Adomnán (d. 704), ninth abbot of Iona, could command all the important kings and clerics of Ireland to guarantee the *Lex Innocentium* or *Cáin Adomnáin*, legislation protecting non-combatants (women, children and clerics), and church property. This law was proclaimed at a synod held in Birr, Co. Offaly, and the list of guarantors is headed by Loingsech mac Óenguso (d. 704), king of Ireland, and Flann Febla, bishop and abbot of Armagh (d. 715).[54] There is no clearer evidence of a new order than the joint promulgation of Adomnán's law by the leading secular and ecclesiastical authorities on the island and, in Adomnán's own case, the western isles of Scotland. From this period onwards, texts advising kings continued to laud the fundamental tenets of a prosperous reign, justice, peace and truth, but a king could only be successful if blessed by God and the church. The text *Tecosca Cormaic* 'The Instructions of Cormac', part of which at least was compiled in the ninth century, is unambiguous in this belief: 'What is best for a king? ... Worshipping great God ... many alms ... Let him improve his soul' (*Cad as dech do ríg?... Adraid Dé móir ... Almsana ile ... Lessaiged anmain*).[55]

Such a radical change to perceptions of kingship might have led to the complete purging of the *banfheis*, the physical mating of the land goddess and the king, and the belief system that accompanied this ceremony. However, as with much of early Irish culture, goddess and ritual were transformed but not obliterated. Old and Middle Irish literature is replete with allusions to sovereignty goddesses and strong elements of their cultic and fecund, often promiscuous, nature. These goddesses are often relegated to women subject to kings as their spouses and lovers, or are attested as historic queens who retain the personification of sovereignty in personal names such Eithne, Gormfhlaith or even Temair. The environment was also a reminder of the potency of the fertile and female aspect of the land. Many prominent places reflected this connection in their names, as found for example in the river names Eithne (Inny) and Bríd (Bride), or in Dún Baoi (Dunboy, Co. Cork), Sliabh na mBan Fionn (Slievenamon, Co. Tipperary) and *Dún Caillighe Béirre*, an unidentified inauguration site of the O'Byrnes in Co. Wicklow.[56] The learned classes also maintained an understanding of the original form of kingship, although the fundamental question remains as to how much was simply transmitted unconsciously or with full knowledge of the layers of associations encoded in their texts. A classic example of this conundrum relates to the kingship of Tara, an exceptional kingship that preoccupied kings and the learned alike throughout the medieval period.

The kingship of Tara: from prehistoric sacral kingship to medieval kingship

The kingship of Tara was not defined by a specific territorial kingdom, but the ceremonial focus of this exceptional kingship was a low-lying hill at the end of a ridge overlooking the River Boyne.[57] The Hill of Tara was located in the east midland kingdom of Brega, the land of low hills and fertile plains, which along with the plain of Kildare (*Currach Life*) in Leinster, Mag Femin around Cashel in Munster, and the Rosommon Plain (*Mag nAí*) around Cruachu in Connacht, was one of the most sought after territories in Ireland. The hill and its hinterland are particularly rich in archaeological monuments dating from the fourth millennium BC to the late medieval period. Many of these monuments can be identified as prehistoric: a Neolithic passage tomb, Bronze Age barrows, temples and henges, a large number of which have only come to light in the past two decades, due to the use of sophisticated modern topographic technologies and rescue excavations.[58] The name *Temair* – anglicized to Tara – incorporates the Indo-European root **tem-* 'to cut' and is cognate with Greek *temenos* 'sanctuary', and Latin *templum* 'temple'. This place was a space cut off or demarcated for sacred purposes, a hilltop sanctuary, and its prehistoric archaeological remains are the surviving physical imprint of its sacral importance. Successive generations through the Neolithic, the Bronze Age, the Iron Age and into the early medieval period constructed significant public structures in this landscape and were often careful to incorporate, and not to destroy, those of earlier generations in their quest for legitimate possession of the sanctuary. The configuration of the Rath of the Synods, which in its final phases dates to the late Iron Age (first to fourth centuries AD), is irregularly shaped because it deliberately embraces an earlier Bronze Age barrow.[59] A similar phenomenon can be detected in the outer configuration of the conjoined earthworks known as the Forrad and Tech Cormaic, in which the north-eastern section of the outer enclosure embraces another barrow (fig. 9). Constant respect for earlier burial monuments and reverential reuse of them reveal a great deal about the beliefs of the communities that shaped Tara.

From the construction of the earliest substantial structure, known as the Mound of the Hostages (Duma na nGiall), a Neolithic passage tomb,[60] Tara developed as a necropolis. During the early Bronze Age, for example, burials were inserted into the soil covering the mound and into the passage tomb itself. One exceptional grave was that of an adolescent buried with a necklace of jet,

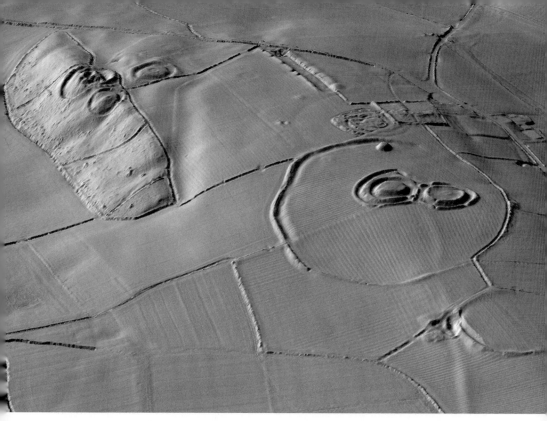

9 The Hill of Tara, Co. Meath: Tara was the most renowned ceremonial capital in Ireland. It was the focal point of an exceptional kingship that was fought over by kings from all parts of Ireland. A king who aspired to be recognized as *rex Temro* 'king of Tara' had to hold the hostages of most of the provincial kings of the northern half of Ireland, and to have some form of affirmation from the king of Cashel. Few Irish kings succeeded in claiming such extensive power although many claimed to be kings of Tara. Archaeologically, Tara is a prehistoric complex comprising dozens of funerary monuments dating as far back as the Neolithic, henges, ceremonial routeways and other religious monuments. © Discovery Programme, Dublin.

amber, bronze and faience, and with a dagger and a bronze awl at the feet. In cultures worldwide, the significance of ancestral graves is commonly acknowledged. The graves of past generations presented a focus for ceremonies involving the legitimization of authority, taking possession of land and marking borders. They were the nexus between this world and the other, as often depicted in early Irish, Anglo-Saxon and Norse literature,[61] and at times were of themselves sacred or holy places in the landscape. This function is best known, for example, from late antiquity and the medieval period in the development of the cult of saints' relics and tombs as foci of considerable devotion in the Christian and Islamic religions.[62] Ancestral graves were known in Ireland as *fertae*, and they were important markers in the landscape.[63] Burial monuments at Tara were undoubtedly incorporated into ceremonies of legitimization of kings and new dynasties, and into rituals demarcating the hill's liminal position between the sacred and the profane. One might surmise that passing over or around the graves of illustrious ancestors represented a challenge, or an ordeal, that a king was required to undertake before he was proclaimed the great king at Tara.

What evidence survives to suggest that the kingship of Tara was a supreme kingship in Ireland and can it be proven that the king who was proclaimed *rex Temro* 'king of Tara' ruled the whole island? Archaeological evidence would suggest that other sites were as extensive and consisted of similarly impressive monument complexes in prehistory. This is particularly true of Rathcroghan (Cruachu), Navan Fort (Emain Macha), Cashel and Uisnech.[64] There is no surviving detailed historical account of an inauguration ceremony of a historic king of Tara, although the ceremony known as *Feis Temro* 'the feast of Tara' probably continued to be celebrated until the mid-sixth century. It is difficult to discern from medieval literature, which refers frequently to *Feis Temro*, if this was a form of the *hieros gamos*, the mating of the king and the goddess of sovereignty. The eminent Celtic scholar D.A. Binchy regarded *Feis Temro* as 'an archaic fertility rite of a type associated with primitive kingship the world over',[65] which seemed 'to mark the culmination of a reign rather than its beginning'.[66] On the basis of the less fantastic accounts of *Feis Temro*, it is likely that the celebration was a highly significant event directed by a powerful king who desired to be proclaimed the most important king in Ireland.[67] The eighth-century legal text *Bretha Nemed Toísech* states that 'abundance, Feis Temro, binding of kings constitutes a king of kings' (*roimse, feis temrach, fonaidm rig [ruirech] nemtiger righ ruirech*).[68] This statement captures the essential elements of this exceptional kingship. To be proclaimed king of Tara, a king had to demonstrate his munificence through generosity, truth and peace, and his reign had to be prosperous and abundant. He had to be able to celebrate *Feis Temro*, and to do so, he had to gain the submission – presumably by holding their hostages or dominating their territories – of a sufficient number of kings to be recognized as worthy of the title *rí Temro* 'king of Tara'. To achieve this accolade, a king needed to be skilful in military tactics and political intrigue, and to be supported by a strong dynasty. If the exceptional kingship of Tara was governed from a place that was regarded as the centre of the world (*axis mundi*), then its king was supreme and was viewed as the king of the world. As Doherty has demonstrated, the earliest surviving Irish literature preserves enough allusions to the existence of the concept of a world king, not least in the personal name *Domnall* 'world ruler' (similar to Gaulish *Dumnorix* 'world king'), to support its authenticity in prehistoric Ireland. Survival of the office of a supreme ruler and its gradual transformation in the early medieval period was dependent on the agents of a new religion – Christianity. Along with the process of conversion came the reworking of aspects of kingship and the emergence of powerful new dynasties in the fifth and sixth centuries.

Prehistoric and medieval societies did not distinguish starkly between the political and religious or sacral aspects of life as modern societies tend to do. This is an essential key to understanding the kingship of Tara and how it moved from a prehistoric sacral kingship to a medieval royal honour. The landscape of Tara was recomposed in later prehistory and took on a more militaristic aspect, whereby the Hill of Tara was encircled by overtly defensive monuments including Ringlestown Rath, Rathmiles, Ráith Lóegaire, the Riverstown earthwork, and the promontory forts at Rath Lugh and Edoxstown.[69] A further recomposition of the hill's hinterland seems to have occurred between the fourth and seventh centuries. At this stage, Tara as a central focal ceremonial site diminished as kingship in Ireland gradually assumed more Christian characteristics, and Tailtiu (Teltown, Co. Meath), a ceremonial site 20km north of Tara, was favoured by the church and the newly emerging powerful midland and northern dynasties of Uí Néill. There is no evidence of an important church, indeed any early church at all, in the core landscape around Tara, as it is defined by the hills of Tara and Skreen and the Gabhra Valley between them. Significant churches such as Dunshaughlin, Ardbraccan, Trim, Trevet and Duleek, all associated with early missionaries and mentioned in Patrician literature, encircle the Tara landscape but do not encroach on it.[70] This disapproval of Tara by the church and the consequent further recomposition of the landscape find echoes in Muirchú's Life of Patrick. Given the numerous noteworthy monuments with religious or mythological resonances in present day Co. Meath – the early medieval kingdom of Brega – Muirchú's description of this territory may not have been an exaggeration. In celebrating his first Easter as a missionary in Ireland, Patrick 'divinely inspired, decided that this great feast of the Lord, being the principal feast of all, should be celebrated in the great plain of Brega, because it was there that there was the greatest kingdom among these tribes, the head of all paganism and idolatry (*quod erat [caput] omnis gentilitatis et idolatriae*)'.[71] Whatever about the historicity of Patrick's journey to Brega, Muirchú's setting of the dramatic confrontation between Patrick and Lóegaire mac Néill, king of Tara, and his druids, is a combination of a scene with obvious biblical influences[72] and a genuine attempt to grapple with a type of kingship that could not be tolerated within a Christian order. Nor could the ceremonial site linked with that kingship, Tara, be tolerated.

It is at this juncture that the political and military aspect of the kingship of Tara must be considered. When written sources begin to be produced to any significant extent in the seventh century, testimony regarding the polity of the kingship of Tara emerges, albeit fairly shrouded in bombastic propaganda generated for competing dynasties. An official list of kings of Tara was compiled during this period – as represented in the prophetic poem *Baile Chuinn Chétchathaig* – and it primarily reflects the interests of the Síl nÁedo Sláine, a group of dynasties who attempted to rule Brega and Tara until the early eighth century.[73] The ancestors of these dynasties are listed as heroic kings of Tara, but notably absent are kings from among the eastern and midland Laigin and the north-eastern Ulaid. This omission is deliberate, as other early sources that reflect the interests of both these peoples suggest that they contended for the kingship of Tara until the fifth and seventh centuries respectively.[74] Midland, northern and western dynasties came to prominence from the sixth century onwards. They claimed to be the descendants of Niall Noígiallach ('Niall of the Nine Hostages'), an assertion that is most unlikely, but is still a matter of dispute among scholars.[75] They identified themselves as the Uí Néill 'the descendants of Niall'. Their target became the kingship of Tara. They succeeded in gaining a monopoly on the kingship by the eighth century through military strength, the ability of some exceptional kings, and clever alliances with important churchmen. This latter move gave them access to a literate class versed in vernacular literature and tradition, as well as Latin culture that, in turn, led to the creation of dynastic propaganda that established the claim of the Uí Néill to the kingship of Tara in prehistory. This propaganda did not go unchallenged, especially in the south, where a similar coalition of dynasties known as the Éoganachta gradually monopolized the kingship of Cashel. This exceptional kingship in Munster had many analogous characteristics to that of Tara.[76] Such was the influence of southern dynasties that it is unlikely that any king could claim to be king of Tara without their support, and when this was not forthcoming, a frequent occurrence, a king claiming the title 'king of Tara' was often in reality only pre-eminent in parts of the east, the midlands and the north.

The career of Fínnachta Fledach mac Dúnchado, king of Tara (d. 695)

What makes a king famous enough to become a heroic figure in medieval sagas? As elsewhere, people were attracted by a violent and dramatic life, punctuated by bouts of repentance and holiness. In medieval Irish history, some kings gained more fame than others, not alone on the basis of genuinely illustrious careers, but also due to starring roles in the national narrative. Brian Bórama, king of Ireland (d. 1014), slain in the Battle of Clontarf, and Diarmait Mac Murchada, king of Leinster (d. 1171), credited with bringing the Anglo-Normans to Ireland, count among the most renowned of all kings. There were many more such kings, and one of the most colourful of early medieval kings, whose life can be traced both in historical sources and sagas, was the late seventh-century king of Tara, Fínnachta Fledach, 'Fínnachta, the bountiful'.[77]

Fínnachta was born into the dynasty of Síl nÁedo Sláine ('the descendants of Áed Sláine') that had forged a dominant place in the kingdom of Brega. His grandfather, Áed Sláine (d. 604), whose sobriquet *Sláine* suggests some connection with Slane, Co. Meath,[78] was deeply involved in inter-dynastic kin-slaying in his attempt to gain the kingship of Tara. He is recorded as having killed his nephew, Suibne mac Colmáin, in 600, and for that killing earned a fierce rebuke from the monastic community of Iona, whose founder, St Columba, belonged to the northern dynasty of Cenél Conaill. They were also contenders for the kingship of Tara at the same time.[79] Áed Sláine was assassinated in 604 on the orders of his grandnephew Conall Guthbinn ('Conall of the Sweet Voice'; d. 635) at the lake settlement (crannog) of Lough Sewdy, Co. Westmeath. Áed's sons, Diarmait and Blathmac,[80] who were Fínnachta Fledach's uncles, continued the bitter dynastic wars in the midlands, and were not successful in gaining the kingship of Tara until the mid-seventh century. The sphere of influence of Blathmac and his sons, two of whom were killed in 651, was in the lakelands of Westmeath, while his brother Diarmait pursued a military career west of the Shannon. Blathmac may have become king of Tara in the 640s, with Diarmait defeating him in 658.[81] Both died in the great plague that swept through Ireland in 664–5. Fínnachta was born, therefore, into a noble, but particularly violent and fractious, family and even though his own father does not feature to any great extent in the annals, undoubtedly he would have become entangled in dynastic disputes and military campaigns at an early age. There is no record of who Fínnachta's mother was, nor where he might have been fostered. His uncle Diarmait was fostered by the important, but subject, dynasty of Mugdorna, whose territory straddled the modern Meath/Monaghan border.[82] Fínnachta was probably fostered among a similarly subject people. He would have survived two periods of the bubonic plague that spread to Ireland from Britain or the Continent in 664–6 and 684–7. He would have witnessed its effect on the population and the landscape. These plagues caused famine, desertion of parts of the countryside, and the deaths of prominent members of society. Fínnachta Fledach's close connection with Adomnán, abbot of Iona, in the 680s has usually been linked to the latter's role as emissary in negotiating the release of prisoners taken by Anglo-Saxons from Brega in 685. Adomnán is the earliest witness to the seventh-century plagues 'the great mortality which twice in our time has ravaged a large part of the world',[83] and it is possible that Fínnachta sought the great abbot's consolation when Irish society was subject to intense pressure.

When the king withdrew into clerical life in 688, he may have done so for political reasons – as he was being threatened by a kinsman, Niall mac Cernaig Sotail – or as an act of supplication to God to rid Ireland of the plague, or in thanksgiving as the plague waned. Withdrawing into religious life at times of crisis was a common phenomenon among Irish kings of the seventh and eighth centuries. That Fínnachta was militarily active again in 689 suggests that he had not intended to end his life in religion.

Fínnachta's military prime and his campaign to become king of Tara began in earnest in the 670s when he defeated his cousin Cenn Fáelad mac Blathmaic in a skirmish at *Aircheltair* (possibly in the parish of Dulane, Co. Meath) in 675. Such skirmishes were commonplace in the incessant feuding between kindreds of Síl nÁedo Sláine – and many other dynasties throughout Ireland at the time. This endemic petty warfare did not require large armies, and probably normally consisted of small bands of men carrying swords, shields and spears seeking out their enemies in surprise attacks.[84] Warfare and feuding was also ritualistic and terror was instilled in the population by these men with their terrifying cries and sinister clothing.[85] Fínnachta's victory at *Aircheltair* in 675 introduces another feature of warfare at the time; that of fighting battles on boundaries. If *Aircheltair* was in the north of modern Co. Meath, this area in the River Blackwater Valley was a frequently used battleground, especially among Uí Néill midland dynasties.[86] For example, Fínnachta's uncle defeated his rival Conall Guthbinn in 635 at Cúil Chóeláin (near Kilkeelan, Co. Meath); Niall mac Cernaig Sotail, Fínnachta's second cousin, defeated another kinsman in 688 at Imlech Pích (Emlagh, Co. Meath); and, the northern king Fergal mac Maíle Dúin killed the Síl nÁedo Sláine king of Brega, Conall Grant, in 718 at Kells. Not only was the feuding intense and bloody, creating a somewhat unstable ruling class, but those living in the vicinity of battlegrounds must have been used to endemic violence and displacement. This district was also part of a royal demesne associated with the great assembly site of Tailtiu (Teltown, Co. Meath) and, as such, it may have had a population who were used to an aristocracy tramping over their fields.

The high point of Fínnachta's reign came in 677 when he managed to hold *óenach Tailten* 'the assembly of Tailtiu', a prerogative of a king successful in his claim to the kingship of Tara. How had he come to gain this elevated status? Any king with ambitions to proclaim himself king of Tara in 677 needed to have dealt with his own closely related dynasties, as well as with the emerging Northern Uí Néill dynasties, and the kings of the Laigin and Ulaid, all of which coveted the kingship themselves. If the annals are to be believed, in four years (675–9), Fínnachta Fledach defeated all rival dynasties – the Northern Uí Néill in their own stronghold of Ailech, Co. Donegal (676),[87] the Laigin close to the royal residence of Lagore, Co. Meath (677), and the Ulaid at Tailtiu (679). In the last instance, the Ulaid were probably attempting to prevent Fínnachta from holding *óenach Tailten* and attempting to reaffirm that he was king of Tara. He was king of Tara, however, with a remit for the northern half of Ireland only, for, as with many of these early kings of Tara, there is no evidence that he succeeded in being recognized by the province of Munster, or even Connacht. Fínnachta, despite later propaganda, was not king of Ireland. Nor could he have ever been secure enough in his kingship to have made such a claim. In the final decade of his career, he was plagued by dissenters from among his cousins, the Síl nÁedo Sláine, who finally killed him and his son, Bressal, in 695.

Fínnachta Fledach had two known wives (not an unusual arrangement for a king of his time). His queens came from the royal households of his provincial rivals, the Laigin and the Ulaid. The sequence of his marriages is not clear, but it is likely from the circumstances of his reign and his relations with both provinces that his first wife, Conchenn, was of the Ulaid and his second wife, possibly named Derb Fhorgaill, belonged to the Laigin.[88] Conchenn's own connections and life follow a pattern common to many royal women in early medieval Ireland. She was the daughter of Congal Cennfhota of the Dál Fiatach, who became king of the Ulaid between 670 and 674. As such, an alliance with Congal through marriage with Conchenn would have been advantageous to an ambitious king aiming for the kingship of Tara, as Fínnachta was at this time. Conchenn was probably only a teenager when she was brought to the midlands to marry Fínnachta. The marriage may not have lasted very long, and Conchenn is not acknowledged as mother of Fínnachta's sons. Once divorced, she seems to have returned to the north and married Bécc Bairche, her father's killer and next king of the Ulaid. This was another marriage of political convenience that was designed to end a thirty-year feud between their two dynasties. Conchenn was the most important of Bécc's three wives, and reputedly the mother of seven of his sons. Once Conchenn had been sent back north, Fínnachta probably sought Derb Fhorgaill, the daughter of Cellach Cualann, king of Uí Máil of Leinster. Like Fínnachta, Cellach Cualann was ambitious, and in 680 he became king of Leinster when Fínnachta killed Cellach's rival, Fiannamail mac Maíle Tuile. A marriage alliance between Fínnachta and Cellach was mutually beneficial and such marriages formed part of Cellach's strategy of securing power. Other daughters were married to various Síl nÁedo Sláine kings and Cellach's own wives also came from midland Uí Néill dynasties.[89] Derb Fhorgaill was most likely the mother of Finnachta's three sons. She died in 684 and was outlived by Fínnachta by more than a decade. As no other wife is recorded, this situation may have facilitated Fínnachta's brief entry into religious life in 688.

Fínnachta had three sons, one of whom, Áed, continued his father's line, but without any great success. His descendants played a part in the politics of Brega until the late ninth century without attaining the kingship of Tara again. Fínnachta's association with Adomnán of Iona ensured that he was remembered in sagas, most especially in the epic saga the *Bórama*, which emanated from Leinster, in which Fínnachta was tricked by St Moling into liberating the Laigin from a heavy tribute that had been imposed on them by the king of Tara from time immemorial.[90]

THE OBLIGATIONS AND POWER OF KINGS

Laws and reality

Early Irish legal texts and instructions to kings, the Irish versions of the universal *speculum principum* 'mirror of the prince', classify the various ranks of kings, their obligations to one another, to the people they rule, and the rights due to them. The underlying approach to royal authority is based on the idea that there was a contract between the ruler and the ruled, and that a king's status, like that of other nobles, relied on men in clientship, and particularly in base clientship.[91] The eighth-century law tract on status, *Críth Gablach*, provides a useful introduction to the relationship between king and people, and between greater and lesser kings.[92] In a society in which the taking of oaths was at the centre of lawmaking, and thus was a particularly powerful act, a king's oath could override the evidence of all but a bishop, a sage and an anchorite.[93] His oath had the power to exonerate the actions of his people (*túath*) against other peoples, and presumably to refute accusations against them. He was expected to provide them with a just judge, if he did not assume the role himself.[94] He could give pledges on behalf of his people to other kings, often to one superior to himself, and receive pledges from his own people to ensure that they fulfilled their public duties.[95] These pledges related to providing military service (*slógad*), and the observance of an edict (*rechtge*) and a treaty (*cairde*). A king could convene his people to an assembly (*óenach*) and to a hosting to a border territory, although the laws suggest that the assembly could only be proclaimed with the assent of the people as a whole.

How was a king's life organized (*córus ríg*)? As is so often the case, the laws are somewhat schematized in describing the *córus ríg*. For example, the order of the royal week (*sechtmonáil*, borrowed from Latin *septimanalis*) at first sight seems somewhat far-fetched: a king drank ale on Sundays, judged legal cases on Mondays, played boardgames (*fidchell*) on Tuesdays, went hunting on Wednesdays, had sexual relations on Thursdays, went to horse-races on Fridays and judged legal cases again on Saturdays.[96] Thomas Charles-Edwards has argued that this list imposed the Christian seven-day week on the royal week and also enforced Christian moral practices on kings. Thus, Thursday is chosen as the day for sexual activity probably because that day was *dardaín* 'the day between two fasts', Wednesday (*cétaín*) and Friday (*aín*), when such pursuits were prohibited by Irish church canons. These prohibitions were not necessarily that alien to kings, however, considering that royal lives had always been subject to ritualistic restrictions. Restrictions on kings are common in early Irish sagas. In the saga *Togail Bruidne Da Derga*, the heroic king Conaire Mór refused to sleep with a woman because a taboo prevented him from receiving the company of a lone woman after sunset.[97] It may be no coincidence that the majority of battles listed in the prophetic text asserting the rights of the Uí Néill dynasty to the kingship of Tara, *Baile in Scáil*, occurred on Tuesdays, but none on Thursdays and Fridays.[98] No more than the taboos mentioned in the sagas or the bizarre ordering of the royal week in *Críth Gablach*, the phenomenon of battles being fought on particular days of the week or seasons of the year reflects a universal practice in societies that divided time in a ritual order.

Do other sources corroborate the laws in their portrayal of a king's functions and activities? The military aspect of royal lives predominates in the annals. Kings are continually recorded as being involved in skirmishes and attacks on neighbouring kingdoms and fighting significant battles.[99] A graphic – and probably relatively realistic – picture of the devastation resulting from a hard-fought battle is given in the Annals of Ulster's entry in Latin on the Battle of Áth Senaig fought between the Uí Néill and the Leinstermen in 738:

> The Battle of Áth Senaig [or the Battle of Uchbad 'battle of the groans'] between the Uí Néill and the Laigin was sternly fought, and the two kings respectively, leaders firm and exalted, namely, Áed Allán [Uí Néill king of Tara] and Áed son of Colgu [king of Laigin]. One of them [Áed Allán], though wounded, survived triumphant, but the other [Áed son of Colgu] was beheaded by a battle-sword. Then the descendants of Conn [the Uí Néill] enjoyed a tremendous victory, when in extraordinary fashion they rout, trample, crush, overthrow and destroy their Leinster adversaries, so much so that almost the entire enemy is well nigh annihilated, there being a few messengers to bring back the tidings. And men say that so many fell in this great battle that we find no comparable slaughter in a single onslaught and fierce conflict throughout all preceding ages.

This depiction of a bloody battle rings true, as archaeological evidence corroborates elements of it. For example, kings were subject to beheading by rivals, as happened to Máel Mórda mac Gairbíth, king of Conaille [modern Co. Louth] in 893. They also inflicted punishments on their enemies, as in 970, when

Ardgar mac Matudáin, king of the Ulaid, with the Vikings attacked Coinnire
(Connor, Co. Down) 'leaving many beheaded there' (co fargaibh ár cenn: AU).
Archaeological evidence of beheadings has been discovered in early medieval
cemeteries. The large cemetery at Owenbristy, Co. Galway, was in use from the
sixth to the tenth century. Of seventy-nine inhumation burials, seven were
decapitated. At Mount Gamble, Co. Dublin, two young men, buried together
sometime during the period 656 to 765, met with violent deaths by weapons
and one of them was decapitated.[1] In the same cemetery, a high proportion of
the identifiable adult males died violently, and their general stature was taller
and more robust than the rest of the male population. These men may have
belonged to a warrior class who protected the kingdom and the king's household
(teglach). This class may be compared with the medieval Welsh teulu 'household
troop' led by the penteulu 'the captain of the household troop'.[2]

Other forms of death faced by kings, as recorded in the annals, included
strangulation (AU 742), drowning (AU 864) and burning (AU 891, 901). In the
entry for 901, Máel Ruanaid mac Flainn, heir-apparent of the kingship of Tara,
was burned by a lesser people, the Luigne, along with other kings and Dub
Cuilinn, the head (princeps) of the church of Ros Ech. The fate of kings and
heroes being subjected to threefold death by wounding, fire and drowning
(gonad, loisced, báided) is a common motif in early sagas and although often
regarded as an expression of ancient sacrificial ritual killing, the motif clearly
had resonances for contemporary medieval audiences.[3] Another ultimate
sanction against a royal rival – be he within the king's own family or an outsider
– that is prevalent in sagas and history, was that of blinding. Once blinded, and
hence blemished, a king was no longer regarded as fit to rule. This mutilation
befell the heroic king of Tara, Cormac mac Airt, and led to his expulsion from
Tara, but it also happened to historic kings such as Áed úa Maíle Sechnaill, who
was blinded by his brother, Donnchad Donn, in 919. Áed was excluded from
competing for the kingship of Mide or Tara, both kingships falling into the hands
of Donnchad until 944.

Kings were often preoccupied with defending their kingdoms and when
successful continued by expanding their authority into neighbouring and even
distant kingdoms. This meant that they had to impose and exact tributes from
these kingdoms, normally of cattle, but also of other livestock, wool, wood and
other commodities.[4] Exacting a tribute could lead to conflict and is the
overriding theme of many early sagas including the tána 'cattle raids' of which
Táin Bó Cúailnge 'The cattle raid of Cooley' is the most renowned. Genuine
binding tributes did exist and were regularly claimed by kings enforcing their
supremacy over external kingdoms. The classic instance of such a tribute is the
bórama 'cattle-tribute' collected by kings of the Uí Néill from the province of

Leinster. As with the *tána*, the *bórama* was a central theme of literature emanating from Leinster throughout the early medieval period. It was redacted finally into a Middle Irish heroic saga, *Bórama Laigen*, told from the bombastic and defensive standpoint of the Leinstermen. This cattle-tribute was genuinely extracted in 721 when Fergal mac Maíle Dúin, king of Tara from the northern dynasty of Cenél nÉogain, imposed the *bórama* and secured the hostages of Leinster. Unfortunately for Fergal, his victory over the Leinstermen was short-lived, as he was slain by Murchad mac Brain, king of Leinster, at the Battle of Almain in the following year. Such was the precarious life led by even the most powerful of early Irish kings.

Relationships between dynasties or kingdoms often led to alliances, or, in the case of a defeated kingdom, to submission to a greater authority. Both sides had to fulfil obligations and respect the rights of the other party. This was a fundamental tenet of both individual and collective legal relationships. For example, an eighth-century poem on the mutual contractual obligations between the Uí Néill dynasties and the Airgialla, a group of dynasties in the north who claimed a common ancestry, sets out the rights and obligations of both parties.[5] The Airgialla were obliged to provide significant military service to the kings of the Uí Néill as part of a grand alliance, and, as remarked by Thomas Charles-Edwards in his analysis of the so-called charter poem of the Airgialla, 'war had its own particular legal regime with its own guarantors'.[6] The army was to follow prescribed routes and to set up camps at designated locations. Loss or theft of Airgialla livestock was penalized and the latter were not expected to provide military service in spring or autumn, the periods of sowing and harvesting. In return for these privileges, the Airgialla were also expected to entertain and acknowledge the high status of Uí Néill kings. Such public transactions were often guaranteed by hostages (*gíalla*) and there are many references in the annals to kings binding defeated kingdoms to their obligations by taking hostages. Kings regularly handed over their sons or important nobles as sureties for good behaviour and, in many cases, it seems that these hostages were not well treated, especially if their own people revolted against their master. *Críth Gablach* depicts these unfortunate 'forfeited hostages' as on public show in chains in the king's banqueting hall.[7] In warfare between the Picts and the Dál Riata in 736, the sons of the king of Dál Riata, Dúngal and Feradach maic Selbaig, were bound in chains and taken as hostages. Their fate is unknown. Other sources suggest that the two sons of Selbach did not survive their capture. There is a telling episode in the *Vita Prima* of Brigit in which the saint pleaded with a king on behalf of a prisoner for whom she offered a ransom. The king refused and ordered that the man be executed, whereupon Brigit succeeded in winning him a reprieve for one night. Some of the king's companions attempted to circumvent the saint's protection by snatching him from the king's hands to kill him. Brigit learned of this ruse, and said to the prisoner 'when the chain is removed from your neck for you to be executed, turn to the right towards us and you will find us immediately for we're waiting for you'. The man followed Brigit's instructions and, 'as soon as he was unshackled, he went to Brigit, whereas they [the king's companions], as they thought killed the man and cut his head off'.[8] Since some saints' Lives often mirrored the moral and social concerns of certain sections of society, Brigit's action in this episode possibly reflects a concern for hostages and prisoners in the same way as Adomnán of Iona's concern for women, children and clerics in warfare was enshrined in the *Lex Innocentium* 'Law of Innocents'.

Assemblies, law-giving and protecting the kingdom

An impression is often given in modern historical commentaries that early medieval Ireland was lawless and chaotic, and that with the exception of the church, society was petrified in a 'Celtic' and prehistoric backwater. The reasons for this are usually explained by Ireland's position outside the Roman Empire, and the absence of Roman influence on society. Since Ireland was small, it is argued, its kings, unlike Anglo-Saxon or Carolingian kings, did not need sophisticated royal households or centralized administrations. As an example, Janet Nelson in her consideration of kingship and royal government in western Europe, *c.*700–*c.*900 comments:[9]

> Nearly everywhere, some traditions of late Roman imperial government survived. Ireland was an exception, not only because Roman traditions were lacking, but because kingdoms were so small: an Irish king scarcely needed agents to act on his behalf at court or away from it because he could act in person, through face to face meetings and confrontations; and legal business was dealt with in part by members of the indigenous learned class, the brehons.

This may be the initial impression created by the Irish sources, many of which are in the vernacular, but both historical sources and archaeological evidence suggest that a more complex form of governance existed in Ireland, and one that was not wholly uninfluenced by Roman imperial traditions. Ireland, in common with many regions on the frontiers of the Roman Empire, had extensive contacts with many aspects of imperial life, trading, political negotiation, military expeditions, cultural contacts and personal relations. Indeed, late Roman imperial power structures, as well as Byzantine, Merovingian and Carolingian practices, often find their parallels in Ireland, albeit on a much smaller scale. Materially, there is evidence from the fifth to the seventh century, for example, that an elite in society asserted their status by possessing imported goods, such as tableware from the late antique world, wine and oils, and elaborate brooches modelled originally on Romano-British prototypes.[10] While particular laws or ordinances are not associated with individual kings, as in the case of Anglo-Saxon kings, Irish kings were involved in issuing edicts and in the administration of justice. The relationship between king and jurist – and others such as poets and clerics – was vital to the administration of law in early medieval Ireland, and as noted by Robin Chapman Stacey in her discourse on the subject:[11]

> Jurists, poets, clerics and others within the community appear in the [law] tracts as a normal part of the dispute-resolution process, and often they seem to be functioning outside the presence of the king. However, the consolidation of justice under royal authority was a priority for kings and their advisers everywhere in Europe in this period, and the same must have been true as well for Ireland. The difference was that there existed in Ireland what did not exist elsewhere: an entrenched juristic class, conscious of its standing and privileges.

Críth Gablach declares that during an *óenach* 'assembly of his people' a king could compel his subjects to observe certain public obligations and it specifies *slógad* 'a military hosting', *rechtge* 'an edict, exercising the function of government' and *cairde* 'a treaty'. The *rechtge* was agreed between king and people in times of defeat, plague and in subjecting lesser kings. Exceptional situations in which the king had the authority to direct his people included the expulsion of foreign people – such as Saxons, the example mentioned in *Críth Gablach* – preparing agricultural produce and imposing a religious law. Adomnán's 'Law of Innocents' is cited as an example.[12]

How kings reacted to a genuine crisis in society is particularly clear from two episodes in the eighth century. The annals often record that kings retreated to religious life (*in clericatum exiit*), in some instances as a genuinely pious act of penance, in others following expulsion from their kingship. There are cases in which it seems clear that kings entered religion to seek divine intervention to save their people from plagues, famine and natural disasters. In 740, Domnall mac Murchada, king of Mide and a contender for the kingship of Tara, took on a religious life following a heavy loss of his retinue the previous year. Ireland was hit by disease (*lepra* and *bolgach*) in the 740s and in 748 snow of unusual depth fell 'so that nearly all the cattle of the whole of Ireland perished, and the world afterwards was parched by unusual drought'. The relics of Trian of Cell

Deilge (Kildalkey, Co. Meath, or Kildellig, Co. Laois) were brought on a circuit in 743, when the *bolgach* was rampant, and Domnall entered the church again in 744. As the possession and public veneration of relics was associated with the *stabilitas regni* 'stability of the kingdom' and peace, and probably by extension, in an agricultural community, prosperity, the use of Trian's relics in times of crisis was undoubtedly the result of some *rechtge* directed by Domnall as a dominant king. This was not unlike the use of relics by Merovingian, Carolingian and Byzantine kings and emperors, whereby the relics, along with constant prayers by monks and pious nobles, brought blessings and stability upon a kingdom.[13] Thirty years later, between *c.*772 and *c.*786, Ireland was overwhelmed by disease, famine, loss of livestock and grain crops, and extreme weather. The constant burning and raiding of major monasteries, particularly in the east, midlands and north, may reflect a society in turmoil. The church responded in the same way as did provincial kings. In 772, there was a period of widespread fasting, and the laws of Comán and Áedán were enforced on parts of Connacht. The relics of two major midland saints, Erc of Slane (Co. Meath) and Finnian of Clonard (Co. Meath), were brought on circuit in 776, the law of Colum Cille was declared by Donnchad mac Domnaill, king of Tara, and Bressal, abbot of Iona, in 778, and a significant meeting was convened by senior clerics at Tara to negotiate peace between the Uí Néill and Laigin in 780. Artgal mac Cathail, king of Connacht, retired from his kingship and went to Iona in 782. In the following year, Patrick's law was promulgated in Cruachu by his successor, Tipraite mac Taidc, along with the abbot of Armagh. A royal meeting (*rígdál*) was held between Donnchad, king of Tara, and the north-eastern king, Fiachna mac Áedo Róin, at Inis na Ríg in eastern Brega and the relics of Erc of Slane were brought to the great ceremonial complex of Tailtiu (Teltown, Co. Meath) in 784. This was followed by a circuit of the relics of Ultán of Ardbraccan (Co. Meath) in 785. Finally, in the following year, 'a horrible vision [was seen] in Clonmacnoise, and great penance [was done] throughout Ireland' (*AU* 786).

Various types of assembly from the local to the national were convened at sites throughout Ireland.[14] There are many vernacular terms for an assembly or a meeting, but the most common are *óenach*, *dál* and *airecht*. The *óenach* might be a local assembly, possibly held at harvest-time, and, while it often involved some form of royal governance, the event usually also comprised other activities including horse-racing, entertainment, trading and drinking. Such a communal event would have placed the various strata of society in their rightful positions, with the nobility separated from the unfree, and men and women segregated. The composite Tripartite Life of Patrick, which narrates the saint's progress from kingdom to kingdom, often uses the setting of communal meetings for Patrick's encounters with local kings. For example, when in southwest Munster, he was in the kingdom of the Uí Fhidgenti, where the king Lonán mac Maicc Eirgg prepared a feast for him at Mullach Cáe (Knockea, Co. Limerick). The circumstances for a communal gathering, as perceived from this text, were associated with major events in a kingdom: choosing a king; a decision to convert to Christianity or the foundation of a church. In Patrick's Life, the event was the recognition of Nessán, founder of the church of Mungret, Co. Limerick.[15] The highest level of assembly that involved provincial, if not national, gatherings and proclamations took place at óenaig such as óenach Tailten (Teltown, Co. Meath), óenach Carmain (possibly Carnalway, Co. Kildare)[16] and óenach Cruachan (Rathcroghan, Co. Roscommon). Similarly, royal assemblies (rígdála) were provincial or national phenomena that were infrequent and normally marshalled by particularly powerful kings. For example, the law of Patrick was enforced by the northern king Áed Allán and the southern king Cathal mac Finguine at their meeting in 737 at Terryglass (Co. Tipperary), a prominent church on the Shannon.

During the ninth century, at a time of both provincial conflicts and an increasing threat from the Vikings, a series of royal assemblies were held, most of which were presided over by the abbot of Armagh. They included royal assemblies held in 851 and 859 under the auspices of the most powerful king in Ireland, Máel Sechnaill mac Maíle Ruanaid of the midland Uí Néill dynasty of Clann Cholmáin. He attempted – often successfully – to rule the northern and midland Uí Néill dynasties and to extend his rule into Munster, Ulaid and Osraige. He also faced the Vikings in 856, who along with one of his enemies, Cináed mac Conaing, the Uí Néill king of the eastern kingdom of Ciannachta, had plundered his lands and churches in 850. Apart from using force, Máel Sechnaill advanced his ambitions through shrewd political moves, including the convening of major royal meetings. In 851, a royal conference was held in Armagh between Máel Sechnaill accompanied by the nobles of the northern half of Ireland and Matúdán son of Muiredach, king of the Ulaid, who was accompanied by the nobles of that province. The abbot of Armagh, Diarmait úa Tigernáin, and Fethgna mac Nechtain, bishop of Armagh (who later became abbot), with the community of Patrick, and Suairlech mac Ciaráin, abbot of Clonard (Co. Meath), with the clerics of Mide, were in attendance. Effectively, Máel Sechnaill succeeded in bringing the nobles and clerics of the whole northern half of Ireland together to one location, the primatial 'city' of Armagh. This was a demonstration of his authority and it also seems to have been a clear declaration by the king of Ireland of his recognition of Diarmait as abbot of Armagh and of Fethgna as his successor. Diarmait's abbacy had been marked by rivalry with Forannán mac Muirgile between 834 and 852, when both men died. Fethgna succeeded them and ruled until 874.

In 859, Máel Sechnaill convened another important *rígdál* at Ráith Áeda meic Bric (Rahugh, Co. Westmeath), which once more was attended by Fethgna and Suairlech and the nobles of the southern half of Ireland. The Annals of Ulster record that the assembly's aim was 'to make peace and amity (*síd 7 caínchomracc*) between the men of Ireland'. One of its primary results was to move the buffer kingdom of Osraige (roughly co-extensive with modern Co. Kilkenny) from the political and military sphere of Munster to the jurisdiction of Máel Sechnaill's own sphere of influence in the east and midlands. In her detailed study of the context and location of the *rígdál* at Rahugh, Elizabeth FitzPatrick summarizes its importance as 'a highly significant event that successfully brought Osraige into the jurisdiction of the Southern Uí Néill, declared Máel Sechnaill's dominance over Munster, reinforced the primacy of Armagh, and emphasised the pre-eminence of Clonard among the churches of Mide …[and] it could also have been the very occasion on which the king of Tara was acclaimed by the gathering of kings and churchmen as the "king of Ireland"'.[17] She argues that Máel Sechnaill's *rígdál* is likely to have been held on Cnoc Buadha (Knockbo), a ridge with a bowl-barrow perched on top of its northern end and in direct line of sight with the church of St Áed mac Bric.[18]

Óenach Tailten and Máel Sechnaill's *rígdála* were national or provincial gatherings that were not necessarily the same as smaller, local assemblies of *túatha* or smaller kingdoms. What happened at these assemblies, where were they held, and what role did the king play in the proceedings? No detailed description of a local *óenach* survives, but we can surmise from legal texts, saints' Lives and archaeological evidence as to the conduct of an *óenach*. A kingdom or group of kingdoms probably had a designated site for the holding of an annual *óenach*. As with the more important *óenaige*, it is likely that they were held on boundaries. This would have been convenient if the assembly involved more than one kingdom. One likely type of location would have been the site of a *ferta* 'ancestral grave', many of which appear to have been located on boundaries overlooking rivers and on ravines.[19] Fergus Kelly has noted from legal glossaries that it was a king's duty to hold a regular assembly on 'king's land' (*mruig ríg* or *ferann ríg*).[20] It is possible that this royal demesne included a *ferta*, as might be inferred from the complex of monuments at Holdenstown and Dunbell, Co. Kilkenny, which incorporates Iron Age and early medieval cemeteries, including a *ferta* overlooking the River Nore, a possible medieval church and a cluster of large ringforts.[21] The place-name *Dún Bile* (Dunbell) suggests that it was also the site of a *bile*, a symbolic tree associated with inauguration rites and assemblies. Paul MacCotter notes that the *óenach* was often associated with a hill or a mound, a traditionally revered tree (*bile*), or a prehistoric hilltop site. He lists places such as Carn Oilella near Lough Arrow,

Co. Sligo, Monasteranenagh, Co. Limerick, and Dunkellin, Co. Galway, as possible early *óenaige* sites.[22] One of the duties of a king's clients was to prepare the assembly site and to clear roads to enable horses to travel easily to the assembly.[23] Considering that horses and horse-racing (*grafann*) formed an essential component of the *óenach*'s activities, this task was necessary and the location of a site must have been determined by the requirements for a racing circuit. Indeed, the use of the Latin translation *circus* for *óenach* underpins this equine aspect of the assembly and also suggests the use of a circular or oval space. One might imagine an event such as the Bellewstown Races held at the end of August on the Hill of Crockafotha, Co. Meath, as the nearest modern equivalent to a regional *óenach*. Exchange of goods and trading were also part of the function of an *óenach*, as any gathering of people might normally entail, and considering the emphasis on horses in relation to *óenaige*, the likelihood is that they were primarily horse fairs. If they were held at the beginning of harvest, as the evidence suggests,[24] much had to be considered in a local community at that time: the state of the harvest and the abundance or scarcity of food for winter, the organization of the reaping party (*meithel*), the threshing and drying of corn. The importance of a successful organization of the harvest is depicted in Cogitosus' Life of Brigit, where the saint summoned reapers and labourers to help with the harvest. When the *meithel* had assembled, it began to rain and the whole surrounding countryside was inundated, while Brigit's harvest remained dry, allowing her reapers to work miraculously from dawn until sunset.[25] The drastic outcome of a rainy autumn for food supplies is worthy of note in the annals, as recorded in *AU* 858, when 'a rainy autumn destructive to the fruits of the earth' caused concern. No doubt a king was obliged to call an assembly to establish the success or otherwise of a harvest and the implications of the situation for himself, his various clients and the general populace for the next half year. A shortage in food supplies could have triggered raids on neighbouring kingdoms or on large ecclesiastical settlements, and could also have impinged on the renders owed to him from his clients, and the tributes owed to superior kings from his kingdom.

In his influential paper on exchange and trade in early medieval Ireland, Doherty argued that by the eighth or ninth century, as smaller kingdoms were absorbed into overkingdoms, the function of the *óenach* was taken over by some larger monasteries.[26] This would make sense in the case of Armagh, Kildare, Durrow or Clonmacnoise, where over-kings had residences, varied craft activities were pursued, and their economic capacity was greater than that of other settlements in the countryside. The annals record, for example, that a man was killed in Armagh in 870 in front of the house of Áed Findliath, king of Tara, suggesting that Áed resided there, probably at certain times of the year. The

monastery of Kildare was attacked by Cellach mac Brain, a contender for the
kingship of Leinster, on St John's Day (29 August) in 833. Many were killed on
that occasion, an indication that there may have been a fair or harvest gathering
in the vicinity of the monastery, and that it afforded Cellach an opportunity
either to appropriate or to destroy the fruits of the harvest. In 921, Godfrid
grandson of Ímar and the Vikings of Dublin raided Armagh on the Saturday
before the feast of St Martin (10 November), a traditional time of winter
celebration that probably involved the holding of a fair in the monastery. The
gathering of crowds for the fair no doubt attracted the Vikings in their search
for provisions and slaves. Notably, the annals (*AU*) state that Godfrid spared
the *céli Dé* and the sick of Armagh, and also the monastery buildings, except for
a few dwellings that were burnt through carelessness. Yet, while there is evidence,
as Doherty suggested, for *óenaige* held in monasteries, this change did not
necessarily preclude the holding of assemblies elsewhere at a local level to discuss
and organize many other practical aspects of life.

Crop production was an important agricultural activity that involved
harnessing water and the construction of corn-drying kilns and mills.[27] These
activities were undertaken both in large monasteries and in rural settlements,
examples of which are the significant seventh-century milling complex at the
monastery of Nendrum, Co. Down (pls 4, 5),[28] and the crop production
settlement at Raystown, Co. Meath, that appears to have been in use primarily
between the sixth and eighth centuries.[29] At Raystown, there is evidence for the
production of wheat, barley, oats and rye, along with the physical remains of
many structures associated with drying and milling corn. Milling on an industrial
scale was undoubtedly the basis of a local economy that included exporting
products to other kingdoms and abroad, and as such, activity at Raystown must
have been regulated by some controlling authority such as a regional king. Mills
had to be kept in order, ditches and gullies cleared, and an adequate supply of
water had to be available. While a well-organized production centre might have
operated smoothly and did not require royal intervention, undoubtedly there
were occasions when disputes arose or an emergency occurred. And it is at these
times that a king might have held an assembly, not necessarily a fair (*óenach*),
but a public forum on how to address a problem or deal with a dispute. This
type of assembly may have been the *airecht*, a term often used to describe legal
disputes concerning ownership or trepass. The law on the transfer of water
across land owned by different neighbours to a mill, *Coibnes Uisci Thairidne*, is
mainly concerned with rights to the use of mills by landowners and with the
obligations of the miller to his neighbours.[30] The text, for example, decrees that
it was improper to conduct water through the sanctuary of a church (*nemed
cille*), a fortress (*dún*) or the precinct of an ancestral grave (*maigen feirt*).[31] The

level of compensation paid to a neighbour for use of his land depended on the quality of the land, whether it was arable or rough land.[32] As some localities must have been traversed by many water-courses, gullies and mill-races, and as the law demonstrates that this activity was carefully regulated, the need for debate, arbitration and planning must have arisen frequently and must have been aired at public assemblies. *Coibnes Uisci Thairidne* alludes to the legal principles of inherited custom and how a dispute might be resolved. It cites the general legal maxim that[33]

> There are three rules which heirs are not capable of altering if their father and grandfather have acknowledged them throughout their lifetime: the rule of every watercourse (*cáin cach uisci thairidne*), and the rule of an estuary (fishing weir) (*cáin inbir*), and the rule of a bridge (*cáin drochit*) … If they have been acknowledged, they are to remain so forever, whether they be gratis or whether a fee is due(?) according to the decision of a judge.

Watercourses, estuaries and bridges, though they might be on private land, were public utilities and, therefore, required careful regulation. The reference to the decision of a judge in this text directs us to the *airecht* 'court, assembly', and the relative roles of kings and judges in the administration of justice and other legal matters. An Old Irish text on court procedure sets out the arrangement of a court session (*airecht*) in which the judges (*brithemain*) sat in a central position with the king, the bishop and the chief poet. Others present included sureties, witnesses, litigants, hostages, advocates and custodians of tradition (*senchada*).[34] In his discussion of this text, Fergus Kelly surmises that in such a court session, the judgment was arrived at by a judge or judges, but that the judgment was promulgated by one of the dignitaries in the back court – the king, the bishop or the chief poet, and that this was most likely the king. The role of the *senchaid* can be clearly deduced from the provision in *Coibnes Uisci Thairidne* relating to the legal position of an heir in relation to a watercourse, an estuary or a bridge. If the *senchaid* determined that a father or grandfather had acknowledged the situation, then their heir was bound by that rule. Whether written or oral, this memory of tradition was the equivalent of legal precedent and was vital to the administration of early Irish law. Given the possible number present at such a session, up to thirty participants, Kelly assumes that an *airecht* was held in the open air. From descriptions in sagas and in the laws, it is likely that such proceedings took place in open spaces in front of a king's residence (*faithche*), on a hill or perhaps at a boundary *ferta*. There is also a possibility that temporary buildings or awnings were erected for the occasion. The term *pupall* 'a tent' is

10 Baronstown, Co. Meath: this large defensive fort overlooking the River Gabhra in the valley between the hills of Tara and Skreen may have been used as an assembly site. It consisted of a circular ditch with an internal diameter of 40m with large wooden planks forming a bridge at the entrance between the inner and outer ditch. A horse's skull was buried in a pit at the entrance. © National Roads Authority.

one of a number of words that describe temporary structures, often related to royal, ecclesiastical and military assemblies. Other terms include *both* 'a hut' (possibly made of wood), *sosad* 'a camp, terrace, rampart' and *forad* 'a mound, platform', often associated with royal assemblies. Tara had its *Forad*, a mound presumably of similar morphology to the mounds of Navan and Rathcroghan, while the use of *forad* in the plural to describe assemblies at Tailtiu implies not only the existence of a single mound from which the king proclaimed or viewed events, but the construction of earthen or wooden platforms for spectators at an *óenach*.[35]

While the discovery of objects from assembly sites is rare, normally consisting of stray finds of lost objects such as pins or brooches, a potential model for identifying assembly sites has been suggested for Anglo-Saxon England that might be relevant to Ireland. Sarah Semple has suggested that the combination of funerary landscapes and square or sunken structures (possible shrines), other buildings, standing posts and deviant burials could be regarded as 'microcosms, places where perhaps all the ritual functions and concerns of a pre-Christian tribal society were played out: religious belief and practice, displays of aristocratic power, enactment of justice and forms of assembly'.[36] The large defensive fort discovered at Baronstown, Co. Meath, has all the hallmarks of an *óenach* site (fig. 10, pl. 3). It consisted of a circular ditch with an internal diameter of 40m, and was situated on high ground overlooking the River Gabhra, 2.5km east of the Hill of Tara. Finds from this impressive site were relatively meagre and do not suggest that it was a habitation. They included pins, a seventh-century penannular brooch – of a type found at the royal site at Lagore, Co. Meath – bucket staves, and a considerable amount of animal bones that were deposited in the deep ditch. Large planks formed a bridge at the entrance between the inner and outer ditch, and at this point, a horse's skull was buried in a pit. It is not implausible that Baronstown was the place where an important local king, or even an aspirant king of Tara, gathered his people to administer justice or to decide on a military campaign. Buckets, barrels and animal bones may be the remnants of feasting associated with these assemblies, while brooches and pins could be personal belongings lost on an *óenach* day.

THE EXTENDED ROYAL FAMILY

The structure of the royal kindred

Lawyers and churchmen were deeply interested in the structure of the kindred and family from the highest to the lowest in society. This concern related to the key institutions of honour-price, fosterage, marriage, inheritance and succession. As a result, a large corpus of law tracts, legal glosses and canon law developed around the functioning of these institutions and many different terms survive in Old Irish and Latin that describe their many constituents.[37] Other sources, such as saints' Lives and sagas, touch on dramatic events in the lives of the nobility, narrating themes of the abandonment of children, abortion, the strong bonds of fosterage, relationships – both legal and illicit – between the sexes, and kin-slaying.[38] Early Irish tales were also used as vehicles for dialogues about these fundamental institutions, especially during the seventh and eighth centuries, which heralded a period of social change consequent on the ultimate adoption of Christianity.[39] How all these texts relate to the reality of family life in early Ireland is largely unexplored, despite the existence of true-life evidence available in the annals and from archaeology.

The *fine* 'kindred': the fundamental unit of society

The *fine* was the entity to which individuals and communities owed their existence. This unit operated as a nuclear family, an extended family, a legal and economic entity, and, in the case of the royal kindred, it encompassed the wider community. The nuclear family, which was patrilinear, was descended from a common ancestor with generations progressing from fathers to sons and grandsons (table 1). This meant that one ancestor could, through his sons and grandsons, create a group of collateral or parallel kindreds that, in royal circles, could often lead to fierce competition for supremacy. Legally, these distant cousins might claim rights to inheritance or to succession from one another, especially when one *fine* died out with no heirs. A person was also attached to his or her maternal kindred (*máithre*), and in particular to their mother's father or brother. A woman was always tied either to her own kindred or to her husband's kindred, depending on her marital status. Hence, she was almost always dependent on her father or brothers when unmarried or divorced, and on her husband or sons when married or widowed. A woman who vowed to follow a religious life was attached to her church, but maintained strong connections with her own *fine*. As always in life, there were many variations of the *fine*, and the lawyers attempted to classify many of these variations as they deemed necessary for the purposes of legal culpability and for rights of inheritance.[40] However, these classifications may not reflect actual reality or may have been designed to cover eventualities among noble families. Further down the social scale, even if individuals had blood ties of kin, they were very dependent on their lord for legal status and protection.

TABLE 1. The nuclear family as part of the *fine*.

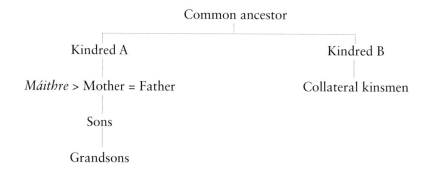

The royal kindred or the *fine* of a lord extended in its obligations and its rights beyond that of the nuclear noble family to the wider community. Many people depended on a king and his honour-price (*lóg n-enech*), which established his status, and reflected his role as ruling the privileged class (*nemed*),[41] the free (*sóer*) and the unfree client (*dóer*).[42] In the laws, a king was often ranked as equal to a cleric and a poet, as clearly set out in *Críth Gablach*, the law on status:[43]

Cía as sruithiu, in rí(g) fa epscop? Is [s]ruithiu epscop, húare arnéraig rí(g) fo bíth creitme; tuarga[i]b epscop dano a glún ria ríg.

Who is more illustrious, the king or the bishop? The bishop is more illustrious, because a king does reverence to him because of faith; hence a bishop raises his knee to a king.

This scene suggests that it was incumbent on a king to rise before a bishop to greet him in recognition of the superiority of an ecclesiastical rank over a secular rank, but that bishops respected kings – hence the bishop raising his knee to the king.[44]

In its role at the head of a community, therefore, the king's *fine* extended beyond his own immediate blood relatives to collateral kindreds and to those dependent on him in society (table 2). The Irish canon laws (*Collectio Canonum Hibernensis*) describe his role precisely in their adage *justitia regis pax populorum* 'the justice of the king is the peace of the people'.[45] The head of a kindred acted on behalf of his kin (and in the case of a king on behalf of a wider community) to enforce their rights, to make contracts and give pledges, and to ensure good behaviour. If his authority was ignored or questioned, the situation undermined his position and destabilized the kindred and kingdom.[46]

TABLE 2. The king's *fine*.

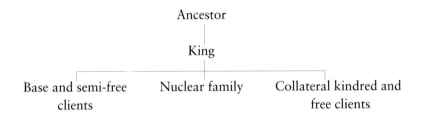

The royal kindreds of the Loígsi (fig. 11)

The early Irish secular genealogies, the pedigrees of the pre-Norman noble families, are full of information on kingdoms, dynasties and lands held by these families. The topographical information embedded in these texts can be very detailed about the different kindreds of a particular dynasty. They cover their obligations to over-kings, their own hierarchical structure, their lands, and the churches maintained on these lands. The genealogies of the midland dynasties known as the Loígsi illustrate the fragmentation of kindreds and their common bonds in considerable detail.

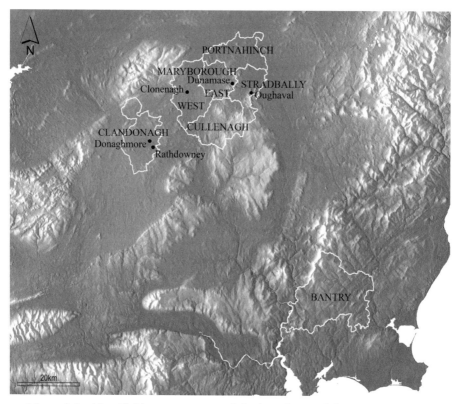

11 Map of the identifiable components of the kingdoms of the Loígsi, comprising the modern baronies of Clandonagh, West Cullenagh, Maryborough, Portnahinch and Stradbally, with the outlier of Bantry, Co. Wexford. Map prepared by Robert Shaw; © Discovery Programme, Dublin.

The lands of the Loígsi at the height of their power extended between the two plains of Mag Réta and Mag Roichet, which equates in general with the modern baronies of Stradbally, Cullenagh, Clandonagh, Maryborough East and West, Portnahinch, all in modern Co. Laois. The core of their kingdom became the medieval cantred of Leys.[47] The dominant royal kindred were the Loígsi Réta. Certain concentrations of archaeological sites in this region are indicative of intense prehistoric and early medieval activity. One outstanding area incorporates Greatheath, Morett (Mag Roichet), Ballydavis and Dunamase. This area has a similar profile to the plain of Kildare and even the Tara landscape. There is a spectacular series of ring-barrows on Greatheath,[48] while the impressive rock outcrop of Dunamase (Dún Másc), fought over by kings belonging to many dynasties in Leinster and the midlands, is reminiscent of the Rock of Cashel.[49] At Ballydavis, the central burial of four Iron Age ring-ditches contained cremated human bone in a tinned bronze box buried with other artefacts, including a bronze fibula and eighty stone and glass beads. The decoration and shape of the bronze box has been compared with a similar object from a female chariot burial in Wetwang Slack, Yorkshire.[50] The possibility that people with close links with northern Britain resided in this area during the Iron Age is not necessarily surprising, and might even explain the Loígsi's claim to have originated from the north-east of Ireland.

The extensive genealogical tracts on the Loígsi seem to have been compiled during the reign of Gáethíne mac Cináeda, a mid-ninth-century king of the Loígsi, whose son Cennétech (d. 903) was very active against the Vikings. This royal kindred were known as Síl mBeraich 'the descendants of Berach'. Berach mac Mescill probably reigned in the late eighth century. Síl mBeraich's chief fort seems to have been Ráith Baccáin near the early church of Domnach Mór Maige Réta (probably Donaghmore, Co. Laois). The ninth-century Tripartite Life of St Patrick mentions Gáethíne mac Cináeda in a somewhat whimsical tale about this church. It relates that the saint came to Domnach Mór and found a labourer digging the ditch of Ráith Baccáin (*rígdún inna tuaithe* 'the royal fort of the kingdom') on a Sunday. Patrick tried to prevent him, but the work continued, and as a result the saint foretold that the fort would not be occupied until a wind (*gáeth*) blew from the pit of hell. This was a prophecy relating to Gáethíne – and a play on his name – as the text finishes by saying that the fort was rebuilt during his reign.[51]

The seven noble kindreds of the Loígsi, including the immediate royal family, were descended from Barr mac Cáirthind, who was reputedly converted to Christianity by the early missionary Bishop Íbar. Whether this is historically true or not cannot be verified, but Barr is regarded as having lived sometime during the sixth century:[52]

> The noble families (*sóerchlanna*) of the Loígsi are all the descendants of Barr mac Cárthind wherever they are located.
>
> The royal kindred (*rígrad*) from whom are the kings [of Loígsi Réta] are Síl mBeraich meic Mescill, that is, Berach of the blessings. Sóergus Doithnennach blessed Berach mac Mescill's twelve sons.

The Loígsi Réta were due military service (*fecht*), a hosting (*slógad*), tribute (*cáin, cís*), debt (*cobach*) and food-render (*bés*) from the seven free kindreds of the Loígsi under their authority.[53] The king of Loígsi Réta alone dealt with their over-king, the king of Leinster, or at least that was what he strived to do.[54] As pointed out by Charles-Edwards, it was in the interest of the king of Loígsi Réta to hold onto as much as possible of these tributes and renders himself rather than seeing them going to the king of Leinster, 'or, even worse, bypassing him entirely and going straight to the king of Leinster'.[55] The king of Leinster was given the freedom of passage through the territory of the Loígsi Réta on his way to Munster, and no more than one hundred and fifty men from the seven kindreds of the Loígsi participated in the hosting of the provincial over-king.[56]

The genealogical tract on the Loígsi is remarkable for the detail recorded about the landownership and land divisions between the various noble kindreds. If plotted on a map – and it is difficult to do so, as many of the place-names mentioned are unidentified – they provide a clear view of the extent of the farmsteads of free clients and their proximity to that of the royal kindred (fig. 11).[57] The genealogies divide the Loígsi into their main kindreds and their sub-groups. They also provide some detail about estates and familial churches held by these kindreds. For example, Loígsi Réta consisted of thirteen kindreds Síl mBaccáin, Síl Mescill, Síl Dochlú, Síl mBeraich meic Mescill, Clann Beraich, Clann Duinechda, Clann Chairpri, Síl nAilella, Uí Fachtnai, Uí Dúnlaing, Clann Ruaidíne, Clann Indrechtaich, Clann Chathasaich. Síl mBeraich meic Mescill were the reigning royal line when the genealogies were compiled. Their lands were in Mag Réta, Feib (a territory around Donaghmore, Co. Laois[58]), and their main residence at *Ráith Baccáin*. The churches most clearly associated with them were Cluain Eidnech (Clonenagh, Co. Laois) that was controlled by Clann Ruaidíne, and Domnach Mór (Donaghmore).[59] Other Loígsi subject to Loígsi Réta included Loígsi Raimne, Dubloígsi, Loígsi Tulcha Breguin, Loígsi Uí Chuilúin, Loígsi Lethnada, Loígsi Cúile Buichle. The Loígsi Síl nAduair were more exalted than the rest, and may once have been in contention for the over-kingship of the Loígsi. On the margins of nobility were kindreds who were distantly related to the Loígsi or clearly not related to them at all. Some were Laigin, including the Uí Broccáin, who controlled the important church of Tulach meic Comgaill or Nuachongbáil (Oughaval, Co. Laois). The Benntraige are named at the end of the genealogy. They were an early people who clung onto lands in Wexford and Cork and whose name survives in the place-name Bantry, Co. Wexford, an anglicization of Benntraige. This is one microcosm of similar structures that were replicated throughout the island.

Noble women: consorts, sisters, mothers

> Question. How many pairings are there in Irish law? Answer. Eight: a lord and his base clients, a church and its tenantry, a father and his daughter, a girl and her brother, a son and his mother, a foster-son and his foster-mother, a teacher and his pupil, a man and his wife.

The law on status, *Críth Gablach*, rarely mentions women, and when it does, they are viewed as essential participants in a free or noble household. The preferred status of a noble woman was that of *cétmuinter* 'chief wife, legal spouse' of equal grade and with no rivals. The *mruigfher* 'farmer' was to have a *cétmuinter*, daughter of a father of equal rank in a proper marriage contract.[60] A king's consort (the word *rígan* 'queen' is not used in the text) held an equal position beside the king with his judge in the king's house (*tech ríg*).[61] An *ócaire* 'the lowest grade of freeman', and indeed all others recognized in the text, were to be compensated for the rape of his wife or daughter.[62] There were exceptions to this provision, but these often related to the perceived participation by the woman in the crime. The existence of women other than a *cétmuinter* of equal rank, or his daughters, in an *ócaire*'s household is fleetingly mentioned. The honour-price of his *dormuine*, a concubine probably recognized by his chief wife, was a quarter his own honour-price and half that of his wife.[63] And the household comforts or luxuries of a free woman are itemized: her bed, her saddle and her pet dog (*orcae*). The dangerous and devious nature of women, a characteristic so often conveyed in sagas, was also to be reckoned with by freemen, and especially kings. The king was warned not to go about alone, but was to be accompanied by his retinue, consisting at least of a judge and two attendants. If he went about alone, he might encounter a woman who could claim later that he had fathered her son 'the day on which nobody (else) need give testimony for her'. Otherwise, her unsupported oath would have had no chance of success.[64]

Certain texts concentrate on the status of women, especially women of free or noble status, but like so many such texts in contemporary societies, they place these women in relation to their fathers, brothers, sons, kindreds and the church. Inevitably, they deal with marriage, divorce, inheritance and status. Queens were daughters, wives and mothers. There is extensive coverage of marriage, property and inheritance in early Irish legal and canonical texts in which the status, wealth and morals of women are considered at great length.[65] The title *rígan* 'queen' begins to appear in the annals in the mid-eighth century in obits of historical royal women, and then they normally use phrases such as *regina regis* or *rígan ríg* 'the queen of a king'.[66] In a recently converted Christian society, some noble daughters chose to remain virgins and join communities of nuns. This status was often a useful alternative for a father with too many daughters.[67]

Two texts form the basis for our understanding of women's roles in society: *Cáin Lánamna*[68] ('the law of the couple') and the provisions on marriage as laid down by Irish ecclesiastical canons.[69] Sagas and saints' Lives supplement our knowledge of noble women, but by their nature are difficult to date and cannot be regarded as historical, although they may at times echo changes in society. The annals and genealogies contain records of historical women, but they tend not to provide much detail. As in law, these women are mentioned because of illustrious fathers, spouses or sons. A typical entry follows the format as in the Annals of Ulster 890 'Flann [Lann] daughter of Dúngal, queen (rígan) of the king of Tara, fell asleep in penance'. Behind this terse entry lies the unsettled life of Lann daughter of the king of Osraige, who in her youth moved from her father's court to become wife of three kings in succession.[70] Her first marriage was to a neighbouring king, Gáethíne king of the Loígsi, to whom she bore a son, Cennétech (d. 903). Her second marriage was to the formidable midland king of Tara, Máel Sechnaill mac Maíle Ruanaid (d. 862), to whom she bore Flann Sinna (d. 916), later to become king of Tara. This marriage was probably engineered by Lann's ambitious father Dúngal as he sought to build an alliance with the king of Tara and to detach his kingdom from the grip of the kings of Munster. Lann's brother, Cerball mac Dúngaile, was a particularly successful king of Osraige, and he and Máel Sechnaill, her second husband, concluded a significant alliance in 859 in which Osraige became subject to the kings of Tara and to the primatial church at Armagh. Three years later, Máel Sechnaill died and was succeeded by the northern king Áed Findliath (d. 879), who took Lann as his wife. She was subsequently put aside by Áed, who then married Máel Muire daughter of Cináed mac Ailpín (d. 868), in what seems to have been a strategic alliance between the Northern Uí Néill and the king of Alba. To add to the complexity of family ties, Lann's son, Flann Sinna, later married the same Máel Muire, his step-father's widow. Máel Muire's son with Áed Findliath, Niall Glúndub (d. 919), became king of Tara on Flann Sinna's death, if not earlier.

How could this system of serial royal marriages continue in an ostensibly Christian society, and what effect did such a system have on women such as Lann and Máel Muire? The likelihood is that Lann was taken out of fosterage at fourteen, the probable standard age for a girl to marry, and married to Gáethíne, to whom she probably had been betrothed from an early age. Gáethíne, or possibly his father Cináed, gave Lann's father a bride-price (coibche) of land, cattle and household goods, some of which was given to Lann. She would have entered this marriage as one of equal partners known in Cáin Lánamna as lánamnas comthinchuir ('a marriage of equal contribution'), in which the contribution to the marriage by both parties was the same. Cáin Lánamna recognized different types of unions, not all of which amounted to full marriage status.[71] The basic premise of a union was that of an economic contract between two kindreds and the more legal the contract, the more legal the union. The most frequent types of marriage were the ones of equal partnership and the marriage in which the husband contributed most to the household (lánamnas for ferthinchur 'a marriage of greater contribution by the man'). On occasion a man could marry a banchomarba 'heiress', and in such cases the woman brought more goods into the marriage. This was a lánamnas for bantinchur ('a marriage of greater contribution by the woman'). In such instances, a woman could only hold a life interest in her inheritance before it reverted back to her father's kindred. The woman's land or property was inherited by her sons, but to ensure the continuity of her paternal kindred's possession it was common that she would marry a close relative from among that kindred.

Lann's three marriages were undoubtedly regarded as valid marriages, even if she was not the sole wife of each king. Her first husband, Gáethíne, may have had other wives. By the time she married Máel Sechnaill, Gáethíne may have been dead, leaving her free to marry again. Her marriage to Áed Findliath on Máel Sechnaill's death is an example of a royal widow marrying the successor in order to secure their claim to a kingship. This follows a pattern noted elsewhere, in particular among the Merovingians and Lombards.[72] These women were 'conduits of power, as women who, although they could not rule in their own right, could transmit rightful claims to their new husbands'.[73] This would also explain the marriage of Flann Sinna, Lann's son, to his step-father's widow, Máel Muire. To complicate matters further, Flann Sinna also married Áed Findliath's daughter, Eithne (table 3). Clearly, to enable kings to enter into such complicated relationships, and indeed to use royal women as political collateral, a parallel system of divorce had to exist. After all, Lann was alive when Máel Muire married her former husband Áed Findliath.[74]

TABLE 3. The marriages and relationships of Lann, queen of Ireland (d. 890). Numbers indicate the sequence of marriages.

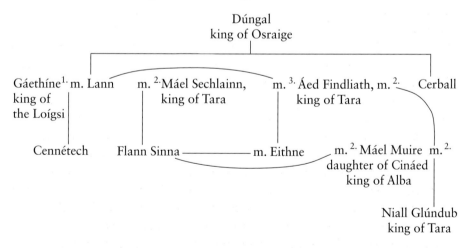

As in many societies from the late antique period onwards, Irish society operated two interlinked and yet at times opposing sets of rules on marriage: native custom and canon law. Whereas there must have been considerable accommodation between native and canon lawyers – indeed they often drew on the same class – their texts, as laid down in *Cáin Lánamna* and the *Collectio Canonum Hibernensis*, diverged in their moral attitude to serial monogamy, divorce and the maintenance of concubines or other unions during marriage.[75] The audience for such tracts was the nobility who had to deal with inheritance and succession, both of which were dependent on the stability of marital unions. *Cáin Lánamna*'s approach to marriage and other unions was contractual and economic, and as such dealt with property and goods brought into a union and divided on divorce. *Collectio Canonum Hibernensis* adopted a moral Christian approach and its fundamental attitude favoured monogamy and condemned adultery, especially when the perceived culprit was a woman.[76] The guiles of women provide the narrative for the beautifully crafted saga, *Fingal Rónáin*, in which the young wife of an old king attempted to seduce the king's son with catastrophic consequences.[77] A short entry in *Chronicon Scotorum* suggests that royal women were genuinely at risk if their conduct was seen as wanton. It records that Órlaith daughter of Cennétech – Brian Bórama's sister – was slain by the king of Tara Donnchad mac Flainn in 941, 'having been charged with illicit sexual relations with Óengus, his son (CS)'. Óengus died in 944. The circumstances of the relationship and Órlaith's death are otherwise unknown, although the enmity between Donnchad and her kindred, the Dál Cais, cannot have helped her cause. This may be an isolated and extreme incident, but nonetheless it demonstrates that, despite provisions in the laws for all sorts of unions, politics or human emotions could lead to brutal outcomes. *Cáin Lánamna* explains the reasons for divorce on the part of both spouses and the economic and hereditary consequences of the parting. In summary, types of divorce included:[78]

(i) Divorce by mutual consent in which the contribution of each partner and the profits thereof were divided by mutual agreement.

(ii) Divorce by a man from his wife on grounds of adultery, damaging his honour, carrying out an abortion, infanticide or if she neglected her household.

(iii) Divorce by a woman from her husband on grounds of being sexually unsatisfactory, a vagrant, for mistreating or slandering her.

In the case of Lann, who married two kings of Tara, Máel Sechnaill and Áed Findliath, her divorce from Áed must have been by mutual consent and negotiated by her kinsmen. Her position must have been complex and precarious once she was no longer Áed's official first wife. Her life may have become even more difficult when her son Flann Sinna married Máel Muire, who had replaced her as the king of Tara's *cétmuinter* 'first wife'. When the labyrinthine pattern of intermarriages of Uí Néill kings is examined, one can only conclude that royal women were prepared for an unsettled life, moving from one royal court to another and bearing sons to different men. Their status depended on their fathers, husbands and sons. In this context, Lann probably lived in the court of her son Flann Sinna once she was put aside by Áed, and if later tradition is correct she was an active patron of churches. The late 'Fragmentary annals of Ireland', which portray Lann as a scheming queen who incited her husband Áed into war against the Vikings and other Irish kings, mention that she had 'many carpenters in the wood chopping down and shaping trees' for a church in Kildare.[79] When she died 'in penance' in 890, she may have been resident in Kildare or in the vicinity of Clonmacnoise, the favoured monastery of her second husband, Máel Sechnaill, and their son Flann Sinna.

Royal women did not have to deal merely with being set aside as official wives, they also had to contend with official or betrothed concubines (adaltrach airnadma), and less official relationships between their husbands and other women. As many of these relationships were recognized in law, especially for purposes of inheritance and succession, the main priority of these women was to protect their sons' claims from the rival offspring of other official wives or indeed women of lesser status. There is no more compassionate portrayal of such a situation than in the Life of Brigit:[80]

> There was a nobleman of Leinster stock named Dubthach. He bought a bondmaid named Broicsech and she was of comely appearance, good living and a good slave. Her master desired her and slept with her and she became pregnant by him. When Dubthach's wife came to know of this she was sorely aggrieved and said to her husband, 'Cast out this bondmaid and sell her lest her offspring surpass my offspring'. But her husband refused to sell the maid since he loved her very dearly, for she was a person of irreproachable conduct.

This brief passage encapsulates all the human emotions that must have been played out in many aristocratic households: love, jealousy, rivalry and submission. Laws and sagas also acknowledge that bitter disputes could erupt in royal courts as a result of the interests of rival queens. As pointed out by Anne Connon in her extensive study of early queens of Tara, the rivalry between the jealous wives of Diarmait mac Cerbaill (d. 565) in the Middle Irish tale Geinemain Áeda Sláine 'The Birth-tale of Áed Sláine' depicts the tensions between royal wives, especially with regard to their children, and corresponds with what we know of the dangers of multiple royal marriages in early medieval England and Francia.[81]

Noble children: from birth to adulthood

The care of children of the noble and even lower classes is unusually well documented in early Irish sources and in particular in the laws. In her survey of child-centred law in medieval Ireland, Bronagh Ní Chonaill remarks that 'throughout this source [the laws], the treatment and safety of the child remained central and was [sic] underscored by the legal profession's desire to protect the right of the unborn child and the health of the expectant mother; to protect the standard of education and maintenance; to protect the child from neglect or attack; to protect the (foster-)parent from a charge of neglect or financial ruin; and even to protect children from one another during play'.[82]

Children are mentioned in many law tracts, and two fragmentary laws on children, *Cáin Íarraith* ('The law of the fosterage fee')[83] and *Macshlechta* ('Son-sections'),[84] dating probably to the eighth century, survive. Concern with the circumstances of birth and of rearing and fostering children also permeates early sagas and saints' Lives. Despite this legal concern, it is evident from other texts such as *Cáin Adomnáin* and from archaeological evidence that life was not easy for children in early Ireland, no more than it was for adults.

Early childhood from birth to fosterage, at about seven years, is best represented in the literature for royal children. The pangs of childbirth even disturbed the monastic routine of St Columba as described in Adomnán's Life of the saint. He was reading when he suddenly got up and declared that he had to hurry to the church to pray 'for a poor girl who is tortured by the pains of a most difficult childbirth'. This woman was a noble of Columba's maternal kindred. The saint's prayer was successful as the Lord showed 'favour on the poor girl and brought timely help to deliver her from her difficulties'. She safely gave birth and was in no danger of death.[85] The reality of childbirth can often come through episodes in the literature, despite the detached nature of many texts. Eithne, the mother of St Máedóc, held onto what seems to have been a weaver's sword (*bacan na bainfighidh*) while giving birth to the saint, a position commonly used by many women in childbirth, even if the object is something other than a weaver's sword.[86] Archaeological evidence provides graphic illustrations of the dangers of pregnancy and childbirth. For example, the rates of young adult female deaths between the ages of seventeen and twenty-five are often higher than male death rates, reflecting the hazards of this age for women. This is strikingly demonstrated in the discovery during excavations in a large cemetery at Mount Gamble, near Swords, Co. Dublin, of a complete skeleton of a woman in her twenties that had a fully developed neonatal foetus in birth position within the woman's pelvis (fig. 12). Both woman and child probably died due to complications in childbirth.[87] This common phenomenon is

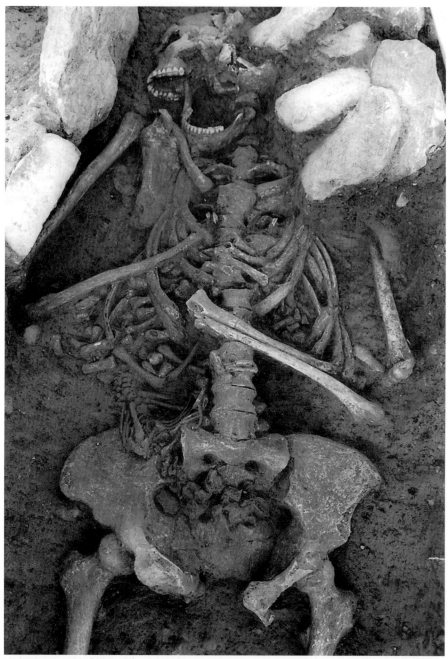

12 Mount Gamble cemetery, Co. Dublin: burials were discovered in an extensive cemetery that was in use between the sixth and twelfth centuries. Burial ccxlviii, pictured here, is that of a woman with the foetus in birth position within her pelvis – a burial that signifies the dangers of childbirth. © Edmond O'Donovan/Margaret Gowen & Co. Ltd.

recognized in the laws and the removal of a child from the breast of its dead mother was sometimes necessary.[88] Early childhood mortality rates seem to have been relatively high, with many children dying before the age of five. Death could be due to disease or starvation, possibly due to famine, as evident in the burial together of three children between two and nine years in Mount Gamble,[89] or the 25 per cent of those buried in a cemetery at Cherrywood, Co. Dublin, who died within the first two years of life.[90] The annals also record particular years of child mortality, in 683–4 and again in 825, when Ireland was hit by disease, famine and a great shortage of bread. Children were breastfed. The law tract *Bretha Crólige* notes that one of the three categories of persons who had to be accompanied by a woman was 'the mother of every child at the breast'.[91]

Infanticide was probably prevalent, especially for children born with a disability. An episode in the *Vita Prima* of Brigit is stark in its depiction of the practice:[92]

> Another day a woman came to Saint Brigit and said 'What am I to do about my child? You see, his father wants to kill him because he is almost a stillborn child for he is blind from birth and with a mental disorder.'
>
> Thereupon Brigit took pity on the woman. She told her to wash the child's face in the water nearby and at once the boy who was called a 'cretin' became normal and they say that until his death he had no eye-disease but always had healthy eyes.

The canon laws mainly follow Augustine with regard to abortion and infanticide in viewing them as serious crimes for which a woman was severely punished.[93] A relatively common topos in saints' Lives is that of saints taking abandoned children into their care. Cellanus, the blind monk who was a learned holy man in Colmán Elo's church at Lynally, was son of an Uí Néill noble who had rejected him and had asked a servant to kill him. He was saved by the servant and the saint.[94] Whereas the laws deemed that the welfare of orphans was the responsibility of the head of a kindred who acted as a father-figure on their behalf, it is unlikely that this extended to all children.[95]

Fosterage

When the child of a freeman or noble family reached seven years – or often even at an earlier age – he or she was normally sent to spend the next seven years with a foster family. Fosterage was one of the most important institutions among the nobility and their clients in early Irish society, and many fundamental human bonds were created during these childhood and adolescent years. A child was bound to its foster parents, to their own family and to other foster children cared for by the foster family.[96] Two types of fosterage existed: a fosterage of affection and a contractual fosterage. As children were often fostered with a family of lower rank, the institution also instilled a form of cohesion between the free classes, as this was one way in which the different elements of that section of the population mingled and formed loyal attachments. Royal dynasties depended on fosterage to build alliances, and in many cases multiple fosterages of royal families were effective in creating networks of alliances.[97] The case of Áed Sláine, who aspired to the kingship of Tara, illustrates the loyalty instilled among foster-brothers. Áed killed his nephew and rival Suibne mac Colmáin Máir in 600 at Brí Dam (perhaps in the vicinity of Geashill, Co. Offaly). Áed was killed in 604 at the instigation of his grand-nephew Conall Guthbinn in revenge for his father Suibne's death. It would appear, however, that the deed was done by Conall's foster-brother Áed Gustán, presumably as a loyal companion expected to carry out such actions. Conall did not attain the kingship of Tara for his dynasty and was killed in 635 by Áed Sláine's son, Diarmait.

Fosterage did not simply function as a form of childcare. Its other vital purpose was to provide education to children according to their class and gender. Most children were taught 'the usual arts', which in the case of boys meant riding, swimming, board-games and bearing arms.[98] While somewhat exaggerated, the depiction in the epic *Táin Bó Cuailnge* of Cú Chulainn's arrival as a boy at Emain provides an impression of this type of education being conducted among noble boys in which games, both physical and mental, were used to teach discipline, physical training and leadership.[99] Noble girls were taught sewing, cutting-out and embroidery, essential skills needed to manage the production and utilization of cloth in any household. Equally practical was the training of the sons and daughters of lower grades in agricultural practices and food production. The son of an *ócaire* 'lowest grade of freeman' learned livestock-herding, kiln-drying and wood-cutting, while his daughter learned to use a quern, a kneading trough and a sieve. The importance of these activities to the early Irish economy is clear from the range of objects and structures often found at settlement sites: corn-drying kilns, mills and millstones, querns and spindle whorls of bone and stone, loom weights and weaving tablets.[1] Children going into a contractual fosterage brought with them a fosterage fee – the amount depending on the child's social status – and nursing clothes, while the sons of kings went with a horse. Nursing clothes consisted of a blanket (*brat*) and a black tunic (*inar dub*). Additional later glosses to the main law on fosterage suggest that children of different classes were distinguished by the colour of their clothes: grey, yellow, black and white for the lowest class (*aithig*), red, grey-green and brown for middle ranks (*airich*), and purple and blue for the sons of kings.[2] Whether these particular colours were worn by various ranks is open to question. However, sagas often describe the clothes of the nobility in great detail associating purple, gold and bright red with royalty.[3]

What happened when problems arose as a child was being fostered? The laws deal with discipline, misbehaviour and maltreatment of children, both in the environment of their own biological families and when fostered.[4] As children grew older, they were expected to behave more responsibly, particularly beyond the age of twelve. A key element of discipline taught to noble children, as suggested by the laws, was the maintenance of social stability and the imposition of restorative penalties for misdemeanour. A child who misbehaved persistently became a liability to his kin, as they had to compensate a foster family for any damage or injury caused by his actions. It did not necessarily mean that he or she returned to their biological family, as it was open to a foster-father to continue to discipline and rear them, while at the same time seek further payment from the natural father. Bad fosterage was recognized and seems to have been put down to neglect, especially deprivation of food, clothing or medical attention. In such cases, a child could be restored to its natural family and its kin compensated for the neglect. It seems that a foster family could have cause 'without necessity' (*cen dethbiri*) to return a child who was ill or not otherwise fit for fosterage, and 'out of pride' (*ar diumus*), which presumably followed either family's loss of status. A fosterage contract was legally terminated on the death of a child or due to a dispute over compensation for a child's crime or a dowry. The child's nursing clothes, milch-cow and excess fees were returned to its father in such cases.

The role of druids and prophets in the fosterage of noble children is such a common theme in early Irish sagas and saints' Lives that it is likely to have been one of the genuine functions of this religious caste. Cathbad, the druid, acted in Conchobar mac Nessa's court at Emain as the king's advisor and tutor to the troupe of boys (*macrad*), among them Cú Chulainn. He taught divination and his prophecies related to two aspects of a foster-son's education, bearing arms and riding a chariot.[5] Cormac mac Airt's foster-father was Lugna Fer Trí, who was a prophet, and who, in a manner similar to Cathbad, foretold the heroic career of his foster-son.[6] The involvement of a shamanic caste in the rearing of the classic hero of sagas is a common universal role and is to be expected in such an extensive corpus of heroic literature as that from Ireland. Their appearance in hagiography may perhaps reflect a situation closer to reality. Adomnán, for example, has Columba outwit and indeed terrify Broichan, the foster-father of the Pictish king Bridei.[7] The *Vita Prima* of Brigit illustrates how the detached world of the laws and the complex nature of noble families operated in reality.

Brigit's father was a nobleman, her mother a bondsmaid, and therefore, unfree. Dubthach's wife – supported by her brothers – insisted that he get rid of the bondsmaid, most especially as there were portents that her offspring would surpass the queen's sons. He finally sold Brigit's mother to a poet but not the child in her womb for whom he was responsible. The poet returned to his own region and then sold the bondsmaid to a druid who, after Brigit's birth, moved to Connacht and later to Munster – an indication of how the privileged classes were not confined to one kingdom but had the freedom to move around the country. As Brigit was filled with the Holy Spirit she could not digest the druid's 'unclean' food and 'thereupon he chose a white cow and set it aside for the girl, and a certain Christian woman, a very God-fearing virgin, used to milk the cow and the girl used to drink the cow's milk and not vomit it up as her stomach had been healed. Moreover, this Christian woman fostered the girl'.[8] When Brigit indicated that she wished to return to her father, the druid sent her back as a free person with her Christian foster-mother. This episode is replete with both mythological and Christian motifs, but one of its important aspects is that it illustrates how Christianity was assimilated into the native practice of fosterage. It has been argued that spiritual Christian kinship, as it evolved in sixth-century Francia and seventh-century Anglo-Saxon England, did not make headway in Ireland.[9] Presumably Brigit was not only taught to keep a house by her Christian foster-mother, as required by law, but she also raised her as a Christian with the druid's permission. He accepted this situation as his own sense of divination led him to understand that the child's future renown would stem from her Christian sanctity. This transfer of role from one religious caste to another may have related in particular to the education of noble foster-sons destined to join a religious life. Hence, the equivalent of a druid in the *Vita Prima* in Adomnán's Life of Columba was Cruithnechán, a priest, and Columba's foster-father. Cruithnechán also had to contend with a miraculous child who was visited by an astonishing portent at which the priest 'began to tremble, and bowed his face to the ground for he recognized that the grace of the Holy Ghost was poured from heaven upon his foster-son, and he stood in awe'.[10] The transition from the role of non-Christian spiritual guide to that of Christian spiritual foster-parent may have been seamless for some, as was the transition from guardianship of sacred sites to churches.[11]

Noble sons: succession to the kingship

The issue of succession from one king to another has been a key debate in early Irish historiography since Eoin MacNeill, the founding father of the subject, discussed it in his book *Celtic Ireland* published in 1921.[12] Two questions have formed the basis of the debate since MacNeill wrote: who was qualified to be considered for kingship, and what qualities determined who among them would become king?[13] MacNeill concluded:[14]

> In ancient Irish law, a person eligible to succeed (rigdomna) to a kingship must belong to the same DERBFINE as a king who had already reigned.
>
> The DERBFINE was a family of four generations, a man, his sons, grandsons and greatgrandsons.
>
> Among the persons thus lawfully eligible, the succession was determined by election.

Whatever about the subsequent complex arguments on the law and the reality of succession to early Irish kingships, MacNeill covered the main elements of dynastic succession, not only in Ireland but in many other cultures: suitability for the position, relationship with a preceding king or kings, seniority, or otherwise, of the individual and his family, and the process of proclamation as king. Who was entitled to claim a kingship (*flaithes, ríge*), to be accepted by a people (*túath(a)*), to represent his kin (*fine*) and to inherit the mensal lands of a kingdom (*cumal senorba, ferann ríg*)? In an effort to offer a clear description of succession, the following discussion addresses some of these topics in detail.[15]

Fit to be king: the concept of 'febas'

One passage in *Audacht Morainn* lists the attributes of a lord: he is to be merciful, just, impartial, conscientious, firm, generous, hospitable, honourable, beneficient, capable, honest, stable, steady and true-judging.[16] The text continues by listing the ten things 'which extinguish the injustice of every ruler': rule and worth (*flaith 7 febas*), fame and victory (*cluith 7 coscar*), progeny and kindred (*cland 7 cenél*), peace and long life (*síd 7 sáegul*), good fortune and people (*toceth 7 tótha*).[17]

Many of these attributes are common characteristics sought in leaders to this day and many of the same traits are found to be lacking in leaders who are elected. The annals are littered with elegiac obits to prominent kings that praise them for their generosity, their justice and mercy, and their prowess in defending their people. A verse from the obit of Máel Finnia mac Flannacáin (*AU 903*) is typical:

The son of Der bFáil, fighting for Brega's plain,
Was wont to smash every deceitful band,
Generous Mael Finnia, mighty and valiant,
A stout hero, very noble and warlike.

And yet the records of the careers of kings, as described in the same sources, relate incidents of kin-slaying, attacks on churches, and bloody contests within their own dynasties and with neighbouring dynasties. One of the essential requirements to be eligible for kingship in the laws was *febas*, a term that has a range of meanings and one that is difficult to translate. *Audacht Morainn*'s phrase *flaith 7 febas* encapsulates the concept succinctly. A king had to be an excellent and worthy individual and to be wealthy and powerful enough to fulfil his obligations towards his kindred, his clients and the people he ruled. To what extent did this requirement determine who might be eligible for kingship and who in the end became king? This forms a core of the succession debate about early Irish kingship with, for example, Charles-Edwards arguing for a greater significance of *febas* as a pre-requisite for eligibility than Bart Jaski, who argues for the importance of a range of qualifications including seniority, importance of kindred, maternal connections, age and so on. Whatever about the theoretical debate about *febas*, the requirement in practical terms could have been used to rule out a wide range of individuals, especially when combined with the other 'theoretical' attributes listed in *Audacht Morainn*. Hence those of unsound mind, those with a perceived disability, and those showing signs of inability to perform in legal or military spheres could be deemed ineligible for kingship. The idea of *febas* is embedded in another term, *rígdamna* 'material for a king', or the later *tánaise ríg* 'heir-designate'. Were the many men whose deaths are recorded in the annals holding these titles potential candidates for a kingship, noble and upright individuals or actually designated to be heirs to a kingship? The sources suggest that these titles could cover a wide range of individuals, not necessarily all succeeding to kingships, or even likely ever to become kings. What distinguished a successor to a kingship did not depend on his *febas* alone. The *febas* of his kindred and his relationship with his predecessor or predecessors was also of considerable importance.

The 'febas' of the kindred and relationship with a predecessor

It is essential to our understanding of the structure of authority in early Ireland that we distinguish between the least important king – the *rí túaithe* – and the most important, the provincial king and the claimant to the kingship of Tara or Ireland. The *rí túaithe* was the representative of his people in his dealings with other kings and *túatha*, and succession to such a kingship may have been relatively straightforward, progressing as *cenn* or *ágae fine* 'head of the kindred' from father to son, unless a collateral kindred attempted to seize the kingship or a kindred fragmented and declined. Outside forces could also interfere in a succession, and often did. Time and again the genealogies provide detailed insights into the fragmentation or survival of dynasties throughout Ireland at a micro-level. They describe noble families as *sáerchlanna* 'noble and free descendants', *prímaicme* or *prímsloinniud* 'chief kindred' or *rígrad* 'a line of kings' of a province or a people. A typical example of the division of a territory between the descendants of a single ancestor is that of the Uí Chonaill Gabra, whose over-kingdom extended west of Limerick to the borders of Cos Limerick and Kerry. The genealogies explain that the mid-eighth-century king Flann mac Eircc had nine sons and from them a host of minor noble families descended (table 4).[18]

TABLE 4. The nine sons of Flann mac Eircc.

1. Ledbán	2. Scannlán	3. Sathgel	4. Gallchobor	5. Aurthuile
(Uí Ledbáin)	(Uí Scannláin)	(Uí Sathgil)	(Uí Gallchobuir)	(Uí Aurthuili)
6. Murchad	7. Bécán	8. Artgal	9. Conchobar (?Olchobar)	
(Uí Murchada)	(Uí Bécáin)	(Uí Artgaile)	(no issue)	

Of these, Scannlán (d. 786) was the most important, as his descendants held the over-kingship of Uí Fhidgenti, which, at the time, stretched from the lands around the Shannon Estuary into Co. Clare. Indeed, Scannlán's brother Olchobar (d. 796/7) – perhaps the Conchobar of the genealogies who had no issue – became abbot of the powerful monastery of Inis Cathaig (Scattery Island, Co. Clare). He may have held the provincial kingship of Munster. Scannlán is listed as having had six sons: Máel Cellaig, Dúnadach, Muiredach, Dúbartach, Flannabra and Bran. The descendants of Dúnadach were the dynasty who clung onto the Uí Fhidgenti kingship until the tenth century. In two generations, it can be surmised that at least those listed in the genealogies had some claim to the kingships of Uí Chonaill Gabra and the over-kingship of the Uí Fhidgenti. *Febas* was indeed attached to that dynasty as it was regarded in legal tracts as one of the leading dynasties of Munster.[19] Scannlán's eminent brother Olchobar did not succeed him either in his immediate kingship of Uí Chonaill Gabra or in the over-kingship of Uí Fhidgenti. If he was proclaimed king of Munster – and this is far from certain – he was chosen as an exception, and possibly a compromise candidate in time of stress in the province. Another of Scannlán's brothers, Murchad (d. 807), however, was over-king and also the king of Uí Chonaill Gabra. He, in turn, was succeeded by Scannlán's son Dúnadach (d. 835). It is possible that Dúnadach was considered too young or inexperienced compared to his uncle Murchad on the death of his father and that it was decided that Murchad would be the more competent to represent the people of the kingdom. Not that Dúnadach was incompetent; he defeated the Vikings in battle in 834.

The maxim *areirig osar sindsear* 'the junior rises up before the senior' impinged on many relationships in society: lesser kings before greater kings, kings before great abbots and bishops, and brothers in competition for succession. While seniority among those eligible for a kingship, and in particular among brothers, was the common prerequisite for elevation, it did not stand in the way of a younger son achieving a kingship over his older brothers. Interestingly, the church favoured primogeniture as the *Canones* explicitly lay down that the eldest of a father's sons was to inherit his patrimony, and that on that son's death the patrimony was to be divided among his heirs, his brothers and their successors.[20] As outlined by Jaski, however, there are many instances of younger sons succeeding to a kingship in literature.[21] Succession to provincial kingships was less certain, as it involved more than one dynasty, often many, and military might and political cunning was also necessary to be proclaimed a king of kings. The number of free and base clients who swore allegiance to an individual king was a further indication of his strength and ability to rule a kingdom successfully.

Patterns of alternation between dynasties have been detected for a long time by historians in relation to the succession patterns of certain provincial kingships. The cases most often cited are the overlordship of the Uí Néill that alternated from the eighth to the eleventh century between the midland dynasties of Clann Cholmáin and the northern Cenél nEogain, and the kingship of Leinster, which alternated during the same period between three dynasties, the Uí Dúnchada, Uí Fháeláin and Uí Muiredaig.[22] King lists of the major kingships for the period are constructed to give the impression of a smooth system of alternation, but this often belies periods of great strife and instability. If the reigns of three successive ninth-century powerful Uí Néill kings of Tara, Niall Caille (Cenél nEogain, 833–46), Máel Sechnaill mac Maíle Ruanaid (Clann Cholmáin, 846–62) and Áed Findliath (Cenél nEogain, 862–79) are examined, it becomes apparent that threats to their authority came not only from the rival dynasties for their kingships but also from within their own kindreds. All had to contend with an external threat from kings of Munster to the extent that, in reality, Niall Caille had to share his rule of Ireland with Feidlimid mac Crimthainn, king of Munster (d. 847). Given the number of potentially eligible candidates for a kingship, and especially a regional or provincial kingship, violent rivalry and kin-slaying (*fingal*) was rife. In this period, two examples illustrate how local this rivalry could be and, indeed, that it was probably frowned upon by the church from an

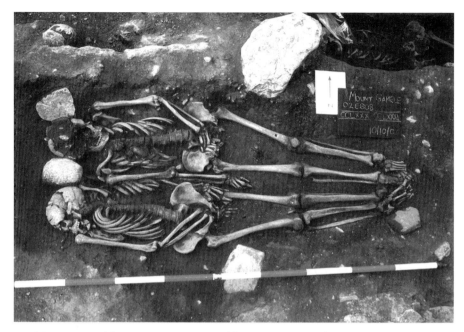

13 Mount Gamble cemetery, Co. Dublin: one grave (burials cclxxx–cclxxxi) contained the bodies of two adolescent males who died due to violent trauma – one was decapitated and the other received blows to the left side of his head. They may have been the victims of battle or of rivalry among families within a kindred for succession to a kingship. © Edmond O'Donovan/Margaret Gowen & Co. Ltd.

early stage. The strictures of Adomnán against Áed Sláine for his involvement in kin-slaying provide compelling evidence of the church's view of *fingal*.[23] It nevertheless continued as a practice – as indeed happened in relation to many dynasties elsewhere. In 839, Cennétech mac Congalaig, king of the east midlands kingdom of Uí Moccu Uais of Brega, was deceitfully killed (*dolose iugulatus est*) by his brother or kinsman Céile. Céile's over-king, Máel Sechnaill mac Maíle Ruanaid, was involved in ruthless kin-slaying some years later when, during the succession struggle to his father's kingship in 845, he killed his brother Flann and his cousin Donnchad mac Follamain. In the following year, he succeeded Niall Caille, who was drowned in the river Callann near Armagh.

The archaeological record (as found in burials) may reflect such internecine struggles in the evidence for violent struggle, trauma and ritual killings. Decapitation followed by a decent burial may indicate that the dead were victims of a succession dispute, as in the case of the two individuals buried in one grave in the cemetery at Mount Gamble, Co. Dublin – one was beheaded, the other executed by receiving blows to the left side of his head (fig. 13).[24] Two decapitated males linking arms were buried in one grave in the seventh-/eighth-century cemetery at Knoxspark, Co. Sligo,[25] possibly representing two unsuccessful candidates to a kingship. Theoretical alternation could be disrupted by an ambitious aspirant to a kingship or by an aspirant who feared the challenge of the reigning king's son. This seems to have been the case with Áed Findliath, Máel Sechnaill's successor to the kingship of Tara. In 860, Máel Sechnaill led a formidable army from the midlands, Leinster, Munster and Connacht towards Áed's own northern kingdom, presumably in response to menacing moves by the latter. His army camped outside Armagh and it was attacked by Áed and his ally Flann mac Conaing (d. 868) from the east midlands dynasty of Síl nÁedo Sláine of Brega. Flann was Áed's nephew, his sister's son. Máel Sechnaill fought off Áed and Flann's attack on that occasion, but, in the following two years, Áed invaded Máel Sechnaill's own kingdom of Mide with his allies Flann mac Conaing and the Vikings. Since Máel Sechnaill died in 862 – apparently of natural causes – Áed had probably decided to move against him in 860 either because he knew that the king of Tara was suffering from ill-health or because Máel Sechnaill was growing old. Equally, he may have been concerned by the strength of Flann Sinna, Máel Sechnaill's son. By marrying Lann, Máel Sechnaill's widow and Flann Sinna's mother, Áed secured the kingship of Tara both militarily and symbolically. Áed Findliath died in Druim Inasclainn (Dromiskin, Co. Louth) in 879 and was succeeded by Flann Sinna.

How a king was chosen by his people

Most narratives relating to the public proclamation of a king concentrate on the inauguration rituals, especially those of the kings of Cashel and Tara. The discussion also centres on the 'royal' landscapes in which these public events took place, not just at great sites such as Tara, Cruachu, Caisel and Tailtiu, but also at many local sites throughout the country.[26] *Críth Gablach* states *is túath oirdnither ríg* 'it is a *túath* which exhalts a king'. The sources offer occasional glimpses of other elements in the process of the proclamation of a king. In the description of the proclamation of the king of Cashel in *Longes Chonaill Chuirc* ('the Exile of Conall Corc'), the Múscraige, a subject people to whom the swineherd Cuirirán belonged, were conferred with a privileged position in the ceremony:[27]

> It is he [the swineherd or his descendant], too, who raises the cry of the kingship for the king of Cashel, and is given a blessing by the king, and straightway receives the garment of the king (*dechelt ind ríg*). Hence it is, then, that Corc's Cashel exists, and it is the progeny and the seed of Corc mac Lugthach that abides forever in Cashel from that time forth.

Interestingly, in the story of *Senchas Fagbála Caisil* 'The history of the founding of Cashel', the privilege of blessing the provincial king was accorded the descendants of another people, the Éile, in whose territory the provincial capital, the Rock of Cashel (pl. 6), was located:[28]

> And Duirdriu gave him (Corc) the blessing at Ráith na nIrlann by the lawn (*faithche*) of Cashel, and he was proclaimed king at once.

The special role of vassal people in being the guardians of ritual capitals and their associated royal mensal lands has never been properly recognized. The literature suggests that people such as the Múscraige at Cashel, the Déssi Temrach at Tara and the Senchineóil Chonnachta at Rathcroghan, not only played a significant part in the actual ceremonies, but also protected the ceremonial complex itself. A reflex of this role occurs in the topographical tale relating to Odra Temrach (Odder, Co. Meath), which is located near the Hill of Tara. In his bid to take possession of Tara, the heroic king, Cormac mac Airt, went to dig out a ditch on the hill – no doubt part of the ritual associated with declaring oneself king of Tara. While digging, he heard three cries. The cries came from Odrán, who belonged to the vassal people known as Déssi Temrach. Odrán complained that Cormac had insulted him by violating his land and taking possession of it. Cormac bargained with him and offered him Odra Temrach, at the foot of Tara, which Odrán accepted.[29] Although Déssi Temrach were vassals, the import of this tale is that they continued to make their mark within the ceremonial complex at Tara.

A further example of this phenomenon is found in the Tripartite Life of Patrick. It tells of the contest for the kingship of Uí Amolgada (in north Mayo) among the seven sons of Amolgaid mac Fiachrach. In an aside, the text relates how the twenty-four *senchenéla* 'old, vassal peoples' would rise up if a man with a nickname were to rule them.[30] A nickname was an equivalent to a blemish and would have drawn attention to a deformity or an undesirable trait in a potential king. Óengus, 'the most arrogant of the brothers', used this stipulation laid down by these vassal peoples to gain the kingship by giving nicknames to all his brothers and, thereby, secured possession of the kingship himself. Ultimately, his deceit was unsuccessful as he also deceived St Patrick and, as a result, his descendants were denied the kingship forever. While this episode appears to be somewhat far-fetched, given the number of kings who had descriptors such as *menn* 'dumb' or *cáech* 'squinting' added to their names, the role of the free clients among vassal kindreds, who after all must have made up a considerable number of a *túath*'s population, in a king's election was probably important. A possible historical reflection of the episode in the Life of Patrick occurs in 777 (*AU*), which records a skirmish between Niall mac Conaill Grant (d. 778) and Cummascach mac Fogartaig (d. 797) of Uí Chernaig Sotail (Síl nÁedo Sláine) over the kingship of southern Brega. The skirmish occurred on the green (*faithche*) of a royal residence at Caladruim (Galtrim, Co. Meath). Among the dead was Echtgus mac Baíth, king of Déssi Breg (alias Déssi Temrach), the most important client people of the kingdom. The gathering of a crowd on the *faithche* of Caladruim implies that an assembly was being held there, perhaps involving the proclamation of one or other of the protagonists, Niall or Cummascach. Echtgus mac Baíth's participation is likely to have been in his role as the king of Déssi Breg and an important person involved in the election of the king of southern Brega. Unfortunately for Echtgus, it cost him his life.

In a highly stratified society, and one also very prone to internecine violence, the recognition of a king and his inauguration must have often caused tension in a community. This was obviously lessened if there was no dispute about the succession and the new king was inaugurated with the agreement of his people. It was also eased by the various free clients and their leaders holding a traditional role in the succession process and the inauguration. Their assent and willingness to participate in an inauguration or royal assembly was a clear indication of the acceptance of a king by his people.

Who were the people of a kingdom?

Social order under the rule of a strong king is the fundamental basis of a good functioning society in early Irish law and in the instructions on good kingship such as *Audacht Morainn* and *Tecosca Cormaic*. This meant that a kingdom's people, theoretically at least, knew their place in their communities from their honour-price and their legal status. The ideal society, consisting of the privileged class, known collectively as *nemed*,[31] and of other free but lesser classes is proclaimed in the Middle Irish poem *Diambad messe bad rí réil* 'If I were an illustrious king'.[32] This text also lists the professions valued in society:

> For each his task has been appointed …
> the craftsman uses bronze,
> the abbot's son is in the church,
> the farmer's son is on the land,
> the king's son is binding hostages,
> the carpenter's son follows the adze,
> the smith's son takes to the coal,
> the trumpeter's son carries the horn,

the hero's son follows arms,
the cleric's son goes on circuit,
the harper's son carries the harp,
the potter's son takes to the clay,
let the physician's son be a physican,
the son of the string player sings clear tunes,
the mariner's son takes to the sea,
the husbandman's son tills soil,
the poet's son practices poetry,
the jester's son practices satire,
let the judge's son be without decadence,
let the pirate's son take to evil-doing from harbour to harbour,
let the comb-maker's son follow combs,
the butcher's son, his work is slaying …
… it is from the young man comes forth the king.

Idealized though this view of society may be, it, nevertheless, makes sense when considered in the context of other sources. The *nemed* were the ruling class who were made up of the royal dynasty, the higher religious (particularly bishops) and professional elite (especially judges, poets and craftsmen). Many were hereditary families whose crafts or professions were handed from father to son or, where this was not possible, through other male lineages. Even seemingly lower crafts, such as comb-making, were hereditary, and given the need for combs, reflected in their prevalence in the archaeological record, were probably valued crafts.

Certain groups were vital to the smooth operation of a kingdom's governance and economy, and none more than that of the judge, the poet and the farmer. Judges (*brithemon*) and poets (*filid*) could confirm a king in his royal position, or could cause his downfall. The laws and literature are replete with anecdotes of kings losing their kingships as a result of giving bad judgments and of being victims of satire. According to the laws, judges were not qualified unless they were proficient in just about every branch of law. This situation may not reflect reality, but the texts can be used at least to demonstrate the extent to which law governed this society. Judges had to be able to adjudicate, for example, in neighbourhood law, laws relating to property, succession, contracts, sick-maintenance, injury, the ownership of bees down to laws regulating dogs and cats.[33] The wealth of early Irish legal texts proves that these were genuine requirements as the actual laws survive in all these legal domains.

As clearly demonstrated by Breatnach in his study of satire and praise, 'in a society where honour (*enech*) was so valued, the weapon of *áer* 'satire' was especially to be feared', and indeed needed to be regulated.[34] Praise poetry, on the other hand, was almost an antidote to satire, *molad do-nig aír* 'praise which washes away satire'.[35] The power of the highest grade of poet, the *ollam*, extended beyond sanctioning or praising his king. He was also the custodian of a community's memory which formed legal precedence. This is clear from the law on the grades of poets:[36]

> an *ollam* ... he is knowledgeable in all historical science, and he is knowledgeable in the jurisprudence of Irish law (*is éola i cach coimgniu, 7 is éola i mbrithemnacht fénechais*).

As custodians of history and memory, considerable importance accrued to the poets in their legal capacity, as they could confirm the ownership of land. This power is explicit in laws and legal glosses. Among many examples, Liam Breatnach quotes from an Old Irish text on prescriptive rights which lists various means by which evidence of title was served:[37]

> There are ten immoveable rocks which hold fast every ownership of estates: one estate is covered by three [generations of] lords, another land is confirmed by the words of poets [*ala tonn fo toruib filed fosaigther*], one estate [*íath*] has remained under households [*fo trebaib*] of clerics, another land is attained by prowess with swords.

This text may seem highly legalistic, but when viewed from a practical perspective, this procedure was essential to the stability of a kingdom as it regulated claims to land. One gloss on this form of regulation brings us closer to reality where it details the actual evidence for ownership of every mound (*ferta*):[38]

> if he was seen making a trench around it, i.e. as for example every assembly mound [*fert áenaigh*]; or if custodians of tradition [*senchaide*] demonstrate that it was by the kindred [*fine*] that the trench was made.

Communal memory was maintained by the hereditary nature of the office, for, as the law on the grades of poets states, 'When is a family a family of poets? Not difficult; their father is a poet and their grandfather'.[39] And while poets could accumulate great wealth, sometimes theirs was a precarious profession, especially if they used their power of satire injudiciously. This may have happened to one of Ireland's leading ninth-century poets, Flann mac Lonáin, in 896 when he was killed by the local dynasty of Uí Fhothaid Tíre in Waterford. He may have taken sides in a conflict for succession to the kingship of Déssi Muman that was raging at the time, and was assassinated for his activity.

If memory and judgment were essential to the administration of the kingdom, farming was its economic bedrock, and key to this were the different grades of landowners. This was particularly true of the *bóaire*, the prosperous middle-ranking farmer of early Irish agriculture. He was a freeman (*sóer*), but was a commoner and subject to a king to whom he owed food-rent (*bés*) and a certain number of man-days of labour annually.[40] The laws provide a fairly full account of the *bóaire*'s possessions and his agricultural practices.[41] He owned between fourteen and twenty-one *cumal*s worth of land. It is difficult to measure the exact extent of land involved, but the possibility that one *cumal* was a unit of value needed for three cows or more suggests that he owned a fairly extensive farm. While his land was primarily inherited, he had the legal power to purchase land and as a result to improve his status. His primary activity was rearing stock, as he was expected to have twenty cows, six oxen and two bulls. He was also involved in growing cereals – the extent of his acreage under seed presumably depending on the quality of his land – and owned his own plough-team, a corn-drying kiln, and either owned or shared a mill. His rank allowed him to keep two horses – one for riding and one for farmwork. *Críth Gablach*'s description of the house, farmyard and contents belonging to a *mruigfher* – the highest rank of *bóaire* – is sufficiently detailed to compare with archaeological evidence.[42] The house was twenty-seven feet in diameter and in it there was a cauldron with a spit, a vat for brewing beer, iron vessels, kneeding-troughs, a washing bucket, a bath-tub, a candlestick, a knife for cutting rushes, sackcloths, an adze, an auger, a saw, wooden shafts, an axe, a whetstone, a billhook, a hatchet and spears for killing livestock. The house was thatched and there were rushes strewn on the floor. One of his obligations was that he had to have the means to welcome into his house a king, a bishop, the head of a monastic school or a judge, with their retinues. There were various buildings on his land – a corn drying-kiln, a barn, a mill, an outhouse, a pigsty, a calf-pen and a sheepfold. The veracity of *Críth Gablach*'s description of the layout, size and contents of this type of house is supported by the extensive excavations undertaken at the settlement known as Deer Park Farms in Glenarm, Co. Antrim. The chronology of this settlement stretched from the seventh to the tenth century and it appears to have been occupied by one family unit involved in crop cultivation (cereals, flax), woodland management and woodworking, carpentry and basketery, spinning and dyeing cloth, cooking, milling, fishing, metalworking, and bone and antler working.[43] Farmers such as the *bóaire* do not appear in the annals and, apart from archaeological evidence, the closest that we come to gaining a genuine sense of their lives is often in hagiographical episodes of miracles happening on farms and in the fields. A salutary tale is told of Molua of Clonfert: he was sent out to mind his parent's calves that were kept close to the farmstead. The boy fell asleep, and while he was soundly sleeping, the cows returned from the fields, and the calves went to suckle them. This was witnessed by his mother from her house and she became angry as she was afraid that the calves would drain the cows dry of their milk. She went to strike her son but, as she lifted her hand, she fell, and Molua had a chance to separate the cows from the calves. And, of course, such was the boy's sanctity[44] that the cows' milk was saved and everyone blessed Molua.

Kings and the aristocracy are likely to have been in the minority in a kingdom, and yet, the rest of the population is inconspicuous both in the sources and seemingly in the archaeological evidence. Ireland is no different from elsewhere and, perhaps, the absence of the majority is as much to do with scholarly disregard for them as with their complete invisibility. Beneath the free classes were those in unfree or base clientship (*doíre*), some of whom had a restricted independence from their lord, but others who were completely dependent on their lord.[45] Although the laws might give the initial impression that there was no fluidity between classes, this was not so: it was more likely that people were pushed down the social scale, but there were opportunities for individuals to become free clients and to move into the aristocracy. Base clients known as *fuidir* were positioned between the free and unfree, and under certain circumstances could rise in status. A gnomic text, possibly dating to the ninth century, includes wise sayings that reflect a society's attitude to honour and status, and to those regarded as being on the margins of their communities:[46]

> Three free ones that make slaves of themselves: a lord who sells his land, a queen who goes to a boor, a poet's son who abandons his father's craft.
>
> Three women who are not entitled to a fine: a woman who does not care with whom she sleeps, a thievish woman, a sorceress (*ben aupthach*).
>
> Seven prohibitions: to go security for an outlaw, for a jester and for a madman, for a person without bonds, for an unfilial person, for an imbecile, for one excommunicated.
>
> A chief (sic: *flaith*) does not grant speech save to four: a poet for satire and praise, a chronicler of good memory for narration and story-telling, a judge for giving judgements, an historian for ancient lore (*fer cerda fri hair 7 molad, fer coimgne cuimnech fri haisnéis 7 scélugud, brethem fri bretha, sencha fri senchas*).

Literature classifies those on the margins of society as a mass of humanity, the *doéscarshlúag*, who might be found as camp-followers, or the *aithig*, commoners in society. A sense of shared identity of the *déssi* or *aithechthúatha* 'vassal peoples' of Ireland, who had declined in power and were often subject to unjust burdens imposed by their lords, is expressed in the eighth-century text 'The expulsion of the Déssi'.[47] The historians, so lauded in the above-quoted triad, could not resist combining certain groups of people together (notably those whose names ended with *–r(a)ige*) and also creating a narrative around their expulsion from Tara, and their migrations to the south-east and to Britain. There is some historical truth in the tale, as in the migration of Irish people to south-west Wales in the fifth century, but there is an underlying message that successful and dominant dynasties needed the support of the *aithechthúatha* to maintain their authority. This message is directed specifically at the Uí Néill dynasties in the northern half of Ireland and the Éoganachta in the southern half. And as seen in the previous section, the *déssi* performed important duties in a kingdom, not least the choreography of the proclamation and inauguration of a king.

Beyond the *fuidir* and the *aithig* or *déssi*, who had a legal status and, albeit difficult, some prospect to improve themselves, there were others who had no legal status and little or few material possessions. In certain cases, they were simply bound to their lord and worked on the land or performed hard manual labour, but were provided for with shelter and provisions. These were people known as *bothaig* and *senchléithi*. In other instances, some of them were slaves who could be sold on from master to master, as was the case with Brigit's pregnant mother, who was sold by her master, Brigit's father, at the insistence of his wife and her brothers, no doubt in order to save their honour.[48] The *Vita Prima*, along with many other saints' Lives, brings us as close as is possible in medieval texts to the destitute and those outside the law. Saints by their very status often placed themselves outside the law and challenged authority, often escaping censure through miracles. In her dealings with her father, Brigit is portrayed as enraging him by her actions, which ran contrary to the acceptable prescriptions of a noble daughter. Her relations with the poor provoked his wrath on occasion, no more so than when she handed over the royal sword that had been presented to him by a superior king, and, therefore, formed part of the royal regalia that was a sign of his status. His reaction seems severe, but in the context of his position and the circumstances of her birth was not exceptional:[49]

> Then Dubthach said to the king, 'Buy my daughter to be your slave'. The king replied, 'Why are you selling her?' Dubthach said, 'Whatever she lays her hand on she steals'. And the king said, 'Let her come to us'. Dubthach went out to her and said, 'Where is my sword?' She replied, 'I gave it to

Christ'. Her father became furious and felt like killing the maiden. But the king said to her, 'Why did you give my sword and your father's to the poor?' She replied, 'If God were to ask me for yourself and him, I would give you and all you have to him if I could'. Then the king said, 'This daughter of yours, Dubthach, is a great responsibility for me to buy and a greater one for you to sell'. Then the king gave her another sword to give to her father. And Dubthach went home with his daughter rejoicing.

Whether the *Vita Prima* is a seventh- or eighth-century text, this episode exposes grave issues that must have been addressed by the church, kings and lawyers. Although a noble woman, Brigit had no legal status beyond her dependency on her father, and, therefore, should not have handed his sword, a gift from his superior, to a poor man, another person with no legal status. Brigit's authority was God and she represented the poor man as Christ. Little wonder that the king refused to buy her as, in effect, she was challenging his own authority and was crossing fundamental societal controls relating to authority, possessions, legal status and relations between the powerful and the weak. The difficulty created by Brigit can be deduced from *Bretha in Gatta*, the law on theft, which decrees that if there is a theft of a valuable item belonging to a king or one of the *nemed* class from the house of a vassal (*aithech*), a labourer (*bachlach*) or a concubine (*airech*), full compensation was given to the noble. The equivalent of their honour-price was given to those whose houses had been raided.[50] The king's dilemma in the *Vita Prima*, which he clearly did not wish to confront, was that Brigit and the poor man were thieves, but that Brigit judged the situation in a completely different light.

The *Vita Prima*, and many other hagiographical texts, suggest that once established, churches became refuges for those rejected by society, or at least portrayed themselves as such. Dislike of the sick and disabled could pervade even the church, again as the *Vita Prima* illustrates:[51]

Saint Brigit went to another church in the Tethbae area in response to an invitation, to celebrate Easter Day there. However, the superioress of the church said to her nuns on the day of the Lord's Supper, 'Which of you is going to do the washing of the feet today for our old people and our sick?' But as none of the young nuns wanted to do it, they made excuses.

Then Brigit said, 'I am willing to wash the poor and sick women'. Now there were four sick women in the one house: one a paralytic who was a helpless invalid, the second a possessed woman completely taken over by the demon, the third blind and the fourth a leper. Then Brigit began to wash the paralytic first and the latter said, 'O holy Brigit ask Christ to

heal me'. And Brigit prayed and at once the woman was healed, the leper
was cleansed and the deranged nun was cured.

Care for the sick who had means was not the preserve of the church, however,
as is clear from the law tract *Bretha Crólige* and also from the archaeological
record. A woman buried in a *ferta* in Ballymacaward, Co. Donegal, sometime
during the fifth or sixth century lived up to twenty years beyond her menopause,
despite suffering from post-menopausal osteoarthritis of the spine.[52] Her burial
in an ancestral mound confirms her likely lofty status, her survival in such a
condition to a relatively old age being testimony to care within her family. At
the other extreme was the burial of an elderly woman with Paget's disease, a
chronic bone disorder, in a corn-drying kiln amid debris and burning at Corbally,
Co. Kildare, sometime between the fifth and seventh century. Her burial may
have been a hasty disposal of the body outside the main circular enclosure of
the nearby familial cemetery.[53] Perhaps this unfortunate woman was deemed to
be an outcast, either due to her disability and her community's fear of her. We
can be relatively certain that she had no legal status and that she had not been
entitled to sick-maintenance by the end of her life. She may even have been one
of those outcast women listed in the triads as reviled by society.

THE ROYAL HOUSE AND HOUSEHOLD

The royal house in laws and literature

There are many colourful descriptions in early Irish literature of the palaces and
courts of early Irish kings, but these are not matched by archaeological evidence.
The halls of heroic and mythical kings take on otherworldly and exaggerated
characteristics that often do not reflect reality. It may even be the case that
descriptions in Irish literature were sometimes based on images and buildings
encountered abroad, such as in Anglo-Saxon or Carolingian royal courts.[54] In
reality, however, and as most skilfully presented by the late ninth-century
Carolingian Hincmar of Reims in his treatise *De Ordine Palatii*, the laws of the
court and the physical position of various office holders in relation to the king
were essential for the orderly management of royal governance.[55] It was no
different in Ireland. Legal and annalistic descriptions and the numerous terms
associated with a king's residence conjure up a more realistic image than that
provided in sagas of the arrangements at court and the living conditions in a
royal household.[56] A key description on which to base this study is the
description of the *tech ríg* 'king's house' in *Críth Gablach*.[57] The household of a
rí túaithe consisted of four servants or guardsmen (*amuis*), a hostage given by

14 Tara: the ceremonial routeway on the hill was known as *Tech Midchuarta* 'the house of the mead court'. This monument was visualized in the medieval period as a royal banqueting hall, the ultimate royal residence. © National Monuments Service, Department of Arts, Heritage and the Gaeltacht.

the king's unfree clients as a pledge to fulfil their responsibilities (*fer gill*), messengers or envoys (presumably from other *túatha*), his own retinue and guests, poets, musicians and various entertainers. All of these people were consigned to one part of the king's house, thus revealing that various precincts in the royal residence were confined to particular classes or inhabitants. Placed closer to the king were a guardsman to guard the door, two further guardsmen to prevent 'conflict of the ale-house', the king's free clients and hostages on his watch. Closest to the king were his judge and his wife. Finally, kept in chains were the *géill díthma*, hostages whose lives had been surrendered to the king because of the treason of those who had offered them as pledges for loyalty to the king. This description, while somewhat idealized and dictated by the law tract's overriding need to portray the hierarchal structure of society, nonetheless probably offers a reasonable insight into the likely residents of a king's household (fig. 14). Various terms are used to describe this community, the most common being *muinter* – equated with Latin *familia* and also frequently used to describe a monastic community – *teglach* which literally means 'the residents of a house', *tellach* 'hearth, household, family' and *treb* 'farmstead, people, household'. The ninth-century *Cáin Domnaig* 'Law of Sunday', which stipulates how Sundays should be spent and what penalties were incurred for transgressing the rules, incidentally provides a pen-picture of the routine activities of a household and a kingdom:[58]

> 'This is what I forbid', saith the Lord: 'On Sunday there shall be no dispute, or lawsuit, or assembly, or strife, or bargain, or horse-driving, or sweeping the floor of a house, or shaving, or washing, or bathing, or washing [clothes], or grinding in mill or quern, or cooking, or churning, or yarn-weaving, or adultery, or journeying by anyone beyond the border of his own territory, or racing, or shooting with spear or arrow, or riding on horse or ass, or boiling food, or swimming, or horse-riding, or splitting firewood, or coracle on water …'

Many of these household chores in a king's residence were undertaken by different servants:[59] cooks (*benchoic, ferchoic* 'a female or male cook') who boiled or roasted meat and kneaded and baked bread, the staple foods of the royal household. The common term for an attendant, or servant, is *gilla*, but there are many compounds of *gilla* that suggest a wide variety of servants – *gilla con* 'a minder of hounds', *gilla cupáin* or *deogbaire* 'a cup-bearer', *gilla echraide* 'a groom', *gilla gaí* 'a minder of the spear' and *gilla scuir* 'a stableman'. A *gilla urláir* or *echlach urláir* and the *gnáth lucht* were the household servants who did the menial tasks around the royal house.[60] An important person in a royal household, and indeed in the kingdom as a whole, was the *rechtaire* 'steward', who functioned as an overseer and who ensured that the seating arrangements, sleeping accommodation and food were all in good order. The *rechtaire* also gathered in the king's food and other tributes. He had control of the servants and along with the *techtaire* 'messenger' was accorded half the honour-price of his master.

Críth Gablach's description of the royal household clearly indicates that a king needed bodyguards to protect his person and to defend his residence. The law tract cautions that the king's bodyguards should be men whom he could trust: a man he saved from violent death, from capture, from captivity, from service and servitude, 'lest he betray him or slay him through feelings of grievance or patriotism'.[61] A king had to be careful and watchful and to balance between trusting such men to protect him – given that he had saved or spared them – and fearing that they might act violently towards him. And that is what sometimes happened. The king of Leinster, Fiannamail mac Maíle Tuile, was killed in 680 (*AU*; ATig.) by Foidseachán, a member of his own household, at the instigation of the king of Tara, Fínnachta Fledach. Similarly, Fócarta mac Lachtnáin, king of Tethba, was 'wickedly' killed by an unnamed member of his household (*dolose a sua familia occisus est*) in 927 (*AU*).

Along with the *rechtaire*, the king or noble's first wife (*cétmuinter*) was also central to the smooth running of a household. One of the reasons that a man could divorce his wife was on the grounds that she neglected her household duties. Apart from keeping the residence in order, what were the economic activities of such a household? *Cáin Lánamna*, a very pragmatic law tract, is a useful source in this respect, as it details the economic contribution of a couple to their marriage measured by their respective property and belongings. It also explains how proceeds from the partnership were divided by both parties if they happened to divorce.[62] In explaining what goods and land were brought into the various categories of union and how the proceeds were divided following a divorce, the text provides a fair idea of the common activities of a well-to-do household. The higher the status of the couple, the greater the brideprice brought into the marriage by the woman, and wealth by the man, and the less manual labour undertaken by them. Partners who were of equal status and respectability agreed a contract for common ploughing with the assistance of their kinsmen, for leasing land and for providing food and entertainment for their lord as required by law. They also agreed to prepare food for feast-days, as they were also expected to entertain the head of their own kindreds' churches. They paid stud fees and furnished their household. If the union had to be dissolved, division was made in proportion to the entitlement of each partner in regard to land, stock and labour. The stock mentioned includes cattle and pigs. The proceeds of rearing cattle and of dairy produce were not only divided between the couple, but some went to the herders and dairy workers. The text recognizes that the woman was likely to have been in charge of the fattening of the pigs and keeping the pig sties clean and involved only in spring ploughing. In the case of the wife of a king, she was unlikely to have frequently visited pig sties but oversaw such activities with the assistance of a *rechtaire* and servants – most particularly when her husband was away on long military campaigns. The industry most closely associated with women was textile production. *Cáin Lánamna* stipulates that 'the wife takes half of clothing and woven fabric, a third of fibre combed and ready for spinning; a sixth of fleeces and sheaves of flax; a third of woad in steeping vats, half if it is caked'. There is considerable archaeological and linguistic evidence for the production of textiles, and for spinning, weaving and sewing. Shears, spindle whorls, pin beaters, loom weights, weaving tablets and needles occur on Irish sites, among them the stone fort of Cahercommaun,

Co. Clare, the royal crannogs of Lagore and Moynagh Lough, Co. Meath, and the Iron Age and medieval levels at Knowth, Co. Meath.[63] These objects are matched by words such as *abras* 'yarn, yarn-spinning', *fige* 'weaving, plaiting', *indech, slat fige, garman* 'weaver's beam', *sním* 'weaving', *úaimm* 'sewing'. The value of this industry to society is reflected in the rather extreme prohibition and penalties for weaving on Sunday or eve of Monday in *Cáin Domnaig*:[64]

> Yarn-weaving on the eve of Monday; if it be weaving in a loom, the loom-beam and all other material shall be burned, and seven ounces are paid as fine. If it be hand-weaving, a half-ounce of silver [is the fine] for it.

The heavy-duty work relating to the production of cloth was for girls and women of lower ranks, while noble women are often portrayed sewing and embroidering fine cloth. In the tale *Compert Con Culainn*, the hero Cú Chulainn sets out to woo Emer daughter of Forgall Manach, a native of Búaigne (probably Galtrim, Co. Meath). He finds her with her company of young women (*bantellach, bantrocht*) who were learning embroidery and needlework from Emer (*oc foglaim druine 7 deglámdae la hEmir*). The text continues that Emer had many gifts: beauty, a singing voice, sweetness, wisdom, love and embroidery (*búaid ndruine*). These were the reasons why Cú Chulainn had come to woo her – she had all the traits required of a woman, despite her somewhat unbearable haughtiness![65] And in many of these tales, the nobility are depicted as wearing fine clothing and jewellery. While the archaeological record leaves us in no doubt that the Irish were able to produce exquisite metalwork at the time, there is little evidence of the existence of cloth other than woollen and linen garments, which were not particularly brightly coloured. There is textile evidence for decorative borders made with small tassels and tablet woven braids from Ballinderry 2 crannog, Co. Offaly, and Lagore, Co. Meath.[66] This paucity of materials may not be a true reflection of the array and colours of cloth available to the nobility. Niamh Whitfield has matched the plethora of details regarding clothing and ornamentation of the main characters in the Middle Irish tale *Tochmarc Becfhola* with real objects and clothing from Ireland, and descriptions borrowed from Roman, Anglo-Saxon or Carolingian material culture.[67] Becfhola wears a purple cloak (*brat corcra*), a sign of her royalty – she is the malevolent form of the sovereignty goddess – and one often associated with kings, heroes and otherworldly beings in early Irish sagas. Of course, Irish society was not alone in recognizing purple as a royal colour and, as Whitfield notes, purple was also the colour of power in the Mediterranean. The Byzantine emperor wore a purple cloak at his inauguration. The Irish term *corcra* 'purple' was possibly borrowed from Latin *purpura* as early as the fifth century.[68] Unlike in the Mediterranean,

15 The Garryduff gold bird: this object was discovered in a ringfort at Garryduff, Co. Cork. This beautiful, tiny bird was perhaps once part of a larger object such as a pin. It dates to the seventh or eighth century and is testament to the craft of early Irish metalworkers who were accorded a noble status in their society. © Cork Public Museum.

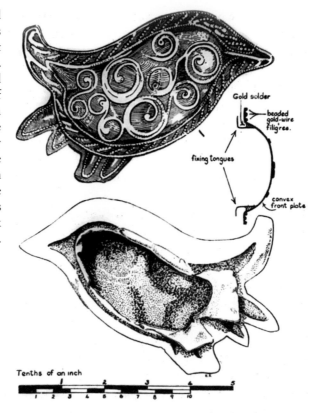

murex, the shellfish from which the purple dye was extracted in the Roman and Byzantine world, was not available in Ireland. If purple was genuinely used as a dye, it may have been extracted from dog whelk (*nucilla lapillis*) or from lichen. The latter would have produced a redder dye – hence the explanation for the term *corcra* meaning 'crimson' as well as 'purple'. Intriguingly, evidence for the production of purple dye from dog whelk occurs mainly along the west coast at shellmidden sites such as Inishkea North, Co. Mayo, Dooey, Co. Donegal, and Doonloughan and Dog's Bay, Roundstone, Co. Galway.[69] A fragmentary text possibly dating to the eighth century claims that a tax on madder – a plant used to produce red dye – was due to the king of Munster from the Burren, Co. Clare, and the Aran Islands, Co. Galway.[70] This reference suggests that places commonly perceived as isolated could have been important in the 'royal' economy of early Ireland and that they may have gained their wealth from the production of exclusive materials.

High-class metalworking was one of the activities undertaken within the precincts of certain royal residences. Some of the finest objects from early medieval Ireland were found at such sites, including the small gold bird from

Garryduff ringfort, Co. Cork (fig. 15, pl. 7), a gold filigree panel from Moynagh Lough crannog, Co. Meath, a gold filigree panel from Lagore crannog, Co. Meath, and a goldworking crucible and gold-rubbing stone from Clogher, Co. Tyrone.[71] All these objects date to sometime in the seventh or eighth centuries. A yellow enamel block was discovered at Moynagh Lough and crucibles with droplets of red enamel turned up at Garranes ringfort, Co. Cork. Yellow enamel was used for ribbon inlay, while red enamel was used as a background colour.[72] The distinction made between the smith (*goba*) and goldsmith (*cerd*), which is evident from the archaeological record, is also apparent in the laws. The commentary on the tract on accidental injury *Bretha Éitgid* declares that gold, silver and bronze found in a smith's forge had to be forfeited as by right they should not be there, but belonged to a goldsmith's forge, where they were necessary for his craft.[73] Presumably such precious metals would only be kept in a smith's forge if they were stolen and were being concealed.

The royal household was not devoid of lively entertainment and drinking sessions. Both *Críth Gablach* and *Audacht Morainn* warn kings about the dangers of the ale-house and excessive drinking: the king was to station two men with spears in front of him to protect him from the conflict of the ale-house (*fri cumascc cuirmthige*),[74] and he was immune from paying compensation to anyone injured in the *cuirmthech*: 'the ale-house with friends and great abundances of mead-circuit, where foolish and wise, familiars and strangers are intoxicated'.[75]

The text *Lánellach tigi rích 7 ruirech* 'The full complement of the house of a king and overking'[76] offers an animated representation of a greater king's household in which it details the house's furnishings. It is not as lavish as the palace described by Hincmar of Reims, but is similar in its view of the proper arrangement of a court, with the notable absence of clerics:

> Conchobar sat in the chief seat.
> Goibne [the smith] sat by his knee.
> Forinde [the druid/seer/poet] sat beside him [between two cubicles (*imdae*)].
> Tot mac Éogain Orbrecht [the judge] sat in front of him [beside the king's throne].
> Augune [possibly a second judge] sat behind the king's cubicle/couch (*imdae*).
> The spearman sat by the houseposts (*cletha*).
> The sureties [hostages] sat before the king.
> Búanond [the ruling queen?] in the level rush-strewn place (*blaí aíne*).
> The hospitallers (*briugu*) sat by the bounteous king's forearms [serving him].
> All the leeches (*lege*) sat with the drink-measure beside the cupbearers (*dáilemon*).

The leather-bottlemakers (*cairemain*) and the brewers (*cirpsiri*) sat on the great threshing-floor (*magen márthúaircne*).

The jesters (*drúth*) and the [other entertainers?] sat between the two candle-holders (*etir in di chondelbrai*) [on the front floor of the house].

Other dependent people (*dóernemed*: satirists and tricksters) sat by the door-posts (*aurchoilli*).

The horn-blowers (*cornairi*), charioteers (*áraith*), and flute-players (*cuslennaich*) sat in the front part of the house.

The attendants (*fois*) took up position in front of the pillars of the upper level (*úaitne*) sitting and standing.

The hunters (*selcthi*), fishermen (*íascairi*), trappers (*cuthgairi*), and fence-makers (*etarpuigi*) sat in a cubicle apart [among the vessels in the company of the attendants and the cooks].

The royal house in archaeology

Does the image of the king's household depicted in *Lánellach tigi rích 7 ruirech* in any way match the archaeological evidence for royal and noble residences? Many difficulties arise in identifying a site as a royal residence. The great provincial capitals – Navan Fort, Tara, Knockaulin, Rathcroghan and Cashel – have yet to yield evidence of domestic habitation for this period, although Rathcroghan and Cashel probably incorporated some such settlements. The royal site at Clogher, Co. Tyrone, included a raised univallate ringfort built within an earlier hillfort that was reconfigured into a very strong defensive rampart. A metalled roadway ran over a causeway under a six-post tower and through a stone-revetted entrance. A wooden gate guarded the entrance. Richard Warner, who excavated the site, interprets this as a royal fort (*rígráith*) that was possibly occupied between the sixth and ninth centuries, and was at the heart of the important northern federation of kingdoms known as the Airgialla.[77] It was the residence of the dynasty Síl nDaimíni. Traces of a large circular building, about 40m in diameter, were discovered inside the bank of the ringfort. The cultural assemblage and industrial activity at Clogher resembled that found on other royal sites – imported B and E ware pottery, penannular brooches, an iron bull-head mount and a hoard of other iron objects and bronze-working debris. While archaeology confirms the historical record that Clogher was a royal site, such social distinctions are not evident in all settlements. Chris Lynn, in his study of houses in rural Ireland (that is, non-Viking settlements) between AD 500 and 1000, comments on this difficulty:[78]

Attempts to rank sites socially, to determine the different status of the occupants of contemporary dwellings at a single site and to distinguish confidently between houses, outbuildings and internal activity areas (crafts, stores, stacks, pens etc.) are frustrated by poor preservation and disturbance at some sites and at others by excavations of inadequate scale.

The large round house at the crannog at Moynagh Lough is a case in point. While this crannog is presumed to be a 'royal' residence, the extensive and high-class metalworking carried out on the site might also suggest that it was the house of a master-craftsman whose status in society and wealth was certainly close to, if not higher than, that of a *rí tuaithe*. The large round house (*cruinntech*) at Moynagh Lough was 11.2m in diameter externally and 10m internally. The foundation was of gravel on top of a platform of redeposited peat. The circular wall was defined by a double row of post-holes and the entrance was in the eastern side of the house. Over 250 post-holes were found inside the house, apparently demarcating the internal partitions and supports for benches and bedding areas – no doubt these features equate to terms such as *colba* 'platform, bench', *iarcúl* 'back of the house', *iardom* 'western part of the house', *imdae* 'bed, cubicle, bench' and *lepaid* 'bed, cubicle'. The habitation debris in the house consisted mainly of ash spreads raked out from the central hearth that was an open hearth into which a rectangular stone-lined setting was placed. A further hearth was added at a later stage. As might be expected, these hearths had a central position in the lives of the inhabitants. Not only did the ash debris build up, but there was a noticeable concentration of animal bone in the vicinity of the hearths.[79] Living conditions in Moynagh Lough, and indeed in many large residences, were not ideal. Walls were constructed in the main from wickerwork, planks and posts or drystone walls. They were roofed with thatch of reed or straw, and sometimes turves, and may have been deliberately kept relatively small to allow for easier heating. The existence of conjoined structures, often in a figure-of-eight plan, probably provided more space and privacy and facilitated various activities.[80] Hygiene was undoubtedly a problem and was probably not helped by damp conditions. There is probably a genuine message regarding sanitation in the otherwise fantastic otherworld tale *Echtra Nera* 'The adventure of Nera'.[81] The hero Nera had released a prisoner from the gallows. The man was desperate for a drink, for a great thirst had come upon him when he was hanged. He clung onto Nera's neck and asked him to go to the nearest house. There they found no drink and the hearth-fire raked. The next house had no drink, as there was no water left in that house from washing and bathing, and cleaning of the tub of slops. Finally, they found a house and there the prisoner not only drank from the washing and bathing-water, but also from the tub of slops 'and he drank from it and then spat the last mouthful from his mouth into the faces of the people who were in the house, so that they all died'. And the text then cautions:

> Hence it is not good for there to be water left over from washing and bathing, or a hearth-fire which has not been raked, or a tub with slops in it, in a house after bedtime.

It is hardly surprising, given such conditions, that early Irish sagas depicted royal households as living in splendour and surrounded by luxurious goods and materials. Kings may have dreamt of palaces with sparkling roofs, colourfully festooned walls and sumptuous furnishings. They may have heard of the existence of rich royal residences in Britain and on the Continent, but they never encountered them in reality. If they attempted to replicate exotic items, it was through their fine metalwork and in splendid brooches that they commissioned for themselves and their families. The splendour of royal palaces was mostly imaginary and formed part of a royal court's make-believe entertainment.

THE LIFE AND DEATH OF THE KING

The king's annual circuit

The early Irish king did not reside in one place throughout the year. There was a constant need to ensure that his clients dutifully handed over their tributes and that he granted them the required gifts in return (*taurchrecc 7 ráith*). Even the lowliest of kings and middle-ranking nobles had the right to be entertained by their clients, particularly during the period between New Year's Day and the beginning of Lent (Shrovetide). This winter period, when food could be scarce, was known as *aimser chue* and was a time when a heavy burden was placed on sections of the population who had to provide a feast for a king or a noble and his retinue.[82] The law tract *Cáin Lánamna* signals how seriously clients took their obligation to provide hospitality for their superiors. The contract between partners of equal status in a marriage provided for 'getting together food for a coshering (*coí*), getting food for feast-days'.[83] Generous hospitality was an essential component of this society and refusal of hospitality was taken as an insult to one's honour-price. Yet if advantage was taken of the host, and in most instances this situation seems to have involved the appearance of a lord accompanied by an excessive retinue (*tromdám*), the law provided for the client's protection: 'everybody is fed and hospitality is not refused up to the legal number

16 Traces of a raised road running between Skreen and Tara: early Irish sagas claim that the main roads of Ireland converged at Tara. While not necessarily true, ceremonial routeways in the immediate landscape did meet on the hill. This raised road between Skreen and Tara existed in the thirteenth century and is described then as a *via regale* 'a royal road'. It may mark the line of the earlier road from the north Leinster coast known as Slige Chualann 'the road of Cualu'. © Joe Fenwick, NUI Galway.

of his retinue. Refusal of hospitality in the case of a guest accompanied by an excessive retinue does not damage one's honour for, though one refuse, this is not deemed refusal of hospitality if the retinue is excessive'.[84] Considering that the highest grade of king mentioned in *Críth Gablach*, the *rí ruirech* (a provincial king), had a retinue of thirty, one annual visit was probably sufficient.[85] Once a king and his retinue took to the roads and made a circuit of his clients' houses, many tasks had to be completed by his clients. For example, roads were cleared 'that they may not soil chariots going on a *cue* [winter circuit]'.[86] A *lámraite*, 'a by-road between two highways', was constructed for errands and winter-visiting.[87] Archaeological evidence for communication networks in early Ireland has been recognized to a greater extent in recent decades. Gravel and wooden trackways (toghers) across bogs appear to have been commonplace.[88] It has been suggested that some linear monuments in ceremonial landscapes were ceremonial routeways. A raised earthen road running in a straight line on a north-east–

south-west axis has been recorded between the hills of Tara and Skreen. Where best preserved, it consists of a raised, flat-topped bank on either side of which is a shallow ditch (fig. 16). This may be one of the roads leading to Tara and may indeed be the Slige Chualann described in a thirteenth-century charter as the *regalem viam qua itur de villa de Skryn versus Taueragh* 'the royal routeway that goes from the manor of Skreen towards Tara'.[89] At the other end of the scale are the wooden trackways, constructed with different layers of brushwood, round-wood and planks in Castletown Bog, Castelarmstrong, Co. Offaly. Excavation yielded a poignant cameo of daily life in the seventh century with the discovery of a leather ankle shoe with front-lacing at the heel and the toe. The sole was worn through, probably due to the wear and tear on the pedestrians' feet as they wended their way through the bog.[90] Rivers were also vital elements of the communications' network, and no greater evidence of their use exists than the many incursions made by the Vikings into the country's interior by their navigation of major rivers such as the Barrow, the Boyne and the Shannon.

Hospitality for a king or superior entailed a considerable amount of preparation by the host, who was required to abide by certain customs of hospitality.[91] One of the maxims in the tenth-century text known as the 'Triads of Ireland' declares: 'Three prohibitions of food: to eat it without giving thanks, to eat it before its proper time, to eat it after a guest'.[92] Other texts and descriptions of entertaining royal guests are clear that etiquette was important and that these feasts were not unruly drunken occasions – not that sometimes this may have not been the end result. Washing facilities awaited guests on their arrival, and bathing was an integral part of the occasion. The host provided a washing-trough (*ambur indlait*), a bathtub (*long fhoilcthe*) and a comfortable bed (*imid*), as well as food and the heat of a fire for his guests. The *Vita Prima* of Brigit relates how a large episcopal retinue in chariots and laden with gifts was guided miraculously by Brigit through a storm:[93]

> And she took them straight into a big house after unhitching the horses and chariots, washed their feet and regaled them with plenty of food. As well as that she made up the beds and put the guests to rest, and, as they thought, Brigit and her nuns performed all the services required for guests.

Unbeknown to her guests, Brigit had conjured up a phantom guesthouse for them in the middle of the wood and once they awoke, finding themselves sitting in the wood, the saint had to explain what had happened. In this instance, Brigit was the client to her superior, Bishop Brón, and she provided for him according to custom. Detailed provision is also made in the laws for compensation in cases of food poisoning and the distribution of bad ale, which was probably a frequent occurrence. The intention of the host was crucial to the penalty for bad hospitality. Ignorance on his part met with a lighter penalty than deliberate provision of bad food and ale. The host either had to make restitution by giving an equal quantity of wholesome food to the injured party, or in the case of food poisoning, the price of the cure was paid for by the host. If the food was deliberately given to the party to cause injury or worse, a fine was imposed which depended on the honour-price of the injured party.[94]

Bad hospitality could gain a bad reputation and loss of status and, worse, the sanction of satire. Although the episode in the Middle Irish tale *Cath Maige Tuired* 'The Battle of Moytura' is not true, the dread of sanction is understood from the uttering of the first satire in Ireland by the *fili* Cairpre against the mythical and destructive Fomorian king, Bres mac Elathan, for his inhospitable treatment of the Túatha Dé Danann.[95] Any early Irish king listening to Cairpre's revenge on Bres would understand clearly the consequences of niggardliness and negligence in following proper etiquette:

> The next day he [Cairpre, the *fili*] arose, and was not thankful. As he went across the yard, he said, 'Without food quickly on a dish, without cow's milk on which a calf grows. Without a man's habitation after darkness remains, without paying a company of storytellers – let that be Bres' condition. Bres' prosperity no longer exists', he said, and that was true. There was only blight on him from that hour; and that is the first satire that was made in Ireland.

Of course, worse could happen to a king. A banquet could cost a king his life, as happened in 795 in the case of Conn Cétadach, the unfortunate son of the king of Tara, Donnchad Midi (d. 797). Conn was killed by his rival Flann mac Congalaig in the house of Cumalcach in Crích Ua nOlcáin in Brega. The more fulsome entry in the Annals of the Four Masters explains that bad ale led to Conn's death:

> A feast was made by Ua Olcáin, which was partaken of with odious ale; dregs were given to him by Flann, so that he bore away his head after his death.

> *Coirm do ronadh la hUa Olcáin issedh doth chath de linn gráin,*
> *Tuctha descaid dó ó Flann co ruc a cend o bebail.*

There was a difference in scale and intent between the circuit of a lesser king and that of a regional or provincial over-king. The minor king traversed his kingdom implementing a system of granting fiefs of cattle or land (*sóer-rath*, *taurchrecc*) and exacting personal service (*manchuine*) and food-rents (*bés tige*) from his free and unfree clients (*sóer-chéle*, *gíallnae*). In the main, this was probably a relatively peaceful cycle of seasonal activities interrupted by natural disasters, internal dynastic dissension and, more seriously, the exactions of his over-king. This greater imposition could manifest itself in an obligation to provide material goods – food, clothing or hospitality – and, more likely, manpower for heavy labour and warfare.[96] Anecdotes in early saints' Lives suggest that heavy labour was regarded as a form of unwelcome forced drudgery that needed to be regulated by the church. There is no starker account of the system of forced labour mustered by a king and the toil and potential strife ensuing from a royal command than the episode in Cogitosus' Life of Brigit regarding the construction of a major road. It is also instructive about the techniques of road-building in early Ireland. It is likely that the king involved was the provincial king of Leinster or a least an over-king within Leinster who had the capacity to muster a workforce for an important public scheme:[97]

> Once an edict of the king of the country where she [Brigit] was living came into force throughout the *tuatha* and provinces which were under his jurisdiction and dominion, to the effect that all the peoples and *tuatha* should come together from all the territories and provinces and build a solid wide road. They were to lay a foundation of tree branches and rocks and some very solid earth works in the deep and virtually impassable bog and in the sodden and marshy places through which a large river ran so that, when it was built, it could bear the weight of charioteers and horsemen and chariots and wagon-wheels and the rushing of people and the clash of enemies from all sides. When many people had gathered, they divided into their own sections by kinship groups and households the road which they had to build so that each clan and household built its own allotted section.
>
> But when the exacting and really difficult part of the river happened to fall to the lot of one of these *tuatha*, this *tuath* wanting to avoid the very hard work, used its strength to browbeat Brigit's weaker *tuath* [the Fothairt] so that it would have to work on this difficult section of the road-building. This cruel and unfair *tuath*, having chosen an easier section than it had got in the draw, would then build it without any trouble from the river.

Needless to say, once Brigit had learned from her kinsmen that they were being maltreated, she miraculously caused the river to leave its course and move to the section of the road being built by members of the arrogant *túath*. An empty dried up gorge was left in the landscape as proof of Brigit's miracle.

Military campaigns, whether incursions on a small scale into a neighbouring territory or a large-scale movement that caused lengthy periods away from the core of his kingdom, were unavoidable for an early Irish king.[98] Violence was endemic, albeit probably on a petty scale, and this is borne out in the historical sources and archaeological evidence. *Críth Gablach* provides a fair insight into the type of disturbance that the inhabitants of the early Irish countryside endured as kings proceeded through their localities with violent intent or exacting tribute. A king could impose a levy (*errech*), normally stock, on the inhabitants of a rebellious *túath* in recompense for a disputed tribute and to cover the outlay of the expedition to extract that tribute. The many instances of Uí Néill over-kings bringing an army south to Leinster to exact the *bórama* (cattle-tribute) from the kings of Leinster attests to the reality of such disputes. In 721, the king of Tara and Northern Uí Néill king, Fergal mac Maíle Dúin, went to Leinster and imposed the *bórama* on the Laigin and took their hostages as a guarantee. In a later instance, in 999, Áed mac Domnaill, son of the king of Tara, raided the north-eastern kingdom of Uí Echach and took away a great tribute in cows. A marginal note in the Annals of Ulster calls it *creach mór Maighi Cabha* ('the great raid of Mag Coba'). A lesser king would often be obliged to make a circuit of the main residences (*dúne*) of his kingdom with an over-king and, during that circuit, could impose an *errech* on the inhabitants of the locality to support the royal party. No doubt this type of burden often caused resentment and a king was obliged to return the *errech*. He could requisition a similar levy when he was returning from an expedition against another *túath* and was resting with his army in border territory – often the location for battles and regarded as waste or liminal land.[99]

Considering the distances covered by over-kings and their armies on military expeditions, it is likely that they were absent from the heartland of their kingdoms and their homes for long periods. The perils and anxiety of such absences for those at home is delightfully illustrated in the tale *Compert Mongáin* 'The birth of Mongán'.[1] The king of Ulaid, Fiachna Lurgan (d. 626), went to Scotland to assist his ally the king of Dál Ríata, Áedán mac Gabráin (d. 606), to fight the Saxons. Fiachna left his queen at home, and while her husband and his ally were fighting in north Britain, a visitor came to their chief residence at Ráith Mór in Mag Lena (Rathmore, Co. Antrim). The tale continues:

> He asked the woman to arrange a meeting place. The woman said that there were not in the world possessions or treasures for which she would disgrace her spouse's honour. He asked her whether she would do it to

save her husband's life. She said that if she were to see him in danger or difficulty, she would help him with whatever might be in her power. He told her to do it 'because your spouse is in great peril. A frightful hero has been brought against him over whom no one may prevail. And [your husband] will die by him. If I make love with you, you will bear a son from it. The son will be renowned and marvelous. Moreover, he will be Fiachna's. I shall go into the battle which will be fought tomorrow at the third hour after sunrise in order to save him. And I shall overthrow the [enemy] soldier in front of the men of north Britain. And I [shall] tell your spouse what has gone on and that it is yourself who have sent me to aid him'.

Fiachna's wife surrendered to the visitor and he, in turn, saved Fiachna. The queen gave birth to Mongán (d. 625), having admitted what she had done. The visitor was the sea god Manannán mac Lir and Fiachna's queen was Caintigern, who is reputed to have been British.[2] One suspects that queens were often lured into unfaithfulness during their husbands' lengthy absences and that the visitors to their chambers were not always sea gods.

The death and burial of a king

There is a cycle of tales in early Irish known as the *aideda*, which narrate the dramatic deaths of heroic mythological and early historic kings: Cormac mac Airt, Conaire Mór, Diarmait mac Cerbaill, Lóegaire mac Néill and Muirchertach mac Erca.[3] In most instances, their deaths are violent and are brought upon them by their own deeds or words. Whereas their reigns began with many favourable portents and they were recognized as just and rightful kings, their lives ended dogged by portents of doom and, as noted by Muireann Ní Bhrolcháin, 'many of these are the malevolent opposite of those very elements that accompany the ruler's accession to kingship: women, water or alcoholic drink and the hitherto peaceful landscape which now reacts negatively'.[4] Diarmait mac Cerbaill, a king who is reputed to have reigned as king of Tara in the middle of the sixth century and to have been the last to hold *Feis Temro*, the inauguration banquet of a king of Tara, was subjected to a threefold death by wounding, fire and drowning.[5] Most interestingly, one version of his death (ATig. 563.4) claims that the king's body was buried at Clonmacnoise and his head in Coinnire (Connor, Co. Down), awaiting his resurrection in the latter site. Unlike Diarmait, the other heroic kings were not buried in churches but in mounds that were monuments in exceptional landscapes such as the Boyne Valley. One version of his death claims that Cormac mac Airt was buried overlooking the Boyne at Ros na Ríg.[6] Rosnaree, Co. Meath, on a bend in the Boyne opposite the Neolithic tomb of Knowth, is the site of a small mound that, when excavated, revealed a decapitated flexed female burial with a foetus. The burial dated to sometime between the third and fifth centuries and the woman was buried with a silver ring. Nearby were two other female burials.[7] While this is not the grave of Cormac mac Airt, it is certainly a very intriguing late Iron Age/late antique burial. In the literature, early historic kings were perceived sometimes as being buried facing their enemies. Lóegaire mac Néill was reputedly buried at Tara facing the Laigin,[8] and Óengus mac Nadfraích buried standing up in the royal tomb at Cashel.[9] The Irish, unlike the Anglo-Saxons, did not have sentinel burials, and therefore, these allusions were either transferred into literature with knowledge of Anglo-Saxon practices or were a metaphor for kings facing their enemies in death.[10]

The overall impression from the annalistic record is that historic kings often came to violent ends either in battles with neighbouring kings or predatory over-kings, or in bloody internecine episodes. This may have been the case, but we must be mindful that the annals record noteworthy events and the death of a king in battle is more remarkable than the peaceful demise of a king in his bed. Nonetheless, such peaceful deaths are occasionally recorded: in 880 (*AU*), Máel Ciaráin mac Conaing, king of Tethba, died of old age having retired into religion (*in clericatu uitam senilem finiuit*). Retreat into religion was a common feature for kings, especially when they had been ousted by rivals or even when under pressure in their kingship.[11] As in life, there were unexpected deaths from natural causes, as seems to have happened in 814 (*AU*) to Niall mac Áedo, king of Uí Chormaic (in Leinster) (*repentina morte moritur*). There are instances of deaths from long illnesses, as in the notable case of a certain Niall mac Illáin, 'who suffered from paralysis for thirty-three years and was disturbed by frequent visions both false and true'.[12] The prevalence of disease meant that kings as much as their people were affected by periods of famine and pestilence: in 685, Congal mac Guaire of the Airgialla and Bressal mac Ferguso, king of Coba, died of disease. As they belonged to neighbouring kingdoms in the mid-north and north-east, this is likely to indicate the prevalence of a disease in that region in the 680s. In the two previous years (683–4), the annals record the 'mortality of children', possibly an outbreak of measles, that may have also killed adults such as Congal and Bressal. Similarly, Innrecht mac Cathail, king of Connacht, died of dysentery, known as 'the bloody flux', in 768, at a time when famine and disease were particularly rampant in Ireland.

Drowning and wounding are among the various fates met by historic kings. In 622, Conaing mac Áedáin meic Gabráin, king of Dál Ríata, was drowned, and the poet Nindine sang:[13]

The sea's great pure waves
And the sun that pursued him,
Into his weak wicker coracle they flung themselves
Together on Conaing.

The woman that cast her white hair
Into his coracle against Conaing,
It is her smile
That smiled today on Tortu's tree.

Violent rather than accidental drowning befell other kings, as happened in 851 when Cináed mac Conaing, king of the eastern coastal kingdom of Ciannachta was 'cruelly drowned in a pool by Máel Sechnaill [king of Tara] and Tigernach [king of south Brega], in spite of the guarantees of the nobles of Ireland, and the successor of Patrick in particular' (*AU*). The Annals of the Four Masters add that he was drowned by Máel Sechnaill's people in the river Ainge (Nanny) 'to revenge upon him the evils he had committed against the laity and the church'. In 849, Cináed had rebelled against the king of Tara with his allies, the Vikings, and had plundered churches and *túatha*. He had also levelled Tigernach's royal residence at Lagore and burned the nearby wooden church (*darthech*) at Treóit (Trevet, Co. Meath), causing many deaths. It is clear from verses added to both annalistic entries that Cináed's death was a formal execution, as he was taken 'bound to a pit' and 'was in a sack approaching a pool'.[14] Beheading was another form of violent death and execution: in 980, Dubgall mac Donnchada, a *rígdomna* of Ailech belonging to the northern dynasty of Cenél Conaill, was killed by his cousin Muiredach mac Flainn, and a month later Muiredach was beheaded by his own people (*AU*).

The burial places of historic kings are not often recorded in the annals and we have to seek hints elsewhere in archaeological evidence, ecclesiastical texts and early literature for the locations of royal graves. Since Irish late Iron Age and early medieval burials are rarely accompanied by significant grave goods, it is difficult to distinguish social status in burials. There are a number of indications, however, that point to possible royal graves: burial in ancestral grave mounds (*fertae*); the rare occurrence of certain grave goods such as neck rings or toe rings; decapitated skeletons; and the existence of a central grave around which a cemetery develops. Many *fertae* dating approximately from the Iron Age (occasionally reusing Bronze Age mounds) to the eighth century are located overlooking rivers and ravines at places in the landscape that were boundaries between territories.[15] A typical example of a *ferta* was discovered at Pollacorragune, Co. Galway. This monument consisted of four graves, three male and one female, inserted intermittently into a mound between the fourth and seventh centuries. The mound was located on a natural elevation on an esker ridge close to a Bronze Age mound. That two of the skeletons were of some importance is suggested by the grave goods that accompanied them: a male buried sometime between the fifth and seventh century had an iron disc close to his skull and a fragment of iron on his chest, while a female, buried between the fourth and sixth century, had two small fragments of iron beside her right elbow.[16] An intriguing burial, given the connections between women, horses and sovereignty,[17] is that of a woman whose extended inhumation burial was inserted into a mound that contained a Bronze Age cinerary urn in Farta, Co. Galway. This woman was buried with the complete skeleton of a horse possibly sometime in the fifth or sixth century. The mound was approximately 500m to the west/north-west of the Rath of Feerwore, the original site of the famous highly decorated Turoe Stone (fig. 17).[18] One might imagine that this woman was a queen, or at least somehow regarded as the personification of sovereignty, who was buried in an ancestral grave that marked a focal point in the landscape. A crouched male buried in the cemetery of Owenbristy, Co. Galway, was wearing a tubular neck-collar,[19] possibly a ceremonial item of dress such as the *nasc niad* 'a champion's collar' mentioned in early literature.[20]

Memorial stones, which are common in Roman Britain and on the Continent, were not adopted in their traditional form in Ireland. It has been suggested, however, that ogam stones, which record so many personal names and patronymics, may occasionally have marked a burial.[21] Other ogam stones probably functioned as memorial stones without an associated burial, as in the case of the Painestown ogam stone in Co. Meath that appears to commemorate a fifth-century Leinster king of Tara, Mac Caírthinn, of the Uí Enechglais.[22] Uninscribed standing stones or even wooden posts may also have marked important graves or familial cemeteries, as was discovered at Kiltullagh Hill 2, Co. Roscommon, where a standing stone marked the grave of an adult male buried there in the fifth or sixth century.[23]

The attraction for kings to be buried in ecclesiastical cemeteries increased with the growing power of the church from the late sixth century onwards. This shift did not lead to the immediate abandonment of ancestral graves or familial cemeteries, which were either cared for with the church's blessing,[24] or continued to be used until the eleventh or twelfth century. As kings became more ardent adherents of Christianity and patrons of the church, they were given privileged positions in death by being buried in the inner sanctum of ecclesiastical cemeteries. The prophetic text *Baile in Scáil* 'The Phantom's Frenzy', probably originally compiled in the ninth century and revised in the eleventh, lists the Uí Néill kings of Tara from the mythical Conn Cétchathach to Máel Sechnaill mac

17 Turoe Stone, Co. Galway: this highly decorated stone has been regarded as one of the rare examples of Iron Age art in Ireland. It originally stood close to the mound at Farta, Co. Galway, which is known to have contained a Bronze Age burial and an additional grave of a woman buried with a horse in the fifth/sixth century AD. The woman's burial and the stone may be connected suggesting that this was a site of some form of inauguration rite. © Discovery Programme, Dublin.

18 Base of North Cross at Ahenny, Co. Tipperary: a scene of the ceremonial procession of a decapitated body thrown over a horse with ravens pecking at it. The procession is led by a figure holding a processional cross. The panel has been interpreted variously as a biblical scene or an episode from a saint's life or the death of a royal figure. The most probable explanation is that it depicts the return of a fallen king from battle for burial in a church cemetery. © Rachel Moss, Trinity College Dublin.

Domnaill (d. 1022). On some occasions, it mentions the burial places of kings.[25] Congal Cinn Magair mac Fergusso (d. 710) and his successor Fogartach mac Néill are the first kings to have been buried in Clonard. A later king of Tara, Donnchad Midi (d. 797), died of a tumour in the same monastery and was buried there, as was his son Conchobar (d. 833). The northern king, Áed Allán mac Fergaile, was killed at a battle on the shore of Loch Sailchitain (Loughsallagh near Dunboyne, Co. Meath) in 743 and was buried in Clonmacnoise. The powerful king of Tara, Máel Sechnaill mac Maíle Ruanaid (d. 862), and his son Flann Sinna, were both buried at Clonmacnoise. Indeed, it might be conjectured that their graves were among the male burials discovered close to the Cross of the Scriptures or the South Cross at Clonmacnoise.[26] Whoever these men were, they were worthy of burial in the *sanctissimus* of that monastery. Flaithbertach mac Loingsig (d. 765), who was deposed from his kingship in 734, retired to the monastery of Armagh and, according to *Baile in Scáil*, 'the cleric will die at the burial place of the kings' (*at-bath clericus i n-ailaid na ríg*).[27] If this allusion has any historical foundation, it suggests that there was a special area set aside in the monastic cemetery for royal graves. In addition to Flaithbertach, Áed Oirdnide (Ingor) mac Néill (d. 819) and his son Niall Caille mac Áedo (d. 846) were buried in Armagh. Áed Findliath (d. 879), Niall Caille's son, died at a place called Ráith Adomnæ and was brought for burial to Armagh. Niall Glúndub (d. 919) was buried at Kells after his death in battle on the outskirts of Dublin. Other monastic locations for royal burials included Durrow (Fergal mac Maíle Dúin, d. 722), the lesser known Imlech Fía (Emlagh, Lower Kells, Co. Meath) between Kells and Tailtiu (Domnall Midi, d. 763), Iona (Niall Frossach mac Fergaile, d. 778) and Monasterboice (Congalach Cnogba, d. 956). Little visual or material evidence of such royal burials have either survived or have been recovered, with the possible exceptions of the Clonmacnoise burials and a few inscribed slabs that may mark the grave of a king such as that at Seir Kieran, Co. Offaly, commemorating a certain Cerball, possibly Cerball mac Dúngaile, king of Osraige (d. 888).[28] The elaborate ceremony of a slain king's burial procession is depicted on a panel of the base of the North Cross at Ahenny, Co. Kilkenny (fig. 18): two religious leading a procession, one carrying a ringed-cross, the other a crosier, a decapitated body being carried on a horse with ravens picking at it and another religious bringing up the rear. As evident from the archaeological record, no matter how mutilated a body might have been in battle or in other conflicts, the king was brought back for proper burial in a familial cemetery or a preferred church cemetery among his ancestors.

CHAPTER 3

Religion, ritual and ritualists

SEEKING THE OLD BELIEF SYSTEM

The narrative of religion in early Ireland is dominated by Christianity. This approach to belief systems and rituals should cause no surprise, since Christianity was the dominant element of a cultural and religious transformation that began in fifth-century Ireland. Literacy, a new language (Latin) and new ideologies relating to morality and authority came with the new religion and, as occurs with any change of religion, Christianity went to the heart of the society's beliefs in the sacred and the cosmos. The coming of Christianity to Ireland and its apparent rapid progress and dominance over society have been central to the narrative of this period, drawing mainly on exegetical, historical, linguistic and literary evidence. Material and palaeographical evidence such as the production of fine metalwork (altar plate), deluxe manuscripts (Gospel books) and intricate stone monuments (high crosses) are represented as the icons of early Irish Christianity. Monasticism, often ascetic monasticism, is depicted as the norm of religion, while well-known saints – Patrick, Brigit and Columba – have been promoted as Ireland's senior holy people since the seventh century. The 'old religion', if it was even considered, often emerged as a set of vague beliefs drawn from Irish prehistory, the evidence of Celtic and Roman Britain and the Continent, and from medieval Irish literature. Gods and druids dominate this narrative.[1] Too often, the complexities of the religious human experience and the complexity of a society's conversion from one religion to another have been lost in the frequently naïve and confrontational discourse on pagan and Christian in Ireland.[2]

Religion comes under the scrutiny of many disciplines, some of which have been rarely introduced to early medieval Irish religious studies. These include anthropology, comparative religious studies and cognitive science.[3] The extension of the narrative of religious beliefs in early Ireland into these fields has the potential to offer new and rational insights into the practice of religion, custom and ritual in this society, which, in turn, elucidates aspects of its distinction between 'the sacred and the profane', if that distinction existed at all.[4] It is argued that the need for religion and ritual in society is a response to the constant social events and processes that humans encounter during their lives that need to be explained either scientifically or existentially. These might include events such as a couple making a relationship a public event through a wedding, a community's offering to a god or ancestor seeking a good harvest, and an initiation ceremony. Hidden forces or agents outside the human domain are often seen as being involved in such events, and although not always the case, rituals normally lead to social effects. For example, a marriage is a public declaration of the existence of a couple and, therefore, they are expected to behave in a certain fashion by society. Emotional involvement in ritual can range from the charged and dramatic to the sober and repetitive.[5] It is often the case that rituals conducted by special agents, more often than not organized into priesthoods, are more public occasions, thus leaving an imprint or a stronger memory in their wake. Memorable and dramatic ritual forms, to which the emotions respond, are more likely to be transmitted to a new generation or new population, and to be culturally successful. Anthropologists and cognitive scientists often identify a distinction between abstract theology (often the 'official' form of religion) existing side-by-side with intuitive forms of religion (the 'popular' form of religion).[6] Hence, for example, the existence of a hierarchy of gods from the great god of creation to those essential to daily domestic life responds to the varying plea bargaining of humans.

This theoretical approach may seem very distant from the coming of Christianity to Ireland, but if we are to recover our understanding of the old belief system that coexisted with Christianity for a number of centuries, and finally conceded to the new belief system, these models prove invaluable in comprehending the process of conversion and the survival of traces of the older religion into the Middle Ages. This subject is fraught with difficulties, and scholars in recent decades have stressed the many pitfalls when attempting to define or disentangle earlier belief systems from an omnipresent medieval Christian culture.[7] These difficulties include the tendency to frame 'paganism' with reference to biblical or classical allusions (*interpetatio Romana*) that aimed at standardizing formulations of pagan practices, often creating a conflation between what modern scholars might call pagan and folk superstition.[8] This wary approach has been adopted in relation to defining 'paganism' in Ireland, most forcefully expressed by Kim McCone in his monograph *Pagan past and Christian present*. While it is clear that Christian literate culture inspired many early Latin and vernacular Irish texts, the range of texts in Ireland, especially in the vernacular, is so varied and also close in date to the continued existence of strong elements of the old religion that, combined with archaeological and other evidence, and with the use of models from other disciplines, it is possible to identify genuine non-Christian religious practices and practitioners.

The rites and rituals of two religions

> The three waves which go over a person in baptism, he renounces three
> renunciations in them: he renounces the world with its vanities, he
> renounces the devil with his snares, he renounces the passions of the flesh.
> It is this that changes a person being a son of Death to being a son of Life,
> from being a son of Darkness to being a son of Light. When he breaks
> those three renunciations in the three waves which go over him, unless he
> should go again through the three waters he cannot go into the kingdom
> of God: a pool of tears of repentance, a pool wrung out of blood in
> penance, a pool of sweat in labour.

This very evocative extract comes from the early Irish Christian text *Apgitir
Chrábaid* 'The Alphabet of Devotion', a short manual on religious life, and
especially monastic life, attributed to Colmán Elo of Lynally (Lann Elo), Co.
Offaly (d. 611).[9] Christianity at the time of composition was competing with the
old religion. One of the four darknesses expelled by faith was 'the darkness of
paganism' (*dorcha ngendtlechta*).[10] The extract is imbued with ritual: the water
of baptism, the renunciations, transformation from being a son of Death (*mac
báis*) to a son of Life (*mac bethad*), from darkness to light. But what did such
prescriptions mean in reality? What was the darkness of paganism and what
were the three waves of baptism replacing in the old religion? A tangible way of
establishing the practice of the old religion – and its replacement by the new –
is to examine categories of rites known universally to be associated with rituals.
These rites have been classified in various studies as:[11]

- rites of passage: birth, male and female initiation, marriage, death;
- calendrical rites: rites associated with the solar and lunar calendar (seasonal
  celebrations of sowing and reaping);
- commemorative rites (the commemoration of 'historical' events as in the life
  of Christ, the life of a saint);
- rites of exchange and communion: making offerings, giving gifts to the divine
  in the hope of intervention (various levels of devotion), ritual sacrifice (*sacer
  facere* 'to make holy') to placate deities, communion (a sacrifice that unites
  the human and divine);
- rites of affliction: the need to rectify a disturbed or disorderly cosmos by acts
  of cleansing, healing and purification (penance, pilgrimage and prayer);
- rites of feasting, fasting and festivals;
- political rites.

If forms of these rites are identified as universal 'religious' phenomena, and given the wealth of sources available, it would seem possible to advance the study of the pre-Christian belief system in Ireland by detecting evidence in the archaeological and historical records. This is best approached by examining rites performed to mark important transitions in the human life cycle.

Rites of passage: birth and initiation

The Christian ritual most prominent in St Patrick's *Confessio* and *Epistola* are the rites of baptism and confirmation, which were rites of passage and initiation. In the *Confessio* (§40), Patrick defended his mission from criticism on the basis of the great numbers of Irish being baptized:[12]

> Therefore it is very right that we should cast our nets, so that a great multitude and crowd will be taken for God. Also that there should be clerics to baptize and encourage a people in need and want ...

When condemning the British king Coroticus, who had enslaved members of Patrick's newly baptized community, he describes their appearance (*Epistola* §3):

> The newly baptized and anointed were dressed in white robes; the anointing was still to be seen clearly on their foreheads when they were cruelly slain and sacrificed by the sword of the ones I referred to above.

Baptism and confirmation are rites of passage: the birth (or rebirth) and initiation of a person into the Christian church. By performing this new rite of passage, was Patrick replacing existing rites, or did two ritual systems continue to exist in parallel? Where did Patrick perform his apparent mass baptisms and what imprint did these events have on the landscape? By receiving a Christian baptism, Patrick's 'neophytes' were given a new identity that, in the fifth century, would have probably set them apart from their own society, as had happened with many Christian communities during periods of conversion. Indeed, Patrick admits that this was the case (*Confessio* §42):

> There was a blessed Irish woman of noble birth, a most beautiful adult, whom I baptized. She came to us a few days later for this reason. She told us that she had received a word from a messenger of God, who advised her that she should become a virgin of Christ, and that she should come close to God ... [she became a virgin of Christ as others had] ... Their

fathers don't like this, of course. These women suffer persecution and false accusations from their parents, and yet their number grows! We do not know the number of our people who were born there. In addition, there are the widows and the celibates. Of all these, those held in slavery work hardest – they bear even terror and threats, but the Lord gives grace to so many of the women who serve him. Even when it is forbidden, they bravely follow his example.

Patrick had introduced a public ritual that had social consequences. In its essence, whatever about in practice, Christianity embraced an open attitude to participation by all classes and both genders.[13] Patrick appears to have implemented such openness, at least in his dealings with women and slaves. His own experience as a slave probably informed him on their plight. He deprived a noble father of a potential bride-price or a good economic or political alliance by attracting his daughter into a religious and celibate way of life. Baptism could have effectively broken the bonds of a female slave, a woman without status but necessary in a household, on a farm or in begetting children for her master. Little wonder that this theme recurs so forcefully in the early Lives of Brigit, where her mother's status as a slave to the king and his reluctance to part with her as she (although a Christian) was carrying his child form the core of Brigit's early life. In terms of anthropology and cognitive science, as expounded by Mircea Eliade and by Pascal Boyer and others,[14] the form of Patrick's rituals would have involved memorable pageantry (water, chrism, white clothes) that must have appealed to the senses, and would have been more exciting than existing habitual rituals. His success (and that of other missionaries), therefore, was rooted in conducting new ritual forms sufficiently memorable and frequent to lead to their transmission into the existing culture.

Patrick baptized adults, and by giving them a new identity, created a community within a community. The rite of baptism consisted of various elements: exorcism, renuciation, instruction, fasting, the invocation of Jesus' name, anointing with chrism, submersion or immersion in water, and taking of communion. The 'neophytes' emerged from the rite (as Patrick mentions in the *Epistola*) wearing white clothes. Whitfield, in her study of holy wells in early Ireland, makes a very cogent argument that wells were used instead of baptisteries in Ireland, and hence the proliferation of holy wells throughout the country.[15] The physical possibility of using wells for baptism was made feasible by the fact that submersion or immersion was rare in late antiquity, although not out of the question, and that affusion (water poured over the head) was more widespread. If Patrick and other missionaries, and their successors, appropriated sacred wells for their Christian rite of passage, did this not signify an encroachment into a 'sacred' space already associated with rituals? Early Irish texts and Latin hagiography suggest that the holy well may have remained associated with non-Christian rituals and was even protected by the old ritualists. While saints' dedications of holy wells are common and well-known, the use of abstract names of wells has not been generally observed: *slán* ('healthy, noble'), *sine* ('udder, pap'), *óenadarcae* ('one-horned'), *clébech* (< *cliabach* 'slender, deer, boar, wild animal'?) and *nemnach* ('heavenly, holy, venomous'). These somewhat elusive names hint at a different belief system that was replaced by that of the cult of the holy Christian. Sacred springs are no surprise, nor are wells associated with particular animals: all are easily recognizable from Britain and the Continent, where they are often linked to healing and fertility.

   The literary traditions associated with the well of Segais, the source of the river Boyne (Bóind), allude in an oblique way to its religious significance. It is overlooked by Carbury Hill, Co. Kildare, the location of a cemetery that included Iron Age cremations and later inhumations, dating to between the fifth and seventh century. One male inhumation from the circular enclosure Site B at Carbury Hill was accompanied by an iron shears. A radiocarbon date of AD471– 643 was obtained for this burial.[16] The burial enclosure might be an ancestral grave, a *ferta*.[17] Carbury Hill is Síd Nechtain, the home of Nechtan, the deity consort of Bóind, the river-goddess of the Boyne (which rises at the well of Segais at Carbury). The well of Segais is associated with magical hazelnuts that induced *imbas*, poetic or prophetic inspiration. With this attribute in mind, it is interesting that the eighth-century 'Cauldron of Poesy' decribes the human experience of joy in the following terms:[18]

> As for human joy, it has four divisions (i) the force of sexual longing and (ii) the joy of safety and freedom from care, plenty of food and clothing until one begins *bairdne* and (iii) joy at the prerogatives of poetry after studying it well and (iv) the joy at the arrival of *imbas*, which the nine hazels of fine mast at Segais in the *síds* amass and which is sent upstream along the surface of the Boyne, as extensive as a wether's fleece, swifter than a racehorse, in the middle of June every seventh year regularly.

Whoever ate the nuts or drank the well's water or the salmon that consumed the nuts gained the power of *imbas* 'inspiration, divination, supernatural knowledge' as Finn mac Cumaill did or as Cormac mac Cuilennáin, the king-bishop of Cashel (d. 908) and author of *Sanas Cormaic* ('Cormac's Glossary'), reputedly did.[19] Hence, divination, prophecy and inspiration, all very powerful skills, could be acquired from sacred water and foods (hazelnuts, salmon) fished from it. Archaeology provides evidence of the type of watery places that Patrick or any other missionary had to gain access to if they were to compete with existing rituals. Excavation of a late Bronze Age site at Inchagreenoge, Co. Limerick, seems to have uncovered one such place:[20]

> [the site was] … on the western end of a low-lying bog, at the base of a steep hill. To the east, the area was bounded by a stream, and several springs were encountered during excavation. The site was characterised by two fulachta fiadh with wood-lined troughs, a spring with a deposit of a human skull, several layers of peat containing numerous wooden artefacts, and a post-medieval stone trackway … In the edge of the spring, in a thin deposit of peat above the burnt stone spread, was a human skull, apparently deliberately deposited. The skull was overlain by a layer of unburnt stones, which capped the spring and gave the impression of a platform … a further layer of peat covered the entire site … rich in wood, with plentiful preserved branches, twigs and seeds, particularly hazelnuts. As with the upper peat, large numbers of worked wood pieces and animal bones were recovered.

And it is precisely such a scene that the seventh-century bishop Tírechán depicts when Patrick comes to the well of Slán in Findmag to baptize many and to establish three churches. There he found a square well covered with a square stone 'and the infidels (increduli) said that some wise man (profeta, propheta 'augur, poet: one imbued by imbas') had made for himself a shrine in the water under a stone to bleach his bones perpetually because he feared burning by fire: and they worshipped the well as a god'.[21] Following a common hagiographical topos, Patrick countered the beliefs of the local people that there were bones under the capstone and claimed that gold and silver from the wicked sacrifices of the druids had leaked into the well. This is a clear reference to votive offerings being made at the well, and also to the possibility that human bones were concealed in the well. The well of Slán and the well of Sine were in the territory of the Corcu Temne, otherwise known as the Temenrige. The church of Cell Tóich was in regione Temenrige i Ceru contra solis 'in the territory of the Temenrige in Cerae in the west' (Carra, Co. Mayo).[22] Mac Giolla Easpaig has made the very important observation that the name-stem temen may be cognate with Greek temenos (root *tem- with -en- suffix), and that the Corcu Temne/Temenrige may have been 'the people of the sanctuary', namely, the ritualists who conducted rites in their religious sanctuaries.[23] If druids were to be found in early Irish society, they are likely to have been these people.

As Ireland moved from a society undergoing Christianization to a Christian society, and as infant baptism became the norm in western Christendom,[24] what older rites did this new ritual replace? Naming ceremonies and protective rites are universal rituals performed at the birth of a child. The Life of Brigit offers a hint, which can be compared with other texts, of the operation of the first rites of passage in a dual-belief society. Brigit was born on the threshold of a house, as had been foretold by a druid:[25]

> This is how the prophet said the bondmaid would give birth, neither in the house nor outside the house, and the infant's body was washed with the warm milk she was carrying.

A short time later, Brigit's baptism happened:[26]

> The same druid also as he was asleep one day saw two clerics clothed in white garments pouring oil on the girl's head. They were performing the rite of baptism in the customary way. One of them said: 'Call this virgin Brigit'.

In these extracts, we find the anointing of the child as a Christian through the holy oil of baptism, but also possibly as a member of her own non-Christian community by being washed as a baby in milk, as perhaps required by her mother's circumstances. An incident recounted in the early Munster genealogies offers some corroboration that washing a baby in water or other liquids may indeed have been a form of purification at birth. Óebfhind, the personification of the sovereignty goddess and the consort of Conall Corc, the most important prehistoric king of Cashel, had a dream that she gave birth to four pups. These pups were the progenitors of future Éoganachta (Munster) dynasties. The first and favourite, Nadfróech, was bathed in wine, the second, Mac Cas, in beer, the third, Mac Brócc, in milk and the fourth, Mac Iair, in water. A fifth pup, Coirpre Cruithnechán, which appeared from under her bed, and is clearly not favoured in the text, was bathed in blood.[27] This tale is clearly a commentary on the hierarchy of Éoganachta dynasties – possibly in the eighth century – and is also highly symbolic. Neverthless, the ritual of bathing a baby is at its core, even if the liquids involved are most unlikely. Apart from some form of purification, Brigit undergoes the vital rite of passage of being named, which in her case is unusual, as, at the same time as she is brought into the Christian community through baptism, she is given an utterly non-Christian name. The ceremony of naming is significant in that it involves the public recognition of a child's status, descent and sex. As noted by Charles-Edwards, 'the first moment of transition is the naming of the child'.[28] In many cultures, an individual, and especially a male, can be given a series of names as he goes through life. This pattern occurs in the life cycle of Irish heroes. Finn mac Cumaill was originally named Deimne, while

Cú Chulainn was Sétantae. Christianity may have led to the adoption of the name Colmán (the diminutive of *Colum* borrowed from Latin *Columba*) by two generations of Irish kings who reigned between AD 550 and 650, and then it was almost exclusively used as a common ecclesiastical name.[29] Taking such a name was a definite public statement, and the name may either have been given to royal sons deliberately, or adopted by them on their succession to a kingship as a declaration of their adoption of Christianity.

A third rite universally associated with infancy is the protective rite. In his analysis of the heroic biography of Cormac mac Airt, Tomás Ó Cathasaigh discusses the protective rite as narrated in the Cormac story: Olc Aiche, Cormac's maternal grandfather who is a herdsman and druid-smith, protects the child against death by wounding, drowning, fire, sorcery and wolves, and against every evil.[30] These are very common motifs, but the brief sentence describing the rite is intriguing:[31]

> When Cormac was born, the druid-smith, Olc Aiche, put five protective [magic] circles about him (*fo-caird ...cóic cresa imdegla fair*), against wounding, against drowning, against fire, against enchantment (?), against wolves, that is to say against every evil.

Ó Cathasaigh interprets the phrase *cresa imdegla* as 'protective girdles', but suggests that this is metaphorical and that Olc Aiche uttered an incantation or spell, 'a pagan counterpart of that portion of the *lorica* which contains a list of dangers against which protection is asked'.[32] And if that is so, the power of words is a fundamental element of this protective rite and these incantations influenced their Christian reflex, the *lorica*:[33]

> *Ocus is luirech hirse inso*
> *Fri himdegail*[34] *cuirp 7 anma ar demnaib 7 dúinib 7 dualchib ...*
>
> And it is a breastplate of faith,
> To protect body and soul against demons and people and vices.
> If anyone recites it every day, with his mind fixed wholly upon God,
> Demons will not stand against him,
> It will protect him against poison and envy (= the evil eye),
> It will guard him against sudden death,
> It will be a breastplate for his soul after death.

Objects that might compare with *cresa imdegla* do not occur in the archaeological record, and grave goods are relatively rare in infant burials in Ireland. An exception is an infant burial from Parknahown, Co. Laois, dating to between the seventh and ninth century, which was accompanied by an antler bead, a perforated horse tooth and a quartz pebble. The power of quartz pebbles to protect a person is strongly conveyed in an episode in Adomnán's Life of Columba.[35] The saint was competing with the druid Broichan in the court of the Pictish king Bridei. Broichan refused to release his Irish slave-girl and, as a result, the saint threatened that he would not have long to live. Coming to the River Ness, Columba picked up a white pebble and said 'Mark this white stone through which the Lord will bring about the healing of many sick people among this heathen race'. Meanwhile, Broichan was struck by an angel and his glass cup broke in his hand just as he was drinking from it – resulting in a near-fatal seizure. Columba was called back to the king's fortress. He handed over the stone and ordered that the white pebble be dipped in water. Broichan was to drink the water, and if he was willing to relent about the slave-girl, he would live. He relented and Adomnán continues:

> The stone was dipped in some water, where, in defiance of nature, it floated miraculously on the surface of the water like an apple or a nut, for that which the saint had blessed could not be made sink. When Broichan drank from it, though he had been near to death, he recovered completely his bodily health ... The stone itself was kept in the royal treasury.

It healed many, but not those whose natural end had come, and that included king Bridei. When he was dying, the stone was sought, 'but it could not be found in the place where till then it had been kept'.

What was the function of a protective rite? No doubt it was hoped that an incantation and accompanying ritual would shield an individual from curses and the ever-present 'evil eye' that functioned as a social or moral censure based on fear.[36] Clearly, curses could be powerful and terrifying, as suggested by the curse in Cormac's Glossary *Bé Néit fort* 'the wife of Nét upon you'.[37] Bé Néit is equated to the war goddess Badb or Nemain (Gaulish *Nemetona*) and her consort Nét, a war god, and in Cormac's words, *ba neimnech tra in lánamain sin* 'that couple were indeed poisonous'. The conflation of Christian custom and earlier customs surfaces in the medieval Irish legal commentary on the evil eye (*in drochrusc*). Four legal circumstances are explained in relation to destruction by an evil eye, and various penalties are imposed on individuals depending on whether they were habitual offenders or they blessed themselves to counter the effects of their evil eye. For example, if a person known to have an evil eye neglected to utter a blessing, his legal liability might be increased. Three categories of herbs were used to prevent the evil eye, depending on a person's status: *ríglus* 'royal herb', *tarblus* 'bull herb' and *aithechlus* 'plebian herb'.[38] What these herbs might have been is not specified in the text, but they must have acted like garlic or saliva, which are known from other cultures to ward off the evil eye. The beliefs around a phenomenon such as 'the evil eye' and its dangers, which are universal and based on the power of fear, were complex and, as concluded by Jacqueline Borsje in her study of the subject, 'those things in life that are feared are not mentioned by name explicitly but are designated by euphemisms, metaphors, gestures and other means in order "to keep a safe distance" from these causes of fear and not to "call them forth" by naming them'.[39] They were countered by the power of words and objects. This use of words as a defence against evil would have caused little difficulty in a Christian milieu in which invocation of Christ's name, especially in baptism, operated as 'the efficacious power invoked'.[40]

Rites of passage: from puberty to death and rebirth

The narrative of Patrick's *Confessio*[41] gives an account of a missionary trying to convince his seniors that he was succeeding in converting a barbarian society despite many dangers and setbacks. Doherty has drawn on Patrick's writings to show to what extent this British missionary understood Irish society and used his knowledge to his advantage. He surrounded himself with kings' sons as a form of protection and, by enticing these young nobles to follow him, he had access to the next generation of kings who he may have educated into Christianity and literacy, and often into the celibate life.[42] He was also involved in introducing a fundamental change in society, that of challenging existing rites of passage for young men and women of all classes.

Inititatory rituals were common in many societies, and they have been classified as two distinct events in an adolescent's life: the rites associated with puberty, and ceremonies relating to entering an exclusive group.[43] All adolescents undergo an age initiation during puberty and this is especially true of girls once they begin to experience menstruation. In some societies, this may involve a girl's forcible removal from her familiar surroundings,[44] but female initiation rituals 'tend to be more evocative of the cocoon metamorphosis of a caterpillar into a butterfly than a boy passing through dangerous and purifying ordeals to return as a warrior'.[45] Hence a girl's transformation into a woman could be a very dangerous event for the community, as is so dramatically portrayed in the early saga of Deirdre whose beauty and transgressions caused tumult and the death of her lover Noísiu.[46] With menstruation came fertility and the need to confine a girl's sexual activities within an acceptable union, and hence the need for a girl to be married around the age of fourteen. The very public aspect of menstruation is reflected in the Old Irish Penitential and other similar texts in western

Christendom, in which women could not take communion and anyone who had intercourse with them during their 'monthly sickness' did penance for twenty nights.[47] Their parents' angry reaction to Patrick's recruitment of young girls – both free and slave – was to be expected, as his ideal life of permanent virginity for them upset a girl's normal rite of passage to full womanhood.

Initiation rituals worldwide, especially for boys, were a fundamental transition in the religious life of man and often reflected a change in their status as they moved closer to becoming legally responsible. Commenting on this stage in a person's life, Eliade asserts that 'to become a man in the proper sense, he must die to this first (natural) life and be reborn to a higher life, which is at once religious and cultural'.[48] The initiate goes through a ceremony of death and rebirth, into darkness emerging at the end into a new life of knowledge. Christian baptism incorporated this vital aspect of initiation rituals using aquatic symbolism of sanctification, which was enriched by new meanings associated with Christ.[49] Can any ceremony of pre-Christian male transition be detected in the Irish sources? Once a boy reached fourteen or seventeen – depending on the interpretation of the laws – fosterage came to an end and he was regarded as a *fer midboth* 'a man of middle huts'.[50] This term suggests that he was a man who had not yet inherited land or his own property and was living temporarily on his father's land. At points between fourteen, seventeen and twenty ('the age of beard encirclement'), he attained various legal powers, including the power of oath-making and providing legal protection, depending on his rank. The existence of a distinctive ceremony of initation, which separated young men from normal society and educated them in the mysteries of knowledge and a 'new' life, has been identified in early Irish hagiography and sagas.[51] The terms *díberg* and *láech* in Irish, and *laicus* or *latronus* in Latin, came to signify a member of a band of brigands who sought to disrupt normal society with their violence, either by killing sprees or in raiding churches. Early Irish penitentials single them out, along with druids and satirists (*díbergga 7 druídechta 7 cáintechta*), as being unable to gain remission of their sins through penance.[52] There has been much discussion about the nature of these *díberga* 'brigands' and their relationship with the more acceptable *fían*, and the connection between Irish *láech* 'warrior, hero' and Latin *laicus* 'layman'.[53] McCone concluded that the *fían*, and even *díberga*, were 'a typical enough instance of the widely attested phenomenon of the "Männerbund" or association of wild young warrior-hunters that can be linked in various ways to systems of age grading'.[54] Members of this warrior-brigand group are recognized in Irish literature by their distinct insignia, described as a *signa diabolica* or *stigmata*, and bound by an oath or vow, sometimes described in saints' Lives as a *uotum mali* 'a vow of evil'. This has been interpreted by Richard Sharpe as a pagan practice that 'evidently has its own ritualistic code of conduct'.[55] A typical episode is related in the Latin Life of Lugaid, in which a devilish band (*scola diaboli*) came towards the saint and his community wearing *vexilla* on their heads. The Latin *vexillum* normally means a banner or flag, but this text and others suggest that this was some form of headgear. Evidently, it could be seen from afar and was recognizable for what it was, as Lugaid caught sight of the brigands and blessing his community turned them into wood to protect them.[56] Cogitosus' Life of Brigit offers a clear outline of their ritualistic code of conduct:[57]

> [Brigit] saw nine men in a peculiar guise required by a godless and diabolical superstition, shouting in a grotesque tone of voice and showing signs of utter insanity, and in their paths lay destruction and misfortune. With the most wicked vows and oaths to the ancient enemy who reigned over them, they thirsted for bloodshed and planned the slaughter and murder of others before the calends of the following months should arrive.

This code comprised distinctive garb, threatening and, presumably, loud noise, frenzy, common vows binding them to a non-Christian troop, and violent activities at certain times of the year. To this list may be added the *fled demonda* 'the devilish feast' celebrated by these groups. Symbolism, multilation, killing, death and final rebirth form part of a universal code for initiation rites and undoubtedly the description by Cogitosus is the Irish reflex: as elsewhere, for example, initiates were probably tattooed or scarred, renamed and donned animal skins in the various steps towards their second birth. A trace of such practices may have survived in personal names, among them Cennfáelad 'wolfhead', Fáelán 'little wolf' and Fáelgus 'wolf vigour'. While these names survive among early medieval dynasties, occasionally as saints' names, their use in a Christian milieu is relatively rare and not as widespread as the use of other names such as Áed, Ciarán, Colmán and Finnén. There is a contrast between Patrick's efforts to recruit the sons of kings – the most likely candidates to be *díberga* – and Brigit's conversion of the nine brigands to the Lord through repentance on the one hand, and the outright condemnation of *díberga* in the penitentials and other later saints' Lives on the other. This difference suggests two stages of conversion: at first, an attempted accommodation and hence dilution of the practice; thereafter, condemnation and disconnecting those continuing the practice from normal society.

Archaeological evidence from burials of this period shows indications of extreme violence being used towards adolescent males. This might be an indicator of the genuine existence of frenzied marauding young men inflicting death and mayhem on their own age group.[58] If Christian baptism and rebirth into a less violent fraternity was desirable, it took at least two centuries (to the late seventh and beyond) and much condemnation to dislodge this rite of passage from society and, ultimately, to transform the *díberga* into the more beneficial, Christian and often fictional Männerbund of Finn mac Cumaill and his *fían*.

The final rite of passage: death and burial

The anthropologist Pascal Boyer observes, as have many of his discipline, that in any human group, there are prescribed rules and common explicit norms about what is to be done upon the death of a group member. 'There is a wide spectrum here, from places where such prescriptions are minimal and the representations associated extremely bare, to places where far-fetched death-rituals are associated with precise and complicated descriptions of what death is'.[59] In practical terms, funerary rites are all to do with what a society and family do with the body of the deceased, whether this involves rapid burial or cremation, or a lengthy, public decomposition. At another level, the dead are often active ancestors who have their own cults and who become important in a genealogical tradition. This tendency was very prevalent in medieval Ireland, where genealogies were powerful tools for legitimizing dynastic or ecclesiastical power and for the ownership of land. Like genealogies, certain grave mounds, *fertae* 'ancestral graves', were used as boundary and territorial markers.[60]

The law tract *Din Techtugud* describes the legal process of *tellach* 'legal entry' or claiming land: a claimant entered the land in the presence of a witness, taking two unyoked horses across the boundary *ferta*, the ancestral grave mound. He did not unyoke his horses and only allowed them to graze on half of the land. He then withdrew and waited for five days for a response from the occupant as regards arbitration. If there was no response, ten days later the claimant entered the land again, with four horses and two witnesses. He unyoked the horses and allowed them to graze freely. The occupant had three days to respond. If he did not do so, then the claimant entered for the third and last time, ten days after the second entry. The third time he brought eight horses and three witnesses with him. If the occupant did not respond immediately, the claimant then went to the house, where he looked after his animals, kindled a fire and stayed the night. The claimant had now established the right to occupy the land as the legal owner.[61]

Fertae were significant markers in the prehistoric and medieval landscape. Increasing numbers of such sites have been identified and excavated: they are usually located in prominent positions, overlooking rivers, coast, bogs or ravines. They occur as mounds, ring-barrows or circular ditched enclosures and stretch chronologically from the Bronze Age to the seventh century. At different periods during the late Iron Age and between AD400 and 700, burials were inserted into prehistoric ancestral *fertae*. Many of the fifth- and sixth-century inserted burials were female. In her study of *fertae*, Elizabeth O'Brien proposes that such burials 'were probably inserted either by the legitimate occupants of a territory in order to reinforce their valid title to their land when others sought to make a claim, or by intrusive groups, who by introducing their own "guardians" into the *ferta* created a contrived form of continuing as a means of legitimizing a claim to territory'.[62] The site at Ballymacaward, Co. Donegal, overlooks the mouth of the River Erne and Ballyshannon Harbour.[63] It began with a Bronze Age cairn with two cists datable to *c*.2000–1500BC and seems to have remained undisturbed for over a millennium. Two Iron Age cremations, dating to the second or first century BC, were inserted into the surface of the earlier cairn. Sometime between the first and third centuries AD, an extension was added to one side of the cairn into which deposits of charcoal and cremated bone were spread. The cairn was revisited in the fifth or sixth century and four women were buried in slab-lined long cists following the burial rite of extended inhumation, a rite that was introduced to Ireland in the late fourth or early fifth century. Nine further extended inhumations, all females lying in west–east positions, were placed in unprotected graves in the sixth or seventh century. Six of these burials were wrapped in shrouds, which might suggest that these women were Christians, although there is no strong indicator to identify any of the post-fourth-century women as either pagan or Christian. Apart from its prominent location overlooking Ballyshannon Harbour, which would have ensured its strategic position in the landscape, this cairn was located in a frequently contested territory in the early medieval period. The Tripartite Life of Patrick narrates the bitter conflict between the northern dynasties of the Uí Néill, the Cenél Coirpre and Cenél Conaill, in this region, probably during the sixth and seventh centuries, in which Cenél Conaill ultimately prevailed.[64] It is in just such a landscape that *fertae* would have acted as a constant reminder of the power of ancestors, and would have attracted reuse by both conquerors and conquered as they attempted to legitimize their claims through those ancestors.

The process of Christianizing death and burial took a long time in western Christendom. In his consideration of this process in the late Roman world, Peter Brown makes the case that in Christian communities in the fourth and fifth centuries, as among non-Christians, death, burial, and the subsequent 'care' of the dead were matters for the family. The Christian clergy were not involved at all and pagans and Christians were buried alongside one another in family graves. 'A proper Christian burial was the proper "Roman" burial of someone who happened to be Christian'. During the fifth and sixth centuries, however, burial practices for the nobility – clerics, kings and other aristocrats – began to change due to the advance of the cults of saints:[65]

> To be buried near a holy grave was to gain the hope of standing beside the saint, one's patron and protector, on the day of the resurrection. Like iron filings suddenly regrouped around a magnet, the ancient cities of the dead changed, as Christian graves pressed in around the shrines of holy persons. Even the immemorial boundary of the city of the living and the city of the dead, outside its walls, was broken down. In many towns, the dead came to be buried inside the city, so that they could rest near the altars of urban churches.

Christian cemeteries or 'holy ground', in which the greater number of the population was buried, developed from the late seventh century onwards. At this stage, the family care of the dead, which had operated independently of the church, gradually conformed with rituals defined by the clergy.[66] The Irish situation follows a very similar pattern. This is explicit in various sources and in archaeological evidence: the widespread use of *fertae* peters out in the eighth century. At some point in the middle or late seventh century, Bishop Tírechán described the encounter between Patrick and Eithne and Fedelm, daughters of Lóegaire mac Néill, king of Tara, beside the well of Clébach on the slopes of Cruachu to the east, located in the ceremonial complex of Rathcroghan, Co. Roscommon. Unlike their father Lóegaire, who had attempted to destroy Patrick at Tara, the young girls, once they had established that the saint and his followers were neither from the otherworld, earth-gods nor phantoms (*sed illos uiros side aut deorum terrenorum aut fantassiam estimauerunt*),[67] were instructed by the saint and embraced Christianity. Such was their fervour for the Chrisitan message that on receiving the Eucharist they died. Tírechán continues his account:[68]

> … and their friends placed them on one bed and covered them with their garments and made a lament and great keening … And the days of mourning for the king's daughters came to an end, and they buried them beside the well of Clébach, and they made a round ditch in the manner of *ferta* (*et sepilierunt eas iuxta fontem Clebach et fecerunt fossam rotundam in similitudinem fertae*), because that is what the pagan Irish used to do, but we call it *relic*, that is, the remains of the maidens. And the *ferta* was handed over to Patrick with the bones of the holy virgins, and to his heirs after him for ever, and he made an earthen church there.

This passage reflects succinctly what was occurring elsewhere: the conversion of two pagan noble girls, their receiving of communion, their death and burial according to existing customs, and finally, the appropriation by the church of their graves and bones. These then became the focus of a cult of relics over which a church was built. The significance of this Irish account is its early date: Ireland was in line with changes elsewhere. The eighth-century Irish canons, the *Collectio Canonum Hibernensis*, highlight changes in the care of the dead from the kin to the church. The canon 'Concerning the rule that lots should be cast to decide between the church and the ancestral tomb' quotes Origen, the third-century theologian from Alexandria, when dealing with the upkeep of ancestral cemeteries:[69]

> If any secular person has so wished, let lots make the division between the church and the ancestral tomb, but he ought to contribute the greater gift to his church, a few (items), however, to the ancestral cemetery in honour of the ancestors.

The triumph of the church in ensuring that the laity was buried in or close to consecrated ground is expressed in the prologue to the ninth-century *Féilire Óenguso* 'The Martyrology of Óengus'. It declares triumphantly:[70]

> *Borg Ailinne úallach*
> *atbath lia slog mbágach*
> *is mór Brigit búadach*
> *is cáin a rrúam dálach.*

> Ailenn [Knockaulin, Co. Kildare] proud fortress
> has gone with its warlike host,
> great is victorious Brigit,
> fair is her multitudinous cemetery (*rúam*).

Even more impressive is the martyrology's claim *ar-rúama cen tádel it bordgala míle* 'their [the hosts of Christ] unconcealed graveyards are the meeting places of thousands', in which two borrowed place-names, *rúam* and *bordgal*, are used to add to the superiority of the churches as assembly places of the living and dead.[71] The church's cemeteries were full and the old practices of burial had ceased.

Despite this clerical triumphalism, some non-Christian funerary customs continued to be practiced, including burial in cemeteries not obviously associated with a church. Burnt grain, antler tine and animal bones turn up in graves.[72] The deposition of antler tine and pig bones in graves signifies some form of rite. At Collierstown, Co. Meath, a male burial had an antler tine placed in his left hand, while a female had a pig bone in her pelvic area. The woman was buried sometime in the fifth or sixth century.[73] At Ballygarraun West, Co. Galway, a lone female, dating to sometime between the fifth and seventh century, was buried on a layer of burnt alder, hazel and grain. A piece of red deer antler was placed over her pelvic girdle.[74] Quartz pebbles were scattered over bodies, some intentionally on the chest or in the pelvic area. A burial in the extensive cemetery found at Cabinteely, Co. Dublin, had a stone box or cist constructed around its head and a pillow stone. A quartz pebble was deposited with the pillow stone. As mentioned previously, the infant burial dating to sometime between 680 and 890 from Parknahown, Co. Laois, was found with an antler bead, a perforated horse tooth and a quartz pebble. While grave goods are uncommon, the repeated occurrence of a particular object suggests some form of practice and one that could withstand conversion to a new religion and the strictures of canon law. Usually, such customs relate to healing or fertility. In the case of the Parknahown infant burial, the grave goods were amulets. A resonance of some awareness of the curative or even maledictory powers of quartz stones, and of their association with the realm of the dead, appears in the Modern Irish *clocha uaisle* (or *clocha geala*). Although *uasal* normally means 'noble, gentle', it can also mean 'hallowed, sacred to the dead' and *clocha uaisle* 'quartz, white stones' are often found in prehistoric graves, saints' 'beds' and sites associated with the *síd* 'otherworldly beings'.[75]

The funeral feast or wake and family commemorations of the dead were customs connecting the living with the dead. A range of early Irish phrases and words exists that describe the rituals that went with burials: *feis la marb, fled crólige* 'the death-feast', *cluiche caíntech* 'the grieving games'. These rituals must have involved feasting, hence the common occurrence of animal bones in the vicinity of burials and in cemeteries. This is borne out by Adomnán. He tells how Columba took pity on a thief and, after admonishing him for his sins, had a gift of 'a fat beast and six measures of grain' sent to him. The thief died before he received the saint's gift 'and the gifts that had been sent were used at his funeral'.[76] Columba himself tried to ensure that his own funeral was purely monastic. On his deathbed, one of his monks declared that after his death, 'all the population of these provinces will row here and fill the whole island of Iona to attend your funeral ceremonies', but the saint responded, 'only the monks of my own community will carry out my burial and perform the funeral duties'.[77] And the saint had his way as a storm blew for the three days and three nights of Columba's funeral and no one could reach Iona. Nevertheless, Adomnán states that the saint's funeral rites lasted three days and three nights, 'befitting one of his honour and status'. This would tally with the length of an abbot's funeral, involving, as it still does today, all night vigils and the office of the dead. Yet, as he was a member of the Uí Néill royal dynasty, perhaps not all traditional practices were set aside by the monks of Iona for Columba's funeral.

Ritualists in Ireland before Christianity

Consideration of priesthoods or other spiritual intermediaries in pre-Christian Ireland to date has been dominated by a debate about druids that, in turn, invariably depends on classical Continental sources that are somewhat temporally and geographically disconnected from Ireland. Rather than continuing to match these sources with medieval Irish sources, as so many scholars have done,[78] a different approach to our understanding of how pre-Christian religion was organized in Ireland may be productive, if the Irish evidence is exposed to comparative anthropological, liturgical and cognitive analysis. Instead of seeking a uniform priestly institution operating on the basis of a set of doctrines throughout Ireland – a druidic elite that cleverly transferred its authority to a new Christian sacerdotal elite – it might be useful to distinguish between the various levels of religious intermediaries who conducted different rites. This could range from ritualists who negotiated with local ancestors and cults on behalf of a community, to those who dealt with the sacro-political ceremonies of great kings. Fragmentation of priestly functions, and an amalgamation of many belief systems, is often the hallmark of even the most seemingly organized societies. The various 'priesthoods' of the Roman Republic are a case in point.[79] The powerful *pontifices* advised the Senate on religion and administered 'tomb law'. The *augures* ascertained the approval, or otherwise, of the gods for political and military actions, and demarcated sacred space on earth to the *Salii*, who conducted ritual song and dance through Rome in March and October. A potential survival from the era of the monarchy in Rome was the *rex sacrorum* 'king of the sacred rites' – and his wife the *regina sacrorum* 'queen of the sacred rites' – who was chosen by the *Pontifex Maximus*. These performed two particular rites: the *regifugium*, the anniversary of the expulsion of the last king from Rome; and the *agonalia*, a festival at which the *rex sacrorum* sacrificed a ram at the Regia in Rome. The Regia was the house of the *Pontifex Maximus* and contained a number of shrines to various deities including Mars.[80] This type of rite combined political and religious powers at their highest level in Roman society. In Ireland, such ritual agents were undoubtedly necessary to orchestrate events at sites such as Tara, Cashel, Navan Fort and Rathcroghan, and, as with the *rex sacrorum* and other priesthoods after the imposition of imperial power by Augustus in Rome, their functions cannot have remained static, but evolved with changes in society and in power structures.

We should also be mindful that the formation of the Christian priesthood was neither a swift process nor completely independent of influences from other religions. Clearly, sacerdotal concepts such as that of Christ as the 'high-priest' were transmitted from the Old Testament, and terminology such as 'priest' (*hiereus*, Greek; *sacerdos*, Latin) were introduced from the Graeco-Roman world.[81] As P.F. Bradshaw stresses, 'the concept of sacerdotal office in the early Church went far beyond merely the offering of sacrifice' and was not confined to focusing on the Eucharist, or other sacraments, 'even more significantly [it] was understood to extend to both preaching and teaching'. By the fourth century, the bishop exercised the vital sacerdotal functions in a Christian community, although there were diverse interpretations of the extent of priesthood and clergy throughout Christendom.[82]

What can be deduced about religious agents operating in Ireland at the arrival of Christianity? Who conducted the *banfheis* or *hieros gamos* at Tara and other 'royal' sites until the sixth century?[83] Who organized – and presumably profited from – the deposition of valuable offerings at Newgrange in the fourth century?[84] Did they adapt to new Christian ministries or did they fade away? The Irish word *nemed*, cognate with Celtic *nemetos* 'holy, sacred', has been shown to have a range of meanings, from sanctity to defining a privileged status in society and a legal position of temporary exclusion from normal obligations during a crisis or transitional phases in life, such as a pregnancy or a bereavement.[85] *Nemed* could also mean a sanctuary or consecrated place (cognate with Gaulish *nemeton*) and is transferred into hagiography to mean a church. Those who were recognized as holding a higher status of *nemed* were a king, a poet and an ecclesiastic.[86] Indeed, these embody the functions of pre-Christian religious agents: the sacro-political represented by the king, divination and historical memory and the interpretation of laws represented by the poet and judge; and ritual performance and organization represented by the Christian cleric. If the physical consecrated space could become a church, a Christian *nemed*, can we identify the guardians and ritualists who supervised the earlier *nemed*? The Irish sources are close enough to the conversion period not to have erased the memory of such people. An illustration of how they are to be found in an oblique way in the sources relates to the relatively unknown Cattraige in Munster. Ó Riain has made a good case that Tírechán's mention of the baptism of the Éoganachta royal dynasty by Patrick at Cashel *super Petram hi Coithrigi hi Caissiul* is not to be read as 'on Patrick's Rock at Cashel' but as 'on the rock of the Cattraige [*alias* Coithrige] at Cashel'.[87] The Cattraige belonged to one of the oldest population groups in Munster that are recorded in the early genealogies, whose ancestral territory was in Cliú (east Limerick/south-west Tipperary), and who are associated along with a group of related 'older people' (*sencheneóil*) with Emly, the original primatial church in Munster. Furthermore, the founding saint of Cloyne, Co. Cork, Colmán mac Léinín, renowned not just as a cleric but significantly as a poet, is likely to have belonged to the same Cattraige.[88] Cliú, including Emly and other important sites, such as Lough Gur and Knockainey, has yielded considerable archaeology from the Neolithic to the period under consideration.[89] Equally, the place-name Imblech Iubair 'Emly of the Yew Tree' suggests a link to some sacred tree cult. The reputed founder saint of Emly, Ailbe, whose own historicity is suspect, is associated with the Daulrige, an early people like the Cattraige who tenaciously held on to power as an hereditary ecclesiastical family in Emly despite their likely pre-Christian adherence to the god Lug.[90] The sum of this evidence, albeit shadowy, brings us as close as possible to a potential group of pre-Christian religious agents active at important regional sites. The Corcu Temne or Temenrige, mentioned earlier,[91] as the 'people of the sanctuary' who controlled two sacred wells, were also religious agents, at least one of whom converted to Christianity and became a bishop at Cell Tóich.

The more elusive agents were those who negotiated between local communities and the gods and spirits, and their ancestors, individuals who were regarded 'as capable of handling the delicate relations people entertain with spirits and gods'.[92] They are often described as shamans, healers, mediums or witch-doctors, whose main functions related to fertility, healing and dealing with the dead. Their authority was based on local power and they are often seen as having operated a 'low' and flexible ritual system unlike those operating a 'high' system who normally were members of a canonical order concerned with the universal and eternal.[93] Can these local agents be identified either in the sources or the archaeological evidence? The sources invariably associate the non-institutional – and hence non-Christian – variants of ritual with women, and their activities are often depicted as disruptive. For example, the following excerpt from *Bretha Crólige*, the law on sick-maintenance with its later commentaries, lists a series of women and actions deemed as unacceptable. Yet they are indicative of the types of individuals and practices disliked by mainstream lawyers, either secular or canonical:[94]

> There are twelve women in the territory whom the rule of nursing in Irish law excludes: a woman who turns back the streams of war [the abbess of Kildare]; a ruler entitled to hostages [Medb of Cruachain], one who is abundant in miracles [e.g., the virgin or female 'exile of God'], a woman satirist (*bé rinnuis*) [a poetess], a woman wright (*bansáer*), a woman revered by the territory (*túath*) [in origin possibly a prophetess], a woman leech of a territory, a sharp-tongued virago (*birach briatar*), a vagrant (?) woman (*bé foimrimme*), a werewolf in wolf's shape (*confæl conrecta*), an idiot, a lunatic. It is by a fee to their kin that these women are compensated: they are not brought away [to be nursed].

Notably, the *bansáer* 'woman wright or craftswoman' is glossed as either being a midwife who attends births or an embroideress, and the *bé foimrimme* is said to be gone with the fairies (*téit lasna sídaigibh*). The werewolf is a woman who 'likes to stray in wolf's shapes, such as the Í Chon Erca'. Most significantly, the *dásachtach* 'lunatic' is a woman 'about whom the magic wisp is put' (*fo tabarr in dlai fulla*). A *dlaí fulla* was some form of magic wand seemingly used in divination. A further commentary on the text suggests that these various women could not be brought away on sick-maintenance because a host could not assume responsibility for 'a crime of their audacity', and this is understood by the commentators to mean that among their crimes were satire, killing stock and summoning up demons.[95] Undoubtedly, demons and other supernatural beings were called upon well into the medieval period. John Carey has noted the strange reference to Mongfhinn, who, according to the tale *Aided Chrimthainn* 'The Death of Crimthann', was a woman of the *síd* who died at Samain. The text continues:[96]

> Samain is called the feast of Mongfhinn by the rabble, for she was powerful, and was a witch, for as long as she was in a body; and that is why women, and the rabble, utter prayers to her on the night of Samain.

A remarkable entry in the Annals of Tigernach for 1084, if true, demonstrates this type of activity quite dramatically:[97]

> A great pestilence this year, which killed a fourth of the men of Ireland. It began in the south, and spread throughout the four quarters of Ireland. This is the reason for that pestilence, namely, demons came out of the northern isles of the world, that is, three battalions, and there were three thousand in each battalion, as Óengus Ócc son of the Dagda told Gilla Lugan, who used to frequent the *síd* every year at Samain. And he himself saw one battalion in Maistiu, a battalion that was destroying Leinster. Thus they were seen by Gilla Lugan's son and wherever their heat and fury reached, it is there that their venom assailed. For there was a sword of fire out of the gullet of each of them, and every one of them was as high as the clouds of heaven. So that is the cause of this pestilence.

From these extracts we can begin to experience a ritual culture, replicated in so many other societies, that existed outside, and was feared by those who sought to control social and religious mores in early Irish society. And while Christianity became the dominant and higher religious system, it did not wipe out other practices, or even ritualists, who had their roots in an earlier belief system.

The earliest phase of Christianity in Ireland

The coming of Christianity to Ireland is traditionally linked to two individuals, Palladius sent by Pope Celestine in AD431 to minister as bishop 'to the Irish believing in Christ', and Patrick, the Briton, who laboured as a bishop converting the Irish probably sometime during the early fifth century.[98] Patrick left a testament of his mission in two forceful Latin documents, his *Confessio*, a defence of his mission against critics in Britain, and his *Epistola*, a letter condemning a British king, Coroticus, for attacking and enslaving some of his newly converted Christian flock.[99] Concentration by scholars on Palladius and Patrick, and the chronological link between the two missions, has tended to detach the Christianization of Ireland from that of the rest of the contemporary known world, and to have accentuated Ireland's uniqueness in that world. This approach has led to the creation of a phantom institution popularly described as the 'Celtic church'. Ireland was different in many ways: it had its own language, it developed its own political structures, customs and laws, it had not seen Roman legions invade its shores, and it was located at the furthest reaches of the known world. Indeed, Patrick alludes to Ireland's extreme geographical location on a number of occasions in his writings: 'may God not let it come about that I would suffer the loss of his people who have become his in the furthermost parts of the earth (*in ultimis terrae*)'.[1] It is likely that Patrick and others, among them Pope Celestine and his emissary Palladius, would have regarded the conversion of Ireland as a triumph, as it meant that their goal of Christianizing the world had successfully reached its westernmost extent.

Ireland, however, was not totally isolated or immune to changes in society and beliefs happening in its closest neighbour, Britain, and further afield as far as the eastern Mediterranean. In late antiquity (from the fourth century onwards), when Christianity began to take a proper foothold beyond the Mediterranean rim, the Irish and many other similar peoples occupied the *limes* 'frontier-zones' of the late antique Roman world and were influenced by the multi-faceted culture of that world, often identified with the cultural term *romanitas*. Clear evidence for Ireland's connections with the late antique world is manifest in the archaeological, dynastic and linguistic records.[2] The large collection of Roman objects found clustered around the entrance to the Neolithic passage tomb at Newgrange, Co. Meath, attests not only to the deposition of votive offerings at a pagan cult site, a common Romano-British practice, but also to military links between Ireland and the Continent in the early fourth century. Gold medallions of Constantine and Constantius (both Christian

19 Map showing distribution of find spots of Mediterranean amphorae in Ireland and Britain. These amphorae were shipped to Ireland from the Cypro-Syrian region and around Asia Minor in the late fifth and sixth centuries. The coastal distribution, especially in the kingdoms of Brega and Cualu, points to the likely centres of cultural and economic interaction with the wider world. Map prepared by Ian Doyle and Robert Shaw; © Ian Doyle/Heritage Council.

20 Map showing distribution of find spots of E ware in Ireland and Britain. Bowls, jars and jugs produced in central and western France were imported during the sixth and seventh centuries. Map prepared by Ian Doyle and Robert Shaw; © Ian Doyle/ Heritage Council.

emperors), dating to the 320s and 330s, were based on coins struck in Trier and were produced on special occasions as *donativa*, presentation gifts by the Emperor to high officials or military officers in the imperial army (pl. 8). These medallions are rare, with only a small number known from Britain and the Continent. Their appearance in Ireland suggests either the return of Irishmen who had gained high rank in the imperial army of *Belgica Prima*, with its capital in Trier, or as diplomatic gifts exchanged between an Irish king and a visiting emissary. Two hoards of Roman silver, dating to the late fourth/early fifth century, have been found in Ireland, from Ballinrees, Co. Antrim, and Balline, Co. Limerick, and rather than regarding them as loot lost by marauding Irish raiders, they are now classified as the standard type payment for military service found around the northern frontiers of the empire at this time. While there is no hint of Christianity in the deposits from Newgrange, and, indeed, the very circumstances of the offerings are a sign of cultic practice, they nevertheless point towards the lines of transmission of ideas from the empire to Ireland. Depositing jewellery is known from cult centres in Roman Britain.[3] Raghnall Ó Floinn has argued that a similar, if smaller, rural shrine, possibly devoted to fertility and healing, at which imported Roman objects were deposited, functioned at Freestone Hill, Co. Kilkenny, in the late fourth and early fifth century.[4] If, by any chance, an Irishman served in the imperial army in Trier or its surrounding regions, he could have encountered Christians among the ranks and might even have noticed the veneration of relics at Trier Cathedral, built on a momumental scale by the Emperor Constantine and Bishop Maximin in the mid-fourth century, or even encountered the small community of Christian monks living there.[5] While this might seem improbable, it is noteworthy that a fifth-century Christian memorial from the cemetery of St Matthias in Trier, now unfortunately lost, was dedicated by his wife to the memory of *Scottus* 'an Irishman'.[6]

Pottery imports are the best confirmation of trade between Ireland and western Britain and the Continent as far as the eastern Mediterranean (figs 19, 20).[7] Amphorae of various shapes and sizes – predominantly the types classified as Bi (LRA2), Bii (LRA 1) – from the Cypro-Syrian region and around Asia Minor (modern Turkey) respectively – were shipped to Ireland in the late fifth and sixth century. They most likely contained wine and olive oil. Tableware in the form of Phocaean Red Slip Ware (PRSW), which was produced from the fourth century at Phocaea in Asia Minor (Turkey), has also been found in Ireland, although it is much rarer than sherds of amphorae. How did these imports end up in Ireland and who were they for? Two models of distribution have been suggested – they came either from a small number of direct shipments from the Mediterranean to Ireland, or as part of a secondary distribution network from western Britain.[8] The distribution of B ware in Ireland and western Britain is particularly significant for its clusters in Cornwall, Devon, Dorset and Somerset, the southern Welsh coast and along the north Dublin and Meath coast. These regions incorporate the important gateways of Bantham, Tintagel, Caldy Island, Tenby, Dalkey Island and Colp on the Boyne Estuary, distribution centres that may be the key to understanding not only a trade network, but also lines of cultural and religious influences. Words borrowed from Vulgar Latin into Irish are associated with trade, and especially the wine trade, and are regarded by Damian McManus as 'a very early transfer to Irish'.[9] They fit remarkably well with the world of merchants and buyers of imported pottery and other exotic items: *sesra* (< *sextārius*) 'a measure of capacity', *muide* (< *modius*) 'a vessel for holding liquids', *esarn* (< *exhibernum* (*vinum*)) 'year-old wine', *cann* (< *panna*) 'vessel', *cess* (< *cista*) 'basket' and *dírna/dinnra* (< *denārius*) 'weight'. Such were the close connections between regions in Ireland, particularly all along the east coast, that certain groups in society were multi-lingual and particularly open to different cultural influences. As argued by Amanda Kelly in her extensive study of PRSW and Bii ware, the delicate tableware – and also imported glass – and wine or olive oil that occurred in places such as Garranes and Clogher were ostentatious displays that served 'to consolidate strict social hierarchical frameworks, effectively distinguishing the highest stratum of society'.[10] It is to this world that Patrick belonged, and glimpses of it are portrayed in his writings. He is insistent on his *romanitas* and difference from the Irish:[11]

> My name is Patrick … My father was Calpornius. He was a deacon; his father was Potitus, a priest, who lived at Bannavem Taburniae. His home was there, and that is where I was taken prisoner. I was about sixteen at the time.
>
> I declare that I, Patrick, – an unlearned sinner indeed – have been established a bishop in Ireland. I hold quite certainly that what I am, I have accepted from God.
>
> I live as an alien among non-Roman peoples, an exile on account of the love of God – he is my witness that this is so.

He had been taken captive by these non-Roman people and, as a British slave, he rediscovered his faith:[12]

> After I arrived in Ireland, I tended sheep every day, and I prayed frequently during the day. More and more the love of God increased, and my sense of awe before God. Faith grew, and my spirit was moved, so that in one day I would pray up to one hundred times, and at night perhaps the same. I even remained in the woods and on the mountain, and I would rise to

pray before dawn in snow and ice and rain. I never felt the worse for it, and I never felt lazy – as I realize now, the spirit was burning in me at that time.

He finally escaped from Ireland by ship, despite the taunts of a hostile crew:[13]

> The day I arrived, the ship was about to leave the place. I said I needed to set sail with them, but the captain was not at all pleased. He replied unpleasantly and angrily: 'Don't you dare try to come with us'. When I heard that, I left them and went back to the hut where I had lodgings. I began to pray while I was going; and before I even finished the prayer, I heard one of them shout aloud at me: 'Come quickly – those men are calling you!' I turned back right away, and they began to say to me: 'Come – we'll trust you. Prove you're our friend in any way you wish'. That day, I refused to suck their breasts, because of my reverence for God.[14]
>
> They were pagans, and I hoped they might come to faith in Jesus Christ. This is how I got to go with them, and we set sail right away.

This was the context in which Patrick became familiar with the Irish, and although he returned to his family in Britain, he felt compelled by his faith to become a missionary among the Irish and to teach them the Gospel.

Palladius came to Ireland in very different circumstances and even possibly to contain the activities of missionary bishops such as Patrick.[15] He was sent as a bishop by Pope Celestine in 431, as recorded in his chronicle by Prosper of Aquitaine:[16]

> To the Irish believing in Christ, Palladius, having being ordained by Pope Celestine, is sent as first bishop.

Prosper of Aquitaine, in his text *Contra Collatorem*, explains the stategy driving the pope's initiative:[17]

> He [Pope Celestine] has been, however, no less energetic in freeing the British province from this same disease [the Pelagian heresy]: he removed from that hiding place certain enemies of grace who had occupied the land of their origin; also, having ordained a bishop for the Irish [Palladius], while he labours to keep the Roman island [Britain] catholic, he has also made the barbarian island [Ireland] Christian.

These are the first indications of official contacts between Irish Christians and the papacy in Rome. They occur in the wider context of Rome trying to counter a heresy spread by the Briton Pelagius, establishing itself as the axis of all Christianity, as opposed to Constantinople in the east, and of missions to people beyond the frontier of the empire, to barbarians who were not regarded as Romans. In 429, Pope Celestine had sent Germanus, bishop of Auxerre in Gaul, to Britain to counter Pelagianism. He had done so at the instigation of Palladius. This activity was orchestrated by aristocratic and influential officials of the church. Prosper was an important polemicist and possible adviser to Pope Leo the Great. Germanus of Auxerre was a Gallic bishop, an aristocrat and a former provincial governor, and Palladius, of whom little is known,[18] was a deacon in Rome. Of Palladius' mission and the rest of his life beyond 431, we know nothing. His mission may have been primarily in the east of Ireland and there are hints that his activities were conflated with those of Patrick in the latter's later Lives. And yet, despite the paucity of information about Palladius' mission to Ireland, it suggests a context for the advance of Christianity in Ireland in the early fifth century. The existence of an Irish Christian community was known in Rome, and indeed Charles-Edwards has suggested that contacts with them may have preceded the decision to send Palladius to them.[19] Apart from his concerns about the Pelagian heresy in Britain and Gaul, Pope Celestine was also a keen legislator with regard to the election of suitable candidates as bishops and, as noted by Robert Markus, 'was worried about the extent of the monastic takeover in the Gallic Church, and warned the Gallic bishops not to allow a "new college" to emerge as a source of future bishops'.[20] This warning was declared in 429/30, just before Palladius was sent to Ireland. The 'new college' of bishops had already begun to dominate in the form of powerful, influential aristocratic monks from the island monastery of Lérins off the southern coast of Gaul. Given the pope's anxiety about the proliferation of monks as bishops and also his general concerns about church legislation, Palladius was also undoubtedly sent to Ireland to organize the Christian communities along the lines outlined in Celestine's numerous *epistolae* 'letters' on the subject.[21]

Equally, the activities of Germanus of Auxerre, who visited Britain in 429 to counter Pelagianism, are instructive in our efforts to reconstruct Palladius' mission to Ireland. In Auxerre and elsewhere in Gaul, Germanus collected relics and encouraged cults of local martyrs. While in Britain, he visited the site of veneration of the martyr Alban 'the Briton' – possibly at Verulamium – accompanied by Lupus of Troyes. There, he deposited the relics of the apostles and martyrs, a clear signal of Britain being part of the universal church, and he took Alban's blood (dried in the earth) back with him to Auxerre. A basilica was dedicated to St Alban there and the *Passio S. Albani* 'The martyrdom of St Alban' was displayed on *tituli* 'notices' in the basilica.[22] Palladius probably visited the Irish Christians with relics and plans to dedicate churches to the apostles and the martyrs. The later Tripartite Life of Patrick claims that Palladius left a casket (*capsa*) with the relics of Peter and Paul at the church of *Cell Fine*.[23] This assertion might be a complete fabrication, as many later references to Palladius seem to be, or it could reflect a faint understanding of what his mission entailed, and that it was not dissimilar to Germanus' to Britain. Is there a trace of this mission and its subsequent suppression by Armagh in the story of Sachellus, who is mentioned in Patrician literature as associated with *Bassilica Sanctorum* (Baslick, Co. Roscommon). Sachellus was reputedly ordained by Patrick in Rome and there he gave him a portion of the relics of Peter, Paul, Laurence and Stephen that were housed in Armagh. Sachellus, and another bishop Caeticaus, were chastized by Patrick for ordaining bishops and clergy without his consent, a possible echo of the universal controversy in the Christian church about authority to ordain priests and consecrate bishops.[24] Archaeological investigations at Baslick, one of the very rare occurrences of the place-name in Ireland, have revealed the existence of considerable activity there pre-dating the existing medieval parish church which is supported by the discovery of an ogam stone built into the fabric of that church.[25]

Unlike Britain and Gaul, Ireland had no urban centres and if there were any major foci of authority in the landscape, they were at cult sites often linked to kingship – as at Tara, Rathcroghan, Knockaulin or even Armagh itself. These landscapes were obvious targets for missionary activity and it is no coincidence that bishops who belonged to this first phase of conversion were commemorated close to these places. Hence, Secundinus in Dunshaughlin, Co. Meath, was close to Tara, Auxillius and Iserninus close to Knockaulin (and Kildare), and Sachellus close to Rathcroghan. While none of these bishops is historically linked to Palladius, and they are usually depicted as submitting to Patrick, their existence leads us to explore conversion strategies and the establishment of ecclesiastical structures elsewhere as models for the Irish conversion narrative.

Christianizing a rural landscape

'The landscape, in particular those places where heaven and earth met, was being Christianized'.[26]

Doherty, in his study of Irish kingship, generated a long overdue study of the tangible ways in which Christianity advanced in a non-urban society. Ireland was not exceptional, as is often claimed, as contemporaneously Christian missionaries were engaging with many varied rural communities from the east Mediterranean to Ireland. As scholars often point out, the very word *paganus* 'pagan' actually means a rural dweller who lived in a *pagus* 'rural environment'.[27]

Throughout many regions Christianity was introduced into the countryside through rural estates and the private worship of an elite class. Kim Bowes, in her study of rural estates and private cults, details the variety of forms of estate worship from villa churches, mausolea to 'monasteries' in Britain, Hispania, Gaul, northern Italy and north Africa.[28] A number of Bowes' conclusions form the basis for a different approach to understanding the conversion of the Irish countryside: estate conversion often constituted 'the first Christian monumental presence in many areas of the western countryside' and these Christian buildings 'were prompted by far more ancient seigneurial concerns: the efficient management of human capital and the articulation of status'. This estate-based Christianity quite often operated independently of the control of bishops, who were usually based in cities and who did not have the economic wherewithal to extend their authority into the countryside.[29] The 'life' of Martin of Tours, compiled soon after the bishop's death in 397 by Sulpicius Severus, is a manifesto for a militant Christianization of the countryside quite different from the relatively slow and passive progress of Christianity through its adoption by rural elites. While Martin was Sulpicius' patron, the latter was a member of the rural elite in Gaul. He was an Aquitainian aristocrat who had retreated to Primuliacum, one of his family's estates, to live a life of prayer and spiritual education, while at the same time continuing to manage his estate.[30] His 'community', and that of others such as Paulinus of Nola, were foci of spirituality and Christian rituals but were not monastic in either their routines or their environments, and were not actually involved in a planned Christian conversion of the countryside, as Sulpicius claimed was the intention of Martin of Tours.

How does Ireland fit into this model of conversion, in which a rural elite and private worship were an essential part of the conversion process? To comprehend the earliest phase of conversion in Ireland, it is necessary to consider the pattern in Britain and also how Patrick exemplifies a certain class of British Christian. Evidence for fourth- and fifth-century Christianity in Britain is not as extensive as often thought, or as Sharpe describes it, 'very fragmentary, and its interpretation often speculative and liable to major configurations'.[31] Charles Thomas' study of Christianity in Roman Britain attempted to assemble as much evidence as was available in the 1980s, and since then more has been discovered archaeologically.[32] The only definite evidence for metropolitan centres in Britain comes in 314, when Eborius from York, Restitutus from London and a certain Adelfius, possibly from Lincoln, attended the Council of Arles. Three unnamed bishops travelled from Britain to attend the Council of Rimini in 359. There was enough Christian activity in Britain in the early fifth century for Pelagius, a Briton, to generate a heresy that required a vigorous response from Rome, although Pelagius himself, for the most part, was active on the Continent. Patrick is also an important witness to British Christianity, and his description of his family's status, property and ecclesiastical office makes perfect sense. Patrick's father, Calpornius, held both civic and ecclesiastical offices. He was a decurion and a deacon.[33] Being a decurion, Calpornius was a member of a council (often known also as the *curiales*) of the urban centre of the *vicus* of *Bannavem Taberniae*. By the fourth or fifth century, this position was probably quite onerous and unattractive, as decurions had to pay for their office and had the responsibility of collecting local taxes and maintaining civic standards.[34] As decurions normally resided in their urban centre or nearby, Patrick's description of his father's estate being near the *vicus* of *Bannavem Taberniae* fits well into this category of middling aristocratic class. So does his need to proclaim that he is a free citizen of the empire, as in Bowes' estimation, 'Being Christian in Britain seems to have been very much also about being a contemporary Roman, and faith and *romanitas* seem to have been announced with the same emphatic claxon'.[35] Not only was Patrick a member of the civic aristocracy, he was also a member of an ecclesiastical family: his father was a deacon and his grandfather Potitus a presbyter.[36] Being a member of an ecclesiastical family, Patrick most likely would have been aware of the existence of some form of episcopal authority, and could have had access to a small family estate church in his own *villula*, and also to a church in or near the *vicus* of *Bannavem Taberniae*, either an intramural congregational church or an extramural cemetery church, as classified by Thomas in his discussion of church buildings in Roman Britain.[37] An example of this type of family estate church is Lullingstone villa in Kent, with its painted decoration of praying figures (*orantes*) (pl. 11).[38]

Ireland was not urban, and evidence for *vici* and *villae* does not exist. Hence, Patrick and other missionaries from Britain and Gaul were encountering a landscape of rural communities, but not of totally isolated settlements. There is sufficient evidence of fifth- and sixth-century archaeology in Ireland to propose potential models for the Christianization of the Irish countryside, even if the remains of church buildings are absent.[39] Considering his own familial background in civic administration and the church, it is not surprising to find that Patrick identified kings (*reges*) and sub-kings (*reguli*) as those he needed to deal with and pay to ensure his safety and the success of his mission.[40] In Ireland, the equivalent of the British, Gaulish or Hispanic estate and seigneurial system was the *túath* and its king, while the town or city was probably replaced by the foci of regional or provincial kingships. Fading memories of this model of conversion are very strongly suggested in the notes (*additamenta*) attached to Bishop Tírechán's text, some of which may be dated to the seventh century, and others of which may have been added in the eighth century.[41] The overall theme of these additional notes is Patrick's retrospective sweeping up of churches and land grants associated with saints outside the remit of Armagh. The formula used is consistent: land, often kin-land, is granted to a royal son or daughter or to an ecclesiastic. A church is established and then Patrick arrives to bless the place and hence place it under his – in reality Armagh's – protection.

It would seem, therefore, that estate churches became Patrick's churches. In one example, Binén macc Mugu, a priest, was given land by his mother's kindred:[42]

> Binén macc Lugu, scribe (*scriba*) and priest (*sacerdos*) and also anchorite (*anchorita*), was the son of a daughter of Lugath macc Netach. His mother's kin gave him his hereditary land, on which he founded a church, consecrated to God and offered to Patrick, and holy Patrick marked the place for himself with his staff, and he was the first to offer (there) the body and blood of Christ after Binén had received ordination from him, and (Patrick) blessed (Binén) and left him in his place.

In another instance, part of a king's estate was given to Patrick:[43]

> Patrick came to the territory of the Calraige and baptized Mac Cairthin and Caíchán, and after he had baptized them, Macc Cairthin and Caíchán offered to God and Patrick the fifth part of Caíchán ('s estate), and the king exempted it for God and Patrick ... These are the boundaries of the fifth part, that is Caíchán's Fifth (*coiced Caícháin*): From the stream of Telach Berich out of Braidne (?) as far as ... Tuilgos from the mountain. From the stream of Conaclid to Reiri and from the border of Druimm Nit to the stream of Tamlacht Dublocho, along the stream to Grenlach Fote ... Lord (*flaith*) and vassal granted all this immediately after baptism was conferred upon them.

Can we find the equivalent of Patrick's own *villula* in Ireland – an aristocratic settlement that was in contact with the wider world whose inhabitants could have been receptive to the new religion? An indicator of such settlements, as mentioned earlier, is the presence of imported pottery, which implies the use of luxury items such as fine tableware, wine, oils or foodstuffs. One example is that of the multivallate ringfort of Lisnacaheragh in the townland of Garranes, Co. Cork, which was excavated in the early 1940s and re-explored more recently.[44]

Garranes: an Irish villula open to foreign influences?

Like the 'royal' fort at Clogher, Co. Tyrone, Garranes was a highly defended circular settlement with three substantial banks of earth and stones. It had an elaborate entrance and a complex system of gates. Based on the evidence of artefacts discovered at the site, and in one particular part especially, the fort was probably occupied in the later fifth and sixth centuries. An occupation layer described by the excavator as 'the black layer' yielded most of the artefacts and there was evidence that specialized occupations were carried out in the fort, including metalworking, enamelling and the manufacture of millefiori. The remains of a burnt circular structure was the only evidence for a possible building, but more evidence of habitation may exist, as the site was only partially excavated. While it has been suggested that Garranes is to be identified as Ráith Raithlenn, the royal centre of the southern dynasty of Uí Echach Muman, the connection is not conclusive.[45] Garranes is more likely to have been the hub of high-class craftsmen, who were nobles in the social hierarchy as prescribed by early Irish law. Given the nature of the finds, the settlement could have acted also as a distribution centre for imported goods that were transferred to places such as the provincial royal capital of Cashel, Co. Tipperary. One of the largest collections of sherds of imported pottery in Ireland was found on this site, consisting of the equivalent of thirteen amphorae (Bi, Bii and Bmisc) and one PRSW bowl. This particular bowl from western Turkey has been dated to $c.$AD500,[46] while the various amphorae came from the eastern Mediterranean sometime during the fifth or sixth century. Did Christianity come to Garranes with this outside trade? One indication of Christianity at Garranes, albeit tangential, is a mirror-shaped mould with a raised cross on its face. The land around the multivallate ringfort is fertile, and there is a concentration of ringforts in the area that appear to have some form of planned spatial relationship.[47] The existence of large farmsteads situated in relatively close proximity is a common pattern in fertile parts of Ireland, and, in reality, these constitute the settlements of important families from the fifth/sixth century onwards. An ogam stone, found in a small fort near Lisnacaheragh in the nineteenth century, was deciphered to read C[A]SSITT[A]S MAQI MUCOI CALLITI.[48] Among the genealogies of the Éoganachta, in whose territory Garranes was located, one kindred is listed as Cenél Caíllaide, descended from a certain Caíllaide mac Conaill, reputed grandson of Natfróech, progenitor of many of the Eóganachta dynasties.[49] This inscription commemorates CASSITTAS, who may have lived during the sixth century, and more importantly, signifies that members of the Garranes community were literate or were at least in contact with a literate class. In sum, Garranes and its hinterland offers us the Irish equivalent of the western littoral Roman *villula* from which Patrick came, and its culture hints at a community open to the reception of Christianity and literacy.

Caherlehillan: an early Christian community and 'memoria'?

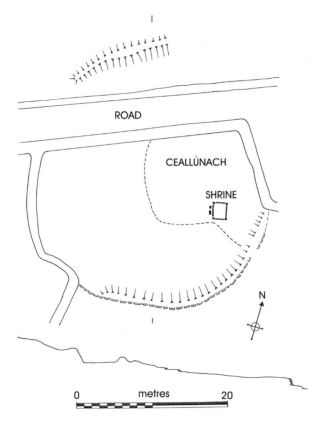

21 Caherlehillan, Co. Kerry: an outline plan of the church settlement and later additions. © John Sheehan, University College Cork.

One of the most significant recent excavations for this period in Ireland was conducted by John Sheehan at Caherlehillan on the Iveragh Peninsula, Co. Kerry (fig. 21).[50] This site was from the beginning a Christian place: it consisted of an enclosed area at the centre of which was a rectangular structure, possibly a small church, with graves aligned on it, including a 'special' primary grave – a *memoria* or founder's grave. Evidence for the performance of liturgical rites, especially the liturgy of the Eurcharist, was also discovered in the form of a wooden table altar supported on a single wooden post. Radiocarbon dates firmly place the foundation and development of Caherlehillan in the late fifth and sixth centuries. This date is supported by the discovery of sherds of two Bii eastern Mediterranean amphorae in an occupation deposit from the site's domestic area.[51] Notably, veneration of the special grave continued for approximately a further two centuries to the eighth century, with the construction of a *lecht* 'shrine'. At some stage, sherds from an E ware lid, imported from western France sometime between the late sixth and early eighth century, were deposited around the *lecht*. It has been suggested that this

22 Cross-inscribed slabs from Caherlehillan, Co. Kerry: these slabs stand beside the *lecht* 'shrine' on the early Christian site. They include a series of symbols often used in early mosaics and paintings, including a liturgical fan of the Eastern Church (*flabellum*) and a stylized peacock, a symbol of Christ's resurrection. © John Sheehan, University College Cork.

represents a deliberate votive act that finds its reflex in hagiographical literature, whereby a monastic cemetery was classified as a *rúam*, a borrowing from *Roma*. Thus, by depositing soil or other items from Rome or the Roman world in the ground, the place itself became an extension of Rome.[52]

A further distinctive feature of Caherlehillan are the cross-inscribed slabs, two of which stand beside the shrine (fig. 22).[53] One slab is inscribed with a linear Latin cross with C-scroll terminals and a roundel beneath it with similar C-scrolls. The second slab appears to represent a *flabellum*, the liturgical fan of the eastern church, in the shape of a disc (an arced cross) surmounting a handle. Above the cross is a stylized profile of a peacock, the symbol of immortality and of Christ's resurrection used in early Christian mosaics and paintings in the Mediterranean world. Two further fragmentary slabs with the same images were discovered on the site, which has led the excavator to conclude that all the Caherlehillan slabs 'have a distinctively exotic background that ultimately lies in Mediterranean Christian culture'.[54] This world also probably included a learned elite who were travelling between the southern regions of Ireland and western Britain. Their learning manifested itself in ogam inscriptions, which occur on the Iveragh Peninsula and which probably span the same chronological horizon as the church at Caherlehillan. This site, which belongs to the formative period of Christianity in Ireland, may not have developed beyond the eighth century, when its function was taken over by some other larger church. What was Caherlehillan? It might be argued that this was a version of an estate church that serviced a *túath* and its nobility, one of whom may have been its *érlam* 'founder', either king or cleric, whose grave was a venerated *locus sanctus* from the time of his death. Indeed, the impressive cashel (stone fort) close to the church site could have been the residence of the founder's family, a suggestion supported by child burials within the ecclesiastical enclosure.[55] Given the presence of the cross-slabs decorated with iconographic Christian symbols that must have been understood by the carvers themselves or those instructing them, and also the paucity of graves on the site (eighteen in all), an alternative interpretation is that Caherlehillan consisted of a small coenobitic community. If established in the late fifth or sixth century, this community is likely to have been influenced by the tradition of the Egyptian desert fathers and a community life influenced by John Cassian's Institutes and Conferences, written in the early fifth century. These highly influential texts, which circulated widely, introduced the desert tradition to a burgeoning western monastic movement. This was also the period during which most major monastic rules were evolving, and it is plausible that the community of Caherlehillan was open to influences from the Mediterranean or Gaul.[56] The attraction of holy places and relics to ascetics became a key movement of monasticism from the fourth century onwards, with individuals such as Paulinus of Nola, Sulpicius Severus and John Cassian creating monastic communities around such foci.[57] Perhaps this was the ascetic model that was transmitted to Caherlehillan? We can only surmise that the iconography, the amphorae and some form of monastic model that manifested itself in Caherlehillan had all followed the same route to the south-west of Ireland in the late fifth century and flourished there for over two hundred years.

Garranes and Caherlehillan are indicative of the types of sites in which early forms of Christianity appear in fifth- and sixth-century Ireland, and undoubtedly they were replicated throughout the island. They may have been organized within a local ecclesiastical structure that in itself was taking shape and took two centuries to become a coherent institution.

ESTABLISHING A CHRISTIAN STRUCTURE

The narrative of early medieval Christianity in Ireland is dominated by three eminent individuals: Patrick the Briton, Columba of Iona and Columbanus of Bobbio. This view has greatly skewed the complexity of the Irish church that evolved from the sixth century onwards. The imprint of Christianity in Ireland consists of a network of thousands of sites, place-names and cults that have survived to the present, as well as many that have left no trace.[58] Christianity in early medieval Ireland was administered by bishops, priests and abbots, some in orders, others who were lay people. Practice of moral and sacramental religion varied from erratic arrangements among the laity, often dependent on promixity to well-organized churches, to the extreme observance of ascetics. All kinds of church buildings were constructed, from simple post-and-wattle edifaces to relatively large stone churches and monumental enclosures. As the church became a powerful institution from the seventh century onwards, most people in Ireland somehow encountered its influence, be it through its provision of pastoral and social care, negotiating peace when violence bedeviled communities, changing economic practices, spreading literacy or replacing traditional religious customs with new rituals. This encounter was not always regular and not always benign, as the church as much as kings levied tributes and triggered dissension in society. While many sources emanating from the most powerful churches – often with the support of their royal patrons – did much to promote an image of an organized and coherent structure, the Irish landscape, reflected by archaeological and place-name evidence, contradicts any depiction of a uniform monolith. This was a church of many houses.

It is apparent that Palladius' mission to Ireland was a well-planned endeavour that formed part of a greater papal enterprise and that, despite his critics in

Britain and his own self-deprecation, Patrick's mission was not a haphazard venture. Both missionaries were involved in organizing existing Christian communities and newly converted people within the church's structure as it was developing elsewhere. Ireland did not lag behind Britain or the Continent in this regard, as the substantial organization of the church emanating from Rome took place primarily from the fifth century onwards, while monastic rules were increasingly codified in Gaul and Italy during the same period. Hence, Ireland is to be viewed as part of this movement and not as an isolated outlier catching up with increased governance in the church. Otherwise, it is difficult to explain the sophistication of the early sources in Irish and Hiberno-Latin that emerge in the late sixth century and demonstrate a command of literacy and exegesis on a par with many other regions in Christendom.

The earliest level of ecclesiastical organization

There are a number of key statements in the composite text known as the *Liber Angeli*, written during the seventh century to proclaim the rights of the heir of Patrick and his see at Armagh. Similarly, Tírechán's work exposes a layer of hierarchical ecclesiastical structures established by an early wave of missionaries. In arguing that God gave Patrick the whole island, Tírechán declares among other claims that 'all the primitive churches (*ecclesiae primitivae*) of Ireland are his'.[59] The use of the phrase *ecclesiae primitivae*, which in this context must mean the foundation churches of Christianity in Ireland, was charged with meaning as it was the phrase probably coined by John Cassian in the fourth century to describe the church at the time of the apostles, and was used by many reformers to hark back to the ideal of the *vita apostolica* 'the apostolic life'.[60] In an even more assertive declaration on behalf of Patrick and Armagh, the *Liber Angeli* states:[61]

> Further, every free church (*aeclessia libera*) and every city (*civitas*) in all Ireland which is seen to have been founded by a bishop, and every church anywhere that is called *domnach* ought – in accordance with the mercy of the kind and almighty Lord towards the holy teacher and with the word of the angel – to belong to the special *societas* of Bishop Patrick and the heir of his see at Armagh, for as we have already said, God gave him the whole island.

This extract singles out the churches called *domnach* for special mention. *Domnach* is a borrowing from Latin *dominicum* 'the house of the Lord, a

23 Aerial photograph of Donaghmore, Co. Kildare: the name *Domnach Mór* (Donaghmore) suggests that this was the site of an early church. It consists of a double enclosure around the churchyard on the spur of a hill. © Cambridge University Collection of Aerial Photographs: CUCAP AYR050.

church' that was in use until the fifth century, and then replaced in Ireland by *cell* (from Latin *cella*).[62] While churches with this element in their names are attested throughout the country, most of those that can be identified are spread around the east, the midlands and the north. Many *domnaig* (plural) are qualified by the adjective *mór* 'great' and follow the pattern *Domnach Mór Maige X* 'the great church of the plain of X'. Doherty has suggested plausibly that, in this particular usage, *mag* means not only 'a plain', but a settled area, and that 'this represents the areas of concentrated population in the fifth century when the first dioceses (with their concern for pastoral care) were established'. These were the churches of independent bishops of the missionary period.[63] Their associations often hint at early connections. Bishop Cethiacus ministered to his mother's people the Corcu Sai or Sairige at Domnach Sairigi near Duleek, Co. Meath.[64] Lomán, possibly of British descent,[65] and Silvester were associated with Domnach Imlecho (Kilmalum, Tipperkevin, Co. Kildare).[66] Domnach Mór (Donaghmore, Co. Laois) is associated with an obscure and possibly foreign bishop Deineth and with Pól (Paul) and Martan (Martin).[67] The physical configuration of these churches is unknown, as they were most likely built of wood or of sods,[68] but some faint traces of their layout survive to the present.

The later church and graveyard of Donaghmore, Co. Kildare, for example, is enclosed by an oval-shaped stone enclosure which may follow the line of an earlier enclosure (fig. 23). The site is located on the spur of a hill and yielded an ogam stone in the nineteenth century. The inscription commemorates a certain Nadfroích descendant of Trénlug (NETTAVRECC [KOI?] MAQI MUCCOI TRENALUGGO).[69] There is a further enclosure nearby. A similar configuration exists at Donaghmore Upper, Co. Kilkenny, identified as Domnach Mór Maige Roigni mentioned in Patrician literature. Here there is a later church and graveyard with a possible earlier enclosure and a ringfort in the vicinity.[70] Some church sites retaining the *domnach* element were clearly chosen for their proximity to important dynastic or ceremonial complexes: this is the case with Donaghpatrick, which is close to the royal settlement of Ráith Airthir in the ceremonial landscape of Tailtiu (Teltown, Co. Meath). This is the first identifiable layer of ecclesiastical organization across a large swathe of the island. It was an episcopal structure probably established in the fifth century, often linked to early foreign missionaries, mainly British, and located in well populated regions. As borne out by Caherlehillan, however, this was not the only model of ecclesiastical structure to be adopted in Ireland during this period and later.

The introduction of monasticism

St Augustine of Hippo (354–430), writing in his Confessions, narrates a tale told by a certain Ponticianus, a north African who was an official in the emperor's court and who introduced Augustine to the story of Anthony of Egypt and monasticism. Augustine continues:[71]

> From this, his conversation turned to the multitudes in the monasteries and their manners so fragrant to thee, and to the teeming solitudes of the wilderness, of which we knew nothing at all. There was even a monastery at Milan, outside the city's walls, full of good brothers under the fostering care of Ambrose – and we were ignorant of it. He went on with his story, and we listened intently and in silence. He then told us how, on a certain afternoon, at Trier, when the emperor was occupied watching the gladiatorial games, he and three comrades went out for a walk in the gardens close to the city walls. There, as they chanced to walk two by two, one strolled away with him, while the other two went on by themselves. As they rambled, these first two came upon a certain cottage [casa] where lived some of thy servants, some of the 'poor in spirit' ('of such is the Kingdom of Heaven'), where they found the book in which

was written the Life of Anthony! One of them began to read it, to marvel
and to be inflamed by it. While reading, he meditated on embracing just
such a life, giving up his worldly employment to seek thee alone.

This extract is a valuable illustration of how monasticism might have spread to
Ireland, if Irishmen in the imperial army were serving in places such as Trier.
Augustine was introduced to Anthony of Egypt and monasticism through
Ponticianus. The latter travelled with the emperor's court and while on his
journeys came across monks, both in highly organized monasteries such as
Ambrose's foundation in Milan, and in smaller communities like the *casa* close
to the city walls in Trier. Monasticism could take many forms and, until the ninth
century, was subject to a variety of legislation.[72] Ponticianus' tale also
demonstrates how a life of poverty and chastity in a community – or even in a
solitary state – attracted recruits from all classes, one of the distinct features of
Christianity in the empire. And finally, the anecdote about the two officials
coming upon the Life of St Anthony in the *casa* illustrates strikingly how texts
circulated and how important literacy was in the spread of a movement such as
monasticism. There is no reason why soldiers of Irish origin in an imperial army
might not have encountered the same text and movement when they were in
Trier, although, as mentioned earlier, the evidence from the Newgrange material
suggests that if they did, they clung to their old beliefs.

In his *Confessio*, St Patrick claims that the sons and daughters of lesser Irish
kings became monks and virgins of Christ (*filii Scottorum et filiae regulorum
monachi et virgines Christi*).[73] He continues with his assertion that many women,
nobles and slaves had been baptized and had chosen to become virgins of Christ
despite threats from their families. If Patrick envisaged any form of monastic life
for his converts, it is highly unlikely that they followed any particular rule, but
were similar to the many small communities that sprang up throughout Gaul
and Italy during the fifth century. These were house and villa communities of
aristocrats who 'took to a life of religion and turned their own homes into
religious retreats for family and friends'.[74] Yet monasticism, as it was mediated
from the Egyptian desert to western Christendom through the works of John
Cassian, Augustine, Jerome, Caesarius of Arles and Martin of Tours, was a highly
complex movement. It combined intellectual thought and education, often
zealous religious ideals, and radical social behaviour. The search for definitions
of the role of the abbot in a community, liturgy, degrees of solitude, humility,
obedience, possessions and many other questions generated considerable
discussion in the early church.[75] The lives of the desert fathers offered a basis
for the creation of institutional monasticism, and the essential elements of their
way of life were gradually codified into monastic rules.[76] As monasticism became

more regulated from the sixth century onwards, Ireland's nascent monastic communities became part of this vibrant force. The sixth century was the century of the great master abbots: Benedict, Columba and Columbanus.[77] Pope Gregory the Great (d. 604), with whom Columbanus corresponded, was the first monk to become pope and was keenly aware of the tension between the contemplative life of the monastery and active involvement in society,[78] a tension that manifested itself throughout the medieval period in Ireland between busy monastic settlements and more remote eremitical foundations. In his correspondence with the pope, Columbanus mentioned that he was aware of the discussion between the sixth-century British clerics Gildas and Uinniau, sometimes identified as Finnian of Movilla (Co. Down).[79] Their fragmentary correspondence suggests that both were grappling with similar difficulties to those encountered by the anonymous monastic legislator known as 'The Master' and by Benedict of Nursia.[80] Among the difficulties that needed to be addressed were the perennial problems of wandering monks who left their monasteries without their abbots' permission, exercising chastity and poverty, the retention of possessions by monks, and dealing with proud and vain monks. Gildas' penitential outlines penances for various sins from the gravest to the lightest, and, in doing so, gives us a fleeting glimpse of life within an early and evolving monastic community. On the sins of monks, Gildas wrote:[81]

> A presbyter or a deacon committing natural fornication or sodomy who has previously taken the monastic vow shall do penance for three years … He shall have bread without limitation and a titbit fattened slightly with butter on Sunday; on the other days a ration of dry bread and a dish enriched with a little fat, garden vegetables, a few eggs, British cheese, a Roman half-pint of milk … also a Roman pint of whey or buttermilk for his thirst, and some water if he is a worker. He shall have his bed meagrely supplied with hay …
>
> A monk who has stolen a garment or any other (thing) shall do penance for two years …
>
> One who has not arrived by the end of the second psalm shall sing eight psalms in order. If when he has been aroused he comes after the reading, he shall repeat in order whatever the breathren have sung. But if he comes at the second reading, he shall go without supper …

The abbot was essential to the proper supervision of his community and, notably, Gildas in his correspondence with Uinniau implies that even by this stage in Britain – and possibly in Ireland – abbots ruled with varying degrees of strictness:[82]

Gildas says: An abbot of a stricter rule should not admit a monk from the monastery of a somewhat laxer abbot; and a laxer abbot should not hold a monk of his back if he is inclined to stricter ways.

Monastic life developed in various forms in western Christendom and Ireland was no exception in adopting these diverse forms: the basilical and often royal monastery, the monastic community directed by an abbot and devoted to an ascetic life, the solitary monk or virgin who survived on the margins of society.

Kildare: a royal basilical monastery

In Gaul and Italy, basilical monasteries developed that were built around the tombs or relics of saints, were sustained by royal patrons and had a community of monks, and sometimes nuns, attached to them. These communities were vital to the growth of monastic worship with their use of psalmody and solemn liturgical celebrations. Among the most significant of these basilicas in Gaul were the churches of St Martin in Tours and St Denis in Paris.[83] Many of the most renowned monasteries in Ireland were in fact forms of basilical monasteries. These included Kildare, Clonmacnoise and Emly. Cogitosus' seventh-century Life of Brigit is quite explicit in depicting Kildare as an episcopal basilica served by a monastic chapter headed by a bishop and by a community of nuns and widows headed by an abbess. This arrangement appears somewhat comparable, and even perhaps contemporary, to that established by Caesarius in the cathedral church at Arles in 512. Caesarius compiled a rule for the nuns of the monastery of St John the Baptist (*Regula sanctarum virginum*) between 512 and 534.[84] No such rule survives for Kildare, nor is there evidence for Caesarius' insistence on absolute reclusion of the nuns until death. Instead, Cogitosus offers an intriguing insight into the functioning of the two communities at Kildare, and their respective places in the basilica:[85]

[The church] is adorned with painted pictures and inside there are three chapels, which are spacious and divided by board walls under the single roof of the cathedral church. The first of these walls, which is painted with pictures and covered with wall-hangings, stretches widthwise in the east part of the church from one wall to the other. In it there are two doors, one at either end, and through the door situated on the right, one enters the sanctuary to the altar where the archbishop offers the Lord's sacrifice together with his monastic chapter and those appointed to the sacred mysteries. Through the other door, situated on the left side of the aforesaid cross-wall, only the abbess and her nuns and faithful widows enter to partake of the banquet of the body and blood of Jesus Christ.

The bodies of Brigit and Conláed, the reputed sixth-century founding bishop whom Brigit had called from a solitary aescetic life to fulfil the episcopal and liturgical needs of her basilica, were enshrined in ornate tombs on the left and right sides of the altar. In his description, Cogitosus also claims that the monastery was 'the safest city of refuge in the whole land of the Irish for all fugitives, and the treasures of kings are kept there'.[86] While Cogitosus' text may have been exaggerated and written when Kildare was seeking to rival Armagh for primacy of the Irish church, the parallels between Kildare and Continental basilical monasteries cannot be disregarded. The issue is whether the author used Continental models as a literary topos to promote Kildare's status or whether he reflected a reality that has left no physical trace. Kildare was a royal church (eigenkirche) of the Uí Dúnlaing kings of Leinster from the 630s, its abbot, Áed Dub mac Colmáin (d. 638), being a brother of Fáelán mac Colmáin (d. 666), aspirant provincial king of Leinster. Earlier dynasties had also associated themselves with Kildare through Brigit and Conláed and this royal connection lasted through the early medieval period. A remarkable example of a royal dynasty's hold on Kildare was that of the family of Cellach mac Dúnchada, king of Leinster (d. 776). His daughter Muirenn ruled as abbess of Kildare from 805 to 831. His sons Fáelán, Muiredach and Áed ruled as abbots of Kildare from 798 to 828 respectively, while their brother Fínshnechta was the provincial king of Leinster from 776 to 808. The king died of an illness in Kildare, which suggests that the monastery was either a royal residence or served as a hospice.[87] As for the truth of Cogistosus' description, Carol Neuman de Vegvar has argued cogently that the basilica did genuinely exist by the seventh century and that it was built deliberately imitatio Romae ('in the Roman fashion') to counter the claims of Armagh as primatial church and to rival Armagh's own architectural imitatio Romae constructed during the same period.[88]

Bangor and Iona: influential and learned ascetic communities (fig. 24)

The development of coenobitic monasticism from the eastern Mediterranean is punctuated by the important contributions of charismatic individuals including Pachomius in Egypt, Basil of Caesarea, John Cassian, Caesarius of Arles, Honoratus of Lérins and Benedict of Nursia. In late sixth-century Ireland, similarly charismatic individuals had a huge impact on the organization of coenobitic life, which led to the foundation of monasteries that thoroughly

24 The Cathach: this is the oldest extant Irish manuscript and the earliest example of Insular Irish script. It is a copy of the Psalter that dates to the late sixth or early seventh century. © Royal Irish Academy.

influenced the political, intellectual and spiritual world of medieval Ireland. Columba of Iona in the west isles of Scotland, who died around 597, and Comgall of Bangor on the north-eastern coast, who died in 601/2, established two such monasteries. Columbanus (d. 614), founder of the Continental monasteries of Luxeuil and Bobbio, a forceful correspondent with Pope Gregory the Great, was educated at Bangor. As a result of the works of early biographers, the careers of Columba and Columbanus have been well documented. It is instructive, however, to chart their early ascetic formation and their perspectives on monastic life. Columba's and Columbanus' early education followed similar paths. In Adomnán's seventh-century Life of Columba, there are only brief allusions to his childhood. He seems to have been fostered by the priest Cruithnechán who, from the text's description – if true – served a church that was near his house.[89] For a noble child of the powerful northern dynasty of Cenél Conaill (Uí Néill) to be fostered by a priest would seem unusual, unless this was a way in which his family, as recent converts, expressed their fervour and handed one son over to the church. As Sharpe has tentatively suggested, however, Columba's biographer Adomnán was keen to depict the saint as Christian from birth and his fosterage with Cruithnechán was designed to stress 'that the holy person's sanctity is unaffected by time: they were as holy at birth as at death'.[90] As a deacon, Columba lived in Leinster studying divine wisdom with a certain Gemmán, and in an episode about the killing of a young girl despite the protection of the saint and his old teacher, Adomnán depicts Gemmán as reading his book 'out on the plain', with Columba also reading a little distance away.[91] While this detail could be stylistic, it is possible that they were indeed out on a plain and that Columba had studied in one of the old *domnach* churches in Leinster. Columba also studied scriptures with the bishop Uinniau,[92] who, if he was the same person who corresponded with Gildas about monastic life, would have probably ordained the saint and taught him a monastic rule and introduced him to the monastic fathers. *Amra Choluim Cille*, a lament supposedly composed in Old Irish on Columba's death, claims that he applied the judgments of Basil, loved the books of Cassian and studied Greek.[93] This intellectual regime, of course, finds its parallel in the Rule of St Benedict, as does the paradigm of the saint being introduced to his monastic education by a master. The very use of the title *Regula Magistri* 'The rule of the master', accorded to the anonymous sixth-century major monastic rule, encapsulates this concept.

Columbanus' early years were not unlike those of Columba. Jonas' seventh-century Life of Columbanus is scant on details regarding his life in Ireland and, as with Adomnán, sets out to demonstrate his patron abbot's sanctity and erudition from an early age. Jonas claims that from his boyhood he studied grammar, rhetoric, geometry and scripture. If true, Columbanus was educated initially in the late antique *liberalia studia* and in Christian scripture,[94] a training that would explain his florid Latin and his capacity to form complex arguments. Jonas portrays Columbanus as warding off the temptations of women 'whose fine figure and superficial beauty are wont to enkindle mad desires in the minds of wretched men'.[95] Ironically, it was a holy and devout woman who exhorted him to leave his home in Leinster, and to place himself under the tutelage of Sinell, 'distinguished among his countrymen for his unusual piety and knowledge of the Holy Scriptures'.[96] He then became a member of the monastic community of Bangor that had been founded by Comgall, who had been 'held in high esteem for the fervor (sic) of his faith and the order and discipline he preserved'.[97] In Comgall's community, Columbanus embarked on a life of fasting, prayer and mortification of the flesh, a journey which he adhered to throughout his life and, in turn, imposed on his own monks, not without causing difficulties among them. Although he was not trained by Uinniau, Columbanus nonetheless knew of Gildas' writings and of the correspondence between him and *Uennianus auctor*.[98] As with the influential aristocratic circle of Lérins, Columba, Columbanus and Comgall appear to have belonged to a similar closely connected ascetic group in late sixth-century Ireland. In one episode in Adomnán's Life of Columba, for example, he and Comgall were washing their hands near a spring when Columba prophesized that the spring would be tainted by human blood spilled at the fort of Dún Cethirn at a battle about to be fought between their respective dynasties, the Uí Néill and the Dál nAraidi in 629.[99] Whatever about Columba's prophetic ability, the inference of the story is that these great abbots did not lead cloistered lives, but travelled between Ireland and Britain, and engaged with kings and nobles, some of whom were their close relatives.

Living the life of a monk: Adomnán's Life of Columba (pl. 10) *and the Antiphonary of Bangor*

Monastic rules have a generic quality about them in that they all deal with similar issues, such as obedience, prayer, poverty, chastity and the relationships between a monastic community and the rest of society. Equally, saints' Lives normally reflect a particular version of monasticism that concentrates on the sanctity of the founder and his or her miraculous powers. Not having direct accounts of his lifestyle leaves us grappling with archaeological and written sources to gain a genuine insight into the authentic life of a monk in early Ireland. Adomnán's Life of Columba, for example, has at its heart the dominant themes of Columba's sanctity and his miraculous and prophetic powers. It also follows the template of Sulpicius Severus' Life of Martin of Tours and Gregory the

Great's depiction of Benedict of Nursia, both of whom were regarded as exemplary abbots. Beneath these strands, however, the actual life of the community at Iona – most likely during Adomnán's time there rather than during Columba's abbacy – can be detected in a surprising amount of detail. Combining this material with archaeological evidence brings us closer to the life of a monk in an early coenobitic community.

Becoming a monk involved a long process of education and penance. This is highlighted in the Life of Columba, when two brothers came to Iona as pilgrims and were instantly professed by the saint to the astonishment of the community. Columba had to justify his action by prophesying that the brothers did not have the time to follow the normal path to profession as they were to die within a month of their arrival in the monastery. And so they did.[1] A longer and possibly more accurate, if exaggerated, entry into the community was imposed on a certain Librán.[2] He came to Iona from Ireland, having 'only lately assumed the clerical habit'. He was put up in the monastery's guesthouse where Columba interviewed him and established who his people were and what the reason was for his journey. Librán had come from Connacht and was on a penitential pilgrimage apparently with the intention of becoming a monk. But Columba 'then set out for him how strict and burdensome were the demands of monastic life, for he wanted to test the strength of his penitence'. Undeterred, Librán spent seven years in penance in the monastery of Tiree (Mag Luinge) and returned to Iona during Lent. He was then sent back to Ireland to gain his freedom from his master and to fulfil familial obligations. After various adventures, he returned to Iona ready to be professed. Columba gave him the name Librán 'the little free one' because he had been freed from his obligations and his sins and, 'during the next few days, Librán took the monastic vow'. The story of Librán illustrates the requirements for entry into a regulated and properly structured monastery ruled by an abbot: a monk had to be free from worldly obligations, cleansed of his sins often through severe penance, and although not mentioned in the Librán story, suitably educated in scriptures and liturgy. On occasion, individuals were sent away, as happened to Fintan mac Tulcháin, who came to Iona and was refused entry by Columba's successor, Baíthéne, on the grounds that the saint had foretold that Fintan would not be an abbot's monk, but an abbot of monks. Fintan or Munnu (d. 635) founded the monastery of Taghmon, Co. Wexford. Notably, Baíthéne followed the same practice with Fintan on his arrival at Iona as Columba had with Librán: 'As soon as he was brought [to Baíthéne], Fintan threw himself to the ground on bended knee, as was proper. Being told to rise by the holy elder, he was given a seat and asked by Baithéne about his still unascertained people and province, his name, his manner of life and for what reason he had undertaken the effort of the journey'.[3]

The Cross of the Scriptures, Clonmacnoise, Co. Offaly: this high cross provides unequivocal evidence of the importance of the monastery as a centre of royal and ecclesiastical power. It replaced an earlier monument – possibly a large wooden cross or stake – and was a focal point of burial in the monastic complex. The cross was erected *c*.909 by Flann Sinna, king of Ireland, and Abbot Colmán Conaillech. © Rachel Moss, Trinity College Dublin.

2 Cahercommaun, Co. Clare: this massive stone fort was built overlooking a narrow, sheer gorge in the fertile Burren. In the eighth and ninth centuries, it may have been the residence of an over king who ruled as far north as the Aran Islands. Cahercommaun is one of many similar stone for that dot the landscape of the western seaboard. © Eamonn O'Donoghue/Claire Cotter.

3 Baronstown, Co. Meath: a large defensive enclosure built on high ground overlooking the Rive Gabhra, east of the Hill of Tara. This may have been used as an assembly site. © National Roac Authority.

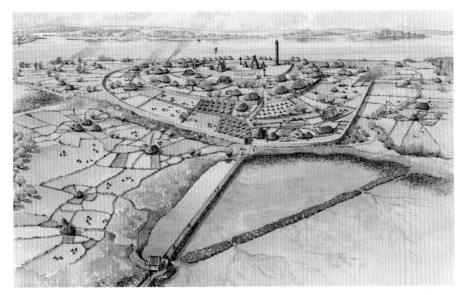

4 The early Irish monastery at Nendrum, Co. Down: the monastery of St Mochai at Nendrum was excavated by H.C. Lawlor in the early 1920s and it yielded considerable evidence for life in the community during the early medieval period. This reconstruction shows some of the essential components of an early Irish ecclesiastical centre: the churches, the saint's shrine, the three enclosures and crosses marking the areas confined to the community and open to the laity, and the homesteads of the community and its tenants. The round tower is a later addition. © Philip Armstrong/Tom McErlean/NIEA.

5 The tidal mill at Nendrum: the monastery is located on Strangford Lough and the lough was vital to its economic vibrancy, as illustrated by the discovery of tidal mills dating to the seventh and eighth centuries close to the monastery. The mills would have provided flour for bread for the community and its tenants and also a surplus that could have been traded for other goods. © Philip Armstrong/Tom McErlean/ NIEA.

6 The Rock of Cashel, Co. Tipperary: this rock stands alone and impressively in the fertile plain of Mag Femin. This was the capital of Munster and the ceremonial seat of its provincial kings. It seems to have gained its name *Caisel* circuitously from Latin *castellum* and, although now recognized by its medieval ecclesiastical buildings, was undoubtedly a centre of ritual activity since prehistory. © National Monuments Service, Department of Arts, Heritage and the Gaeltacht.

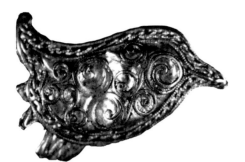

7 The Garryduff gold bird. Discovered in a ringfort in Co. Cork and dating to the seventh or eighth century, this small gold bird formed part of a larger object, possibly a brooch. © Cork Public Museum.

8 A pair of fourth-century AD gold medallions belonging to the reigns of Constantine and Constantius discovered around the entrance of the Neolithic passage tomb at Newgrange, Co. Meath. These medallions were *donativa*, presentation gifts made by the emperor to high officials or military officers in the imperial army. They may have been deposited by Irishmen who had returned following a career in the army or may have been diplomatic gifts presented to an Irish king. © National Museum of Ireland.

9 View of Armagh city by Richard Bartlett, 1601 (NLI MS 2656): this seventeenth-century illustration contains the main elements of the medieval *urbs* of Armagh, its division into three parts (*trian*), the enclosed hilltop site of the main church and the distribution of lesser churches around the hill. © National Library of Ireland.

DE TRANSITV AD
DÑM SCI NOSTRI
PATRONI COLVMBE

10 Adomnán's *Vita Sancti Columbae* (MS Gen. 1 Stadtbibliotek, Schaffhausen): the Schaffhausen manuscript of the Life of St Columba of Iona written by Adomnán, the ninth abbot of Iona (d. 704), is the earliest version of the text and has a direct connection with the monastery, in that the scribe was Dorbbéne of Iona (d. 713). © Stadtbibliotek, Schaffhausen.

11 Part of a fourth-century wall painting from a Romano-British villa at Lullingstone, Kent: the villa at Lullingstone incorporated a family estate church that was decorated with murals, including one of praying priestly figures (*orantes*). © British Museum, London.

12 The Clonmore shrine found beside the River Blackwater, Co. Armagh: this small portable shrine dates to *c*.AD600 and is probably the earliest example of Irish Christian metalwork. It was discovered as part of a river dredging scheme that brought up a considerable amount of metalwork and metalworking debris, possibly associated with a workshop in Armagh. © National Museums of Northern Ireland.

13 Kilmalkedar alphabet stone, Co. Kerry: this complex pillar stone is incised with a linear latin cross with 'C' scrolls at each terminal. Two texts are incised on its left side, dn̄ī for *Domini* 'of the Lord' and the Latin alphabet. © Robert Shaw, Discovery Programme, Dublin/ Dublin Institute for Advanced Studies.

14 Great Sugar Loaf, Co. Wicklow: this spectacular mountain dominates the landscape of north-east Wicklow and seems to have attracted ritual activity since prehistory. © Heritage Office, Wicklow County Council.

15 Illaunloughan, Co. Kerry: a monastic community lived on this tiny island during the seventh and eighth centuries. The island is dominated by a gable reliquary shrine. © National Monuments Service, Department of Arts, Heritage and the Gaeltacht.

Monastic life was determined by the canonical hours of the office. The best evidence for the practice of the canonical hours is found in the Antiphonary of Bangor, a late seventh-century codex written there c.680–91.[4] The codex contains the elements of the monastic office as celebrated at Bangor: hymns celebrating the saints and monastic observance there, versicles, and collects or concluding prayers with which each office ended.[5] This type of codex was commonly found in a monastery. Adomnán tells of the miṛculous recovery of a book of the week's hymns written by Columba with its satchel that had been left in water from Christmas to Easter.[6] On the basis of the office outlined in the antiphonary, and supplemented by information from the rule of Columbanus, who had been trained at Bangor, the monastic office at Bangor, and possibly at Iona, can be reconstructed. The daily hours, corresponding to the classical divisions of the day and night, were marked by the offices of *secunda, tertia, sexta, nona* and *vespertina*, all of which consisted of psalms, collects, communal prayer and, at vespers, the *Gloria in excelsis*. The two offices of nightfall and midnight were particularly long, as they consisted of twelve psalms, collects and devotional prayers. Matins (*matutinum, vigilia*) consisted of even more psalms (depending on the length of night and day in summer or winter), collects, canticles, the reading of the Gospel and the commemoration of the martyrs.[7] In a monastery following such a liturgical timetable, a monk's life was focused on the church building in which he spent much of his life, and his energy and mental capacity were undoubtedly affected by his ability to adapt to sleep deprivation and the chanting of lengthy offices.[8] Despite this hardship, Adomnán recounts episodes about the liturgy that convey the joy of feastdays and a detachment from the material world. Once, when he himself was returning from a synod in Ireland, he was delayed by contrary winds, but wished to reach Iona for St Columba's solemn feast (commemorating his death on 9 June). He prayed to the saint while waiting and, predictably, the wind dropped and he reached Iona after the hour of *tertia*. 'So we were able to wash our hands and feet before entering the church with the brethren to celebrate together the solemn mass at the hour of Sext [*sexta*], for the feast of St Columba and St Baithéne'.[9] On another occasion, Columba stopped the monks from going to work and asked them to prepare for Mass and a special meal, similar to that provided on Sunday:[10]

> The brethren were obedient to his words. That day was made a holiday, the preparations were made for a celebration of the sacred liturgy, and they all went to the church clothed in white as for a major feast. As they were singing the office, they reached the point where the prayer is usually chanted, which mentions the name of St Martin. Here St Columba suddenly said to the singers: 'Today you must chant "for St Colmán the

bishop"'. At this, all who were present realized that Bishop Colmán in Leinster, St Columba's friend, had gone to the Lord.

The eremitical tradition of a solitary existence in penance, fasting and praying was a long-standing component of monasticism that originated among the early desert fathers such as Anthony of Egypt. Ireland's monastic model was no different, and, although the early Irish eremitical tradition is often drawn on to justify a particular form of 'Celtic monasticism', this latter concept is a modern construct often based on romantic reactions to wild landscapes such as those at Skellig and Glendalough and also on a modern uncritical reading of early texts. Columba followed a strict eremitical life, often retreating from the community on Iona. The island of Hinba, somewhere in Iona's sphere of influence, was a smaller foundation given over to penitents, both lay people and members of the monastic community. Such was the lifestyle followed there that Adomnán mentions that, on one occasion, when visiting the island, he granted a relaxation of the rules about diet 'even for those living in penance'.[11] More extremely, Columba once went to live on Hinba, where he remained day and night locked in his house in solitude, neither eating nor drinking. In this state of physical deprivation and heightened mental vigilance, 'singing spiritual chants of a kind never heard before', the saint admitted that 'he was able to see openly revealed many secrets that had been hidden since the world began, while all that most dark and difficult in the sacred Scriptures lay open, plain, and clearer than light in the sight of his most pure heart'.[12] This description is a common topos, but it could also reflect the physical effects of sleep deprivation, extreme fasting and an existence in the dark on the human body. Mary Helms has delved into this aspect of early monasticism and paints a vivid picture of life as a monk in late antique and early medieval Europe.[13] Nocturnal liturgies held in dark and silent churches are natural conditions that have been long regarded 'as qualitatively charged circumstances and extraordinary periods of time when distant spiritual potencies of the universe draw nearer and people may reach out into the limitless shadows to contact unearthly powers and shadows'. For monks, therefore, the dark night was 'the most compelling time to formally acclaim in communal ritual (as well as in private prayer) the presence and the power of God'. Being deprived of sleep, especially core sleep, combined with fasting and repetitive chanting and deep meditation, could lead to a reduction in the natural human drives – thereby helping to reduce the desires of the flesh – and occasionally cause monks to experience euphoric states of bliss.[14] This sense of the deep darkness is wonderfully conveyed in Adomnán's account of Columba's death. The dying saint was alone in the church praying at the altar as the brethren were gathering for the midnight office:[15]

So Diarmait [Columba's servant] entered the church crying in a tearful voice: 'Father, where are you?' The lamps of the brethren had not yet been brought, but feeling his way in the dark he found the saint lying before the altar. Raising him up a little and sitting down at his side, he cradled the holy head in his bosom. Meanwhile, the monks and their lamps had gathered and they began to lament the sight of their father dying ... Then at once he gave up the ghost ... the whole church was filled with the sound of sorrowful lamentation.

In regarding Columba as their father, the monks were recognizing not only his sanctity but also his role as abbot, their spiritual guide and ruler. As monastic life became more institutionalized in the west from the fourth century onwards, the role of the abbot and his relationship with his community became more critical. St Benedict particularly emphasized the abbot's position in the monastery.[16] Columba, for example, disapproved of a monk travelling without his abbot's consent: Cormac Ua Liatháin was unsuccessful in finding a place of retreat because he brought such a monk with him on his voyage.[17] He frequently sent his monks on particular missions to Ireland and could relax rules as well as impose stricter conditions, as occurred when he and Baithéne visited Hinba and relaxed the rules about diet, even for the penitents on the island.[18] It is clear that Baithéne, his kinsman, was chosen by Columba to succeed him as abbot[19] and, during Columba's own abbacy, Baithéne (d. 600) was very active in the community. He was prior of the church of Tiree and, at one point, Adomnán describes him as *dispensator operum* 'distributor of tasks' during the harvest, and as a teacher and scribe.[20]

What of living conditions on Iona? What is known about diet, clothing, living quarters, interactions in the community and relations with the secular world? Fortunately, a number of excavations have been undertaken there, and archaeology can offer some insights into the practical aspects of the monastery at least from the seventh century onwards.[21] Buildings were made of wood and some were substantial and constructed using elaborate carpentry. Adomnán tells of pine trees and oaks being brought to Iona to build a longship and to be used as beams for the great house.[22] The most extensive building discovered to date was a round house 18m in diameter, a very large structure that may have functioned as a communal domestic building, in many ways similar to round houses built within large ringforts and crannogs. Adomnán relates two stories about a great round house being built at Durrow, described by him as a *rotundum monasterium* and a *magna domus*.[23] Given the close links between Iona and Durrow from Columba's own lifetime, it is likely that both monasteries were organized similarly. Large ditches were also uncovered in Iona, dating to at least the seventh century and, although not as spectacularly clear as the circular *vallum monasterii* (monastic enclosure) identified at Durrow, nonetheless, they were sizeable (2m deep and 3m wide) and enclosed certain parts of the monastery. Interestingly, there was no evidence of a bank, which suggests that the *vallum* was regarded not as defensive but as a physical marker of sacred space, be it the church or the whole monastic complex. Nothing of the early medieval church survives, although Adomnán's descriptions imply that the whole community could fit into it, and that it had some sort of side chapel or sacristy.[24] Apart from the church, graveyard, domestic communal buildings and animal pens, Adomnán mentions Columba's own separate dwellings and a guesthouse. Columba worked on his manuscripts in a hut supported by planks, which may have been located on the highest point on the island, Tòrr an Aba.[25] He slept and prayed in a different house.[26] Agricultural activities included rearing and butchering mixed livestock, especially cattle and pigs, clearing trees and growing cereals, mainly barley. As in so many early monasteries, milling was carried out on Iona: large millstones were used to support stone crosses and the pool-basin of a possible horizontal mill was also discovered.[27] Milling on Iona was probably for the community and, unlike at Nendrum, was not an industrial undertaking. There were metalworking, glass-making, wood-turning and leatherworking workshops on Iona, producing items such as wooden bowls and pails, glass millefiori, shoes and presumably boats. Despite its reputation for learning, no evidence for the production of vellum was found, nor were styli or slates present as they were at Nendrum.[28] Finally, excavation revealed the diet of the monastery's inhabitants, a mixed and not necessarily spartan diet that included red meat (beef, lamb and venison), seal, a variety of fish and seabirds.[29] Milk was available and there was a bakery: according to Adomnán, Genereus, the Englishman, was the monastery's baker.[30]

The overall impression gained from Adomnán's depiction of Iona, albeit probably a reflection of the seventh century, and from the island's archaeology and landscape, is that this was a busy community that was well organized and self-sufficient. Its community was ruled by powerful, but mainly considerate, abbots, and the life cycle of the monks was dominated by prayer, offices and work. The sea and wind were the dominant natural forces and they often caused grief due to drowning and limited Iona's communications with the outside world. The community was not at all as isolated as modern pilgrims might assume. It was part of a well-organized maritime network and as part of that network the monastery attracted novices, kings and pilgrims from Ireland and Scotland, most of whom would have been cared for in the island's guesthouse. Although cast in standard hagiographical tropes, Adomnán's sentiments towards Columba in the preface to his Life evokes admirably Columba's own ethos and that of his monastery:[31]

He [Columba] spent thirty-four years as an island soldier, and could not let even an hour pass without giving himself to praying or reading or writing or some other task. Fasts and vigils he performed day and night with tireless labour and no rest, to such a degree that the burden of even one seemed beyond human endurance. At the same time he was loving to all people, and his face showed a holy gladness because his heart was full of the joy of the Holy Spirit.

Clonmacnoise: a large, rural 'monastic' settlement and estate

A shift of authority from small family churches, monasteries and nunneries in cities and the countryside to large, rural monastic estates such as Lorsch and Fulda – the so-called *reichklöster* model – can be detected on the Continent between the seventh and eighth centuries. Matthew Innes, in his study of this phenomenon in the Rhineland, comments:[32]

> In 750 one went to the city to buy or sell, to encounter the sacred, to meet a patron – in short, for virtually any activity which could not be undertaken in the countryside. By 850 one could go to either the city or the monastery to engage in important business, the choice depending on what kind of business it was, and with whom one wanted to interact. This was an increase in social complexity, which led to a corresponding increase in the complexity of the settlement hierarchy.

Powerful patrons endowed the large monasteries, placed members of their kin in important positions in these institutions, and thus created great ecclesiastical lordships that owned land, people and smaller churches. Ireland was different in that there were no cities or towns – in the sense of Roman urban centres – and yet, a similar phenomenon to the large Rhineland monasteries emerged at approximately the same time. The resultant monastic settlements and estates were significantly distant in ethos from their coenobitic origins and the monastic life as lived on Iona in the seventh century – even if Iona participated in high eccleasitical and secular politics. A monastic community that followed some form of coenobitic rule existed in these large foundations, but they were mainly ruled by lay abbots and other officials who negotiated with secular rulers and administered estates and the settlement's income. Did Ireland experience an increase in social complexity in the seventh and eighth centuries, which in turn led to a corresponding increase in the complexity of settlement hierarchy? In an attempt to answer this question, it is worth focusing on one dominant site that is in many ways similar to places such as Lorsch and Fulda: namely, the great monastery of Clonmacnoise.

These large Continental monasteries were located at important strategic sites that also functioned as important social centres: Fulda, although depicted as remote and isolated, was founded on the site of Grabfeld, a likely Frankish centre of lordship, while Lorsch was an aristocratic centre at which public assemblies were held prior to the foundation of the monastery.[33] Clonmacnoise might be depicted as a wilderness surrounded by bogland and hemmed in by the River Shannon, but, in reality, its location was at a strategic point on the great river at the heart of a complex riverine transport network, and toghers (wooden roads transversing the bogland) and gravel roads.[34] Clonmacnoise sits on the line of the Esker Riada, a glacial ridge that runs east–west across the Irish midlands to the Shannon, while the discovery of extensive bridge timbers, some of which have been dated by dendrochronology to AD804, showed that the monastery was beside an important crossing over the river into the west.[35] Archaeological excavations revealed possible Iron Age activity in the form of an arc of post-pits in which the timber posts had rotted over time. There is no indication of the nature of this early activity, but it might be compared with much more extensive cultic occupation at Armagh,[36] and the prehistoric landscape located close to the royal monastery of Emly, Co. Limerick.[37] Politically, Clonmacnoise was in a region that faced changing circumstances throughout the early medieval period. The place-name, Cluain moccu Nóis (Nois) 'the meadow of the descendants of Nós' hints at a connection with an early people, the Nósraige (Noisrige).[38] They may have been Leinstermen, whose province held sway as far west as the Shannon to the seventh century. The Nósraige only left their mark on the place-name, and no trace of their influence can be detected in the monastery's history. Clonmacnoise was in the small kingdom of Delbna Bethra, whose own dynasty does not appear to have had much influence there either, but – to borrow a metaphor coined by F.J. Byrne regarding the situation – was dominated by 'that cuckoo in their nest, the monastery of St Ciarán at Clonmacnoise'.[39] From its foundation, the church became a large entity in its own right and was endowed by competing provincial dynasties who were aspiring to dominate the midlands and the riverine traffic of the Shannon, if not also the kingship of Tara. These competing interests are evident in the familial affiliations of a significant number of the monastic officials.[40]

Little is known about the founder-patron, Ciarán, despite the existence of Irish and Latin versions of his Life.[41] He supposedly died of the plague in 549, Christ-like at thirty-three. One tradition maintains that he belonged to the Latharna Molt, a kindred of the north-eastern Dál nAraide, who left a trace in the place-name Larne, Co. Antrim. It may be no coincidence that a group of

25 Early medieval memorial slab from Clonmacnoise seeking a prayer for Tuathal the craftsman. © Rachel Moss, Trinity College Dublin.

early abbot-founders reputedly originated from this part of Ireland, among them the slightly later Colmán of Lynally, whose kindred were the north-eastern Dál Sailne. If Ciarán was active during the first half of the sixth century, he belonged to the founding generation of monastic rulers in Ireland, a number of whom are commemorated with him as dying of plague in 549: Finnian of Clonard, Co. Meath, Colum of Terryglass, Co. Tipperary, Mac Táil of Kilcullen, Co. Kildare, and Colum of Inis Cealtra, Co. Clare. The obits may not be factually correct, but this cluster of founders suggests that, by this period, a network of foundations that differed from the earlier *domnaig* was coming to the fore. These were the teachers who formed the great abbots Columba and Comgall, as acknowledged by the founder of Iona when he visited Ciarán's brethren in Clonmacnoise during the abbacy of Ailither ('the pilgrim'), third abbot of Clonmacnoise.[42] The foundation's close links with royal dynasties from an early date manifests itself in the annalistic sources, in sagas, in hagiography and also in the large corpus of cross-inscribed slabs that have survived (fig. 25). Ciarán's royal patron was the equally shadowy Diarmait mac Cerbaill, king of Tara, a character who straddles paganism and Christianity in early literature, and who was the ancestor figure of the midland dynasties Síl nÁedo Sláine and Clann Cholmáin, powerful patrons of Clonmacnoise.[43] Similarly, western dynasties in Connacht used the monastery as a royal foundation and occasionally died and were buried there. One such king was Indrechtach son of Muiredach of the Uí Briúin Aí, whose powerbase was in the region around Rathcroghan, Co. Roscommon, and who died 'in pilgrimage' in Clonmnacnoise in 723 (ATig.). It would appear that from the seventh century the foundation incorporated a royal church (*eigenkirche*), an ecclesiastical estate and lordship, and a coenobitic community.[44]

By the seventh century, Clonmacnoise was actively seeking tributes from free churches that had early Patrician connections, or at least from churches which Armagh regarded as belonging to itself.[45] Tírechán complains that Cell Tóich, the episcopal church in the territory of the Temenrige in Cerae mentioned previously,[46] 'is (now) with the community of Clúain [Clonmacnoise], and the men of that place sigh'. In two centuries, this sacred landscape had been transformed from a prehistoric religious place of worship around the wells of Sine and Slán to the *túath* bishopric of the Temenrige, and then to a tribute-paying church subject to Clonmacnoise. In the kingdom of the Uí Ailello, one of the ruling dynasties of Connacht, Tírechán objects similarly to Clonmacnoise's acquisition of two other churches, Senchell Dumiche located at an assembly or burial mound of the Uí Ailello (Shankill, Co. Sligo) and Tamnach (Tawnagh, Co. Sligo). Senchell Dumiche was served by a priest, while Tamnach was an epsicopal foundation. Tírechán maintains that the bishop at Tamnach demanded nothing but friendship from the *familia* of Dumech, 'but the community of Clonmacnoise claims them, as they hold forcibly many of Patrick's places since the recent plague'.[47]

Clonmacnoise's interests west of the Shannon are reflected clearly in the origins of many of its abbots. The monastery's early abbots were recruited from a variety of places in Ireland – Leinster, Munster and Ulster. From the 680s, however, an increasing number of them originated from minor kindreds in Connacht – the Corcu Moga in Uí Maine (in east Galway), Gregraige of Loch Techet (around Lough Gara, Co. Sligo), Conmaicne Mara (Connemara, west Galway). During the eighth century, when ruling dynasties from Connacht, the

Uí Maine, Uí Briúin and Uí Fhiachrach, competed to exert their influence, Clonmacnoise was ruled by men from among these dynasties: for example, Cormac (d. 762) appears to have belonged to a branch of the Uí Maine and Murgal (d. 789) to the Uí Fhiachrach.[48] Such was the extent of its politicization that the annals (*AU*; ATig.) record that the communities of Clonmacnoise and Birr – on the border of Munster – fought a battle in 760 at Móin Choise Blae (a place-name that suggests that it was borderland (*blae*)). Clonmacnoise also fought against the community of Durrow in 764. These battles were part of a power struggle within the dynasty of the Southern Uí Néill whose kingdom of Mide stretched to the Shannon and, despite Connachta interests, included Clonmacnoise.[49] Conflict involving monastic communities is cited as evidence of different rules of engagement in Ireland and has been presented as a precursor to the rise of the coenobitic *céli Dé* movement in the ninth century. This latter group has been portrayed as a reaction to the worldliness of the 'old' monasteries. A comparative approach would suggest, however, that ecclesiastical foundations such as Clonmacnoise functioned as major players in the hierarchies of power operating in Irish society. This role is aptly summarized by Innes in his study of settlement hierarchy in the Middle Rhine Valley during the same period: 'Cities and monasteries were dominated by kings and aristocrats, nodal points in the topography of power'.[50] Once such communities acquired estates and interest in territorial struggles, and were also a source of manpower, they attracted the attention of kings and aristocrats. Clonmacnoise was at the heart of such a topography. If, however, the community of Clonmacnoise, or part of it, participated in violence and other struggles, a community following a devout life existed in the midst of this turmoil. Gormán, the successor of St Mochta of Louth, died there in 758. He was the father of Torbach, the abbot of Armagh who commissioned the Book of Armagh in 807. According to the Annals of Tigernach (a Clonmacnoise-oriented chronicle), Gormán died 'having lived for a year on the water of Fingen's well in Clonmmacnoise, and died in pilgrimage at Cluain'. His family's connection with Clonmacnoise was to endure, as Torbach's son, Áedacán, died there in penance in 834 and his son, Éogan, remained there and from him descended Meic Conn na mBocht, a hereditary family who were influential from the ninth to the twelfth century.[51] The predominance of grave-slabs apparently commemorating churchmen – some with names from an international Christian tradition such as Marcus, Benedict, Martin and Daniel – in the considerable corpus from Clonmacnoise attests further to the existence of this contemplative life,[52] although the structure of this life is not clear.

Modern excavations have been conducted at Clonmacnoise since 1977, and an overview of the results of this work presents a picture of a very busy

26 Clonmacnoise, Co. Offaly: a general view of the inner layout of the monastery with its medieval churches, round tower and high crosses. © National Monuments Service, Department of Arts, Heritage and the Gaeltacht.

settlement.[53] Apart from the ecclesiastical core represented in particular by the high crosses and probably associated wooden churches that were later replaced by stone buildings, evidence for daily economic and social activities abound (fig. 26). The River Shannon was crossed by a wooden bridge and there was a docking area near the river with a cobbled slipway. A metalled roadway running north-east–south-west was constructed towards the higher ground on which the churches and cemetery were located. Round houses with hearths and clay floors were uncovered, as were corn, drying kilns and ovens, metalworking areas and spindle whorls and needles indicative of weaving and sewing. Among the array of objects discovered were glass beads, worked bones, motif pieces and combs, dress pins, knives and animal bones, crucibles – one with a speck of gold – and one intriguing piece of fine plaster that may have been part of a fresco. Sherds of imported pottery bear witness to international trade, as might be expected from the site's riverine location.

The discovery of six male burials buried with beef ribs and oriented on the Cross of the Scriptures, that replaced some form of large wooden shaft or pole, prompted the excavator, Heather King, to speculate that these were either kings or important secular nobles.[54] The reigns of three kings of the period are crucial to understanding the nature of Clonmacnoise and the extent to which Irish kings regarded such places as part of their royal domain. In 820, Feidlimid mac Crimthainn seized the kingship of Cashel and, by 823, declared an alliance with Armagh when he brought Artrí mac Conchobair, successor of Patrick, to Munster to impose the law of Patrick there. Interestingly, the next entry in the Annals of Ulster records that Rónán, abbot of Clonmacnoise, resigned from his office in the same year. His resignation is probably linked to the increasing pressure exercised by Feidlimid on Clonmacnoise, which culminated in his candidate, Flann mac Flaithbertaig, a Munsterman of the Múscraige Tíre from down river on Lough Derg, being imposed as vice-abbot and probably abbot.[55] That Flann's title depended on Feidlimid's patronage must explain his violent demise. He was drowned in the Shannon by Cathal mac Ailello, king of Uí Maine, c.834 and Rónán was reinstated as abbot. But not before Feidlimid had left his mark on the church, its buildings and its estates. The dwellings and oratory of Clonmacoise's estate and masons' workshop at Gallen, Co. Offaly (*Galinne na mBretan*), were burned by Feidlimid in 823 and, in 826, he scorched Delbna Bethra, the small kingdom in which Clonmacnoise was situated. This was undoubtedly a hostile political move, but it also may have been expedient, as a famine and pestilence, and a resultant shortage of bread (*AU* 825: *magna fames 7 defectio panis*), was affecting the country. As often was the case, economic production hubs became targets during food shortages and functioned to feed armies or to shelter the general populace, which of course, must have caused considerable hardship for the settlement's inhabitants. Feidlimid's ambitions went beyond his own provincial kingship and he held a royal assembly (*rígdál*) in 827 with his rival Conchobar mac Donnchada at the church of Birr on the border with Munster, and long in contention with Clonmacnoise. This meeting did not deter Feidlimid in his ambitions, however, and, in 833, he killed members of the community of Clonmacnoise, and, in the words of the Annals of Ulster, 'burned their sanctuary (*termonn*) to the very door of their church (*co rici dorus a cille*)'. He did the same to the church at Durrow. For three consecutive years (833–5), Clonmacnoise was burned. By the 840s, it was attracting the attention of adventurer Vikings. Such attacks did not lead to any decline, but rather they were followed by expansion and a flourishing era for Clonmacnoise. As discussed earlier, the vernacular prophecy, *Baile in Scáil*, mentions that the Southern Uí Néill kings of Tara, Máel Sechnaill mac Maíle Ruanaid (d. 862) and his son, Flann Sinna (d. 916), were buried there.[56] Archaeological evidence is emerging that seems to corroborate the historical narrative that Máel Sechnaill, and especially Flann, were involved in reorganizing the settlement. The enclosing ditch, probably originally constructed in the seventh century, was backfilled sometime in the eighth or ninth century, and a more extensive enclosure was built to accommodate the expanding settlement.[57]

27 Base of the Cross of the Scriptures: a panel above the dedicatory inscription to Flann and Colmán depicts two figures placing a post in the ground. This may be symbolic of the king and the abbot or of their sixth-century predecessors St Ciarán, founder of Clonmacnoise, and Diarmait mac Cerbaill, king of Tara. © Rachel Moss, Trinity College Dublin.

Flann Sinna aspired to the kingship of Ireland, a kingship that his father had attained, but his own reign was not without opposition, particularly from the southern king-bishop of Cashel, Cormac mac Cuilennáin. Flann's ambitions were realized briefly in 908 when he defeated and killed Cormac at the Battle of Belach Mugna. His victory possibly provided the impetus for a large-scale building project at Clonmacnoise. The annals record that the stone church (*damliac*) of Clonmacnoise was built in 909 by him and by its abbot Colmán Conaillech. In his study of the various phases of the surviving cathedral building at Clonmacnoise, Con Manning has argued cogently that Phase 1, the greater part of the north wall and portions of the east and west walls built of yellow/brown sandstone and horizontally laid, can be dated exactly to 909.[58] The inscriptions on the monumental Cross of Scriptures (figs 27, 28, pl. 1), one of the finest high crosses in Ireland, seem to celebrate Flann and Colmán's achievements:[59]

28 Clonmacnoise, Co. Offaly: Cross of Scriptures close to the cathedral. The cross and church formed the core of the settlement that was endowed by powerful midland kings and their ecclesiastical allies. © Rachel Moss, Trinity College Dublin.

> ŌR DO RIG FLAIND MA ... MAELSECHNAILL OROIT DO RIG HERENN
> 'A prayer for king Flann mac Máelsechnaill, a prayer for the king of Ireland'
>
> ŌR DO COLMAN DORRO ... IN CROSSA AR ... RIG FLAIND
> 'A prayer for Colmán who made this cross for king Fland'

A panel above the inscription (fig. 27) depicts two figures – possibly a cleric and a layman – placing a post in the ground. This panel has been interpreted as an Old Testament scene or perhaps the episode in the Life of St Ciarán in which the saint and Flann's shadowy ancestor, Diarmait mac Cerbaill, king of Tara, set up the first post in Clonmacnoise. As pointed out by Elizabeth FitzPatrick, the scene is not unlike that on the later Mathilda Cross made for the nunnery of Essen between 971 and 982, on which Abbess Mathilda holds a processional cross with her brother Otto, duke of Bavaria and Swabia.[60] While that panel is later than the Clonmacnoise panel, the message is similar: it involves religious rite and symbolism and also a proclamation of authority. Mayr-Harting's observation regarding the impact of the Essen panel is equally applicable to the Clonmacnoise panel: 'The important consideration, however, is what effect this kind of art could have had on the self-confidence of the actual persons who ruled, on their sense of the canonization of their own authority'.[61] Where Flann and Colmán were concerned, they were stamping their authority, and therefore declaring their claims to dominant positions publicly, by reorganizing one of Ireland's most important churches. The Cross of the Scriptures was aligned quite spectacularly on the west doorway of the stone church (fig. 28). And while the episode in the Life of Ciarán might be dismissed as fiction, archaeological evidence has revealed that indeed the Cross of the Scriptures had replaced some type of monumental wooden post.[62]

If Clonmacnoise was the archetypal Irish monastery, with its busy lay and coenobitic life coexisting within one complex settlement, which was subject to the vicissitudes of ecclesiastical and secular politics and to good and bad economic cycles, Armagh, the primatial church in Ireland, represented an even more complex institution that laid claim to authority over the whole island.

ARMAGH: THE ROME OF IRELAND

In 697, Adomnán, ninth abbot of Iona, convened the leading kings and clerics of Ireland and Scotland to a synod in Birr at which he proclaimed his *Lex Innocentium* 'Law of Innocents' for the protection of all non-combatants – women, clerics and children – and church property.[63] This law in itself was remarkable, but so was Adomnán's authority in succeeding to gather together from such a seemingly fragmented society so many influential individuals. If the record can be trusted, the guarantor list is a reflection of the prevailing hierarchy at the end of the seventh century. The most senior king was Loingsech mac Óenguso, king of Ireland (d. 704), who belonged to the north-western Uí Néill dynasty, Cenél Conaill, and was Adomnán's fifth cousin and political ally. At the head of the list of clerics was Flann Febla mac Scannláin, learned bishop (*suí-epscop*) of Armagh (d. 715). Flann Febla was son of Scannlán mac Fíngin, king of Uí Méith, whose kingdom lay between south Armagh and the Co. Louth coast. Their name survives in the modern place-name Omeath. The Uí Méith were one of a group of northern dynasties known as the Airgialla, who rendered military service to the Uí Néill,[64] and who also rose to prominence when they took control of Armagh and the cult of Patrick. The Airgialla maintained their grip on the primatial church to the twelfth century through the authority of an ecclesiastical hereditary family, the Uí Sínaich.[65] But how did Armagh emerge to become the most important ecclesiastical seat in Ireland and to boldly declare itself a primatial see in the seventh century (as indeed Kildare did)?[66] What connection did Armagh have with Patrick?

Armagh's rise to prominence exemplifies the consolidation of a British missionary's cult into that of a national apostle,[67] and the absorption of small churches and their patronal families into 'the special union (*societas*) of bishop Patrick and the heir of his see at Armagh throughout Ireland'.[68] Ireland was not alone in going through a complex process of regulation that determined the balance of power between local and central authority in the church between the fourth and seventh centuries. For example, the Visigothic Iberian Peninsula witnessed such a process in the sixth century, during which authority was balanced between the remains of foci of Roman power – the *civitates* that had absorbed the original Iberian *oppida* system – and newly established foci, which were often ecclesiastical sees.[69] It is with that Iberian model in mind that Armagh's initial advance should be approached. In addition, the link created between regional and local kingdoms, churches and founders or patrons was a vital dynamic in Armagh's success in gaining a national status.

Armagh's proximity to the great mound of Navan Fort (Emain Macha) is often cited as the setting for the pre-Christian backdrop to its later development. Both sites were more closely connected, however, insofar as Armagh itself was part of the wider Navan landscape and had a prehistoric beginning.[70] The place-name, Ard Macha 'the height of Macha', Macha being a reflex of the sovereignty goddess, is testimony to the hill's position in this landscape. A remarkable map of Armagh made by Richard Bartlett in 1601 illustrates the undoubted connection between these two sites as the ancient roadway meanders past Armagh city over Legarhill (Mullaghcreevie), crosses the River Callan and past Navan Fort (pl. 9). Human activity from the Neolithic onwards has been detected in this landscape, most especially the late Bronze Age and early Iron Age, when spectacular ceremonies were enacted at Navan Mound, the King's Stables pool and Loughnashade. Not surprisingly, the configuration of the Navan landscape is particularly reminiscent of the Tara landscape. Excavations undertaken at Castle Street on the hillside south of St Patrick's Cathedral, Armagh, revealed the existence of a substantial V-shaped prehistoric ditch that may have enclosed an area of about 50m in diameter, with its centre to the south of the present cathedral.[71] This protective ditch changed function sometime during the fifth or sixth century when material from the outer bank was pushed back into the ditch and the latter was infilled. After that, a stone causeway was built, and debris from an early medieval metal-workshop was tipped into the ditch.[72] Another excavation at Scotch Street, a slight knoll on the east side of the city's hill, uncovered a small oval fire-pit containing a series of burnt deposits, one of which (layer 7: charcoal) dated to the third to fifth centuries and possibly beyond.[73] This activity was followed by burials, some of which might also date to the fifth century, but are more likely to have been inserted in the sixth or seventh century. This area has been equated with the place mentioned in early sources as the *fertae martyrum* 'burial place of the martyrs/saints'. One particular grave (Grave A) was noteworthy: it was wider than a normal grave but too short to contain an extended adult and the evidence suggests that the body was disarticulated and had been transferred from elsewhere. In addition, two squared wooden posts may have been placed over the grave as markers.[74] A burial of disarticulated remains has also been unearthed at the cemetery of Colp, Co. Meath, where the remains of a male adult (B161) were placed in a wooden box with metal corner-brackets and inserted into the outer edge of the bank of a penannular enclosure. The bone has produced a date in the fifth/sixth century.[75] The Armagh burial hints at the possibility that during this period a new focus was located around a 'special' and probably Christian holy grave. This was not exceptional and was happening throughout Christendom, not least in Rome itself. In the composite seventh-century text known as the *Liber Angeli*, probably made up of two parts, consisting of the foundation charter of Armagh and its claims over other churches, we find glimpses of the design and reconfiguration of the *urbs Alti Mache* 'the city of Armagh'.[76] Of course, it is a text that has to be read at different levels – the immediate description of Armagh's physical layout, its ambitious claims over the churches of Ireland and the privileges of its bishop as heir to St Patrick, the national apostle. Of the site, the angel said to Patrick:[77]

> The Lord your God knows that your present place which we see before us, placed high on the hill, is narrow and has (only) a small church (*cellula*), and is also hemmed in by some inhabitants of the region, and the surrounding territory (*suburbana eius*) is not sufficient to give shelter to all.

By the time of writing, the *urbs* was viewed as being divided in liturgy and space between three orders, virgins and penitents, and those serving the church in legitimate matrimony:[78]

> And these three orders are allowed to hear the word of preaching in the church of the northern district (*in aeclessia aquilonalis plagae*) on Sundays always; in the southern basilica (*in australi uero bassilica*), however, bishops and priests and anchorites and the other religious offer pleasing praises.

Like so many other churches in Christendom, Armagh had received the relics of martyrs from Rome:[79]

... it [Armagh] ought to be venerated in honour of the principal martyrs Peter and Paul, Stephen, Lawrence and the others. How much more should it be venerated and diligently honoured by all because of the holy admiration of a gift to us, beyond praise above other things (namely) that in it, by a secret dispensation, is preserved the most holy blood of Jesus Christ the redeemer of the human race in a sacred linen cloth, together with relics of saints in the southern church (*in sacro lintiamine simul cum sanctorum reliquiis in aeclessia australi*), where there rest the bodies of holy men from abroad who had come with Patrick from across the sea, and of other just men.

An addition to the *Liber Angeli* gives a fleeting glimpse of the liturgy performed at Armagh:[80]

A Rule of Prayer: On every Sunday in Armagh, when going to the shrine of the martyrs (*ad sargifagum martyrum*) and returning from it, namely, 'Domine clamaui ad te' to the end, 'Ut quid Deus repulisti' to the end, and 'Beati inmaculati' to the end of the blessing, and the fifteen gradual psalms. The End.

This offers a splendid image of the religious of Armagh sometime in the seventh century processing on Sunday to the southern basilica, which is likely to have been a small wooden church,[81] and venerating the shrine in which were kept the relics of Peter, Paul, Stephen, Lawrence and the linen cloth that preserved the blood of Christ.

Kildare's Cogitosus could claim that his church contained the sarcophagi of its patrons, Brigit and Bishop Conláed, 'adorned with a refined profusion of gold, silver, gems and precious stones with gold and silver chandeliers hanging from above and different images presenting a variety of carvings and colour'.[82] His contempories in Armagh could not make such a claim, even in their assiduous efforts to surpass Kildare or any other church in Ireland in primacy. As a note to Tírechán's *itinerarium* starkly admits about Patrick, that just like Moses, *ubi sunt ossa eius nemo nouit* 'nobody knows where his bones rest'.[83] Muirchú's seventh-century Life of Patrick, and a further supplementary note to Tírechán, claimed that the saint was buried in Dún Lethglaisse (Downpatrick, Co. Down) or close by in Saball (Saul, Co. Down) 'in the church near the sea'.[84]

Patrick himself makes no reference in his *Confessio* or *Epistola* to founding a particular church or being bishop of a *civitas*. If there is any sense of geography in his writings, it would point towards the north-east of Ireland and, indeed, it is in this part of the country that the earliest traces of Patrick's cult can be detected. In his important review of the early cult of St Patrick, Doherty demonstrates that the spread of his cult was 'much more embedded in the realities of late sixth- and seventh-century Irish politics than in assimilation to a pagan cult [of Brigit]'.[85] The early Patrician cult focused on the heartland of the Ulaid, one of the most powerful people in Ireland prior to the mid-seventh century. The Ulaid contended for the kingship of Tara until their king Congal Cáech, contender for the supreme kingship, was defeated decisively by his Uí Néill rival, Domnall mac Áedo at the Battle of Mag Roth (Moira, Co. Down) in 637. This battle began the process of the Ulaid being hemmed in to their north-eastern territories from that time onwards. It also signalled the strengthening not only of the Uí Néill, but also of their allies, the Airgialla, who moved to establish their authority in the southern territories of the Ulaid, including around Armagh. And, as Doherty points out, it is not surprising in this context that 'Armagh assumed the leadership within the Patrician cult from c.640 under the direction of the Airgialla'.[86] There were other factors that reinforced the cult at Armagh. While Patrick's body may have been buried in Downpatrick or Saul, Armagh seems to have had insignia belonging to him, at least by the seventh century.[87] But why would we not expect a Patrician church to be at Armagh from a very early period? If he was the missionary who converted the Ulaid and their subject peoples, then an early church dedicated to him in their most sacred landscape and ceremonial capital around Emain Macha makes sense. It also ties in with a pattern identified elsewhere in the country, as with Secundinus' church Domnach Sechnaill (Dunshaughlin, Co. Meath) at an entry point to the landscape of Tara or Sachellus' church at Baslick, Co. Roscommon, in the Cruachu (Rathcroghan) landscape. Furthermore, the *Liber Angeli* is very emphatic on the church's episcopal nature, and in its second part on the rights of its bishop, it opens with the phrase 'Further, concerning the honour of the bishop of Armagh, the bishop presiding in the see of the perfect pastor' (*Item de honore praesulis Airdd Machæ episcope praesedentis cathedram pastoris perfecti*).[88] Armagh's promotion of Patrick also follows the well-established model, especially in fifth-century Gaul and seventh-century England, of the rise of the cults of great bishop-confessors. Most significant and well-known among them were Martin of Tours, Germanus of Auxerre, two episcopal saints whose cults clearly influenced the Patrician cult, and Augustine of Canterbury, Chad of Lichfield and Cuthbert of Lindisfarne.[89] There could be no better description of this phenomenon at work in Armagh than Ian Woods' observation that in fifth-century Gaul the acquisition of a sanctified episcopal patron represented a defining element in the transition from town (*oppidum*) to city (*urbs*).[90] Armagh was not an urban settlement on the grand scale of Tours, but its proponents, if their perception of themselves can be understood from the language of the *Liber*

Angeli, used urban language (*urbs, suburbana eius, receptio archiepiscopi heredis cathedrae meae urbis, quipped ciuitas*) and built the cult of a bishop-confessor, and even more triumphantly of an apostle, around Patrick.

Once the cult was established at Armagh, how did it gain such momentum to eventually become the most important church in Ireland? The *Liber Angeli* sets out in its various (and not necessarily contemporary) parts the blueprint for expansion. From the very beginning, it speaks of Patrick in national terms of converting the Irish, not just certain people among them. Armagh is an *urbs* that needs to be expanded both locally and physically, and as an entity over the whole island:[91]

> Therefore a vast *termonn* [sanctuary] is being established by the Lord for the city of Armagh ... And further, the Lord God has given all the tribes of the Irish as a *paruchia* [ecclesiastical domain] to you and to this city, which in Irish is named Ardd Machae.

To accomplish this extension of its power, the bishop of Armagh sought to extract a tribute and lands from secular lords, free churches of the provinces, and monasteries of coenobites (*super liberas prouinciarum huius insolae aeclessias et uniuersis cynubitarum similiter monasteriis*).[92] One way in which to implement this policy involved the bishop of Armagh and his company going on visitations, and 'there shall be a worthy and fitting hospitality for each one [of his company], to the same number, as becomingly by day as likewise by night'.[93] Indeed, peripatetic bishops on visitations with their companies travelling throughout their *territoria* were a common sight throughout Europe.[94] The strictures for anyone not providing for the bishop of Armagh and his company and closing his house against him were severe: 'he shall be forced to render seven female slaves or, similarly (do) seven years' penance'.[95]

As elsewhere, relics and the attraction of relics to pilgrims was understood from an early stage in Armagh. It was a place of veneration of some of the church's most important martyrs – Peter, Paul, Stephen and Lawrence – of Christ himself, the linen cloth that preserved his blood, and of holy men from abroad who came with Patrick. Armagh had *insignia* belonging to the saint and undoubtedly used them as part of its bishop's visitations. Insulting or violating these *insignia* led to a fine of four female slaves.[96] How such relics were carried around the countryside can be deduced from the tiny decorated 'house-shaped' shrine and the remnants of a related satchel discovered beside the River Blackwater at Clonmore, Co. Armagh (pl. 12).[97]

Armagh claimed rights over many churches in Ireland, especially those classified as free churches, cities of episcopal rank and any place called

29 A seated figure of an ecclesiastic holding an open book with an inscription (currently illegible), probably from an earlier building and now located in Lismore Cathedral, Co. Waterford. © Rachel Moss, Trinity College Dublin.

domnach.[98] Such an extravagant claim caused dissension with great churches, including Kildare, which for a while made similar claims to primacy (as expressed in Cogitosus' Life of Brigit), Clonmacnoise and lesser churches. More than once does Tírechán reflect these tensions, especially with Clonmacnoise, over who should control early and declining lesser churches.[99] Muirchú's Life of Patrick, which depicts the saint as a triumphant hero, blazing a trail through the land, was written in the context of a lesser church seeking to be included under Armagh's jurisdiction.[1] Muirchú wrote his Life at the request of Áed mac Brocáin (d. 700) of the Leinster dynasty of Uí Bairrche, who, like the Ulaid, were in decline in that province in the seventh century. Áed was bishop, the church of Sleaty (Co. Laois), an old episcopal church dedicated to Fíacc, its first bishop, one of Patrick's reputed disciples, and an apprentice poet. The site itself overlooks a stream and is occupied by a later medieval church and plain high crosses.

Fortuitously, a series of additional notes and documents in the Patrician dossier (referred to as the *Additamenta*) relate the fortunes of Sleaty, its position in Leinster and its agreement (*audacht* 'testament') with Armagh.[2] Fíacc was consecrated as the first bishop of Leinster by Patrick and he established a church at Sleaty on land granted by Crimthann mac Énnai Cheinnselaig, a pseudo-historic fifth-century king of Leinster. Crimthann was baptized by Patrick there, the king granted it to Patrick, and he was finally buried there. This episode is a clear reflection of the fate of Sleaty in the seventh century: Crimthann was an ancestor figure of the Uí Chennselaig, a rising dynasty whose base was along the southern Barrow and Wicklow Mountains, and who along with the other rising – and initially more successful – dynasty, the Uí Dúnlaing, caused the decline of the Uí Bairrche. By attempting to link Patrick and the old church of Sleaty with Crimthann, some politically astute parties among the Uí Chennselaig and Armagh were forging a connection between Patrick and Crimthann, and hence between Armagh and the Uí Chennselaig. No doubt in response to this situation, and probably to the expansionist claims of Kildare, Áed needed to protect his claim and his dynasty's (the Uí Bairrche) claim to Sleaty. He went to Armagh during the abbacy of Ségéne (661–88) and offered Sleaty and his kin to Patrick:[3]

> Bishop Áed was in Sleaty. He went to Armagh. He brought a testament to Ségéne, to Armagh. Ségéne gave his testament back to Áed and Áed granted his testament and his kindred and his church to Patrick for ever. Áed left his testament with Conchad [bishop of Sleaty d. 692]. Conchad went to Armagh. Fland Feblae confirmed its meaning to him and moreover accepted him as abbot.

Here we catch a glimpse of how Armagh built her status in the seventh century. This was not a haphazard process, but was a form of administrative and legal agreement. It would seem that the key element of the agreement was that Áed's successors had to be affirmed in their office by the successors of Patrick. In return, it is possible that Sleaty was given resources by Armagh as stipulated in the *Liber Angeli*.[4] Whatever Armagh gained (a foothold in Leinster on the doorstep of Kildare), Sleaty did not flourish as a result: it remained an insignificant church that continued to function at a local level into the medieval period.

One of the remarkable intellectual discourses of early Christianity was the status and nature of Rome as *caput mundi* 'capital of the world' and *mater omnium ecclesiasarum* 'mother of all churches'. This debate was especially critical between the fifth and seventh centuries, when Constantinople, the imperial capital and 'New Rome', sought to claim an equal status to Rome as *caput mundi*. The decline of the empire in the West changed the balance between

East and West, and the papacy promoted the primacy of Rome on the basis that the apostles Peter and Paul made the city the *caput mundi* and centre of the universal mission of Christianity.[5] Ireland's conversion to Christianity was crucial to the expression that Rome's primacy was not built on an imperial identity or a geographically defined empire, but was dependent on the spiritual mission of evangelizing all nations. Indeed, Ireland's adoption of Christianity was regarded as a triumphant spreading of the gospel to 'the Western regions of the earth's farther strand' (*...in occidua transmundialis limitis loca*), in the words of Columbanus. As such, Christianity had spread over the whole earth and the Irish were bound to St Peter's chair (*devincti sumus cathedrae sancti Petri*).[6] A realization that they were subject to another powerful entity, Rome and the papacy, must have caused significant soul-searching in Ireland, an island that, although on the frontier of the Roman Empire, had not experienced either military intrusions or tax obligations. A new and parallel hierarchy and law were developing, which supplanted or absorbed whatever previous religious order had existed and which threatened the authority of kings and secular lawyers who administered this parallel legal system. The passion of the fundamental debates occurring in seventh-century Ireland is most clearly expressed in the so-called Easter controversy, which related to the cycle to be followed in celebrating Easter. The controversy generated a heated debate and also a series of synods, and led to at least two Irish delegations visiting Rome to seek clarification on various issues.[7] The need of Irish churchmen to appeal to Rome for assistance brought them closer to Rome and its emergent papal institutions, and in a sense they – and, more than anyone else, Columbanus – participated in the universal debate. Three documents offer us an idea of the ferocity, depth and implications of the Easter controversy and of Ireland's new relations with the world elsewhere. These are Cummian's letter to Abbot Ségéne of Iona and the hermit Béccán written *c*.631/3, the letter of John, pope elect [John IV], written in 640, and the *Liber Angeli*'s claim regarding Armagh and Rome.

Cummian's letter, c.631[8]

Cummian wrote his letter in Latin to Ségéne, abbot of Iona, and the hermit Béccán in defence of his standpoint and that of the heads of five major southern churches – Emly, Clonmacnoise, Clonfert, Mungret and Clonfertmulloe – that the Irish church should accept the Easter cycle of Victorius of Aquitaine. This was the practice observed in the Holy City. It seems that he, and others (sometimes known as the *romani*), had been censured for taking this stance, primarily by Iona. Following the process laid down in a canon of Innocent I, Cummian and his fellow religious in the south had deliberated on this doctrinal issue, convened a synod

and sent a delegation to Rome. The letter is a legal document replete with scriptural
and patristic reasoning, and canon law, which, as Walsh and Ó Cróinín point out,
show that Cummian had access to a large library containing texts such as the
decrees of the Nicene and Arles councils in their original form.[9] Cummian's
description of the synod and the Irish delegation's experience in Rome is a vibrant
depiction of Ireland and Rome at the time:[10]

> ... Therefore after a full year (as I said above), in accordance with
> Deuteronomy, I asked my fathers to make known to me, my elders (that
> is the successors of our first fathers: of Bishop Ailbe, of Ciaran of
> Clonmacnois, of Brendan, of Nessan and of Lugaid) to tell me what they
> thought about our excommunication by the aforementioned Apostolic
> Sees. Having gathered in Mag Léne, some in person others through
> representatives sent in their place, they enacted and said: 'Our pre-
> decessors enjoined, through capable witnesses (some living, some resting
> in peace), that we should adopt humbly without doubt better and more
> valid proofs proffered by the font of our baptism and our wisdom and by
> the successors of the Lord's Apostles'. Then they arose in unison and after
> this, as is our custom, they performed a prayer, that they would celebrate
> Easter with the Universal Church the next year. But a short time
> afterwards a certain whited-wall arose, pretending to preserve the
> tradition of our elders, who did not unite with either part but divided
> them and partly made void what was promised. I hope the Lord shall
> strike him down in whatever way he wills. Then it seemed proper to our
> elders, according to the command, that if disagreement arises between one
> side and another, and judgement vary between leper and non-leper, they
> should go to the place the Lord has chosen; and that 'if the matters are
> major', according to the sinodical decree, 'they should be referred to the
> chief of cities [Rome]'. Hence we sent those whom we knew to be wise
> and humble as children to their mother, and having had a prosperous
> journey through the will of God, some of them arrived at Rome, and
> returned to us in the third year. And they saw all things just as they had
> heard about them, but they found them more certain inasmuch as they
> were seen rather than heard. And they were in one lodging in the church
> of St Peter with a Greek, a Hebrew, a Scythian and an Egyptian at the
> same time Easter, in which we differed by a whole month. And so they
> testified to us before the holy relics, saying: 'As far as we know, this Easter
> is celebrated throughout the whole world'. And we have tested that the
> power of God is in the relics of the holy martyrs and in the writings which
> they brought back.

Cummian and his supporters bypassed Armagh as an arbitrator in the dispute, and sought counsel in Rome (*ad caput urbium*).[11] Yet Cummian was mindful of Patrick, whom he calls *papa noster*, and appealed to the saint's use of a particular Easter cycle to support his argument. Apart from the significance of this letter regarding the Easter controversy, it reveals that, by the seventh-century, the Irish church operated an effective organization that could convene synods to resolve disputes and, if no resolution could be found, that they were referred to Rome.[12]

Letter of pope elect John IV, 640

In his *Ecclesiastical History of the English People*, Bede includes the text of a letter addressed in 640 to senior Irish clergy and religious by the pope elect John [IV]. Like Cummian's letter, it dealt with the Easter controversy and an allegation that the Pelagian heresy – a heresy relating to original sin, redemption and grace promoted by the British monk Pelagius in the fifth century – was being revived among the Irish. John's letter is similar to Cummian's in its formality, but notably different in that he recognizes Patrick's successor Tomméne (Tomianus) (d. 661) as holding the most senior religious office in Ireland.[13] Doherty argues that this was a response from the papacy to an initiative by Armagh with other northern churches – in other words, a parallel to the move taken by the southern churches a decade earlier as described in Cummian's letter. John wrote:

> To our well-beloved and holy Tomianus, Columbanus, Cromanus, Dimnaus and Baithanus, bishops; to Cromanus, Ernianus, Laistranus, Scellanus and Segenus, priests; to Saranus and the other Irish teachers and abbots. Greetings from Hilarius, Arch-priest and guardian (during its vacancy) of the holy Apostolic See: John, deacon and (Pope) elect in the name of God: John, First Secretary and Guardian of the holy Apostolic See: and John, servant of God, Counsellor of the Apostolic See.
>
> Certain letters addressed to Pope Severinus, of blessed memory, remained unanswered at the time of his death. Therefore, lest any pressing matters should remain long unconsidered, we opened them and learned that certain persons in your province are attempting to revive a new heresy from an old one, contrary to the orthodox faith, and that in the dark cloud of their ignorance they refuse to observe our Easter on which Christ was sacrificed, arguing that it should be observed with the Hebrew Passover on the fourteenth day of the moon.

Aside from the complexity of the Easter controversy and the consequent association with Pelagianism, the pope elect's letter implies that the bishop and abbot of Armagh, Tómméne mac Rónáin, was viewed by the papacy as the head of the Irish church. He is followed by four bishops (Clonard, Nendrum, Connor and Clonmacnoise), four priests, some of whom were abbots (Movilla, possibly Bangor, Devenish and Iona), and Sárán úa Crítáin, *sapiens* of Tisaran near Banagher, Co. Offaly (d. 622).[14] Along with Cummian's letter, this document presents a fairly comprehensive picture of the mid-seventh-century structure of the Irish church, its procedures and its relations with Rome, which may have been difficult because of geographical distance, but were, nonetheless, intense and meaningful.

The final passage of the 'Liber Angeli'

The end of the *Liber Angeli* is unambiguous about Armagh's primacy and the legal route set down to resolve ecclesiastical contentions:[15]

> Further, any exceptional difficulty which may arise, (the law of which) is unknown to all the judges of the Irish (*ignota cunctis Scotorum gentium iudicibus*), is by law to be referred to the see of the archbishop of the Irish (*ad cathedram archiepiscopi Hibernensium*), that is, (the see) of Patrick, for examination by its bishop; if, however, such a suit in the said litigation cannot easily be decided there by the wise men, we decree that it is to be sent to the apostolic see, that is, to the see of Peter the apostle, who has authority over the city of Rome.

Armagh had assumed a primatial role in Ireland and viewed itself as the intermediary between the church in Ireland and Rome, by-passing other possible intermediaries such as Canterbury, which, at the beginning of the seventh century, according to Bede, was itself placed in a subject position to Arles by Pope Gregory the Great.[16]

Armagh: the growth of a powerful and wealthy entity

Once it had established itself as the primary church in Ireland by the end of the seventh century, Armagh grew to become one of the most powerful ecclesiastical, economic and political institutions in the country. The head of this church – variously its abbot, its bishop or increasingly, by the mid-tenth century, a non-ecclesiastical lay official[17] – negotiated with and challenged kings, travelled the country with the insignia of Patrick imposing the *Lex Patricii*, a form of ecclesiastical tribute, and administered far-flung estates. The settlement at Armagh appears to have expanded and to have been a planned space. While very little of the architecture of medieval Armagh survives, the city's striking street pattern is normally assumed to retain the lines of three enclosures surrounding the hill, with the main church on the top, the focal point of the settlement located within a double-ringed enclosure. The annals are replete with references to buildings and distinct subdivisions (designated as a *trian* 'a third') of the settlement.[18] The frequent conflagrations recorded in its early history undoubtedly were due to the density of wooden buildings on the hill, and were a facet of life that spared no one, including the abbot. In 823, for example, *AU* records that 'fire from heaven struck the abbot's residence (*foruth n-abbadh*) in Armagh and burned it', while the same chronicle records that in 912 many houses in the enclosure (*i rraith*) of Armagh were burned through carelessness. The year 996 seems to have been particularly disastrous, as a fire – recorded by some annals (*AU*; *AI*) as having been caused by lightning, and by others (ATig.) as having been started deliberately by a local king's son – swept through the whole settlement. ATig. provides the most graphic account:[19]

> Cairell's son, with the men of Fernmuige and the Airgialla, plundered Armagh and carried off two thousand cows, that is, Armagh was burnt, both houses and the stone oratory and the round tower and the sacred wood (*etir tigib 7 damliag 7 cloictheach 7 fidhnemidh*) . . .

A stone oratory stood in the settlement from at least the late eighth century, as a man was killed in 789 in front of the stone oratory (*in hostio oratorii lapidei: AU*). As to the various important houses in the settlement, apart from the abbot's residence, at least one king of Tara, the northern king, Áed Findliath, had a house there, as in 870 a man was killed in front of its door (*ante ianuam domus: AU*). In the southern part of the settlement, along with the abbot's residence stood a house of elections (*In Toí*), probably an early form of chapter house, a stone oratory (possibly the same one mentioned in 789) known as *In S(t)aball* and a kitchen (*AU* 916). The use of the word *s(t)aball*, borrowed from Latin *stabulum* 'a stall (for horses), a building', is the same term as in the place-name for Patrick's other church at Saul, Co. Down.[20] Part of the cemetery may even have been allotted to royal pilgrims, who frequently ended their lives in such places, as a marginal note in *AU* records that in 935 Conchobor mac Domnaill, heir-designate of Ailech, was buried in the cemetery of the kings (*in cimitero regum*) in Armagh. This royal cemetery's existence is corroborated by references to the burial of the kings of Tara, Áed Oirdnide, Niall Caille (d. 846) – drowned in the River Callan near Armagh – and, unsurprisingly, Áed Findliath in Armagh.[21]

Armagh in the late tenth or early eleventh century would have been a rather impressive sight. This was a busy settlement consisting of many imposing buildings, as suggested by this brief, but valuable, account in the Annals of Tigernach for 1020:[22]

> Armagh was burnt on the 3rd of the Kalends of May, with all its wooden churches (*cona durthigib uile*) except for the library (*tech screbtra*). Many houses in the trians were burnt along with great stone church (*in damliag mór*) and the round tower with its bells (*in cloiccthech cona clogaib*), the House of Elections (*Damliag na Togha*) and the Stone Church of the Staball (*Damliag in Stabuill*), and the preaching chair (*in cathair proicepta* – pulpit), and abundance of gold and silver and treasures besides.

If this description is in any way reliable, it begins to explain the range and intensity of activities that took place in early medieval Armagh.

Much of the modern commentary on Armagh has tended to centre on speculation as to whether it was primarily an episcopal or a monastic institution.[23] The abbatial list of Armagh gives the general impression that, until the early ninth century, the head of the community often combined the offices of abbot and bishop.[24] This was less frequent an occurrence from then on, as the office of the successor of Patrick became more economically and politically powerful, and was controlled by certain aristocratic families.[25] There were many exceptions to this pattern, and one way in which we can judge the different models of authority exercised there is to examine the careers of a number of prominent individuals, from various periods. The decades between 783 and 812 saw the emergence of some of these outstanding individuals and the interaction between them is a pen-picture of the complexity of power in early medieval Armagh. In 783, Dub dá Leithe mac Sínaich promulgated the Law of Patrick (*Lex Patricii* (Latin), *Cáin Phátraic* (Irish)) with Tipraite mac Taidc, king of Connacht, in the western province's ceremonial capital Cruachu. This was a provocative act on the part of both men. The king of Connacht was allying himself with an emerging faction in Armagh and challenging the authority of Donnchad mac Domnaill, king of Tara, who had allied himself with Iona and the *familia* of Columba. Dub dá Leithe's actions were directed as much towards the existing hierarchy in Armagh, whose authority he was usurping at a time of considerable disturbance there. No fewer than four abbots are mentioned between 783 and 795: Cú Dínaisc mac Con Asaich (d. 791), Dub dá Leithe mac Sínaich (d. 793), Airechtach úa Faeláin (d. 794) and Fáendelach mac Máenaig

(d. 795). In addition, Affiath, bishop of Armagh, died on the same night as Airechtach, the abbot. These were not the only sudden deaths recorded in Armagh during these unsettled years. Fáendelach died suddenly. He may have died of stress, as his position had been usurped by Dub dá Leithe and he managed to regain his abbacy on the latter's death. Waiting in the wings to challenge his successor Gormgal mac Dindagaid was Dub dá Leithe's son Connmach. That Connmach was successful in his ousting of Gormgal is apparent from his presiding in 804 over a very decisive meeting of the Uí Néill under the leadership of Áed Oirdnide, king of Tara, in Dún Cuair (Rathcore, Co. Meath), before Áed invaded Leinster and enforced the submission of the king of Leinster. Like his father, Connmach was clearly deeply involved in provincial royal politics and had allied himself with the northern king whose dynasty, Cenél nÉogain, was becoming increasingly influential in Armagh. He, like many of Armagh's abbots and bishops, belonged to the local aristocracy of the kingdom of Airthir, in which Armagh was located, a situation that often led to dynastic rivalry influencing succession to the headship of Armagh.[26] In any event, Connmach's attempts to establish an ecclesiastical dynasty did not succeed and he died suddenly – an annalistic euphemism for an unnatural death – in 807. It would take more than 150 years for his family, the Uí Sínaich, to gain control of Armagh and to maintain it until the twelfth century.

Armagh was not devoid of scholars and holy men. Following the turbulent years described above, two very different individuals came to the fore: abbot Torbach mac Gormáin (d. 808) and Nuadu, abbot, bishop and anchorite (d. 812). Torbach's abbacy was short-lived, but, despite this, he left an important legacy as the abbot who compiled the Book of Armagh with the scribe Ferdomnach (d. 847) and his assistants in 807–8.[27] This codex contains the fundamental early texts relating to St Patrick – the saint's own *Confessio* and *Epistola*, Muirchú and Tírechán's works, the *Liber Angeli*, and other additional notes belonging to the Patrician dossier. It also includes a copy of Sulpicius Serverus' Life of Martin of Tours, the New Testament and Pauline Epistles (fig. 30). Torbach's family and ecclesiastical background may have prompted him to produce this dossier, and may also have given him access to copies of these early documents. His father, Gormán, whom we have noted earlier as dying on pilgrimage in Clonmacnoise in 757, was the abbot of Louth. Mochta, the founder of Louth, was probably a genuine disciple of Patrick, and there is ample evidence to show that the apostle's cult was fostered there, and spread from

30 (*opposite*) The Book of Armagh (TCD MS 52): this manuscript was compiled during the abbacy of Torbach mac Gormáin (d. 808) by the scribe Ferdomnach (d. 847) and his school. It contains fundamental texts relating to Armagh and St Patrick – the apostle's own *Confessio* and *Epistola*, the seventh-century 'lives' of Patrick by Muirchú and Tírechán, the *Liber Angeli* and the Life of St Martin of Tours. © The Board of Trinity College Dublin, Trinity College Library, Dublin.

Peruenit uſque dē campo
Parthic addiminuit ǣuſ ⁊
ſed nazinin toiſēnunt adailich ꝗ
ꝓachtꝰ ꝫ indiuint illa cum uiri ·
iiii · ā iiii · cumtabuliſ humaniꝫ
ſcriptiſ monſ moyſuco ꝫelumuit
uint ꝫtielẜ ſuꝵ illoꝵ ut ꝑcoꝵ occidiꝫ
id iunt ⁊ gladier humaniꝫ hinc Adoca
dēidoꝵ hominiſ udiuit lignū ſdie aꝓ
illoꝵ ꝗ ſtinuoꝵ gladior iꝗamanuꝵ ad
effundendum ſanguinin uolunt multaꝗ
do ꝗ ma malꝫache ſtyꝓoꝵ ꝗ ꝓuitꝵn
myꝓ ꝗ ucoꝵuꝵ ꝑ illoꝵ hiſicaith nominē de
ꝗ nith nothi ꝑ i ꝓ iudichi ꝗ alidio do
ꝓ iꝗ iꝗ ⁊ bab illum ꝓut ꝗ ſtiadachu
ſiliſ ⁊ ilm molaine ſilum ꝓ iꝗ uico ⁊
ꝗ uuo cum ꝓ iꝗ uco adlꝫaidum xxx an
mſ ꝗ ondiꝗ ur illum inuiꝗbe ꝓ ma ⁊
dedit illi nō nouum ꝑachellum ⁊ ꝓ e
ſcriꝓ e illi librum pſalmoꝵ ⁊ iudiꝗ
ꝓ ſanuit abillo ꝑ achtūn dꝫ ielꝫ aꝗ
ꝑchuꝵ ꝑ auh launenti ⁊ ꝗ iſpani ꝗ ſimul
inmuichi Cuthacuſ ꝗ uaꝗ ⁊ ꝑ achell;
oꝵdinabant huſ ſtꝵꝓt diaconoꝵ ꝫlu
coꝵ ꝑū ꝗ ilio ꝓ iꝗ uich Incampo aſſ ⁊
Acceꝓ iunt illoꝵ ꝓ ut ꝫe miꝗ aꝗ ꝑ
ꝓ iꝗ uolyꝵ illiꝗ ꝯ ui iunt ad ꝑouinainſ
duci adauiꝗ imichi ad ꝑ aꝗ ieichum ⁊
ꝗ ſichunt ꝓ uinairinammonachoꝵ iꝗ pu
hiꝗ ꝓ iꝗ uai ꝓ uimiꝗ ⁊ dſ ꝯ ſniꝗ
ne ſi t ꝯ l uſ

Dicta ꝑ iꝗ uai

Timoꝵ eindiꝗ habin duein kʒiſiuꝵ ꝗ
ꝗ galliaꝵ aꝗ: Italiam cham iſ ꝓ liꝗ
ꝗ ſimin imam ꝗ uico dꝗ ꝗ iculo ꝓ euuiꝗ
ꝗ iſor adꝑ aradiſirum dō ꝗ iaꝗ aꝵ
delꝫ laria ꝓ eotoꝵi Immo nomanoꝵ
ut xꝓ iꝗ uam krauꝗ ꝗ omani ꝗ ꝫoꝵ urde
cantes uobiꝗ e h Oꝓ oꝵtet ut hora
oꝓ uationiꝗ uex illa laudabiliꝵ cuꝗ e
lꝫ ryon xꝓ e lꝫ ryon ommiꝵ · ad
ꝗ ſtiſſi mē canto Cyꝗ e lꝫ ryon xꝓ e
lꝫ ryon dō ꝗ iaꝗ aꝵ;

Tiꝓ echun ꝗ iꝵ li ꝑ euiꝗ ꝓ e ꝫeoꝵe ꝫ libꝓ e
ultain hniꝵ cuiuꝵ iꝓ e alumin: ꝗ diꝗ
puluꝵ ſuit

Huin · iiii · nomina inlibꝓ e ꝓ eꝵ iꝓ
ta ꝑ iꝗ uiꝗ uco uꝗ ultunim hniꝵ ⁊ diꝗ
buꝗ neꝗ eꝓ um ꝓ eſ inaꝗ oꝵuꝵ dꝗ: elauiꝵ
ꝓ ueccuꝗ uꝵ quiꝵ ꝑ iꝗ uiꝗ aꝗuꝵ cothinthaec:
⁊ ſirmuino · uir domiꝗ maꝗ oꝵ ⁊ eꝓ e
illum uinuꝵ ꝫeſi cun uaꝗ ꝗ iat miliue mae
cuboin maꝗ uꝵ ⁊ raumini illi · iiii · amſ
omni ꝗ ſuniꝵ int uedupli ꝗ labore · ꝓ ꝓoꝵ
cuꝓ uum ꝑoꝵ ſuit tum inmontaniꝵ ⁊ ual
liꝫꝫ Dundeꝗ uriꝗ ſitauit illa anꝗ uelluꝵ
diꝗ Inꝑ omiſiꝵ Incacuminiꝫ montiuꝵ ꝑ eiſ eo
iꝗ ueu montin miſi ꝗ ſintuaꝵ anꝗ uelꝗ ꝑ in
tenua ꝯ ꝯ nauiꝗ illa paꝵ atu ꝗ unꝫeꝗ e
rabulu ⁊ ꝗ eꝯ uꝵ iꝵ uillo inllelum ꝓ uꝵ
ꝑ eꝵ it ꝗ ambulauit ꝫ uꝗ illi anꝗ uel: dū
uictoꝵ nominē heun ⁊ tuꝵ uuꝵ anno
captuꝵ ducituꝵ uꝗ dicituꝵ inhithnum In
xꝓ en anno ⁊ iariꝗ laboꝵ uꝵ maꝗ uꝵ ꝑ elinꝗ
ne potuit iii ⁊ auꝵ anniꝵ ꝓ ambulauit
⁊ nauiꝗ ant inꝑ luceꝫꝫ; ⁊ incampiꝵ ꝓ uꝫꝫ
locuꝵ ⁊ Inconuallꝫꝫ montaniꝵ ꝑ ꝗ galliaꝵ
aꝗ: Italiam totum aꝗ uꝗ ſ ꝓ oꝵ iꝵ ꝗ ꝗ iunt
Inmaꝗ i ꝗ ſico uꝵ ꝑ e dē incommemoꝵa
tioneꝫ laboꝵ Eꝓ ath Inunu ꝫeiꝓ ehꝗ e
ꝗ dē apalanchiꝵ ꝵ uinniꝵ xxx mihitꝵiꝵ
tuꝵ unt ultano ꝗ iꝓ eo Omniaꝵ ꝗ ꝗ euꝗ e
niꝵ uunt Inuthichthꝵ Inplana illuꝵ hiꝵ
toꝵꝗ a ꝓ eꝵ iꝓ tu H ꝗ ꝑ enouiſimal
luiꝵ mirabilia Inuꝵ ꝑ eꝗ iꝗ anno loiꝗuꝵ uꝵ
iꝗ nall ſinita aꝗ uꝗ ꝑ elicit ſacin
Aꝑ aꝵ ſione h ꝵ xꝓ ꝵ ii collꝗ eꝗ inuꝗ e cccc ꝗ ꝗ iii
uꝗ uꝵ aꝗ: Admoꝵ tein ꝑ iꝗ uiꝗ uai Duob ꝵ uꝗ ꝵ
iu · anniꝵ ꝑ eꝗ nanu loiꝗuꝵ e ꝗ m011tin
ꝑ iꝗ uiꝗ uai Omniꝵ h ꝵ ꝑ eꝗ uꝵ illuꝵ uimꝵꝗ e
xꝓ en uꝵ ꝑ utantuꝵ iꝵ cuehon ⁊ inꝑ olu
ꝗ int uꝗ ꝑ euꝵ cuꝯ galliꝵ ad inꝑ oluꝵ mac
oꝓ iſtrali ꝗ dū inꝑ ola ꝑ iꝗ uai ⁊ ꝗ eꝯ um ꝑ iuo
miꝗ utudo ꝗ iꝓ eopoꝵ um ꝵ eonꝵ ꝗ ꝑ ꝑ iꝵ i ꝗ iaco
noꝵ ꝗ ſe oꝵ oꝓ erant hoꝵ ꝗ mer inum loe
ꝯ ꝗ ꝗ

Louth to the Continent in the seventh century with the missions of the brothers Fursa (d. 649) and Foillán (d. 655) to Péronne and the Merovingian court at Nivelles, respectively. Indeed, Torbach may have used his position in Louth and the traditions of that church to gain access to the headship of Armagh.[28] His son Áedacán (d. 835) was also abbot of Louth, and like his grandfather Gormán, died in Clonmacnoise. At a later period, their descendants, known as the family of Conn na mBocht, became a very powerful ecclesiastical dynasty in Clonmacnoise.

Three years after Torbach's death, we find Nuadu, abbot and bishop of Armagh, ostensibly trying to impose Patrick's Law on Connacht again by bringing the saint's relic-casket into the province (AU 811). That this event was not sanctioned or approved of by the aristocracy of Armagh can be detected from the comment in the Tripartite Life of Patrick that in fact Nuadu had released Connacht from their obligations to Patrick's heir: 'That they are not given to them is a matter of deep regret to the community of Patrick'.[29] So, why did the abbot of Armagh look so favourably on Connacht? He himself was from Connacht and, therefore, was an intruder into the abbacy. He is commemorated in the church of Eastersnow (Dísert Nuadat), Co. Roscommon, and it is likely that, apart from possibly being a reformer, he was supported in his intrusion in Armagh by the king of Tara, Conchobar mac Donnchada, and the king of Connacht, Muirgius mac Tommaltaig (d. 815).[30] While Cruachu is not mentioned as the place where Nuadu brought St Patrick's relic-casket, it is most likely that, as in 783, this was the location for his momentous release of Connacht from its dues. We can imagine Nuadu's retinue travelling through the countryside from Armagh to Cruachu: if there is any truth in the Liber Angeli, as abbot and bishop of Armagh on a visitation, he could have had up to a hundred in his retinue:[31]

> If this said bishop, in the evening, comes to a place where his reception has been provided, he shall be given once a worthy refection for the said number of a hundred guests, with fodder for their animals, not counting strangers and the sick and those who abandon infants at the church and the rest, whether outcasts or others.

This large crowd probably travelled on horseback, by foot and by chariot. There are many instances of high ecclesiastics such as Nuadu travelling in chariots and depictions on the bases of high crosses of chariots and horsemen with an individual processing ahead of them carrying a cross are likely to replicate genuine scenes of the period. Nuadu and his company were probably accommodated on their journey in ecclesiastical settlements, by local kings or

31 Muiredach's Cross, Monasterboice, Co. Louth: general view. The inscription at the base requests a prayer for Muiredach who erected this cross, and this is likely to refer to Muiredach mac Domnaill, abbot of Monasterboice and deputy abbot of Armagh (d. 924).

most likely by professional hospitallers (*briugu* sg.). The laws maintain that a *briugu*'s status depended on, among other stipulations, possessing a dwelling on a public road and that the wealthy *briugu leitech*'s house was situated at the meeting of three roads.[32] If Nuadu's mission to Connacht led to an assembly being held at Cruachu, no doubt roads would have been cleared and existing monuments at the ceremonial capital would have been adapted to use for the event, as is evident from excavations at the Knockans in Tailtiu (Teltown, Co. Meath), where a prehistoric monument was refurbished and reused at intervals until the tenth century.[33]

One of the most spectacular legacies of Armagh and its aristocracy in the Irish landscape is the early tenth-century high cross known as Muiredach's Cross at Monasterboice, Co. Louth (figs 31, 32). This cross represents the pinnacle of Irish sculpture of the period and was clearly erected as a symbol of authority as much as a reflection of Christianity. It is assumed that the inscription at the base, which credits its erection to Muiredach, is a reference to Muiredach mac

32 Muiredach's Cross, Monasterboice, Co. Louth: the image of Christ in Majesty from one of the most monumental high crosses in Ireland. The image of Christ in Majesty depicts the Last Judgment. St Michael is weighing the souls under Christ, who is holding a cross and a tau crozier. © Rachel Moss, Trinity College Dublin.

Domnaill, deputy abbot (*tánaise abad*) of Armagh 'chief steward (*ardmáer*) of the Southern Uí Néill, and successor of Buite mac Brónaig [founder of Monasterboice], chief counsellor (*cenn adchomairc*) of the men of all Brega, both laymen and clerics' (*AU 924*). Monasterboice's links with Armagh were particularly close in the mid-ninth century, when Éogan Mainistrech (d. 834), *fer léigind* 'lector' of Monasterboice and abbot of Clonard, struggled to hold on to the abbacy between 827 and 834. He was imposed in Armagh with the support of the northern king, Niall Caille of the Cenél nEógain (d. 846), but met with considerable opposition from the local over-king of the Airgialla, Cummascach mac Cathail, who tried to maintain his own half-brother, Artrí mac Conchobair, in his abbacy. Éogan Mainistrech, who deposed Artrí in 827, also had to contend with a hostile king of Tara of the Southern Uí Néill, Conchobar mac Donnchada (d. 833), who in 831 captured his company (*a muinnter*) and stole his horses. As if that was not enough, in the following year (832), Éogan Mainistrech had to contend with three Viking raids in one month. He died in the following year.

Muiredach, as deputy abbot of Armagh and abbot of Monasterboice, was subject to the powerful Máel Brigte mac Tornáin (d. 927), who ruled both Armagh and the Columban monastery at Kells for more than two decades.[34] That both men were involved in erecting monumental crosses, as clear statements of their authority, is suggested by the inscription on the Tower Cross at Kells, which reads PATRICII ET COLUMBE CR[UX], which is thought by Roger Stalley to refer to Máel Brigte.[35] In these crosses at Kells and Monsterboice, as well as in the contemporary Cross of the Scriptures at Clonmacnoise, we see the lasting imprint of some of the most powerful ecclesiastics, kings and aristocracy of tenth-century Ireland.

Dub dá Leithe mac Cellaig: an abbot above kings

No abbot of Armagh wielded more power than Dub dá Leithe mac Cellaig, who assumed office in 965 by replacing the incumbent Muiredach mac Fergusa and who continued to be influential until his death in 998. Dub dá Leithe was born into an ecclesiastical hereditary dynasty: he belonged to Uí Sínaich, local nobility who had held the abbacy of Armagh in the late eighth/early ninth century (see above). His mother, Deolaid daughter of Máel Tuile, came from the church of Inis Caín Dega (Inishkeen, Co. Monaghan).[36] He and his immediate family formed a ruling elite in Armagh throughout the late tenth century, his brothers, Conaing (d. 981) and Muiredach (d. 984), serving as *fos-airchinnech* (lay administrator) and *fer léiginn* (lector), respectively. A third brother, Eochaid (d. 1004), known as Eochaid úa Flannacáin (taking their grandfather's patronymic), was a master poet and traditional historian (*suí filidechta 7 senchusa*) who also seems to have been head of the guesthouse. Through the line of Eochaid's son, Máel Muire (d. 1020), Clann Sínaich held onto the abbacy of Armagh without break until the 1130s.

Dub dá Leithe derived his power not alone from his family's grip on the main offices in Armagh but also from his alliance with the king of Tara, Domnall úa Néill (d. 980), whose northern dynasty, Cenél nÉogain, retained huge influence in the church. Domnall even went to Armagh to die. For fifteen years, Dub dá Leithe and Domnall ruled contemporaneously and they both attempted to extend their authority over the whole island. Domnall, for example, pursued a particularly aggressive policy towards the midland and eastern Uí Néill dynasties of Brega and Mide, and also against the Viking king of Dublin, Amlaíb (Olafr) Cúarán son of Sitric (d. 980). However, given the complexities of military and political alliances in tenth-century Ireland, Domnall's possible collaboration with Dub dá Leithe did not preclude him from attacking four of Armagh's dependent churches – Louth, Dromiskin, Monasterboice and Dunleer – in 970. Two particular incidents during Dub dá Leithe's abbacy highlight his essentially greater power than Domnall's, insofar as he could impose his authority much further afield, and this included a king of Tara submitting to him. In 973, he went on a visitation to Munster to demand Armagh's tribute from that province. As might be expected, the most senior ecclesiastic in Munster, the successor of Ailbe of Emly, challenged Dub dá Leithe's authority to raise the levy and they quarrelled over it. Peace was made between them by the ambitious and calculating king of Munster, Mathgamain mac Cennétig (d. 976), 'and they agreed upon the perpetual right of [the coarb of] Patrick'.[37] This was a clever move on the part of Mathgamain, Brian Bórama's brother, who, by allying himself with Dub dá Leithe, was bolstering his dynasty's ambitions. Mathgamain's people, the Dál Cais, had risen from relatively modest origins around the Shannon, had taken advantage of the Norse settlement at Limerick, and had seized the kingship of Munster from the Éoganachta dynasties who had controlled it since the seventh century.[38] Mathgamain was killed in 976 by the Éoganachta and their allies, but these were to face an even more skilful enemy in his brother Brian Bórama. In the event, Brian continued Mathgamain's alliance with Armagh. In 1005, his confessor, Máel Suthain, noted in a flourish reminiscent of Ottonian practice, in a marginal note in the Book of Armagh:[39]

> Saint Patrick, when going to heaven, decreed that the entire fruit of his labour, as well as of baptism and of causes as of alms, should be rendered to the apostolic city which in the Irish tongue is called Arddmacha [Armagh]. This I have found in the records of the Irish. [This] I have written, namely Caluus Perennis [= Máel Suthain], in the presence of Brian, Emperor of the Irish (*imperator Scotorum*); and what I have written he has determined on behalf of all the kings of Maceria [Cashel, the provincial capital of Munster].

It was on this occasion that Brian is reputed to have left twenty ounces of gold on the altar of Armagh and he was buried along with his son Murchad after the Battle of Clontarf in 1014 in a new tomb in Armagh (*AU*).

If Dub dá Leithe had mutual interests that he fostered with Domnall úa Néill, and with Mathgamain mac Cennétig, his relations with the next king of Tara, Máel Sechnaill mac Domnaill, were not always easy. The most dramatic incident between the two men occurred as a result of their being on opposite sides in a dispute between the kings of Conaille and north Brega, kingdoms within the immediate spheres of influence of both Armagh and Tara. The chronicle *Chronicon Scotorum* records that in 986

The shrine of Patrick was taken by Máel Sechnaill at Áth Ferdiad [Ardee, Co. Louth] to Áth Sige [Assey, Co. Meath] on account of the war of Cairellán's son [king of northern Brega]. Peace was made by them afterwards, and Patrick's due yielded by Máel Sechnaill i.e. the visitation of the men of Mide both church and laity; a feast from every fortress from Máel Sechnaill himself, along with seven cumals [female slave = unit of currency] and full dues as well.

Máel Sechnaill took the shrine of Patrick away from Armagh's core territory and into his own royal demesne near Tara, presumably as a ransom in his bargaining with Dub dá Leithe. It would seem, however, that the abbot got the better of the king and forced him to render his full dues to Patrick and Armagh. Dub dá Leithe ended his long career with his installation as successor of Colum Cille in 989 and his handing over – perhaps in an acting position – of the abbacy of Armagh to Muirecán mac Ciaracáin from Both Domnaig (Bodoney, Co. Tyrone). Muirecán's conferral of kingly orders (*coro erlegh gradh righ*: AU) on Áed son of Domnall úa Néill and also his great visitation (*mórchuairt*) of the north of Ireland, can only mean that he was placed in the abbacy by Áed's dynasty of Cenél nÉogain. Dub dá Leithe died in 998. Muirecán was set aside in 1001 and replaced by Dub dá Leithe's nephew (Eochaid úa Flannacáin's son) as abbot of Armagh. Dub dá Leithe's career epitomizes the dominant stature of early medieval abbots of Armagh, a status that, to a certain extent, surpassed that of any king in Ireland.

THE CHRISTIAN RELIGIOUS EXPERIENCE OF THE LAITY

Models of pastoral care

The text known as 'The teaching of Máel Ruain', which was written in Irish sometime between 815 and 840, is a dossier of the customs and codes of conduct of Máel Ruain (d. 792), the abbot-bishop of the monastery of Tallaght (Co. Dublin), associated with the religious movement commonly known as *céli Dé* 'clients of God'.[40] An episode in this text relates how Caínchomrac, a bishop of the Déise, was with Dublitir (d. 796), an eminent cleric of Finglas (Co. Dublin), when they encountered a poor woman who asked Dublitir to allow her to join the nuns under his rule. The story continues:[41]

Dublitir grew weary of her entreaties and spoke to her roughly, saying: 'Be off now, may you have no luck!' On hearing these words bishop

Cainchomrac immediately bowed himself to the ground. 'What is it Cainchomrac?' said Dublitir. 'Pity', said Cainchomrac, 'it is a terrible act that you have done, to revile the wretched woman'. Then Dublitir bowed himself. 'I will offer what you judge to the poor woman and to God for what I have done', said Dublitir. 'This is my judgement', said Cainchomrac. 'You will allow the poor woman among the devout women, or give her a milch cow and a garment, so that she will be able to survive without their help. And I will further consider what penance is proper to administer to you for the sore abuse and scorn you meted out to the poor woman'. 'I will do so', said Dublitir, 'and will perform all these things according to your will'.

This episode encapsulates many fundamental aspects of early medieval Irish society: its clear class divisions, the elitism of many clerics, and the opposite saintly and charitable mentality of others. It also deals with the abject poverty of many and their dependence on the church for sustenance. This group of texts, identified by Wesley Follett as the 'Tallaght memoir',[42] frequently mentions providing for the poor or making provisions 'if there chanced to be famine in the land'.[43] The most important feature in this episode, however, is the depiction of the relationship between the ascetic and eminent Dublitir and the poor woman. How can the experience of Christianity by these two extremely different classes be detected in historical sources, art and archaeology? And more significantly, how can we measure the extent to which Irish society in general related to Christianity once the process of conversion was successful? This discussion is in essence a continuation of the consideration of the earlier belief system supplanted by Christianity and its survival in an ostensibly Christian society. Having considered the church from within its various hierarchies of authority, it is appropriate to reflect on the experience of the rest of society.

The extent and nature of pastoral care in the early Irish church is a topic that has featured only relatively recently in scholarly discourses. This trend has been due mainly to a concentration on the apparently dominant monastic characteristics of the church, as opposed to its seemingly less significant episcopal characteristics.[44] In recent decades, scholars, most notably Richard Sharpe and Colmán Etchingham, have reassessed in considerable detail how the church was organized and have emphasized the greater role played by bishops in its administration. They have reviewed critically the earlier received scholarship that was based on a dominant and schematic monastic model. Sharpe reinstated the role of the bishop and adopted a different view of the church's ministry, arguing that basic pastoral ministry was undertaken in small single-priest churches which were probably dependent on collegiate or monastic churches. These were similar to the minsters of Anglo-Saxon England. Bishops often lived in these 'monastic' communities, but were not always heads of their communities as these could have been in the hands of clerical abbots following a monastic rule or, increasingly, as we have seen with Armagh, under the jurisdiction of lay 'abbots' (using the common titles *airchinnech* or *princeps*) who controlled the temporalities of the particular church (the income and services due from land, tenants and tithes). The bishop performed the sacraments, ordained priests, consecrated churches, and undertook visitations of churches under his jurisdiction.[45] In a wide-ranging and detailed assessment of the church from 600 to 1000, Etchingham covered all aspects of authority and ministry using annalistic, canonical and legal texts.[46] In the sphere of pastoral care, Etchingham argues for the existence of a 'paramonastic Christian elite' who were closely bound to their churches 'as recipients of more or less frequent pastoral care and, correspondingly, as payers of regular dues'. These people were the frequently mentioned *manaig* (sg. *manach*), a term borrowed from Latin *monachus* 'monk', that came to be used in a wider sense than its original and even modern meaning. Etchingham regards *manaig*, the 'paramonastic' class, as living under a regime of perpetual, perfective penitence, who were converted from the ways of the world. If this model of pastoral care had been the sole model, then the majority of the population would have been left to live lives virtually ignorant of Christian practice.[47]

The sources: the rules of lawyers and zealots

Before it is accepted that this was the fate of the greater part of society, we need to take stock of who wrote our sources and who were the audiences. There are many Irish and Latin prescriptive texts of the period that set out to regulate the various sections of the Christian population and to guide them away from sinful lives. They consist of pentientials, canon laws, synods, edicts and secular laws.[48] Many of their strictures concentrate on sins of perceived sexual deviance, gluttony and violence, as well as on the proper administration of spiritual and temporal aspects of the church. Their relative complexity, and also their common use of Latin with quotations from the Old Testament, scriptures, church fathers and earlier authorities such as Uinniau and Columbanus, must represent the pastoral and legislative outlook of literate and influential religious. The degree to which these strictures extended throughout society in general is difficult to measure, and indeed the dependence on these sources by scholars attempting to grasp the normal Christian experience in early Ireland has directed the debate constantly back to legal and institutional considerations. But were these texts relevant to an elite few: those in orders; those following a rule; kings; nobles and *manaig*? Or did their strictures filter through to even the lowliest in society? And, rather than concentrating on the immediate concerns of their authors, can we imagine the tangible influence of certain rules on the daily lives of various groups in society?

The *céli Dé* or 'Tallaght dossier' was primarily directed towards communities who had decided to follow a particularly severe form of ascetic life. Many of its precepts are common to universal monastic rules, and relate to conduct of the liturgy, dietary regulations, forms of physical and spiritual penance, relationships within the community itself, and relationships with the wider world. The world was divided between the *céli Dé*, the general clergy (*áes gráid* or *áes uird*), the laity (*áes túaithe* 'the people of the *túath*'), penitents (*áes phenidi, áes aithrige*) and the dead. While many of the injunctions detailed are somewhat dreary and lack human warmth, occasionally the reality of life intrudes. Cooks, dairymaids and servants needed to be watched and punished frequently 'because they used to waste much of the produce, both milk and corn'.[49] Máel Ruain of Tallaght forbade his community to seek news from those who visited them on business, 'because great is the harm that is done and the disturbance that is caused by such news to the mind of him to whom it is told'.[50] They were not to drink the local ale of Cualu nor drink anywhere near Tallaght, but could do so in other parts at a distance from Tallaght – a particularly severe restriction as the ale of Cualu is often praised for its fine quality and was the special reserve of the kings of Leinster.[51] Despite their ostensible comfort with death and passing on to Paradise having lived a good life, perhaps the *céli Dé* retained elements of the fear of the dead that were more prevalent among the general populace:[52]

> The food that is in a house when any one dies in it ought to be blessed and distributed among the poor: because food ought not to be kept in the same house with a sick man, or eaten in the same house with a dead man, however holy he may be.

This practice could be the equivalent of the customary funeral feast, which probably continued among the laity at the burial of a family member. Another explanation might have been the very practical consideration that sickness or death could contaminate food, and cause disease. Women get little notice in many of these texts except for their roles as wives who should abstain from sexual activity with their religious spouses or in the ever-present role of temptresses. And yet even in the harshest of rules, such as the seventh-century Penitential of Cummean, the tenderness of human relationships could occasionally be conveyed:[53]

He [a cleric or monk] who loves any woman, (but is) unaware of any evil beyond a few conversations, shall do penance for forty days. But if he kisses and embraces her, one year … He who loves in mind only, seven days. If, however, he has spoken but has not been accepted by her, forty days.

Similarly, the distress and dangers of childbirth, which must have been such a regular occurrence, slip into the Rule of the Céli Dé and even though the language is prescriptive, the situation recalled is graphic:[54]

When disease attacks a pregnant woman so that she is near to death, the baptismal service is read aloud over water, and the woman makes confession on behalf of her unborn child, and the name of Flann or Cellach is given to it (each of these being common to man or woman), and let the mother drink the water, so that it passes over the child and this constitutes baptism for it.

The complications of married life and potential unhappiness and adultery are constant themes in this literature, which has an overriding aspiration for monogamous relationships. A moral tale in Adomnán's Life of Columba relates how a man, whose wife found him repugnant and refused to sleep with him, sought the saint's help. Columba took a dim view of the woman's attitude, and despite her protestations and willingness to join a nunnery rather than sleep with her husband, he admonished her:[55]

It cannot be right what to do you say. For as long as your husband is alive, you are subject to the law of your husband. It is unlawful to put apart those whom God has joined together.

The situation was resolved when the three fasted and the saint prayed, and the woman's heart was changed from hatred to love, 'so that she never afterwards refused the dues of the marriage bed as she used to'.

The prescriptive eighth- or ninth-century texts *Ríagail Phátraic* 'The Rule of Patrick' and *Cáin Domnaig* 'The Law of Sunday', both of which probably emanated from Armagh or from a Patrician milieu, lay down directives as to pastoral ministry and observance among laity and religious.[56] In *Ríagail Phátraic*, the bishop is the central figure in the proper governance of spiritual life, especially of kings, *airchinnig*, priests and *manaig*: the ideal situation was that each *túath* was to have a chief bishop (*prímepscop*) 'for the ordination of their clergy, for the consecration of their churches, and for the spiritual guidance of lords and heads of churches, for the sanctification and blessing of their offspring after baptism'.[57] Furthermore, a bishop was expected to ensure that a *túath*'s oratory (*durrthech*) and burial ground (*relec*) were purified and that the oratory's altar had its proper fittings, including a case for the chalice and paten and linen cloths.[58] Baptism, communion and the singing of intercessions were deemed appropriate to be conducted in every church, and in *Ríagail Phátraic*, these appear to have been ministered in particular to the *manaig* (ecclesiastical tenants and labourers). Below the bishops were priests who ministered in the small churches (*mineclaisi* as opposed to *móreclaisi* 'great churches') of a *túath* and they were entitled to a house and enclosure (*tech 7 airlisi*), bed and clothing, 'a sack with its kitchen', a milch cow, a day's ploughing with its seed and arable land and dinner at Christmas, Easter and Pentecost. As argued by Swift in her study of priests in their own localities, these men lived in agricultural communities on farms and in houses not very different from their neighbours, and often with their own families. They did not labour in the fields, but were provided for by their communities and, in return, they ministered the sacraments and also had an important role as judges and as fosterers of young boys who might go on to further study in the church.[59] Many obits of eminent ecclesiastics in the annals identify them as fosterlings of other individuals, presumably ecclesiastics: for example, Mochta, fosterling of Fethgna, bishop, anchorite and excellent scribe of Armagh, died in 893(*AU*). Bishop Féthgna died in 874 proclaimed by the annals as 'successor of Patrick and head of all religion in Ireland'. On the ecclesiastical island of Inis Cathaig (Scattery Island, Co. Clare), a large recumbent cross-slab incised with an interlaced Latin cross, possibly dating to the ninth or tenth century, seeks a prayer for Móenach teacher (*aite*) of Mugrón. This unique slab identifies an individual in terms of fosterage, *aite* meaning 'foster-father', in an ecclesiastical milieu, and is particularly personal insofar as the pupil, Mugrón, may have commissioned the slab in a pious gesture towards his teacher, and also to ensure prayers for both of them.[60] One of the few ogam inscriptions to include a person's status is the cross-inscribed stone in Arraglen on the slope of Mount Brandon, which commemorates Rónán son of Comgán *cruimther* 'presbyter' (QRIMTIR RON[A]NN MAQ COMGANN).[61] This stone does not necessarily mark Rónán's grave but attests to his importance in his community, among whom were literate people who saw it fit to recall him on a pilgrim path to the top of the mountain.

As with *Ríagail Phátraic*, *Cáin Domnaig* is a prescriptive text by its very nature that highlights that there was a need to put Sunday observance into practice in Ireland in the eighth and ninth centuries, as had been laid down at other councils elsewhere, most notably at the Anglo-Saxon Second Council of *Clofesho* in 747. In effect, many of the provisions laid down at that council and at other Anglo-Saxon eighth- and ninth-century councils echo the concerns of *Ríagail Phátraic* and *Cáin Domnaig*.[62] The restrictions on movement and work on Sundays, and the extensive exemptions to it, imply that, theoretically at least, it was intended to be observed by every level in society. Among the exemptions from a fine for transgressing the law were making a cooking pit (*saigid fulachta*), tracking down thieves and lawbreakers, giving warning before enemies, going in the direction of a cry and a scream, helping cattle against wolves and a quagmire, and fetching a midwife for a woman in labour.[63] These activities are the stuff of normal rural life. The period of observance was defined in monastic terms as from vespers on Saturday to the end of Matins on Monday. A person could travel on Sunday to seek communion and baptism, or clerics and nuns could attend church, hear a sermon and Mass, attend to a dying person, and provide food for guests for the sake of Christ.[64] All these latter activities seem to have been directed in particular at either a monastic community or ordained priests and bishops, but not necessarily at the laity in general.

What is faith for? Christian belief in daily life

Few could subscribe to the strictures of penitentials and canon laws, which, as with both ecclesiastical and secular laws, involved the aspirational codification of life by men in powerful positions who themselves did not always adhere to their own prescriptions. The infatuation with morals and sexual sins, which are so prevalent in these texts, probably meant very little to the greater part of the population, whose lives were harsh and frequently interrupted by violence, disease and famine. Elements of the old belief system were mixed with Christianity to support them in their lives, and there were different levels of faith at work in the community. In his assessment of religion and belief in Anglo-Saxon England, Chris Watkins conveys precisely the substance of this issue:[65]

> But what was faith for? The official message here was clear enough: it was the pathway to paradise, a shape in which the good life could be lived so that the believer achieved salvation. And yet medieval Christian practice did more than pave the way to heaven. It also supplied explanatory and remedial strategies which the faithful might use to counter misfortune in this world … Supernatural as well as natural forces and human agents might be instruments of God's providence: demons might tempt and punish human beings. Unofficial beliefs, neither sanctioned nor anathematized by the Church, twined around such teachings, adding local variation to a core of shared instincts about the invisible world.

In Western Christendom, the medieval Irish had the capacity to be Christian and monotheistic and to maintain a parallel universe, embodied in the *áes síde*, existing underground or under sea and water. This otherworld pervades early Irish literature and provides us with a virtually unique insight into a medieval religious and spiritual mindset.[66] It is important to comprehend that this evidence does not amount to a peculiarly 'Celtic' spirituality: that is a modern construct created to respond to a modern spiritual exploration. The uniqueness of the Irish material is that its diversity, which is expressed in so many different types of texts, in Irish and Latin, and in art, enables us to seek out even the beliefs of a whole society in detail. This world is wonderfully expressed in a colophon at the end of the heroic tale *Serglige Con Culainn* 'The wasting sickness of Cú Chulainn':[67]

> That is the vision of destruction [shown] to Cú Chulainn by the people (*áes*) of the hollow hill(s) (*síde*). For the demonic power was great before the faith, and it was so great that the demons used to fight bodily with the human beings and they used to show pleasures and secret pleasures to them, as if they were permanent. It is thus that they used to be believed in. So that it is those apparitions that the ignorant call *síde* and *áes síde*.

This comment harks back to the veneration of Mongfhinn, a woman of the *síd* and a witch, by women and the 'rabble' at Samain. The daily concerns of the ignorant and the literate or nobility alike were the same the world over: their own fertility and that of the land and their livestock, protection from disease and success in battles and on journeys. A series of Old Irish charms, as well as numerous very polished vernacular and Latin poems, illustrate 'the power of words'[68] and the intertwining of Christianity with popular remedies. Some of these texts bring us particularly close to popular practices:[69]

> *O lux nostra in tenebris ... It iad briga in imuindse ...* These are the virtues of this hymn ... Place it in the right hand and let it be folded round the knee of a pregnant woman and she will not die then ... Place it in a battle-axe or a sword and they will prevail over one's enemies ... Put it on a horse's back and he will go past every horse.

> Five paters and Ave Marias and a credo after them. Put that into oil and the wool of a wether which has not before been shorn, and place it about the wound, and every wound which it is put will become free from soreness ...

A woman who bears daughters, that is what helps: a horse's tooth around her neck in a sealskin thong over which seven masses are sung, and she will bring forth a boy. Mary bore Jesus, Anna Mary, Elisabeth John, Cylinia Remigius. *In nomine patris* etc. For a speedy delivery to a woman.

The administration of such beneficial charms was not confined to ritualists operating on the margins of society, but was part of the wider functions of the priest and, as Swift has suggested, may have even produced a stream of income for them as intercessors with the supernatural world. The penitentials of Finnian and Columbanus include provisions and penances for the use of magic or potions to excite love. As long as nobody was hurt or led astray in the attempt, the penance was relatively light.[70]

But what of the administration of sacraments, doctrine and burial by priests and bishops? *Ríagail Phátraic* regarded baptism, communion and the singing of prayers for the dead as essentials in any church and, if it did not provide these, a church was not entitled to its proper tithes or 'not entitled to the honour-price of a church of God, but it is termed by Christ a cave of robbers and thieves'.[71] So many early Irish and Latin texts deal with baptism and communion that there can be no doubt as to their prominence in the pastoral duties of clerics. Concern among the Irish clergy to introduce revised versions of various liturgical rites can be deduced from the early ninth-century Stowe Missal, compiled in one of the *céli Dé* monasteries of Tallaght or Lorrha. The missal may have been put together originally *c.*800, but a certain Máel Coích revised parts of it *c.*812. He concentrated especially on the rites of the Eucharist and brought contemporary Roman practice into the rite. He was 'at the cutting edge of reform in the ninth century', and working on the same task as Benedict of Aniane, who was adding a supplement to the *Sacramentarium Gregorianum Hadrianum* for Charlemagne. As described by Brendan Coffey in his review of the liturgical traditions of the Stowe Missal, 'Both monks were engaged in a Romanizing process; not a process of uniformization, but one of adhering to Roman customs'.[72] Whether this process was confined to the communities of Tallaght or Lorrha or was disseminated to the *mineclasa* 'minor churches' is difficult to establish due to the missal's uniqueness.

The content and style of preaching in early Ireland is an elusive subject, dominated by the very few sermons and preaching materials that survive, mainly in Continental rather than Irish contexts. Hence, while the late seventh- or early eighth-century sermon known as the Cambrai Homily was clearly composed in an Irish milieu on the Continent, as were Columbanus' highly rhetorical Latin sermons, it cannot be assumed that this style and language filtered down to the laity in Ireland.[73] The value of surviving homilies and other forms of instruction and glosses – marginal notes to texts that may indicate a form of preaching aid – lies in their content, and the likelihood that the same subjects were explained to the most theologically knowledgeable congregation as they were in a rural familial church, albeit in different registers. As apparent from preaching materials throughout medieval Western Christendom, certain themes were fundamental to the church's teaching. These were the core teachings of Christianity, especially on the nature of God as expressed through the creed, on how to live a Christian life and on the importance of good works and morals, and, as previously mentioned, on the road to salvation and eternal life. Sermons were probably preached on major feastdays in the Christian calendar and most especially at Easter and on particular saints' feastdays such as SS Peter, Paul and Martin of Tours.

One homily survives that illustrates a style of preaching and also the message relayed to a congregation.[74] The text is predominantly in the vernacular and is woven around Latin quotations, including quotations from Matthew's Gospel (Chs 10 and 25) on Christ's calling of the apostles and the Last Judgment, and prayers of thanksgiving during the Mass:[75]

> *Ar dlegair donaib huilib dúilib at-lugud buide do Día 7 a bendachad, amal asberar: Benedicite omnia opera Domini Domino.*

> For it is the duty of all the elements to render thanks to God and to bless Him, as it is said: Benedicite etc. Bless the Lord, ye works of the Lord.

> *... Ar intí comaillfes(?) inna timnaesa cotngéra in Coimdiu cucai i llaithiu brátha, a nasmbéra friu: Venite benedicti patris mei, possidete regnum quod uobis paratum est ab origine mundi ...*

> For whoever shall fulfil these commandments, the Lord will call him to Him on the day of Doom, saying to them: *Venite* etc., i.e., Come, ye blessed of my Father, possess the kingdom that has been prepared for you from the beginning of the world.

This is a homily on the Day of Judgment, a common theme for sermons as it covered many aspects of Christian life: the calling to imitate Christ by leading a virtuous life, to be ever thankful to God and to recognize God's nature, 'the one excellent God who is without beginning, without end'. And to whom was this text addressed? There is an impression that it was used for a monastic community as the good works that would bring salvation are listed as 'labour and study, fasting and prayer, righteousness and mercy, faith and charity'. Those living in such a community would have been familiar with its biblical and apocryphal allusions. Could it have been the type of text available to a priest working in a wider community, be it among monastic tenants or the laity in general?[76] It is noticeable that the Latin insertions are all glossed with translations and commentaries that suggest a threefold schema: a Latin scriptural or liturgical text, a translation of that text and a commentary in Irish around the Latin text. This type of schema could have been used as a *vademecum* to instruct priests (monastic or secular) in the art of scriptural commentaries and the task of preaching. As the text was transmitted in written form to the fifteenth century – it is preserved in late medieval manuscripts – it must have circulated as a didactic exemplar of a homily on Doomsday. Nevertheless, it is not devoid of the performative aspect so necessary for oral instruction and its sometimes florid descriptions of heaven and hell are not far from the equally ornate language of early sagas:[77]

> Woe, then, to him to whom the Lord shall say on the day of Doom that he shall dwell for ever in hell with its many great torments. For its site is low, its dwelling is sorrowful, its stench is great, its monsters are everlasting … it is a scourge to lash, it is an edge to wound … Not such, however, is the kingdom which the saints and the righteous strive after. It is a fair blossom for its great purity, it is a course of a great ocean for its great beauty … it is a harp for its melodiousness, it is a banquet for its great abundance of wine (*is crot ara ceolbindi, is fledól ara fínmairi*) …

The power of the spoken and written word was further strengthened in an environment in which such homilies and commentaries were conveyed through the power of the image, and in a particularly commanding way through the medium of high crosses. In these, we see links with texts. The Last Judgment occurs, for example, on the Cross of the Scriptures and Muiredach's Cross at Monasterboice (fig. 31). The latter illustrates centrally Christ in Majesty flanked on either side by the saved and the damned with Michael the Archangel weighing souls beneath him (fig. 32). Other themes such as the Epiphany cycle (the Adoration of the Magi, the Baptism of Christ, the Miracle at Cana, the Multiplication of the Loaves and Fishes), the Eucharist and Sunday observance link known Irish versions of catechetical texts with sequences on high crosses.[78] If these crosses were painted, they would have stood out in their landscape and would have been one dramatic means through which the fundamentals of Christianity were conveyed to those who were allowed to approach them. The question remains as to how far that privilege extended in society.

The Christian landscape: crosses, churches, relics and wells

No part of Ireland lacks place-names that consist of an ecclesiastical element, and the most common and well known of all these include the element *kil(l)*, the anglicized version of *cell/cill* 'a church'. This, in turn, is a borrowing from Latin *cella*. The vast bulk of these place-names, if not simply formed with a descriptor such as Kilmore (*An Chill Mhór* 'the great church') or Kilross/Kilrush (*Cill Rois* 'the church of the wood'), are qualified either by a personal name or the name of a kindred.[79] Other place-name elements point to some form of ecclesiastical associations in the landscape, and the most common include *achad* ('a field' anglic. *agha*), *cluain* ('a meadow' anglic. *clo(o)n*), *dísert* ('a hermitage, retreat, church' from Latin *desertum* anglic. *dysart*), *domnach* ('an early church' from Latin *dominicum* anglic. *donagh*), *lann* ('a clearing' rare in Ireland (for example, Lambeg, Co. Antrim), but very common in Wales as *llan*), *tech/tig* ('a house, a church' probably replicating Latin *domus*, which was used to describe early estate churches and which is anglicized in various forms, such as Stabannan, Co. Meath (*Tigh Beanáin*)). While some of these elements were used throughout the medieval period to create new place-names, especially *cell/cill*, a considerable number of them are attested in pre-twelfth-century sources. Such is their density that no one could have travelled through the early medieval landscape without encountering a church settlement, large or small. And while stone high crosses may not have been particularly numerous, smaller stone crosses and slabs or cross-inscribed pillars were everywhere, as undoubtedly were their wooden equivalents, thus providing an ever-present reminder to all of the Christian God and his saints. As a local or as a traveller journeying northwards, for example, the Kilnasaggart pillar stone in Co. Armagh (figs 33, 34) would have been a focal point in the pass through the Slieve Gullion ringdyke on a north-south routeway.[80] Standing in a small cemetery, it is inscribed with a long inscription in Irish in half-uncial script, which reads in translation: 'This place dedicated by Ternóc son of Cerán Bec under the patronage of Peter the Apostle'. Ternóc may be the Ternóc son of Ciarán, whose death is recorded in 716 (ATig.). Above the inscription there is a large Latin cross and beneath it is a splendid equal-armed cross with spiral terminals enclosed in a circle. The back face of the pillar stone is decorated with ten equal-armed crosses representing the orders of heaven. This is an intricate and finely carved example of Christian stone sculpture that when encountered, might have evoked a prayer for Ternóc, who gifted the place to the church and to Christ and St Peter, who were symbolically depicted in the equal-armed crosses. There might even be some connection between this site and the relic of St Peter at Armagh – perhaps a reminder in the landscape of the great monastery's territorial power? One might even venture to relate the sentiments

33 & 34 Kilnasaggart pillar stone, Co. Armagh: standing in a small cemetery in a pass through the Slieve Gullion ringdyke, this ornate pillar stone commemorates Ternóc who dedicated the place to St Peter in the early eighth century. There may be a link between this site and the relic of St Peter in Armagh, either a demarcation of jurisdiction by Armagh or some form of income source for the relic in the greater church. Sketch from George H. Reade, 'The pillar-stone at Kilnasaggart', *Journal of the Kilkenny and South-East of Ireland Archaeological Society* (1857), 315–18; photograph (*right*) © Northern Ireland Environment Agency.

of the prayer *Sét no tíag* 'The path I walk' with the emotion as one encountered
the pillar stone along the routeway:[81]

> *Sét no tíag*   *téiti Críst*
> *crích i mbeo*   *bíth cen tríst.*
> The path I walk Christ walks it. May the land in which I am be without
> sorrow.

> *Muinter nime*   *noíbdai níuil*
> *Dechmad nert*   *talman tríuin.*
> The nine orders of heaven of holy cloud, the tenth force of the strong
> earth.

At the other end of the country in Kilmalkedar Church on the Dingle
Penninsula, Co. Kerry, an equally complex cross-inscribed pillar stands at an
early ecclesiastical site (fig. 35, pl. 13).[82] Crosses with spiral terminals are incised
on either side of this pillar and running vertically downwards on the left side of
the stone are two texts, dn̄ī (*domini* 'of the Lord') and an incomplete Latin
alphabet. This pillar is usually dated to the seventh century and it is likely to
have been used both as a literary and as a symbolic medium to teach the Latin
alphabet and also the *elementa fidei* 'elements of the faith'. St Patrick is often
described as giving alphabets to converts as a medium of learning the scriptures
and they could also be used as a basic mnemonic method through which
information was retained. Isidore of Seville, for example, defined letters as *notae*
invented in order to remember things and, as observed by Mary Carruthers in
her landmark study on memory in medieval culture, 'writing is a servant to
memory, a book its extension, and like memory itself, written letters call up the
voices of those that are no longer present'.[83] Standing on the western coast of
Ireland a long distance away from the great urban Christian centres of Rome
and Constantinople, the Kilmalkedar stone encapsulated in sculpture the
fundamentals of Christian belief and literacy for its local community.

When the many ecclesiastical place-names are combined with the large corpus
of early genealogies and archaeological evidence, the ecclesiastical settlement
pattern of the country begins to emerge. Two crucial aspects of this landscape
need to be stressed namely, that it was part of the landscape of the kindred
(discussed in Ch. 1) and not a parallel or separate entity, and that local cults and
relics were a major force in this Christian culture. The large corpus of early Irish
genealogies contains many references to churches, holy men and women, lands
gifted to the church, and families who were specifically attached to churches.
Medieval Irish genealogical tracts combined detailed local information with

35 Kilmalkedar alphabet stone, Co. Kerry: this pillar stone stands in the churchyard of Kilmalkedar on the Dingle Peninsula along with a number of ogham stones. On either side of the pillar are crosses with spiral terminals and running vertically down its left side are two texts: *domini* 'of the Lord' and an incomplete Latin alphabet. © Robert Shaw, Discovery Programme, Dublin.

obvious regional dynastic propaganda that supported the claims of dominant or ambitious kings to provincial kingships, and even to national status. By preserving local, and often earlier, material, the genealogists left us with the Irish equivalent of charters, sufficiently detailed to relate to the archaeological record. This topographical information enables us to form an idea as to how the church functioned locally and what physical shape it took in the landscape.[84] The secular genealogies locate churches and ecclesiastical families within kindreds and dynasties, and even if their power contracted, they often maintained an influence in their lost territories through ecclesiastical families and saints belonging to their kindred. St Brigit is a classic example of this process: the historic foundress of Kildare – Brigit or some other woman – belonged to the Fothairt, a people who had little power in Leinster in the historic period and who were dominated by greater dynasties who took over their church. Yet, because of the foundress' origins, the Fothairt succeeded in holding on to offices, and in particular that of abbess, intermittently to the tenth century. Her bishop, Conláed, belonged to a different dynasty, the Dál Messin Corb, who had controlled a considerable expanse of Leinster and the kingship of Leinster until the seventh century. Their power in the church was also significantly bolstered by their connection with St Cóemgen (Kevin), founder of the other great monastery of Glendalough (d. 618) in the late sixth century. The secular and saints' genealogies include impressive lists of holy men and women with Dál Messin Corb connections including Becnat (Dalkey, Co. Dublin), Lóchán and Énna (Kilnamanagh, Co. Dublin), Nath Í (Taney/Dundrum, Co. Dublin), Moshacru (Saggart, Co. Dublin), Berchán (Shankill, Co. Dublin) and Finnbarr (Killegar, Co. Dublin). As the Dál Messin Corb dynasties declined, Glendalough allied itself to the ascending and different dynasty of the Uí Dúnlaing, while using the reputed familial connection with Cóemgen to bring a lot of these small churches under its patronage.[85] Patronage may have been reciprocal, in that a small church, along with its local king and kindred, often supplied the larger ecclesiastical community with foodstuffs, clothing or fuel. Dalkey (Co. Dublin), for example, had two churches dedicated to the seventh-century female saint Becnat, one on the mainland overlooking the rocky coast, the other on Dalkey Island, the site of a trading-post from prehistory. It is not inconceivable that this coastal district supplied fish inland to the provincial king of Leinster or to the large communities of Glendalough and Kildare. This district of Cualu was renowned for its ale – it is regarded as the ale of kingship in the literature – and again is likely to have supplied its prized brew to kings, bishops and abbots. In return, it is possible that Glendalough educated and sent a priest to serve in Becnat's two churches. In an early litany, Becnat is invoked for protection among other holy women, including Mary and Brigit.[86]

The memory of a number of these other women persists to this day: Cúaca of Kilcock (Co. Kildare), Scíre of Kilskeer (Co. Meath), Sinech of Kilshine (Co. Meath), Ciar of Kilkeary (Co. Tipperary), Lúaithrenn of Killoran (Co. Sligo) and Rígnach of Kilrainy (Co. Kildare) and Templerainy (Co. Wicklow). And in most of these cases there is a remarkably common settlement pattern. A late medieval church with a graveyard that functioned until relatively recently is surrounded by an earthen enclosure – possibly of earlier date – with a holy well dedicated to the local saint. In many cases, ringforts are located closeby and a medieval cross

36 Oran, Co. Roscommon: an early foundation with Patrician connections, this site continued to function into the late medieval period and, as shown in this photograph taken by Mrs F.M. Muriel in 1900, it was a pilgrimage site until the modern period. © Victoria & Albert Museum, London.

survives in the graveyard. This topographical model is so standard that it implies that these churches were founded from within a local kindred during the conversion period and were the resting-place of the *érlam*, the patron whose name was associated with that church.[87] The main exceptions to this common model were churches founded by early missionaries or somehow attached to extensive cults. The most obvious were those churches throughout the country dedicated to Patrick and Brigit that were tied by legal agreement with greater churches such as Armagh, Clonmacnoise and Kildare. Undoubtedly, the bond between church and community was formed around the cult of the local holy person often brought to life through a grave, relics or a feastday. The very existence of early Irish litanies and martyrologies, saints' Lives and pedigrees, which mention so many minor saints, attests to the vibrancy of the cult of local holy men and women throughout Ireland.

Churches, crosses and holy wells were but a part of the public manifestation of Christianity visible to all throughout the landscape. Natural features such as rocks and trees could retain the memory of a saint's passing through a place, as in the case of Domnach Sratha (in the Sligo region near Drumcliff) where, according to the Tripartite Life of Patrick, Patrick had a nosebleed on the road and two drops of blood fell and were marked by a stone (*lecc Pátraic*) and a hazelbush (*coll Pátraic*) near the church.[88] A saint's grave was a particular attraction around the feastday and could be the focus of miraculous interventions and supplication. The depiction of Cell Garad and the well of Úarán (Oran, Co. Roscommon: fig. 36) in the Tripartite Life of Patrick conjures up a typical local church setting:[89]

> Patrick founded Cell Garad, where are Cethech and Cethech's tomb together. Then Patrick made the well named Uarán Garad, and he loved that water greatly, as he himself said:
> > Uarán gar, Uarán which I have loved, which loved me! Sad is my cry, o dear God! Without my drink out of clear Uarán!

Here one finds the church, probably made of wood, the saint's grave mound (*ferta*), and the well that could have been used in earlier non-Christian rituals. There is no historic evidence that Patrick actually founded the church and, indeed, it is most likely that Céthech was the real founder of Cell Garad. As for the well of Úarán Garad, it is named in the ninth-century triads as one of the three principal wells of Ireland.[90] The site developed into an ecclesiastical centre in the medieval period, as evidenced by its round tower, graveyard and medieval cross by the well, and by references as late as 1556 (*AFM*) to its incumbent ecclesiastical family, the Uí Chlabaigh, as successors of Patrick at Úarán Maighe Aoí.

One of the most visible and tangible connections between church and laity was based on the relics of the saints and associated pilgrim attractions. Not all holy men and women were honoured with the enshrinement of their bones, but their graves, as we have seen with Céthech at Cell Garad, could be the focus of veneration. The small island of Illaunloughan in Valencia Harbour, Co. Kerry, is a splendid example of how people were attracted to a holy grave (fig. 37, pl. 15). Marked by a gable reliquary shrine surrounded by a mound and scattered with numerous white quartz stones were the disarticulated bones of two adult males and an infant skull, dated between the late seventh and late eighth century.[91] Bones were often disinterred and a *translatio* was conducted and the saint's relics were placed in a decorated casket of gold and silver. This was done to Bishop Conláed of Kildare in 800 (*AU*) and Rónán mac Beraich of Dromiskin, Co. Louth, in 801 (*AU*). Relics were brought around the countryside either to exact tributes or to calm the populace in times of stress, such as during epidemics or

37 Illaunloughan, Co. Kerry: this tiny island close to the shore of Valencia Island, Co. Kerry, was inhabited by a monastic community in the seventh and eighth centuries. The focal point was the gable reliquary shrine in which two burial cists containing the bodies of two men and an infant were sealed under layers of soil, gravel, shells and white quartz. © National Monuments Service, Department of Arts, Heritage and the Gaeltacht.

famine. A curious example of the imposition of Patrick's law through the power of relics is mentioned in the annals in 734, when the relics of SS Peter, Paul and Patrick were disinterred – presumably at Armagh – were enshrined and were brought on tour to enforce the law. By 737, the annals claim that the law of Patrick ruled Ireland. From the eighth century onwards, saints' relics were brought out in times of need. It is noticeable that no such manifestations of intercession are recorded for the seventh century despite repeated instances of outbreaks of disease and famine. The earliest mention of such a tour relates to Trian of Kildalkey, Co. Meath, whose relics went on tour in 743 when smallpox (*bolgach*) was rampant. The late eighth century was particularly harsh, with constant disease and famine among humans and cattle, as well as severe weather. In 748, *AU* records 'snow of unusual depth so that nearly all the cattle of the whole of Ireland perished, and the world afterwards was parched by unusual drought'. Similar entries are recorded in 764 and 799. The Annals of Tigernach comment under the 748 entry that such was the quantity of snow 'that almost all the sins of all Ireland were cleansed', thus making a direct correlation between the sins of the Irish and the harsh weather and ensuing difficulties. This same period saw regular tours of relics to instil *stabilitas* and calm in society. The relics of Erc of Slane (Co. Meath), Finnian of Clonard (Co. Meath), Ultán of Ardbraccan (Co. Meath), Cóemgen of Glendalough (Co. Wicklow), Mochua (Crónán) of Clondalkin (Co. Dublin), Tóla of Dysert (Co. Westmeath) and Trian of Kildalkey (Co. Meath) went on tour at intervals between 776 and 794. There is a distinct midlands and eastern focus to this list: perhaps this reflects the coverage in the sources or a particular custom more prevalent in the east during that period. The sight of a train of people travelling along the roads with a relic must have attracted much attention and undoubted welcome in a society that depended on the power of image and word to seek the mercy of God.[92]

Although a highly political affair narrated through the lense of a seventeenth-century redaction, the escorting of the defeated king of Munster and abbot of Inis Cathaig (Scattery Island) in 909 – a year after he had been captured and held hostage in Kildare for his participation in the Battle of Belach Mugna – to the borders of Munster typifies this kind of lively procession wending its way through the countryside:[93]

> Flaithbertach was brought to Cell Dara then, and the clergy of Leinster reproached him severely, for they knew that it had been he alone who had urged the hosting and the battle, and that Cormac [mac Cuilennáin, joint king of Munster and bishop of Cashel] had come against his will. However, after the death of Cerball, king of the Laigin, Flaithbertach was released, which was at the end of that year, according to some. Muirenn, successor of Brigit, along with a large group of clergy and many relics, escorted him to Mag n-Airb, and when he arrived in Munster he made peace there. Afterwards he went to his monastery on Inis Cathaig, and he spent a while there piously, until he came out again to take the kingship of Cashel, and he was king of Munster for thirty-two years.

Permanent and visiting pilgrims: the dísert and the island phenomenon

Saints' relics, be they their bones in a specially marked grave or shrine, or non-corporeal relics such as an item of dress (for example, a shoe or a belt), a bell or a crosier, attract pilgrims and pilgrimages. Not all pilgrims followed the same style of pilgrimage nor sought the same outcome for themselves and their community. A king could go on pilgrimage into a monastery to intercede for his people during times of distress or could be driven to take the pilgrim's staff once ousted from his kingship. This seems to have been the case with the northern king Flaithbertach son of Loingsech, who was ousted from the kingship of Tara by his rival Áed Allán in 734 and spent the next three decades in Armagh, presumably as a member of the community there. Yet, the desire for repentence lay at the heart of many pilgrims' journeys. Seeking a remission of sins could mean a temporary exile from the normal course of life, or the more fervent pilgrim might opt for complete separation from the material world and become a *deorad Dé* 'exile of God'. The eighth-century Old Irish Penitential expresses the conditions of temporary and permanent pilgrimages in these terms:[94]

> Anyone who persists in avarice to the end of his life must go on a pilgrimage or must distribute the value of seven cumals to the poor and needy for his soul's sake.

> As for him who desires to reach the pitch of perfectness, he distributes all he has to the poor and needy and goes on a pilgrimage or lives in a communal church till he goes to Heaven.

Certain types of ecclesiastical sites in Ireland and Scotland can be identified as places of pilgrimage where pilgrims could purge themselves of sin, either by performing the rituals of a temporary pilgrimage or by enduring a lifelong pilgrimage of penance and poverty. These include churches with the place-name element *dísert* (borrowed from Latin *desertum*) and, most spectacularly, certain islands along the west coasts of Ireland and Scotland. A *dísert* could be located in a major inland ecclesiastical settlement, as in the case of the tiny, compact stone oratory in the centre of a substantial rectangular enclosure outside the main precinct of Lemanaghan Church, Co. Offaly. This small oratory was dedicated to St Mella, reputedly the mother of St Manachan of Lemanaghan, who became an anchoress.[95] Island ecclesiastical communities varied from the very small, as on Illaunloughan, to far more complex communities, as on the Aran Islands, Inishmurray and Skellig Michael. These were microcosms of greater sites such as Clonmacnoise or Iona. Jerry O'Sullivan and Tomás Ó Carragáin, in their comprehensive survey of Inishmurray (Co. Sligo), argue that the occurrence of a Relic Odráin (*Relickoran* 'the cemetery of Odrán') on both Iona and Inishmurray may be no coincidence and that the Inishmurray complex may have been a conscious imitation of the layout at Iona. The community of Inishmurray could have appealed for salvation to those holy people interred among them. These saints included the founder saint Molaise, the intermediary Odrán and, by proxy, the greater saint Columba, one of whose main Irish churches at Druim Clíab (Drumcliff, Co. Sligo) was not too far away on the mainland.[96] When this replication happened is not known, although the satellite cemetery attracted occasional burials from the early eighth to the seventeenth

century. It is worth noting the death of one Mac Laisre the Learned of
Inishmurray in 803 (*AFM* 798). His name suggests that he was a devotee of
Molaise/Laisrén and it is tempting to think of him as the possible guardian of
the earliest church Teach Molaise, which may have been the founder's reliquary
church. Radiocarbon-dated mortar suggests that this building was built as early
as the eighth or ninth century, and Molaise's great iron bell is of the same
period.[97] This concept of replication is even more evident on the Aran Islands in
Galway Bay, on which small churches were dedicated to many of the senior
saints of Ireland as well as to local saints. However, as with Inishmurray and
Skellig Michael, the earliest phase of ecclesiastical activity in Aran was not
primarily a site of common pilgrimage – that happened from the end of the first
millennium onwards – but as the settlement of ascetic communities. Colmán
(Mocholmóc) mac Commáin, who died in Aran in 751 (AI), was a bishop and
is singled out in an early penitential text as one of the four sages of Ireland who
recommended a particular type of penitential position – 'the whole body is
stretched out along the ground face downwards and both arms laid flat by the
sides'.[98] Aran was not as wild and desolate a place as Skellig Michael might have
been, but was heavily settled and cultivated, and was fought over throughout
the early medieval period. It is likely that the saintly Colmán mac Commáin was
a member of a noble family, the Uí Chormaic, whose kingdom lay in the Burren
(north Co. Clare).[99] His father's name may be fossilized in the name of the great
stone fort of Cahercommaun, Co. Clare.

The tiny island of Illaunloughan provides a detailed impression of the life of
a small monastic community living close to the shore just off Portmagee on
Valencia Island, Co. Kerry. It is only a few metres above sea level and, although
somewhat sheltered, is subject to Atlantic gales and spray, and to considerable
amounts of rain. It was thoroughly excavated in the 1990s.[1] The earliest phase
saw the building of three circular domestic huts, two of which were conjoined
and protected by an enclosure. They were built of sod walls and had either stone
or post-and-wattle revetments to secure the base of the walls. Two (Huts A
and B) had hearths in their centre and charcoal from one was radiocarbon dated
to AD640–751. A drystone wall protected the inhabitants from the wind and
seaspray, and the excavators estimated that, based on the size of the two huts
and the need for storage, bedding, tools and possessions (though probably few),
they were occupied by five or six people between them.[2] The third hut was
flimsier and more exposed and may not have been used as a dwelling.
Metalworking debris, including eighty fragments of clay casting moulds and two
brooches, adds to the evidence that the church was central to fine metal
production, even among small communities, as on this tiny island. This discovery

raises issues as to the composition of the Illaunloughan community: were some of them craftsmen (all evidence suggests a totally male community living on the island), either from local artisan families or from further afield, who had joined a monastic community and whose products were exchanged for foodstuffs or clothing with the mainland community? Their diet was not as might be expected from the severe rules associated with ascestics. These men had access to birds and fish from their own environment, as well as calves and lambs, cereals and dairy produce from the mainland.[3] A small rectangular sod oratory with a wooden hipped roof was built during Phase 1. Five closely spaced graves were placed behind its eastern wall.

Considerable change took place when the community reorganized its settlement in Phase 2. The sod oratory was replaced by a drystone oratory of similar proportions and an almost perfectly circular hut with corbelled walls and a sunken level for protection from the elements. The most significant monument of this phase, and the most visible feature on the northern side of the island to this day, was a gable reliquary shrine. The shrine was elevated on a rock and supported by a soil, stone and gravel mound with an entrance on its western side approached by a flight of sandstone steps and surrounded by a paved area. Sealed under layers of soil, stones, gravel, scallop shells and white quartz stones were two stone cists, each shaped like a miniature lintel cist grave, containing the exhumed bones of two male adults. A single scallop shell – the symbol for the resurrection in Christianity and an object commonly found in graves throughout the world[4] – rested on the lid of one cist. An infant was also buried in one of the cists. The bones of all three dated to a period somewhere between 660 and 794.[5] The Illaunloughan gable shrine is a superb testimony to the importance of holy persons and their graves. It is likely that this is the type of *ferta* described by the Tripartite Life of Patrick as covering Céthech, founder of Cell Garad. The Illaunloughan shrine also confirms that, as recorded by the annals, the rite of *translatio* genuinely took place. A small, temporary building erected between the destruction of the sod oratory and building of the drystone oratory may have been a temporary shrine containing the relics of the community's two saints before they were placed in the gable shrine reliquary. The presence of the remains of a small child in one cist is somewhat unexpected: perhaps it was the founder's biological child or a relative's child fostered by the early community or, more likely, a child oblate? Whatever the reason, such a find, and all that was uncovered at Illaunloughan, brings us as close as is possible to the reality of living out a Christian existence on a small wind-swept island off the west coast.

The end of life: graves and cemeteries

Burial in any society is one of the main expressions of belief as it involves the starkest encounter with the unknown. Even a community that does not believe in an afterlife or in death as a passing on to some form of otherworld conducts a celebration of the deceased's life and affords their body a decent burial. It is often when society breaks down, as in times of war or genocide, that respect for the dead no longer exists and that no obsequies are performed. In these circumstances, bodies are frequently destroyed or dumped in mass graves with no ceremony. Irish society of the early medieval period was one that very gradually moved from ancestral and familial rites to rites and cemeteries controlled by the church. Often these practices were not mutually exclusive, and until at least the eighth century, when the church made more demands in this sphere, it is difficult to classify categorically the difference between a Christian and a non-Christian burial or cemetery.

The two prevalent burial types in Ireland from the late centuries BC and early centuries AD were cremation and inhumation, with the former more prevalent in the early period and inhumation becoming common into the first millennium AD.[6] Interestingly, cremation did not become obsolete, and instances of this practice have been dated to as late as the eighth century. The burial complex at Ask Hill, Co. Wexford, began in the Neolithic and ended with two cremations, one inside and one outside a penannular enclosure. The cremation pits inside the enclosure contained burnt human and animal bone dated to the seventh or eighth century and a pit with a gilded copper-alloy cross mount with interlace decoration. While one interpretation might conclude that this is an aberration and may involve foreigners – possibly Vikings – the more likely explanation is that some people continued to bury in the ancestral burial sites (*fertae*) and for some reason maintained the ancient custom of cremation.[7] The rite of extended inhumation burial was gradually introduced into Ireland from about the late fourth or early fifth century, probably as a result of contacts with the western and northern fringes of Roman Britain, where the rite had become established by the fourth century. Irish burials of this early period (fifth/sixth century) tend not to be grouped in formal cemeteries. They occur as single burials, or in small groups in isolated places. They are often to be found inserted into or around prehistoric burial monuments that form the focus for a subsequent familial cemetery. The range of grave structures for extended inhumation burials includes slab-lined cist graves, stone-lined graves, lintel graves, unprotected dug graves and, very occasionally, plank-lined graves. It can be shown that unprotected dug graves were by far the most common type, followed by stone-lined graves. Slab-lined cist graves tend to be less numerous and to be confined to the earlier part of the period. Lintel graves occur in cemeteries datable to the seventh century or later. Plank-lined graves are an unusual phenomenon and occur in very few cemeteries.

Cemetery landscapes range from one or two isolated graves to extensive cemeteries of a few hundred bodies. Various phenomena bring to light society's views of death and afterlife. They include the intermittent reuse of *fertae* from prehistory to the early eighth century, the occurrence of familial cemeteries (otherwise known as settlement cemeteries) and the virtual absence of opulent grave goods. As mentioned throughout this study, *fertae* were an integral part of the landscape and acted as legal and political boundary markers, and as focal points of mythological and toponymic memory. The necessity to remain within the kindred and protected by an eminent ancestor lingered, even if the eminent ancestor was no longer a king or warrior but a saint (often belonging to the same kindred). The desire to maintain the family unit into the afterlife was shared by Christians and non-Christians alike, as is clear from the Irish canons in which the dictum from a Roman synod, 'cursed is every man who is not buried in the tomb of their fathers' (*maledictus omnis homo, qui non sepelitur in sepulcro partum suorum*) prevails in canons relating to burial.[8] The archaeology and monumental culture (grave-slabs) of cemeteries suggest that this approach allowed for flexibility in the choice of burial ground. As seen from the evidence of Clonmacnoise, only the select few, probably as restricted a group as kings, abbots and bishops and the learned, were afforded the privilege of being buried in the holiest section of consecrated ground of a major church. A small excavation at Sheeon Hill, part of the monastic complex at Durrow, Co. Offaly, provides a valuable impression of the configuration of burial 'plots' at such prestigious sites. A group of extended skeletons in dug graves oriented east–west were enclosed by a bank on a low knoll, while 200m further north was a second knoll containing human remains. These graves were close to, but outside, the double ditch and bank that enclosed the core of the ecclesiastical complex and was aligned on one of the high crosses on the site.[9] A smaller ecclesiastical site at Ballygarran (Killeenagh burial ground, Co. Waterford) replicates the larger sites to a certain degree. Five burials were discovered in the south-east quadrant of the inner of two enclosures on a site that contains the upstanding remains of a church, a bullaun stone and a cross-inscribed pillar-stone.[10] Sites with medieval churches and evidence of early medieval cemeteries are rarely unearthed – although such burials are always assumed to exist on these sites – mainly due to the difficulty in excavating heavily populated graveyards. Among the few excavated sites were Killegar, Co. Wicklow, and Solar, Co. Antrim. At Killegar, forty lintel graves were discovered on a sandy esker ridge overlooking the Glencullen River and close to Killegar church. Two small early medieval iron hand-bells were also found on the site. A potentially significant sequence may be present at Solar: eight males dated to the seventh or eighth century were buried in slab-lined cists and burial continued as late as the thirteenth century. This was an extensive cemetery, as a partial excavation uncovered 123 graves. Solar is a reputed church site, although nothing of the building remains, and it has been suggested that this cemetery started as an ancestral or familial cemetery that was later taken over by the church.[11]

Familial cemeteries have been identified recently as striking and relatively common features that have not always remained visible in the landscape and have been uncovered due to development-led excavations. They are characterized by the large number of burials they contain, sometimes amounting to over a hundred graves. Industrial activity occurs on part of these sites, including milling, corn-drying, butchery and metalworking. The cemetery can be located close to a habitation site and usually developed around a primary burial. While the site might be prehistoric in origin, the main date-range for use of the cemetery normally lies between the fifth and eighth century, but some continued to be used into the late medieval period. Even the smallest cemeteries were often laid out according to a plan and this organization is more obvious in the larger sites. For example, the cemeteries of Holdenstown 1 and 2, Co. Kilkenny, were located on a raised plateau overlooking the River Nore (fig. 38).[12] Holdenstown 1 consisted of two groups of burials within ring-ditches surrounded by a large enclosure and totalling eight graves (four male, two female, two unidentified), which were dated to between the fifth and seventh centuries. Antler picks were found in the ring-ditches and they dated to the third or fourth century. Holdenstown 1 has been classified as a *ferta*, an ancestral cemetery fittingly located on a strategic ridge overlooking the Nore.[13] Holdenstown 2 consisted of ninety-four burials, roughly aligned in five rows and containing a mixture of adult male and female burials organized in several distinct groupings. Intercutting of burials was rare, and in most cases deliberate, and it appears that the graves were marked with some form of identifier. Though not as obviously neat as a modern graveyard, nonetheless, there is a plan to this cemetery and if it belonged to a certain kindred, it is likely that responsibility for its upkeep lay with designated members of the kin. Burial 59, of fifth- or sixth-century date, appears to be significant, as it was a male burial accompanied by an antler pick, of the same date as the picks recovered from Holdenstown 1. There is a clear overlap between the two cemeteries, but the concept of how to plan a cemetery had changed between one and the other. Corn-drying kilns were close to the larger cemetery, as might be expected, given the frequency of finding industrial activity at cemetery sites. That the community carried out normal economic activity so close to the dead could have been for the perfectly practical reason that fires could be safely lit in a

38 Holdenstown 1, Co. Kilkenny: aerial view during excavation. This ancestral grave (*ferta*) consisting of two groups of burials in ring-ditches surrounded by a larger enclosure overlooks the River Nore and is the earliest part of a cemetery complex that appears to stretch from the Late Iron Age to the medieval period. Antler picks were discovered in the ring-ditches, and a fifth-/sixth-century male in a larger cemetery adjacent to the *ferta* (Holdenstown 2) was also buried with an antler pick, making a direct connection between the two cemeteries. © Irish Archaeological Consultancy.

cemetery without endangering houses or animal pens. At a communal psychological level, it probably signifies that the dead continued to be an integral part of society. It would appear that Holdenstown 2 went out of use in the seventh century and that people were buried in the churchyard nearby. This church may have been dedicated to St Colmán of Belach Buaidge at Dunbell (Holdenstown), who, along with his brothers or companions Guaire and Máel Dub, is commemorated in the medieval saints' pedigrees.[14] This is not to preclude that many of the individuals buried in Holdenstown 2 were Christians. They most likely were Christians, as many were buried in shrouds, one almost certain indication of imitating Christ in death.

Conclusion

Why Ireland in the medieval world?

Two paintings exist unknown to the majority of Irish people in two historic institutions in Dublin. One, a portrait of the great nineteenth-century antiquarian, John O'Donovan, is in the Royal Irish Academy on Dawson Street, and even the esteemed members of the same academy may not all be familiar with O'Donovan's image. The other, a portrait of the historian, Celticist and politician, Eoin MacNeill, presides over the History Boardroom in University College Dublin. Although MacNeill dominates the room, very few students who pass through there are likely to take much notice of the austere man in his professorial garb, let alone explore his connection with the university's history. The relegation of O'Donovan's and MacNeill's portraits to relative obscurity is a paradigm for the disregard of their scholarship and that of many others in the fields of medieval Irish history, language, literature and topography in modern Ireland. In a preface to his book *Celtic Ireland* published in 1921, MacNeill wrote with fervour on the uniqueness of the Irish tradition: 'The more one knows of Irish antiquity, the more, if he loves the knowledge of his kind, he will desire to know'.[1]

MacNeill's plea for a greater emphasis on the study of Irish history and language continues to be germane, and in the context of the huge pressure on students to choose a scientific or technological path only, to the detriment of their knowledge of culture and heritage, it is worth quoting:[2]

> If so few are in the field where there is room for so many, experience has convinced me that the deterrent forces are mainly economic. Should any benefactor be inspired to promote work that will make our Nation's ancient story attractive to young Irish intellects and that will also give it the place it deserves in the world's history, my appeal would be for the endowment of research based strictly on the joint study of Irish history and archæology and of Irish philology, and for such endowment as will ensure the publication of any piece of research work well done; for at present, the student, howsoever capable, who would give the time required

for preparation in these studies, would find himself, when his time of research and publication had come, face to face with the prospect of having to do the work at his own expense, and in most cases to engage in other and wholly different tasks to provide a livelihood and the surplus required for this work.

Despite the work of many generations since 1921, MacNeill's analysis is as relevant now as when he wrote it. Resources are scarce, students are directed elsewhere, Irish universities no longer value medieval Irish history, and, on the whole, neither Ireland itself nor the greater world has properly understood the expanse of medieval Irish culture and how much of it survives.

This book attempts to present various aspects of the culture and society of early medieval Ireland using the evidence found in our medieval manuscripts, in our archaeological monuments, in our place-names, in our landscapes and even in our own names. It reflects the work of many scholars since MacNeill's day and also the new approaches that have advanced our knowledge of Ireland from the fifth century to the beginning of the eleventh century. Many of these new methods and ways of scrutinizing evidence have been introduced in the past three decades and, of course, the subject has been heavily influenced by the massive scientific and technological progress of recent times. Similarly, Ireland's own economic development has had its impact, good and bad, on the study of the island's medieval archaeology and history. More resources became available for genuine research, while at the same time landscapes and scholarship were no deterrent to rampant development.

MacNeill wrote the materials for *Celtic Ireland* during the turbulent period between 1906 and 1921 when he himself was caught up in the 1916 Rising and the War of Independence. Such periods of turmoil are more often than not violent, but they also lead to reflections on identity and a people's connections with its past, its landscape and its place in the world. Ours is no longer a violent turmoil, and yet there is turmoil – economic and social – that demands more than political and commercial solutions. There is an imperative on those engaged in professions such as history to contribute to creating stability and a sense of belonging among a shaken community. The past may often be a painful narrative from which lessons can be learned, but it can also be a source of dignity from which people can draw inspiration and share with a universal community.

The abundance of material available to study every facet and neighbourhood of medieval Ireland cannot be underestimated. There are medieval manuscripts of Irish origin, or penned by Irish scribes and scholars, deposited in our own great libraries – the National Library of Ireland, the Royal Irish Academy, Trinity College Dublin – in our universities and in smaller libraries throughout the country. Renowned libraries of the world – the Bodleian Library Oxford, the Bibliothèque Nationale Paris, the Abbey Library of St Gallen, Schaffhausen Stadbibliothek, to name but a few – house Irish manuscripts that, in their various ways, echo episodes in the history of the Irish from at least the seventh century. These manuscripts contain an array of medieval texts in Irish and Latin from the vast canon of early Irish law to an equally impressive corpus of genealogies that details thousands of names from almost every part of Ireland. The Irish custodians of *senchas* not only recorded genealogies but also were diligent in their efforts to explain their own landscapes in historical and mythological terms. From this desire to frame places and geographical features within the narrative of the island's population, a genre of literature, *dindshenchas*, was generated that wove place-names with colourful and fantastic stories in which gods, goddesses, saints and heroes left their mark on the landscape. As I write this conclusion, I look out on a mountain popularly known as the Great Sugar Loaf in Co. Wicklow (pl. 14). Its conical shape, draped with white quartzites, standing alone in the landscape, has attracted attention since prehistory when, in the Bronze Age, stone cairns and burnt mounds (*fulachta fia*) were constructed on or in close proximity to the mountain.[3] More importantly, clusters of Bronze Age *fulachta fia*, enclosures and burials seemingly orientated towards the Great Sugar Loaf at a distance of up to twenty kilometres suggest that this solitary mountain had some cosmological significance for the local community.[4] The Great Sugar Loaf stands in the kingdom of Cualu, which is the region lying between the Dublin and North Wicklow Mountains and the coast. This is a landscape of kingship, its ale, *cuirm Chualann*, being one of the king of Leinster's royal prerogatives. It is also a landscape of *Togail Bruidne Da Derga*, the ninth-century tale of the doomed heroic king Conaire Mór, through which the tale's characters trek and raid.[5] In a delightful article in which he attempted to identify the place-names of this tale and others with various natural features, Eoin MacNeill traced the routeway of the British raiders who ultimately caused Conaire's death, through the mountains and valleys of Cualu.[6] Some of these place-names survive: Long Laga (Luggala), Glenn Caipche (Glencap), Digais (Douce Mountain), Malu (Maulin Mountain), Scairb ind Eoin (Enniskerry), Cuilenn (Glencullen) and Dún Brea (Bray Head). And if we delve further, the genealogies and annals tell us that Cualu was divided into two kingdoms – Uí Chellaig Chualann and Uí Briúin Chualann – both of which include the names of the region's ruling dynasties prior to the twelfth century. Not that these people disappeared after that, as both occur as the common modern surnames (O')Kelly and (O')Byrne throughout the same districts to this day. Understanding these profound connections with our landscape and our culture can only deepen our appreciation of our country's past, and out of that depth of knowledge might emerge a new energy and stability. This book is an introduction to this medieval world. It guides its readers to a threshold beyond which there is so much to learn and investigate.

I conclude with the words of the ninth-century bishop of Kildare, Orthanach úa Cáelláma Cuirrich, from his poem on the history of Leinster:[7]

> *Ber lat mo chomraim it chlúis*
> *co farcba i llebraib dot éis*
> *dubithir mo gus bith gúal*
> *gilithir mo dūan bid géis.*

> Bear with you my estimation in your ear
> that you may leave it in books after you;
> black as coal is my nature,
> bright as the swan my song.

Endnotes

Introduction

1 G.S.M. Walker (ed.), *Sancti Columbani Opera* (1957; repr. 1970), p. 3 (letter 1, para. 1).
2 Ibid., p. 7 (letter 1, para. 2). Columbanus describes the ancient learned class in Ireland in Latin as *nostris magistris et Hibernicis antiquis philosophis et sapientissimis componendi calculi computariis*.
3 I deliberately chose the Jungian concept of the 'collective unconscious' to describe the Irish view of history and their role in the world, which contains a constant element of overstatement and unreality. This characteristic may relate to our relative isolation in the world as an island nation and disconnect from different peoples simply due to our geographical location.
4 F.J. Byrne, '*Senchas*: the nature of Gaelic historical tradition' (1974); E. Bhreathnach, 'The *seanchas* tradition in late medieval Ireland' (2007).
5 T.M. Charles-Edwards (ed.), *The chronicle of Ireland* (2006); D.P. Mc Carthy, *The Irish annals: their genesis, evolution and history* (2008).
6 E. Bhreathnach and B. Cunningham, *Writing Irish history: the Four Masters and their world* (2007), p. 9.
7 *FFÉ*, I, pp 81–3.
8 F. Kelly, 'An Old-Irish text on court procedure' (1986).
9 J.T. Koch and J. Carey, *The Celtic heroic age: literary sources for ancient Celtic Europe and early Ireland and Wales* (1994), p. 45, §28.
10 V. Hull, 'Conall Corc and the Corco Luigde' (1947), 62.
11 R. Ó Floinn, 'Early Christianity in Ireland based on the most current archaeological research' (2012), pp 15–17.
12 *Confessio*, §38.
13 J. Carey, 'The Irish national origin-legend: synthetic pseudohistory' (1994), p. 3.
14 For a detailed account of the growth of this origin legend and the various works that influenced it, see Carey, 'Irish national origin-legend', passim.
15 J.H. Todd and A. Herbert (eds), *The Irish version of the Historia Britonum of Nennius* (1848), pp 220–71.
16 Todd and Herbert, *Historia Britonum*, p. 271, §§83, 85.
17 Ibid., p. 249, §52.
18 Ibid., p. 257, §65.
19 J. Carey, 'Scél Tuáin meic Chairill' (1984).
20 Ibid., 105.
21 Ibid., 106.
22 Ibid.

CHAPTER I
The landscapes of early medieval Ireland

1 F. Shaw (ed.), *The dream of Óengus. Aislinge Óenguso* (1934), p. 63; K.H. Jackson (trans.), *A Celtic miscellany* (1951; repr. 1971), p. 97 [§ 39].
2 Ó Floinn, 'Early Christianity in Ireland', pp 15–17.
3 *AL*, IV, p. 142.8 (comm); *CIH*, p. 201.12–14; F. Kelly, *Early Irish farming* (1997), p. 409.
4 M. Gelling and A. Cole, *The landscape of place-names* (repr. 2003).
5 For a very useful index of Irish place-name elements, see P. McKay, *A dictionary of Ulster place-names* (1999), pp 149–56.
6 *VSC*, II:4.
7 *CGH*, p. 265:155b47–8; p. 84:126a39–42.
8 Plummer, *VSH*, I, p. 260, §v.
9 Koch and Carey, *The Celtic heroic age*, pp 101–2 (trans.); J. Carmichael Watson (ed.), *Mesca Ulad* (1941), p. 13:299–301.

10 E. Grogan et al., *The North Munster Project, 2: the prehistoric landscape of north Munster* (2005).

11 Koch and Carey, *The Celtic heroic age*, p. 102; Watson, *Mesca Ulad*, p. 15:340–1.

12 Kenney, *Sources*, p. 130.

13 B. Colgrave and R.A.B. Mynors, *Bede's Ecclesiastical history of the English people* (Oxford, 1993), I (1).

14 Ibid.

15 J.M. Wooding, *Communication and commerce along the western sealanes, AD400–800* (1996).

16 G. Toner, 'Identifying Ptolemy's Irish places and tribes' (2000).

17 Koch and Carey, *Celtic heroic age*, p. 159, §17 (trans.); E. Knott, *Togail Bruidne Da Derga* (1975 repr.), p. 6, §17.

18 Wooding, *Communication and commerce*, pp 19–20, 68–71; Kelly, *EIF*, p. 408.

19 Wooding, *Communication and commerce*, p. 20.

20 CIH, pp 177:35–9, 178:11–12.

21 A. O'Sullivan, *Foragers, farmers and fishers in a coastal landscape: an intertidal archaeological survey of the Shannon Estuary* (2001); T.C. McErlean, R. McConkey and W. Forsythe, *Strangford Lough: an archaeological survey of the maritime cultural landscape* (2002), pp 144–78.

22 McErlean et al., *Strangford Lough*, pp 200–11; T.C. McErlean and N. Crothers (eds), *Harnessing the tides: the early medieval tide mill at Nendrum monastery, Strangford Lough* (2007).

23 T. O'Loughlin, 'Living in the ocean' (1997), pp 11–23:14 (quote from *Confessio*, §39).

24 A.G. Van Hamel (ed.), *Immrama* (1941), p. 29:130.

25 W. Stokes (ed. and trans.), 'The voyage of Máel Dúin' (1889), 91–3, §34.

26 C. Cotter, *The Western Stone Forts Project: excavations at Dún Aonghasa and Dún Eoghanachta* (2013).

27 For summaries and lists of publications, see www.nra.ie/archaeology and www.excavations.ie.

28 M. Moore (comp.), *Archaeological inventory of County Waterford* (1999). For details regarding the place-names, see www.logainm.ie (barony of Decies-without-Drum).

29 P. McKay and K. Muhr, *Lough Neagh places: their names and origins* (2007).

30 Ibid., p. 25.

31 V. Hall, *The making of Ireland's landscape since the Ice Age* (2011), p. 114.

32 Kelly, *EIF*, pp 379–90.

33 Ibid., pp 380–1.

34 M. Stout, *The Irish ringfort* (1997); F. McCormick, 'The decline of the cow: agricultural and settlement change in early medieval Ireland' (2008).

35 McCormick, 'The decline of the cow'.

36 M. Clinton, *The souterrains of Ireland* (2011).

37 McCormick, 'The decline of the cow', 218; C. Lynn and J.A. McDowell, *The excavation of a raised rath in the Glenarm Valley, County Antrim* (2011), pp 570–88.

38 N. Brady, 'Mills in medieval Ireland: looking beyond design' (2006); F. McCormick and E.V. Murray, *Excavations at Knowth 3: Knowth and the zooarchaeology of early Christian Ireland* (2007), pp 112–15.

39 B. Raftery, *Trackway excavations in the Mountdillon Bogs, Co. Longford, 1985–91* (1996).

40 O. Bergin and R.I. Best (eds), '*Tochmarc Étaíne*' (1938), 176–8.

41 Ibid.

42 Kelly, *EIF*, pp 395–6.

43 www.excavations.ie (ref. 2005:1529 Clonfad 3).

44 A. O'Sullivan, *Crannogs: lake-dwellings in early Ireland* (2000).

45 A. O'Sullivan, R. Sands and E.P. Kelly, *Coolure Demesne crannog, Lough Derravaragh: an introduction to its archaeology and landscapes* (2007), p. 71.

46 F. Kelly, *A guide to early Irish law* (1988).

47 C. Cotter, 'Cahercommaun fort, Co. Clare: a reassessment of its cultural context' (1999).

48 L. Bieler, *The Patrician texts in the Book of Armagh* (1979), pp 150–1, §33 (1).

49 N. Ó Muraíle, 'Some early Connacht population-groups' (2000), p. 169.

50 K. Meyer, *The triads of Ireland* (1906), p. 6, §43.

51 Koch and Carey, *Celtic heroic age*, p. 185.

52 C. Doherty, 'Exchange and trade in medieval Ireland' (1980); idem, 'Some aspects of hagiography as a source for Irish economic history' (1982); idem, 'The monastic town in early medieval Ireland' (1985).

53 J. Bradley, 'The monastic town of Clonmacnoise' (1998), pp 45, 50.

54 C. Swift, 'Forts and fields: a study of 'monastic towns' in seventh- and eighth-century Ireland' (1998), 107–8, 112–13, 119.

55 A. Southall, *The city in time and space* (2000), p. 4.

56 Bieler, *Patrician texts*, p. 186 (14).

57 G.P. Brogiolo, N. Gauthier and N. Christie (eds), *Towns and their territories between late antiquity and the early Middle Ages* (2000).

58 K. Neill, *An archaeological survey of County Armagh* (2009), pp 250–1.

59 J. Blair, 'Small towns, 600–1270' (2000), p. 249.

60 I.W. Doyle, 'The early medieval activity at Dalkey Island: a reassessment' (1998), 100.

61 D. Griffiths, 'Towns and their hinterlands' (2011), p. 155.

62 R. Ó Floinn, 'The Anglo-Saxon connection: Irish metalwork, AD400–800' (2009).

63 K. Meyer, *Sanas Cormaic: an Old-Irish glossary compiled by Cormac úa Cuilennáin, king-bishop of Cashel in the tenth century* (1912; repr. 1994), §§1050, 1076.

64 D. Griffiths, 'Sand dunes and stray finds: evidence for pre-Viking trade?' (2009), p. 280.

65 Ibid.

66 R. Ó Floinn, 'The archaeology of the early Viking Age in Ireland' (1998), p. 139.

67 L. Simpson, 'The first phase of Viking activity in Ireland: archaeological evidence from Dublin' (2010), p. 424.

68 Ó Floinn, 'The archaeology of the early Viking Age in Ireland', pp 140–2.

69 E. O'Brien, 'The location and context of Viking burials at Kilmainham and Islandbridge, Dublin' (1998), pp 219–20.

70 Simpson, 'The first phase of Viking activity', pp 426–7.

71 C. Downham, *Viking kings of Britain and Ireland: the dynasty of Ívarr to AD1014* (2007).

72 J. Sheehan, 'Ireland's Viking Age hoards: sources and contacts' (2001).

73 Ibid., p. 56.

74 S.M. Sindbæk, 'Close ties and long-range relations: the emporia network in early Viking Age exchange' (2010), pp 436–8.

75 Downham, *Viking kings of Britain and Ireland*, passim.

76 B. Schulze-Thulin, 'Old Norse in Ireland' (1996).

77 For an indication of the extent of this evidence, see the *Medieval Dublin excavations* series published by the Royal Irish Academy and the National Museum of Ireland and *Medieval Dublin: Proceedings of the Friends of Medieval Dublin symposia* edited by Seán Duffy and published by Four Courts Press.

78 P.F. Wallace, 'The English presence in Viking Dublin' (1986), pp 207–8.

79 S. Geraghty, *Viking Dublin: botanical evidence from Fishamble Street* (1996); P.F. Wallace, 'Ireland's Viking towns' (2001).

80 Wallace, 'Ireland's Viking towns', p. 45.

81 Ibid., pp 39–41.

82 Geraghty, *Botanical evidence*, p. 70.

83 Ibid., pp 42–4.

84 E. Wincott Heckett, *Viking Age headcoverings from Dublin* (2003).

85 Ibid., pp 105–6. See also P.F. Wallace, 'The economy and commerce of Viking Age Dublin' (1987), pp 219–20.

86 J. Bradley, 'Some reflections on the problem of Scandinavian settlement in the hinterland of Dublin during the ninth century' (2009); M. Murphy and M. Potterton, *The Dublin region in the Middle Ages: settlement, land-use and economy* (2010), pp 58–67.

87 Geraghty, *Botanical evidence*, p. 67.

88 Ibid., p. 71.

89 R. Johnson, *Viking Age Dublin* (2004), p. 88.

CHAPTER 2
Kingdoms, kings and people

1 For definitions of land divisions, see P. MacCotter, *Medieval Ireland: territorial, political and economic divisions* (2008), pp 17–25.

2 S. Reynolds, *Kingdoms and communities in western Europe, 900–1300* (1984; repr. 1997), p. 250.

3 T.M. Charles-Edwards, *Early Irish and Welsh kinship* (1993), pp 116–17, 143–7.

4 J.T. Koch, 'Celts, Britons and Gaels: names, peoples and identities' (2003).

5 Toner, 'Identifying Ptolemy's Irish places and tribes'.

6 C. Doherty, 'Érainn' (2005).

7 D. McManus, *A guide to ogam* (1991); A. Harvey, 'Problems in dating the origin of the ogham script' (2001).

8 McManus, *A guide to ogam*, pp 52, 118–20; Charles-Edwards, *EIWK*, pp 147–65.

9 *CIIC*, pp 150, 156, 163, 175, 178; Charles-Edwards, *EIWK*, pp 150–1.

10 *CIIC*, no. 41.

11 Ibid., no. 307.

12 Ibid., nos 112–13.

13 Charles-Edwards, *EIWK*, p. 152; *CIIC*, nos 263, 292, 300.

14 *CGH*, p. 120:136a10–16.

15 Ó Muraíle, 'Some early Connacht population-groups'.

16 J.T. Koch (ed.), *Celtic culture: a historical encyclopedia* (2006).

17 F.J. Byrne, *Irish king and high-kings* (1973; repr. 2001), p. 108.

18 E. Bhreathnach, 'The medieval kingdom of Brega' (2005).

19 For a detailed record of the kings and kingships of Brega, see C. Swift, 'The early history of Knowth' (2008) with contribution by F.J. Byrne. Byrne's list of titles and genealogical tables (pp 55–87) are particularly instructive.

20 P. Byrne, 'Ciannachta Breg before Síl nÁeda Sláine' (2000).

21 Swift, 'The early history of Knowth', pp 10–18.

22 E. Bhreathnach, 'Medieval sub-kingdoms of Brega' (2004).

23 S. Bertelli, *The king's body: sacred rituals of power in medieval and early modern Europe* (2001).

24 N. Brisch (ed.), *Religion and power: divine kingship in the ancient world and beyond* (2008).

25 Ibid., pp 8–9.

26 F. Kelly (ed.), *Audacht Morainn* (1976).

27 Ibid., pp xviii–xix.

28 M. Fomin, 'Classifications of kings in early Ireland and India': www.celto-indica.celtologica.com.

29 Fomin, 'Classifications of kings', p. 8, §4.4 (A); Kelly, *Audacht Morainn*, pp 18–19, §62 (B).

30 Kelly, *Audacht Morainn*, pp 18–19, §59.

31 M. Dillon, 'The Hindu act of truth in Celtic tradition' (1947); C. Watkins, '*Is tre fhír flathemon*: marginalia to *Audacht Morainn*' (1979).

32 Kelly, *Audacht Morainn*, pp 14–15, §51.

33 Ibid., pp 10–13, §32.

34 S. Hellmann (ed.), *Ps.-Cyprianus. De xii abusiuis saeculi* (1909); A. Breen, 'The evidence of antique Irish exegesis in Pseudo-Cyprian, *De duodecim abusivis saeculi*' (1987).

35 J. Bumke (trans. T. Dunlap), *Courtly culture: literature and society in the High Middle Ages* (1986; repr. 1991), pp 277–8. For comments on the similarity between *De duodecim abusivis saeculi* and vernacular tracts on kings, see T.M. Charles-Edwards, 'A contract between king and people in early medieval Ireland? *Críth Gablach* on kingship' (1994), 114; R. Meens, 'Politics, mirrors of princes and the Bible: sins, kings and the well-being of the realm' (1998).

36 D.R. Howlett (ed.), *Liber Epistolarum Sancti Patricii Episcopi. The book of letters of Saint Patrick the bishop* (1994); C. Doherty, 'Kingship in early Ireland' (2005); www.confessio.ie (Royal Irish Academy).

37 J. Carey, 'From David to Labraid: sacral kingship and the emergence of monotheism in Israel and Ireland' (2008).

38 Ibid., pp 3–4.

39 Ibid., p. 8.

40 Doherty, 'Kingship in early Ireland', p. 22.

41 Carey, 'From David to Labraid', p. 11.

42 P.J. Frandsen, 'Aspects of kingship in ancient Egypt' (2008), p. 47. For a consideration of the concept of *maat* from a Celtic and Indo-European linguistic perspective, see K. McCone's very important article '"King" and "Queen" in Celtic and Indo-European' (1998), 9.

43 D. Freidel, 'Maya divine kingship' (2008), p. 192.

44 K. McCone, *Pagan past and Christian present* (1990).

45 McCone, *Pagan past*, pp 109–20. For a brief survey of the *hieros gamos*, see M. Warmind, 'Sacred kingship among the Celts' (1992).

46 The downgrading of the goddess in her role as the personification of sovereignty was noted by M. Herbert in 'Goddess and king: the sacred marriage in early Ireland' (1992).

47 T.F. O'Rahilly, 'On the origin of the names Érainn and Ériu' (1946); P. Mac Cana, 'Aspects of the theme of king and goddess in Irish literature' (1955–6) and (1958–9); B. Jaski, *Early Irish kingship* (2000), pp 63–72.

48 Hull, 'Conall Corc and the Corco Luigde' (1947), 905. The text is available on www.ucc.ie/celt.

49 I follow Byrne's text in *IKHK*, p. 195.

50 For the relationship between horses, women and sovereignty, see Doherty, 'Kingship in early Ireland', pp 15–20; M. Deane, 'From sacred marriage to clientship:

a mythical account of the establishment of kingship as an institution' (2011).

51 E. Bhreathnach and K. Murray (eds), 'Baile Chuinn Chétchathaig: edition' (2005).

52 D. Bracken, 'Authority and duty: Columbanus and the primacy of Rome' (2002).

53 Bieler, Patrician texts, pp 84–5 (I:15 (2)).

54 M. Ní Dhonnchadha, 'The guarantor list of Cáin Adomnáin, 697' (1982).

55 K. Meyer, The instructions of King Cormac mac Airt (1909), pp 2–5. For a survey of later texts, see E. Bhreathnach, 'Perceptions of kingship in early medieval Irish vernacular literature' (2007).

56 E. FitzPatrick, Royal inauguration in Gaelic Ireland, c.1100–1600: a cultural landscape study (2004), pp 96–7. It appears to have been in the vicinity of the Glen of the Downs, Co. Wicklow.

57 E. Bhreathnach and C. Newman (eds), Tara (1995); C. Newman, Tara: an archaeological survey (1997); E. Bhreathnach (ed.), The kingship and landscape of Tara (2005); E. Bhreathnach and C. Newman, Tara, Co. Meath: a guide to the ceremonial complex (2008).

58 J. Fenwick and C. Newman, 'Geomagnetic survey on the Hill of Tara, Co. Meath, 1998–9' (2002); M.B. Deevy and D. Murphy (eds), Places along the way: first findings on the M3 (2009).

59 E. Grogan et al., The Rath of the Synods, Tara, Co. Meath: excavations by Seán P. Ó Ríordáin (2008).

60 M. O'Sullivan, Duma na nGiall: the Mound of the Hostages, Tara (2005).

61 J. Carey, 'Time, memory and the Boyne necropolis' (1993); S. Semple, 'A fear of the past: the place of the prehistoric burial mound in the ideology of middle and later Anglo-Saxon England' (1998).

62 P. Browne, The cult of the saints: its rise and function in Latin Christianity (1981), pp 1–22; I.M. Lapidus, A history of Islamic societies (2002), pp 94, 209, 374.

63 E. O'Brien and E. Bhreathnach, 'Irish boundary ferta, their physical manifestation and historical context' (2011).

64 R. Schot, C. Newman and E. Bhreathnach (eds), Landscapes of cult and kingship (2011).

65 D.A. Binchy, 'The fair of Tailtiu and the feast of Tara' (1958), 134.

66 Ibid., 135.

67 E. Bhreathnach, 'Temoria: caput Scotorum?' (1996), 82–6.

68 CIH, 2219:39–40.

69 C. Newman, 'Re-composing the archaeological landscape of Tara' (2005), p. 378.

70 E. Bhreathnach, 'Transforming kingship and cult: the provincial ceremonial capitals in early medieval Ireland' (2011).

71 Bieler, Patrician texts, pp 82–3 (I:13 (12) (2)).

72 T. O'Loughlin, 'Reading Muirchú's Tara-event with its background as a trial of "biblical divinities"' (2003).

73 E. Bhreathnach, 'Níell cáich úa Néill nasctar géill: the political context of Baile Chuinn Chétchathaig' (2005).

74 Byrne, IKHK, pp 109–14, 137–8; A.P. Smyth, 'Húi Néill and the Leinstermen in the Annals of Ulster, 431–516AD' (1974).

75 Byrne, IKHK, pp 48–105; D. Ó Corráin, 'Historical need and literary narrative' (1986); T.M. Charles-Edwards, Early Christian Ireland (2000), pp 441–68; B. Lacey, Cenél Conaill and the Donegal kingdoms, AD500–800 (2006).

76 D. Sproule, 'Origins of the Éoganachta' (1984); 'Politics and pure narrative in the stories about Corc of Cashel' (1985); E. Bhreathnach, 'Tara and Cashel: manifestations of the centre of the cosmos in the north and the south' (forthcoming).

77 A. MacSamhráin and P. Byrne, 'Prosopography I' (2005), pp 201–3.

78 Ibid., pp 182–3.

79 Sharpe, Life of Columba, pp 122, 263 n. 70.

80 MacSamhráin and Byrne, 'Prosopography I', pp 198–201.

81 Charles-Edwards, Chronicle of Ireland, p. 153 (658).

82 MacSamhráin and Byrne, 'Prosopography I', p. 200.

83 Sharpe, Life of Columba, pp 55, 203.

84 T.M. Charles-Edwards, 'Irish warfare before 1100' (1996); A. Halpin, Weapons and warfare in Viking and medieval Dublin (2008), pp 10–17.

85 See pp 142–3.

86 Swift, 'The early history of Knowth', p. 11 (fig. 1.1).

87 676 'The destruction of Ailech Frigrenn by Fínsnechta Fledach'. Questions have been raised as to the probability of a midland king being capable of destroying the principal royal seat so far north. MacSamhráin and Byrne ('Prosopography I', p. 202) suggest that he may have

destroyed *Ailech Muirinne* in the midlands, once the residence of his uncle Diarmait Ruanaid.

88 A. Connon, 'Prosopography II. A prosopography of the early queens of Tara' (2005), pp 309–12.

89 Ibid., pp 309–10.

90 M. Dillon, *The cycles of kings* (1946; repr. 1994), pp 103–14.

91 Charles-Edwards, 'A contract between king and people in early medieval Ireland?'

92 D.A. Binchy (ed.), *Críth Gablach* (1970), pp 19–24.

93 Kelly, *GEIL*, pp 198–200.

94 Ibid., pp 23–5.

95 *CG*, p. 95 (*gell*).

96 Charles-Edwards, 'A contract between king and people in early medieval Ireland?', 113.

97 Knott, *Togail*, p. 17:566–7.

98 K. Murray (ed.), *Baile in Scáil 'The phantom's frenzy'* (2004), 139.

99 Halpin, *Weapons and warfare*, pp 10–25.

1 E. O'Donovan and J. Geber, 'Excavations on Mount Gamble Hill, Swords, Co. Dublin' (2010), pp 235–7.

2 A.D. Carr, '*Teulu* and *Penteulu*' (2000).

3 B. Ó Cuív, 'The motif of threefold death' (1973); T. Ó Cathasaigh, 'The threefold death in early Irish sources' (1994); Ní Bhrolcháin, *EIL*, pp 129–36.

4 T.M. Charles-Edwards, 'Early medieval kingships in the British Isles' (1989).

5 T.M. Charles-Edwards, 'The Airgíalla charter poem: the legal content' (2005).

6 Ibid., p. 119.

7 *CG*, p. 23:596–7: *Gé[il]l díthma i nglasaib i n-airthiur fhochlai.*

8 S. Connolly, '*Vita Prima Sanctae Brigitae*: background and historical value' (1989), 33, para. 66.

9 J. Nelson, 'Kingship and royal government' (1995), p. 408.

10 R. Ó Floinn, 'Patrons and politics: art, artefact and methodology' (2001), pp 1–8; A. Kelly, 'The discovery of Phocaean Red Slip Ware (PRSW) Form 3 and Bii ware (LR1 amphorae) on sites in Ireland' (2010).

11 R. Chapman Stacey, *Dark speech: the performance of law in early Ireland* (2007), p. 153.

12 *CG*, pp 20–1:514–24.

13 E. Bozóky, *La politique des reliques de Constantin à Saint Louis* (2006), pp 50–72.

14 Kelly, *EIF* (1997), pp 369–70, 403, 458–62; Jaski, *Early Irish kingship*, pp 49–56.

15 K. Mulchrone (ed.), *Bethu Pátraic* (1939), pp 122–3.

16 D. Ó Murchadha, 'Carman, site of Óenach Carmain: a proposed location' (2002).

17 E. FitzPatrick, 'The landscape of Máel Sechnaill's *rígdál* at Ráith Áeda, AD859' (2005), p. 269.

18 Ibid., pp 270–5.

19 Bhreathnach and O'Brien, 'Irish boundary *ferta*'.

20 Kelly, *EIF*, p. 403.

21 R. Ó Floinn, 'Freestone Hill, Co. Kilkenny: a reassessment' (2000).

22 MacCotter, *Medieval Ireland*, pp 49–51.

23 Kelly, *GIEL*, p. 19; Kelly, *EIF*, pp 319, 538–9.

24 M. MacNeill, *The festival of Lughnasa* (1962; repr. 1982), pp 43–66; Kelly, *EIF*, pp 459–60.

25 S. Connolly and J.-M. Picard (eds), 'Cogitosus's Life of Brigit: content and value' (1987), 14–15, para. 4.

26 Doherty, 'Exchange and trade in early medieval Ireland', 81.

27 Kelly, *EIF*, pp 219–47; M.A. Monk and E. Kelleher, 'An assessment of the archaeological evidence for Irish corn-drying kilns in the light of the results of archaeological experiments and archaeobotanical studies' (2005).

28 McErlean and Crothers, *Harnessing the tides*.

29 M. Seaver, 'Against the grain: early medieval settlement and burial on the Blackhill. Excavations at Raystown, Co. Meath' (2010).

30 D.A. Binchy, 'Irish law tracts re-edited: *Coibnes Uisci Thairidne*' (1955).

31 Ibid., 70–1, §11.

32 Ibid., §12.

33 Ibid., 68–9, §9.

34 Kelly, 'An Old-Irish text on court procedure'.

35 FitzPatrick, *Royal inauguration in Gaelic Ireland*, pp 81–97.

36 S. Semple, 'Locations of assembly in early Anglo-Saxon England' (2004), p. 150.

37 For the fundamental commentaries on this subject, see D. Ó Corráin, 'Marriage in early Ireland' (1985); Kelly, *GEIL*, pp 68–91; Charles-Edwards, *EIWK*, pp 23–165, 545–60 (glossary); T. O'Loughlin, 'Marriage and sexuality in the Hibernensis' (1997); Jaski, *Early Irish kingship*, passim; N. McLeod, 'Kinship' (2000).

38 B. Ní Chonaill, 'Fosterage, child-rearing in medieval Ireland' (1997).

39 K. Hollo, 'Fingal Rónáin: the medieval Irish text as argumentative space' (2004); idem, 'Allegoresis and literary creativity in eighth-century Ireland: the case of *Echtrae Chonnlai*' (2011); Deane, 'From sacred marriage to clientship' (2011).

40 Charles-Edwards, *EIWK*, pp 34–6.

41 *Nemed* is a key term in Irish society. Cognate with other words such as Gaulish and British *nemeton* 'sacred place, grove' (Koch, *Celtic culture*, p. 1350), it means 'priviliged', often with a religious connotation.

42 Kelly, *GEIL*, pp 7–10; for a very perceptive definition of classes in early Ireland, see K. McCone, '*Aided Cheltchair maic Uthechair*: hounds, heroes and hospitallers in early Irish myth and story' (1984), 27–30.

43 *CG*, p. 24, §48. My own translation.

44 For discussion of the role and status of a bishop in society, see pp 75, 79, 102, 149, 167–8.

45 *CCH*, p. 77, liber XXV, cap. 4.

46 Charles-Edwards, *EIWK*, p. 39.

47 D. Ó Murchadha, 'Early history and settlements of the Laígis' (1999); MacCotter, *Medieval Ireland*, p. 173.

48 P.D. Sweetman, O. Alcock and B. Moran (comps), *Archaeological inventory of County Laois* (1995), p. 9, nos 51–9.

49 Dún Másc is associated with the Uí Chrimthainn Áin, who were not of the Loígsi but were Uí Failge, their near neighbours with whom they had much interaction. Excavations undertaken by Brian Hodkinson during the 1990s uncovered evidence for the incorporation of the early medieval dry stone walls into the masonry of the Anglo-Norman castle: see B. Hodkinson, 'The Rock of Dunamase' (1995).

50 For a summary report of the Ballydavis excavations, see V.J. Keeley, 'Ballydavis, Co. Laois 95E111' on www.heritagecouncil.ie (unpublished excavations).

51 Mulchrone, *Bethu Phátraic*, p. 117:2263–70.

52 *CGH*, p. 92:127a42–8.

53 *CGH*, p. 93:127b13–14. For the meaning of these terms, see Charles-Edwards, 'The Airgíalla charter poem', pp 107–12.

54 *CGH*, p. 93:12718–19: *Ní-s-toirchet gillae ríg aile do rígaib Lagen acht gilla ríg Laíchsi Réta* 'The servant of another king from among the kings of [the province of] Leinster do not come to him except the servant of the king of Loígsi Réta'.

55 Charles-Edwards, *ECI*, p. 531.

56 *CGH*, p. 94:127b19–26.

57 *CGH*, pp 88–98.

58 P. Ó Riain, *Corpus genealogicarum sanctorum Hiberniae* (1985), p. 324 (Feibe).

59 *CGH*, p. 93:127b4.

60 *CG*, p. 8:199–200.

61 Ibid., p. 23:595–6.

62 Ibid., p. 5:124.

63 *CG*, p. 5:125–7; N. Power, 'Classes of women described in the Senchas Már' (1936), pp 96–9.

64 *CG*, p. 21:533–5.

65 For the most extensive commentaries on this subject, see R. Thurneysen et al., *Studies in early Irish law* (1936); D. Ó Corráin, 'Women in early Irish society' (1978); D. Ó Corráin, 'Women and the law in early Ireland' (1995); B. Jaski, 'Marriage laws in Ireland and on the Continent in the early Middle Ages' (1996).

66 Connon, 'Prosopography II', p. 313.

67 For an introduction to this subject in other societies, see F. and J. Gies, *Marriage and the family in the Middle Ages* (1989); P. Stafford, *Queens, concubines and dowagers: the king's wife in the early Middle Ages* (1983); G. Clark, *Women in late antiquity: pagan and Christian lifestyles* (1993); P. Stafford, 'Queens and queenship' (2009).

68 Edited and translated into German by Thurneysen, *Studies in early Irish law*, pp 1–75; English translation by D. Ó Corráin on www.ucc.ie/celt.

69 H. Wasserschleben (ed.), *Die irische kanonensammlung* (1885) (*CCH*).

70 Jaski, *Early Irish kingship*, p. 70.

71 Ó Corráin, 'Women in early Irish society'.

72 Stafford, *Queens, concubines and dowagers*, pp 49–54.

73 Ibid., p. 49.

74 M. Herbert, '*Rí Éirenn, Rí Alban*, kingship and identity in the ninth and tenth centuries' (2000), pp 69–70.

75 D. Ó Corráin, 'Irish law and canon law' (1987).

76 *CCH*, liber XLVI (*De ratione matrimonii*), pp 185–95.

77 D. Greene (ed.), *Fingal Rónáin and other stories* (1975); Ní Bhrolcháin, *EIL*, pp 74–6.

78 Ó Corráin, 'Women in early Irish society', pp 4–6; Jaski, 'Marriage laws in the early Middle Ages', pp 30–3.

79 *FAIre.*, pp 132–3.

80 *VPrima*, p. 14, §§1–4.

81 Connon, 'Prosopography II', pp 279–80; Stafford, 'Sons and mothers', pp 79–100.

82 B. Ní Chonaill, 'Child-centred law in medieval Ireland (www.eprints.gl.ac.uk).

83 Kelly, *GEIL*, p. 270, §19.

84 Ibid., p. 270, §18.

85 *VSC*, II:40.

86 Plummer, *Bethada*, I, p. 191; 2, p. 185. For comprehensive studies of many aspects of sex and procreation in early Irish literature, see L. Bitel, 'Sin, sex and celibacy in early Christian Ireland' (1987); idem, '"Conceived in sin, born in delights": stories of procreation from early Ireland' (1992).

87 O'Donovan and Geber, 'Excavations on Mount Gamble Hill', pp 234–5.

88 Ní Chonaill, 'Child-centred law in medieval Ireland', p. 5 (quoting *CIH*, 375.7, 400.8–9).

89 O'Donovan and Geber, 'Excavations on Mount Gamble Hill', pp 233–4.

90 J. Ó Néill and J. Coughlan, 'An enclosed early medieval cemetery at Cherrywood, Co. Dublin' (2010), p. 249.

91 D.A. Binchy, '*Bretha Crólige*' (1938), 25, §29.

92 *VPrima*, p. 44, §101.

93 *CCH*, liber XLV, cap. 4–5.

94 Plummer, *VSH*, I, p. 269, §xxvi.

95 Charles-Edwards, *EIWK*, p. 39.

96 Kelly, *GEIL*, pp 87–90; Charles-Edwards, *EIWK*, pp 78–82; Ní Chonaill, 'Child-centred law', pp 10–15.

97 Charles-Edwards, *EIWK*, p. 29.

98 Kelly, *GEIL*, p. 87.

99 C. O'Rahilly (ed.), *Táin Bó Cúailnge: recension 1* (1976), pp 14–15.

1 For an indication of the types of sites on which such objects occur, see www.emap.ie and a particular profile site, see Cotter, 'Cahercommaun Fort, Co. Clare'.

2 *AL*, II, pp 146–7, 160–1.

3 N. Whitfield, 'Dress and accessories in the early Irish tale "The wooing of Becfhola"' (2006).

4 Ní Chonaill, 'Child-centred law', pp 15–19.

5 J. Gantz (trans.), *Early Irish myths and sagas* (1981), pp 141–2.

6 T. Ó Cathasaigh, *The heroic biography of Cormac mac Airt* (1977), pp 51–2.

7 *VSC*, II:33–4.

8 *VPrima*, p. 16, §II.7.

9 Charles-Edwards, *EIWK*, p. 79.

10 *VSC*, III:2. Interestingly, Adomnán uses the same Latin word, *nutritor*, to describe the Christian Cruithnechán and druid Broichan.

11 See p. 176.

12 E. MacNeill, *Celtic Ireland* (1921; repr. 1981), pp 114–43.

13 These questions were formulated by Charles-Edwards (*EIWK*, pp 89–90) in his dealing with MacNeill's hypotheses on succession. While many disagree with MacNeill and indeed Charles-Edwards' conclusions, the debate ultimately revolves around these fundamental questions.

14 MacNeill, *Celtic Ireland*, p. 114.

15 There have been many discussions on this subject, the most extensive and recent of which include G. Mac Niocaill, 'The "heir-designate" in early medieval Ireland' (1968); D. Ó Corráin, 'Irish regnal succession: a reappraisal' (1971); Charles-Edwards, *EIWK*, pp 89–111; Jaski, *Early Irish kingship*; McLeod, 'Kinship'.

16 Kelly, *Audacht Morainn*, pp 16–17, §55.

17 Ibid., §56.

18 *CGH*, p. 388:326i45–327a20.

19 Charles-Edwards, *ECI*, pp 540–1; MacCotter, *Medieval Ireland*, pp 184–7.

20 *CCH*, p. 100, liber XXXI, cap. 19.

21 Jaski, *Early Irish kingship*, pp 130–7.

22 Byrne, *IKHK*, pp 130–64; I. Warntjes, 'The alternation of the kingship of Tara between 734 and 944' (2004).

23 *VSC*, I:14.

24 C. Baker, 'Occam's duck: three early medieval cemeteries or ecclesiastical sites?' (2010).

25 C. Mount, 'Excavation of an early medieval promonotary fort and enclosed cemetery at Knoxspark, Co. Sligo' (2010).

26 Schot et al. (eds), *Landscapes of cult and kingship*, passim.

27 V. Hull (ed.), 'The exile of Conall Corc' (1941), 950. For a new consideration of the character of the kingship of Cashel, see E. Bhreathnach, 'Tara and Cashel: manifestations of the centre of the cosmos in the north and the south' in J. Borsje et al. (eds), *Celtic cosmology: perspectives from Ireland and Scotland* (forthcoming).

28 M. Dillon (ed.), 'The story of the finding of Cashel' (1952), 67, 72:110–12.

29 Greene, *Fingal Rónáin*, p. 31.

30 Mulchrone, *Bethu Pátraic*, pp 79–80.

31 Kelly, *GEIL*, pp 9–10.

32 T. O'Donoghue (ed.), 'Advice to a prince' (1921–3), 48–9 (§§26–34: my own translation).

33 R.M. Smith (ed.), 'Urchuillti bretheman' in J. Fraser, P. Grosjean and J.G. O'Keeffe, *Irish texts*, IV (1934).

34 L. Breatnach, 'Satire, praise and the early Irish poet' (2006), 63.

36 L. Breatnach, *Uraicecht na ríar* (1987), 102–3, §2.

37 Breatnach, 'Satire, praise and the early Irish poet', 72–3.

38 Ibid., 74.

39 Breatnach, *Uraicecht na ríar*, 106–7, §7.

40 For descriptions of the *bóaire*, his status and his obligations, see *CG*, pp 77–8; Charles-Edwards, *EIWK*, pp 354–62; Kelly, *EIF*, pp 447–8.

41 Kelly, *EIF*, *bóaire*, passim.

42 *CG*, pp 8–10; Kelly, *EIF*, pp 361–2.

43 C.J. Lynn and J.A. McDowell, '*Crith Gablach* and the status of the rath occupants' (2011), pp 603–10.

44 Plummer, *VSH*, II, p. 207 (iv).

45 Charles-Edwards, *EIWK*, pp 307–63.

46 Meyer, *The triads of Ireland*, §§167, 185, 235, 248.

47 K. Meyer (ed.), 'The expulsion of the Déssi' (1907).

48 *VPrima*, p. 15, §4.

49 Ibid., pp 17–18, §18.

50 R.M. Smith, 'Bretha im gatta' (1934), p. 20, §5.

51 Ibid., p. 22, §22.

52 E. O'Brien, 'Excavation of a multi-period site at Ballymacaward, Ballyshannon, Co. Donegal' (1999).

53 R. Tobin and J. Sunderland et al., 'Excavations and specialist reports: Corbally 1' (unpublished reports for Kilsaran Concrete Products Ltd. and Margaret Gowen and Co.). Summarized on www.mappingdeathdb.ie.

54 E. Bhreathnach, 'The Tech Midchuarta 'house of the mead circuit': feasting, the royal circuits and the king's court in early medieval Ireland' (1998).

55 T. Gross and R. Schieffer (ed.), *Hinkmar von Reims: de ordine palatii* (1980), pp 64–6 (cap. V).

56 For comprehensive descriptions of both archaeological and documentary evidence of settlements in early Ireland, see Kelly, *GEIL*, pp 360–93; N. Edwards, 'The archaeology of early medieval Ireland, *c.*400–1169: settlement and economy' (2005). See also www.emap.ie.

57 *CG*, p. 23.

58 J.G. O'Keeffe, 'Cáin Domnaig' (1905), 201–3; A. Hamlin, 'Using mills on Sunday' (1982).

59 Kelly, *GEIL*, pp 65–6.

60 T.F. O'Rahilly, 'Eachlach urláir' (1921–3).

61 *CG*, pp 23:578–82; 38, 581n.

62 www.ucc.ie/celt (*Cáin Lánamna*, trans. Donncha Ó Corráin).

63 M. Fitzgerald, 'Textile production' (2012).

64 O'Keeffe, 'Cáin Domnaig', 206, §27.

65 A.G. Van Hamel (ed.), *Compert Con Culainn* (1933), p. 23, §10.

66 M. Fitzgerald, 'Insular dress in early medieval Ireland' (1997), p. 257.

67 Whitfield, 'Dress and accessories' (2006).

68 For the origin of *corcra*, see D. McManus, 'A chronology of Latin loan-words in early Irish' (1983), 42, 48.

69 Whitfield, 'Dress and accessories', pp 11–12.

70 Hull, 'Conall Corc and the Corco Luigde', 900; Kelly, *EIF*, pp 267–9.

71 S. Youngs (ed.), '*The work of angels': masterpieces of Celtic metalwork* (1989), pp 72–124, 209–10.

72 Ibid., p. 201.

73 *AL*, III, pp 192–3; L. Breatnach, *A companion to the* Corpus Iuris Hibernici (2005), p. 420. See also B.G. Scott, 'An early Irish law tract on the blacksmith's forge' (1983).

74 *CG*, p. 23:592–3.

75 Kelly, *Audacht Morainn*, pp 10–11, §28.

76 M. O Daly (ed.), '*Lánellach tigi rích 7 ruirech*' (1962).

77 R. Warner, 'Clogher: an archaeological window on early medieval Tyrone and mid-Ulster' (2000), pp 45–9.

78 C.J. Lynn, 'Houses in rural Ireland, AD 500–1000' (1994), 82.

79 J. Bradley, 'Excavations at Moynagh Lough' (1991), 16–18.

80 A. O'Sullivan and T. Nicholl, 'Early medieval enclosures in Ireland: dwellings, daily life and social identity' (2011).

81 Koch and Carey, *The Celtic heroic age*, p. 118.

82 D.A. Binchy, 'Aimser chue' (1940; repr. 1995).

83 www.ucc.ie/celt.

84 Ibid.

85 *CG*, p. 19:478.

86 Binchy, 'Aimser chue', p. 20.

87 Kelly, *EIF*, pp 538–40.

88 M. Comber, 'Trade and communication networks in early historic Ireland' (2001).

89 Joe Fenwick, pers. comm.; B. Raftery, *Trackways through time*.

90 www.excavations.ie (1999:741).

91 For a detailed study of all aspects of hospitality in medieval Ireland, see C. O'Sullivan, *Hospitality in medieval Ireland, 900–1500* (2004), pp 211–46.

92 Meyer (ed.), *The triads of Ireland*, p. 35, §250.

93 *VPrima*, §86 (3). See also A.T. Lucas, 'Washing and bathing in ancient Ireland' (1965).

94 *CIH*, I, pp 180.34–181.12. See also *AL*, II, pp 33–4.

95 E.A. Gray (ed.), *Cath Maige Tuired. The second Battle of Mag Tuired* (1982), p. 35, §40; O'Sullivan, *Hospitality in medieval Ireland*, pp 68–70.

96 For a detailed discussion of the power of kings, see Charles-Edwards, *ECI*, pp 522–69.

97 Connolly and Picard, 'Cogitosus's Life of Brigit', 23–4, §30.

98 Charles-Edwards, 'Irish warfare before 1100' (1996).

99 *CG*, p. 22, §44; 87 (note on *errech*).

1 Koch and Carey, *The Celtic heroic age*, pp 204–5.

2 Connon, 'Prosopography II', pp 296–8.

3 M. Ní Bhrolcháin, 'Death-tales of early kings of Tara' (2011).

4 Ibid., p. 46.

5 S.H. O'Grady (ed. and trans.), *Silva Gadelica*, I, p. 82; Ní Bhrolcháin, 'Death-tales', pp 52–4.

6 W. Stokes, 'On the deaths of some Irish heroes' (1902), 310–11; Ní Bhrolcháin, 'Death-tales', p. 50.

7 M. Cahill and M. Sikora (eds), *Breaking ground, finding graves: reports on the excavations of burials by the National Museum of Ireland, 1927–2006* (2012).

8 Bieler, *Patrician texts*, pp 132–3, §12 (Tírechán).

9 K. Meyer (ed.), 'Conall Corc and the Corco Luigde' (1910), 60; Hull, 'Conall Corc and the Corco Luigde', 901.

10 E. O'Brien, 'Early medieval sentinel warrior burials' (2008).

11 E. Bhreathnach, 'Abbesses, minor dyasnties and king *in clericatu*: perspectives on Ireland, 700–850' (2001), pp 121–4.

12 *AU* (860.4).

13 ATig. (622.3). Bile Torten was a sacred tree located probably near Duleek, Co. Meath.

14 *AU* (851.2); *AFM* (849.8).

15 Bhreathnach and O'Brien, 'Irish boundary *ferta*' (2011).

16 F.T. Riley, 'Excavations in the townland of Pollacorrgune, Tuam, Co. Galway' (1936–7).

17 Doherty, 'Kingship in early Ireland'.

18 G. Coffey, 'On the excavation of a tumulus near Loughrea, Co. Galway' (1904).

19 J. Lehane et al., 'Three cemetery-settlement excavations in Co. Galway at Carrowkeel, Treanbaun and Owenbristy' (2010), pp 149, 151.

20 *DIL nasc, nia*.

21 C. Thomas, 'Early medieval Munster: thoughts on its primary Christian phase' (1998), p. 15; F. Moore, 'Munster ogham stones: siting, context and function' (1998).

22 *CIIC*, no. 40.

23 F. McCormick et al., 'A pagan-Christian transitional burial at Kiltullagh' (1995).

24 E. O'Brien, *Post-Roman Britain to Anglo-Saxon England* (1999), pp 53–4.

25 Murray, *Baile in Scáil*, passim.

26 Heather King, pers. comm.

27 Murray, *Baile in Scáil*, pp 43, 60, §42.

28 *CIIC*, II, p. 39, no. 590.

CHAPTER 3
Religion, ritual and ritualists

1 For this approach, see M. Aldhouse-Green, *The gods of the Celts* (1986); *The world of the druids* (1992); *Dictionary of Celtic myth and legend* (1997). For a more recent and integrated view of many of these topics, see Koch (ed.), *Celtic culture*, passim.

2 The intense dialogue about native and imported religion is best exemplified by McCone, *Pagan past*.

3 There are many influential works in these fields, some more accessible than others: see P. Boyer, *Religion explained: the human instincts that fashion gods, spirits and ancestors* (2002).

4 M. Eliade, *The sacred and the profane* (1959).

5 Boyer, *Religion explained*, pp 262–302.

6 E. Thomas Lawson, 'Ritual form and ritual frequency: from ethnographic reports to experimental findings' (2005).

7 R. Markus, *The end of ancient Christianity* (1990); P. Brown, *The rise of western Christendom: triumph and diversity, AD200–1000* (2002); McCone, *Pagan past*.

8 J. Palmer, 'Defining paganism in the Carolingian world' (2007), 425.

9 T.O. Clancy and G. Márkus (eds), *Iona: the earliest poetry of a Celtic monastery* (1995), pp 205–6.

10 Ibid., pp 202–3. For the original text (edited by K. Meyer), see www.ucc.ie/celt.

11 C. Bell, *Ritual. Perspectives and dimensions* (1997), pp 91–137.

12 The translation of Patrick's letters used here comes from the Royal Irish Academy's www.confessio.ie.

13 L.W. Hurtado, *At the origins of Christian worship* (1998), pp 44–5.

14 Eliade, *The sacred and the profane*; Boyer, *Religion explained*; H. Whitehouse and R.N. McCauley (eds), *Mind and religion: psychological and cognative foundations of religiosity* (2005); K. Ritari and A. Bergholm, *Approaches to religion and mythology in Celtic studies* (2008).

15 N. Whitfield, 'A suggested function for the holy well?' (2007).

16 www.mappingdeathdb.ie.

17 I owe this suggestion to Elizabeth O'Brien.

18 L. Breatnach (ed.), 'The caldron of poesy' (1981), 66–7.

19 Ibid., 93.

20 www.excavations.ie (Inchagreenoge. Summary report by Kate Taylor, Margaret Gowen and Co.).

21 Bieler, *Patrician texts*, pp 152–5, §39.

22 Ibid., pp 160–1, §47.

23 D. Mac Giolla Easpaig, 'Significance and etymology of the place-name *Temair*' (2005), pp 447–8.

24 'Baptism' in G.W. Bowersock, P. Brown and O. Grabar, *Late antiquity: a guide to the post classical world* (1999), pp 330–2.

25 *VPrima*, §6 (4).

26 Ibid., §9.

27 *CGH*, p. 196:148a33–9.

28 Charles-Edwards, *EIWK*, pp 175–6, 177–8.

29 Bhreathnach, 'Transforming kingship', p. 134.

30 Ó Cathasaigh, *Heroic biography*, pp 48–51.

31 M. O Daly (ed.), *Cath Maige Mucrama* (1975), pp 68–9, §11.

32 Ó Cathasaigh, *Heroic biography*, pp 49–50.

33 W. Stokes and J. Strachan (eds), *Thesaurus Paleohibernicus*, II, p. 354; J. Borsje, 'Druids, deer and "words of power": coming to terms with evil in medieval Ireland' (2008), p. 33.

34 Note the use of the term *imdegail* again here.

35 *VSC*, II:33.

36 J. Borsje and F. Kelly, '"The evil eye" in early Irish literature and law' (2003); Boyer, *Religion explained*, pp 221–9.

37 Meyer, *Sanas Cormaic*, pp 16–17, §§168, 181.

38 Borsje and Kelly, 'Evil eye', 34–9.

39 J. Borsje, *The Celtic evil eye and related mythological motifs in medieval Ireland* (2012), p. 195.

40 Hurtado, *On the origins of Christian worship*, p. 83.

41 www.confessio.ie, §§41–2.

42 Doherty, 'Kingship in early Ireland', pp 4–5.

43 Eliade, *The sacred and the profane*, pp 187–201.

44 Ibid., p. 193.

45 Bell, *Ritual*, p. 56 (quoting B. Lincoln, *Emerging from the chrysalis: rituals of women's initiations* (New York, 1991 rev. ed.), pp 1–3, 94, 100–1).

46 Jackson, *A Celtic miscellany*, pp 49–53.

47 L. Bieler, *The Irish penitentials* (1963; repr. 1975), p. 265, §36.

48 Eliade, *The sacred and profane*, p. 187.

49 Ibid., pp 132–4.

50 *CG*, pp 89–91 (notes).

51 R. Sharpe, 'Hiberno-Latin *laicus*, Irish *láech* and the devil's men' (1979); K.R. McCone, 'Werewolves, cyclopes, *díberga* and *fíanna*: juvenile delinquency in early Ireland' (1986); J.F. Nagy, *Conversing with angels and ancients: the literary myth of medieval Ireland* (1997), pp 293–9.

52 D.A. Binchy (ed.), 'The Old-Irish table of penitential commutations' (1962), 58–9; K. McCone, 'A tale of two ditties: poet and satirist in *Cath Maige Tuired*' (1989), pp 127–8.

53 P. Mac Cana, 'On the word *láech* "warrior"' (1976), 125–8; Sharpe, 'Hiberno-Latin *laicus*' (1979).

54 McCone, 'Werewolves', 22.

55 Sharpe, 'Hiberno-Latin *laicus*', 82.

56 Heist, *VSH*, p. 142, §44.

57 Connolly and Picard, 'Cogitosus's Life of Brigit', 20–1, §23.

58 O'Donovan and Geber, 'Excavations on Mount Gamble Hill', pp 227–38.

59 Boyer, *Religion explained*, p. 238.

60 O'Brien and Bhreathnach, 'Irish boundary *ferta*'.

61 T.M. Charles-Edwards, 'Boundaries in early Irish law' (1976), pp 83–7; O'Brien and Bhreathnach, 'Irish boundary *ferta*', pp 53–4.

62 O'Brien and Bhreathnach, 'Irish boundary *ferta*', p. 55.

63 O'Brien, 'Excavation at Ballymacaward'; O'Brien and Bhreathnach, 'Irish boundary *ferta*', pp 55–6, 59–60.

64 B. Lacey, *Cenél Conaill and the Donegal kingdoms*, AD500–800(2006), pp 61–5.

65 Brown, *The rise of western Christendom*, pp 262–3.

66 Ibid.

67 Bieler, *Patrician texts*, p. 142 (3).

68 Ibid., pp 144–5 (16, 21).

69 CCH, p. 57: XVIII (5); O'Brien, *Late Roman Britain to Anglo-Saxon England*, p. 53.

70 W. Stokes (ed.), *The martyrology of Oengus the Culdee. Félire Óengusso* (1905), p. 25, §189.

71 Ibid., p. 20, §69.

72 E. O'Brien, 'Burnt magic' (2010), pp 195–8.

73 R. O'Hara, 'Final report: M3 Clonee–North of Kells; Dunshaughlin–Navan. Collierstown 1, Co. Meath' (2009). See also www.mappingdeathdb.ie for details of all these burials.

74 P. Randolph-Quinney, 'An unusual burial at Ballygarraun West' (2007), 30–1.

75 T. Thompson, 'Clocha geala/cloche uaisle: white quartz in Irish tradition' (2005). I wish to thank Charles Doherty for bringing this reference to my attention.

76 VSC, I:41.

77 Ibid., III:23.

78 The standard work on the druids, and one that approaches the subject with more caution than most other commentaries, is S. Piggott, *The druids* (1999 repr.).

79 M. Beard, 'Priesthood in the Roman republic' (1990).

80 L. Adkins and R.A. Adkins (eds), *Dictionary of Roman religion* (1996), pp 4, 190–1.

81 P.F. Bradshaw, *The search for the origins of Christian worship: sources and methods for the study of early liturgy* (2002), pp 201–5.

82 Ibid., p. 205.

83 C. Newman, 'The sacral landscape of Tara: a preliminary exploration' (2011).

84 Ó Floinn, 'Early Christianity in Ireland' (2012), p. 15.

85 R. Latvio, '*Neimed*: exploring social distinctions and sacredness in early Irish legal sources' (2008).

86 Kelly, GEIL, p. 9.

87 Bieler, *Patrician texts*, pp 162–3:51 (4); P. Ó Riain, 'When and why *Cothraige* was first equated with *Patricius*?' (1997).

88 P. MacCotter, *Colmán of Cloyne: a study* (2004), pp 23–8.

89 For a detailed study of this archaeological landscape, see M. Doody, *The Ballyhoura Hills Project* (2008).

90 P. Ó Riain, 'Traces of Lug in early Irish hagiographical tradition' (1977), 148; idem, 'Irish saints' cults and ecclesiastical families' (2002), pp 292–7.

91 See p. 136.

92 Boyer, *Religion explained*, p. 309.

93 Bell, *Ritual*, p. 176.

94 Binchy, 'Bretha Crólige', 26–7, §32. I have incorporated a summary of the commentary and some of the Old Irish terms in parenthesis.

95 Ibid., 28–9, §34.

96 O'Grady, *Silva Gadelica*, I, p. 332; J. Carey, 'Tara and the supernatural' (2005), p. 48.

97 ATig., 308–9. I have changed the translation.

98 D. Ó Cróinín, *Early medieval Ireland, 400–1200* (1995), pp 14–40.

99 www.confessio.ie.

1 *Confessio*, §58.

2 Ó Floinn, 'Early Christianity in Ireland', pp 13–17; McManus, 'Latin loan-words'.

3 A. Woodward, *Shrines and sacrifices* (1992).

4 Ó Floinn, 'Freestone Hill, Co. Kilkenny'.

5 M.A. Handley, 'Beyond hagiography: epigraphic commemoration and the cult of the saints in late antique Trier' (2001).

6 C. Swift, *Ogam stones and the earliest Irish Christians* (1997), p. 121.

7 I.W. Doyle, 'Mediterranean and Frankish pottery imports in early medieval Ireland' (2009); Kelly, 'Phocaean Red Slip Ware (PRSW) Form 3 and Bii Ware in Ireland'.

8 For a summary of the various hypotheses, see Doyle, 'Pottery imports', 34.

9 McManus, 'Latin loan-words', 43.

10 Kelly, 'Phocaean Red Slip Ware (PRSW) Form 3 and Bii Ware in Ireland', 73.

11 *Confessio*, §§1, 43; *Epistola*, §1.

12 *Confessio*, §16.

13 *Confessio*, §18.

14 Note from www.confessio.ie: The practice of symbolically coming under the protection of another by sucking the breast was known in Ethiopia, Egypt, Turkey, Armenia, the Caucasus region and Albania as well as Ireland.

15 On papal concern with the origins and activities of bishops in the early fifth century, and on Prosper of Aquitaine's unfavourable comments on the abbot-bishops of Lerins and Arles, see P. Browne, *Through the eye of a needle: wealth, the Fall of Rome and the making of Christianity in the West, 350–550AD* (2012), pp 426–32.

16 From the *Chronicle* of Prosper of Aquitaine, year AD431.

17 For full discussions of the context of Palladius' mission, see Ó Cróinín, *Early medieval Ireland*, pp 14–22; Charles-Edwards, *ECI*, pp 202–14.

18 D. Ó Cróinín, 'Who was Palladius "first bishop of the Irish"?' (2000).

19 Charles-Edwards, *ECI*, p. 205.

20 Markus, *The end of ancient Christianity*, p. 200.

21 P. Coustant, *Epistolae romanorum pontificum* (repr. 1967).

22 A. Thacker, '*Loca sanctorum*: the significance of place in the study of the saints' (2002), pp 26–7; R. Sharpe, 'Martyrs and local saints in late antique Britain' (2002), pp 114–17; I. Wood, 'Varia: Germanus, Alban and Auxerre' (2009).

23 W. Stokes (ed.), *The Tripartite Life of Patrick* (1887), pp 30–1.

24 Bieler, *Patrician texts*, pp 122–4, §§29–32; Sharpe, 'Martyrs and local saints', pp 137–9, 150–1.

25 B. Shanahan, 'Roscommon landscape: Baslick parish centre' (2009).

26 Doherty, 'Kingship in early Ireland', p. 9.

27 J.K. Knight, *The end of antiquity: archaeology, society and religion, AD235–700* (1999), pp 112–27.

28 K. Bowes, *Private worship, public values and religious change in late antiquity* (2008), pp 125–88.

29 Ibid., pp 187–8.

30 Ibid., pp 155–6.

31 Sharpe, 'Martyrs and local saints', p. 76.

32 C. Thomas, *Christianity in Roman Britain* (1981). For a more recent consideration and speculation, see K.R. Dark, *Civitas to kingdom: British political continuity, 300–800* (1994).

33 *Confessio*, §1; *Epistola*, §10.

34 P. Salway, *The Oxford illustrated history of Roman Britain* (1993), pp 393–5.

35 Bowes, *Private worship*, p. 178.

36 For the possible implications of Patrick's familial background in the late/post-imperial administration and the church, see R. Flechner, 'Patrick's reasons for leaving Britain' (2011).

37 Thomas, *Christianity in Roman Britain*, pp 155–201.

38 Ibid., pp 175, 180–1; Bowes, *Private worship*, pp 130–3, 176.

39 T. Ó Carragáin, *Churches in early medieval Ireland: architecture, ritual and memory* (2010), pp 15–47.

40 *Confessio*, §§41, 52.

41 Bieler, *Patrician texts*, pp 167–83.

42 Bieler, *Patrician texts (Additamenta)*, pp 172–3, §7.

43 Ibid., pp 172–3, §8.

44 S.P. Ó Ríordáin, 'The excavation of a large earthen ringfort at Garranes, Co. Cork' (1942); M.G. O'Donnell, 'Lisnacaheragh, Garranes' (1992), p. 16.

45 J. Ryan, 'Historical addendum: Uí Echach Muman' (1942), 145–50.

46 J.W. Hayes, *Late Roman pottery* (1972), p. 337; Doyle, 'Pottery imports', 19.

47 See summary of the Garranes Ringfort Landscape Research Project, NUI Galway, directed by Michelle Comber www.nuigalway.ie/archaeology.

48 *CIIC*, no. 81.

49 *CGH*, pp 203:149a17; 218:150b45.

50 J. Sheehan, 'A peacock's tale: excavations at Caherlehillan, Iveragh, Ireland' (2009), pp 191–206.

52 Doherty, 'Exchange and trade in early medieval Ireland' (1980), 79; Doyle, 'Pottery imports', 33.

53 Sheehan, 'A peacock's tale', pp 200–2.

54 Ibid., p. 202.

55 'Making Christian landscapes: settlement, society and regionality in early medieval Ireland (Part 2:2, 123)' (report to the Heritage Council, 2010: *www.heritage council.ie/AR01049_Christian_Landscapes _Final_Report*).

56 A. De Vogüé, *La communauté et l'abbé dans la règle de Saint Benoit* (1961), pp 15–38; B. Ward and N. Russell, *The lives of the Desert Fathers* (1981); A. De Vogüé, *Regards sur le monachisme des premiers siècles* (2000), pp 275–84; M. Dunn, *The emergence of monasticism* (2000), pp 82–110, 138–40; Ó Floinn, 'Early Christianity in Ireland', pp 24–31.

57 Dunn, *The emergence of monasticism*, pp 90–1.

58 To gain an informed picture of this subject, see C. Etchingham, *Church organisation in Ireland, AD650 to 1000* (1999); P. Ó Riain, *Dictionary of Irish saints* (2011), passim; the database *Monasticon Hibernicum* at www.monasticon.celt.dias.ie.

59 Bieler, *Patrician texts*, pp 138–9 (18). For detailed discussions of this subject and the advance of Armagh's claims to primacy, see R. Sharpe, 'Some problems concerning the organization of the church in early medieval Ireland' (1984); C. Doherty, 'The

cult of St Patrick and the politics of Armagh in the seventh century' (1991).

60 G. Olsen, 'The idea of the *ecclesia primitiva* in the writings of the twelfth-century canonist' (1969), 66.

61 Bieler, *Patrician texts*, pp 188–9 (21); Sharpe, 'The organization of the church', 254–5; Doherty, 'The cult of St Patrick', pp 61–2 (rev. trans.).

62 D.H. Greene, 'From Germania to Europe: the evidence of language and history' (1997); T.M. Charles-Edwards, '*Érlam*: the patron-saint of an Irish church' (2002), p. 270.

63 Doherty, 'The cult of St Patrick', p. 65.

64 Bieler, *Patrician texts*, pp 146–7 (27).

65 Ó Riain, *DIS*, p. 401.

66 Bieler, *Patrician texts*, p. 181 (40).

67 Ó Riain, *CGSH*, p. 114, §670.37; Ó Riain, *DIS*, pp 260–1.

68 Ó Carragáin, *Church in early medieval Ireland*, pp 36–7.

69 *CIIC*, no. 26.

70 All information regarding these sites is available on the Department of the Environment's Sites and Monuments Record (SMR) at www.archaeology.ie.

71 A.C. Outler (ed. and trans.), *Confessions and Enchiridion*, pp 123–4 (www.ccel.org; www.stoa.org/hippo (original Latin text)).

72 De Vogüé, *Regards sur le monachisme*; Dunn, *The emergence of monasticism*.

73 *Confessio*, §41.

74 Dunn, *The emergence of monasticism*, p. 90.

75 De Vogüé, *La communauté et l'abbé*.

76 Ward and Russell, *The lives of the Desert Fathers*, pp 20–8.

77 De Vogüé, *Regards sur le monachisme*, pp 275–90, 439–518; for an excellent survey of early Irish asceticism, see W. Follett, *Céli Dé in Ireland: monastic writing and identity in the early Middle Ages* (2006).

78 J. Leclercq, *L'amour des letters et le désir de Dieu: initiation aux auteurs monastiques du moyen age* (repr. 1990), pp 30–9; Dunn, *The emergence of monasticism*, pp 133–6.

79 D. Dumville, 'St Finnian of Movilla: Briton, Gael, ghost?' (1997); P. Ó Riain, 'Finnio and Winniau: a return to the subject' (1999).

80 Follett, *Céli Dé in Ireland*, pp 28–37.

81 Bieler, *Irish penitentials* ('Preface of Gildas') (1963; repr. 1975), pp 60–3, §§1, 6, 19.

82 M. Winterbottom (ed.), *Gildas: The ruin of Britain and other works* (1978), p. 82, §5.

83 Dunn, *The emergence of monasticism*, pp 92–6.

84 De Vogüé, *Regards sur le monachisme*, pp 60–3.

85 Connolly and Picard, 'Cogitosus's Life of Brigit', 25–6, §32 (2).

86 Ibid., §32 (9).

87 Bhreathnach, 'Abbesses, minor dynasties and kings *in clericatu*', pp 113–19.

88 C. Neuman de Vegvar, 'Romanitas and realpolitik in Cogitosus' description of the church of St Brigit, Kildare' (2003; repr. 2005).

89 *VSC*, III:2.

90 Sharpe, *Adomnán Life of Columba*, pp 10–11.

91 *VSC*, II:25.

92 Ibid., I:1, II:1, III:4.

93 Clancy and Markus, *The earliest poetry of Iona*, pp 107 (IV), 109 (V), 113 (VIII).

94 Leclercq, *L'amour des lettres*, p. 18.

95 Jonas, *VS Columbani*, §7.

96 Ibid., §8.

97 Ibid.

98 Dunn, *The emergence of monasticism*, pp 151–5.

99 *VSC*, I:49.

1 Ibid., I:32.

2 Ibid., II:39.

3 Ibid., I:2.

4 F.E. Warren (ed.), *The Antiphonary of Bangor: an early Irish manuscript in the Ambrosian Library at Milan* (1893); M. Curran, *The Antiphonary of Bangor and the early Irish monastic liturgy* (1984).

5 I wish to thank Colmán Ó Clabaigh for guiding me through monastic terminology.

6 *VSC*, II:9.

7 Curran, *Antiphonary of Bangor*, pp 166–95.

8 H.-W. Goetz and S.W. Rowan, *Life in the Middle Ages: from the seventh to the thirteenth century* (1993), pp 56–106.

9 *VSC*, II:45.

10 Ibid., III:12.

11 Ibid., I:21.

12 Ibid., III:18.

13 M.W. Helms, 'Before the dawn: monks and the night in late antiquity and early modern Europe' (2004).

14 Ibid., 179–80, 186.

15 *VSC*, III:23.

16 De Vogüé, *La communauté et l'abbé*.

17 *VSC*, I:6.

18 Ibid., I:21.

19 Ibid., I:2.

20 Ibid., I:37, III:23.

21 J. Barber, 'Excavations on Iona, 1979' (1981); A.D.S. MacDonald, 'Aspects of the monastery and monastic life in Adomnán's Life of Columba' (1984); F. McCormick, 'Iona: the archaeology of the early monastery' (1997).

22 VSC, II:45.

23 Ibid., I:29, III:15.

24 MacDonald, 'Monastery and monastic life', 282–4.

25 McCormick, 'Iona: the archaeology of an early monastery', pp 50–2.

26 VSC, III:21, 23.

27 J. O'Sullivan, 'Excavations beside Sruth a'Mhuilinn ("the Mill Stream"), Iona' (1994).

28 H.C. Lawlor, The monastery of Saint Mochai of Nendrum (1925), pp 144–6.

29 McCormick, 'Iona: the archaeology of an early monastery', pp 54–60.

30 VSC, III:10.

31 Sharpe, Life of St Columba, p. 106.

32 M. Innes, State and society in the early Middle Ages: the Middle Rhine Valley (2000), p. 105.

33 Ibid., pp 21, 101–3.

34 A. Maloney, 'From east to west: crossing the bogs at Clonmacnoise' (1998), pp 7–10.

35 F. Moore, 'Ireland's oldest bridge' (1996).

36 H.A. King, 'New graveyard, Clonmacnoise' (1995:240): www.excavations.ie; C. Lynn, 'Recent archaeological excavations in Armagh city: an interim summary' (1977); C. Gaskell-Brown and A.E.T. Harper, 'Excavations on Cathedral Hill, Armagh, 1968' (1984); C. Lynn, 'Excavations at 46–48 Scotch Street, Armagh, 1979–80' (1988).

37 Doody, Ballyhoura Hills project, passim.

38 CGH, p. 99:128b4 (Uí Bairrche); J. [E.] MacNeill, 'Early Irish population-groups: their nomenclature, classification and chronology' (1911–12), 79, §46. Mo Lóce m.h. Noise is supposed to have belonged to these people.

39 Byrne, IKHK, p. 237.

40 For a detailed survey of Clonmacnoise's officials and lands, see A. Kehnel, Clonmacnois – the church and lands of St Ciarán: change and continuity in an Irish monastic foundation (6th to 16th century) (1997).

41 W. Stokes (ed.), Lives of saints from the Book of Lismore (1890), pp 117–34; Plummer, VSH, I, pp 200–17; Heist, VSH, pp 78–81.

42 VSC, I:3.

43 Kehnel, Clonmacnois, pp 106–19.

44 Bradley, 'Monastic town'; R. Ó Floinn, 'Clonmacnoise: art and patronage in the early medieval period' (1998); C. Swift, 'Sculptors and customers: a study of Clonmacnoise grave-slabs' (2003).

45 Bieler, Patrician texts, pp 142–3, §25; 160–1, §47 (4); Charles-Edwards, ECI, pp 252–4.

46 See pp 136, 150.

47 Bieler, Patrician texts, p. 143, §25 (2).

48 Kehnel, Clonmacnois, pp 251 (A23), 253 (A31).

49 Charles-Edwards, ECI, p. 594.

50 Innes, State and society, p. 105.

51 J.V. Kelleher, 'The Táin and the annals' (1971), 127.

52 Swift, 'Sculptors and their customers'.

53 See www.excavations.ie (Clonmacnoise 1977–79:0063 to 2008:1009).

54 Heather King, pers. comm.

55 Kehnel, Clonmacnois, pp 96–9, 254 (A37), 273–4 (A4).

56 Murray, Baile in Scáil, §§50, 52.

57 D. Murphy, 'Early monastic enclosure at Clonmacnoise' (2003), p. 19.

58 C. Manning, 'Clonmacnoise Cathedral' (1998), pp 60–3, 71–7.

59 D. Ó Murchadha, 'Rubbings taken of the inscriptions on the Cross of the Scriptures, Clonmacnois' (1980); L. de Paor, 'The high crosses of Tech Theille (Tihilly), Kinnitty, and related sculpture' (1987); Manning, 'Clonmacnoise Cathedral', pp 73–4.

60 E. FitzPatrick, 'Raiding and warring in monastic Ireland' (1993).

61 H. Mayr-Harting, 'Artists and patrons' (1999), p. 219.

62 Heather King, pers. comm.

63 Ní Dhonnchadha, 'The guarantor list of Cáin Adomnáin'.

64 Charles-Edwards, 'The Airgíalla charter poem'.

65 T. Ó Fiaich, 'The church of Armagh under lay control' (1969).

66 For a discussion of the significance of the designation of Armagh and Kildare as archespiscopal sees, see Charles-Edwards, ECI, pp 416–29.

67 Doherty, 'The cult of St Patrick'.

68 Bieler, Patrician texts (Liber angeli), p. 188, §21.

69 S. Castellanos and I.M. Viso, 'The local articulation of central power in the north of the Iberian Peninsula' (2005).

70 C. Lynn, Navan Fort: archaeology and myth (2003).

71 Gaskell Brown and Harper, 'Excavations on Cathedral Hill, Armagh, 1968'.

72 Ibid., 112–17.

73 Lynn, 'Scotch Street, Armagh', 82.

74 Ibid., 80; N. Edwards, 'Celtic saints and early medieval archaeology' (2002), p. 239.

75 E. O'Brien and E. Bhreathnach, 'Burial in early medieval Ireland: politics and religion' (2013).

76 Bieler, *Patrician texts*, pp 184–91.

77 Ibid., pp 184–5 (6).

78 Ibid., pp 186–7 (15)–(16).

79 Ibid., pp 186–7 (17)–(19).

80 Ibid., pp 190–1 (31).

81 This church may have been replaced later by the stone church known as *Damliac na ferta* 'the stone church of the grave mound' (*AU* 1090), although the southern church with the shrine may not have been one and the same as the *Ferta Martyrum*, which is more likely to have been a cemetery of early graves: see Lynn, 'Scotch Street, Armagh'; Sharpe, 'Martyrs and local saints', p. 142 n. 283.

82 Connolly and Picard, 'Cogitosus's Life of Brigit', 25, §32.

83 Bieler, *Patrician texts*, pp 164–5, §54 (iiii).

84 Ibid., pp 120–1, §II:11 (2); 164–5, §55 (2).

85 Doherty, 'The cult of St Patrick', p. 73.

86 Ibid., p. 71.

87 Bieler, *Patrician texts* (*Liber Angeli*), pp 188–9, §26.

88 Ibid., pp 188–9, §24.

89 Thacker, 'Loca sanctorum', pp 25–31; R. Morris, *Churches in the landscape* (1989), p. 17.

90 I. Wood, 'The audience of architecture in post-Roman Gaul' (1986), p. 78.

91 Bieler, *Patrician texts*, pp 184–5 (7)–(8).

92 Ibid., pp 186–7 (12)–(13).

93 Ibid., pp 186–7 (14).

94 Castellanos and Viso, 'Iberian Peninsula', 10.

95 Bieler, *Patrician texts*, pp 188–9 (24)–(25).

96 Ibid., pp 188–9 (26).

97 C. Bourke, 'The Blackwater shrine' (1991); idem, 'Antiquities from the River Blackwater IV: early medieval non-ferrous metalwork' (2010).

98 See pp 168–70.

99 See p. 186.

1 Doherty, 'Cult of St Patrick', pp 75–8.

2 Bieler, *Patrician texts*, pp 176–9 (13)–(14), (16).

3 Ibid., p. 179 (16).

4 Ibid., pp 184–7 (10).

5 Brown, *The rise of western Christendom*. For a detailed discussion of this topic and of the Irish context, see D. Bracken, 'Authority and duty'.

6 Bracken, 'Authority and duty', 175.

7 Charles-Edwards, *ECI*, pp 391–415.

8 M. Walsh and D. Ó Cróinín (eds and trans.), *Cummian's letter 'De controversia paschali' and the 'De ratione computandi'* (1988).

9 Walsh and Ó Cróinín, *Cummian's letter*, p. 47.

10 Ibid., pp 91–5:259–88.

11 Ibid., p. 49.

12 Ó Cróinín, *Early medieval Ireland*, pp 152–4.

13 L. Sherley-Price, *Bede: A history of the English church and people* (1977), pp 136–7; M.P. Sheehy, *Pontificia Hibernica*, I (1962), pp 3–4 (I).

14 Sheehy, *Pontificia Hibernica*, I, p. 3 nn 1–11.

15 Bieler, *Patrician texts*, pp 188–91 (28)–(29).

16 *HE*, 27.

17 Etchingham, *Church organisation*, pp 83–8.

18 For a detailed description, see T.G.F. Paterson and O. Davies, 'The churches of Armagh' (1940).

19 ATig., p. 350 (Llanerch ed. II, p. 242).

20 A possible parallel is Stalls Church or St Maria de Stabula in Bath, which was built on the site of a Roman temple. The remains of an Anglo-Saxon church window were discovered on the site in 1867: see H.M. Scarth, 'Recent discoveries on the site of the Old White Hart Hotel, Bath' (1868).

21 Murray, *Baile in Scáil*, §§47, 49, 51.

22 ATig., pp 358–9 (Llanerch ed., ii, pp 250–1).

23 For a detailed review of scholarly opinion on the wider question (including Armagh's position), see Etchingham, *Church organisation*, pp 13–46.

24 H.J. Lawlor and R.I. Best, 'The ancient list of the coarbs of Patrick' (1919).

25 Ó Fiaich, 'The church of Armagh under lay control'.

26 This is most graphically portrayed in Ó Fiaich's genealogical tables: 'Armagh under lay control', 123–7.

27 R. Sharpe, 'Paleographical considerations in the study of the Patrician documents in the Book of Armagh' (1982); Charles-Edwards, *ECI*, pp 11–13.

28 Doherty, 'The cult of St Patrick', pp 53, 57–9.

29 Charles-Edwards, *ECI*, p. 30.

30 P. Ó Riain, 'The *Táin*: a clue to its origins' (1994); Ó Riain, *DIS*, p. 517.

31 Bieler, *Patrician texts*, pp 188–9 (24).

32 Kelly, *GEIL*, pp 36–8.

33 J. Waddell, 'Continuity, cult and contest' (2011), pp 195–9.

34 M. Herbert, *Iona, Kells and Derry: the history and hagiography of the monastic familia of Columba* (1988; repr. 1996), pp 74–5.

35 R. Stalley, 'The Tower Cross at Kells' (1997); D.N. Dumville, 'Mael Brigte mac Tornán, pluralist coarb (†927)', *Journal of Celtic Studies*, 4 (2004), 97–116.

36 Lawlor and Best, 'Coarbs of Patrick', 328; Ó Fiaich, 'Armagh under lay control', 90–1; Herbert, *Iona, Kells and Derry*, pp 83–5.

37 *AI*, 973.

38 M. Ní Mhaonaigh, *Brian Boru: Ireland's greatest king?* (2007), pp 21–8.

39 Ibid., p. 142 (following Gwynn, *Book of Armagh*, ciii and fo. 16v).

40 Follett, *Céli Dé in Ireland*.

41 E. Gwynn (ed.), 'The rule of Tallaght' (1927), 24–7. I have changed parts of Gwynn's translation.

42 Follett, *Céli Dé*, 89.

43 Gwynn, 'The rule of Tallaght', 37 (60–1).

44 This approach is best articulated in Kathleen Hughes' classic monograph *The church in early Irish society* (1966).

45 Sharpe, 'Problems concerning the organization of church', 263.

46 Etchingham, *Church organisation*. For a shorter review of the scholarship of pastoral care in the early Irish church, see C. Etchingham, 'Pastoral provision in the first millennium: a two-tier service?' (2006).

47 Etchingham, 'Pastoral provision', pp 89–90.

48 T.M. Charles-Edwards, 'The pastoral role of the church in the early Irish laws' (1992), pp 78–80 (appendix: some types of early Irish prescriptive text).

49 E.J. Gwynn and W. Purton, 'The monastery of Tallaght' (1911–12), 8–9, §10.

50 Ibid., 20–1, §33.

51 Ibid., 22–5, §39.

52 Ibid., 74–5, §43.

53 Bieler, *Irish penitentials*, pp 116–17, §§18–21.

54 Gwynn and Purton, *Monastery of Tallaght*, pp 76–9, §49.

55 *VSC*, II:41.

56 J.G. O'Keeffe (ed.), 'The rule of Patrick' (1904); V. Hull (ed.), 'Cáin Domnaig' (1966).

57 O'Keeffe, 'The rule of Patrick', 218, 221, §1.

58 Ibid., 219, 222–3, §§6, 9.

59 C. Swift, 'Early priests within their own localities' (2011), 39–40.

60 E. Okasha and K. Forsyth, *Early Christian inscriptions of Munster: a corpus of inscribed stones* (2001), pp 108–12.

61 *CIIC*, I, pp 140–2, no. 145.

62 A. Thacker, 'Monks, preaching and pastoral care in early Anglo-Saxon England' (1992), p. 165; C. Cubitt, 'Pastoral care and conciliar canons: the provisions of the 747 council of *Clofesho*' (1992).

63 Hull, 'Cáin Domnaig', 160–3, §1.

64 Ibid.

65 C. Watkins, 'Religion and belief' (2011), p. 272.

66 J. Borsje, 'Monotheistic to a certain extent: the "good neighbours" of God in Ireland' (2009).

67 Quoted by Borsje in 'Monotheistic to a certain extent' from an edition and translation by M. Dillon (ed.), *Serglige Con Culainn* (1953), p. 29, §49 and M. Dillon (trans.), 'The wasting sickness of Cú Chulainn' (1953).

68 I use here the very apt title of the project on this topic directed by Jacqueline Borsje, University of Amsterdam.

69 R.I. Best, 'Some Irish charms' (1952).

70 Swift, 'Early priests', 38–9.

71 O'Keeffe, 'The rule of Patrick', 223.

72 B. Coffey, 'The Stowe enigma: decoding the mystery' (2010), 90.

73 For surveys of preaching in early Ireland, see T. O'Loughlin, 'Irish preaching before the end of the ninth century: assessing the extent of our evidence' (2001); B. Murdoch, 'Preaching in medieval Ireland: the Irish tradition' (2001).

74 J. Strachan (ed.), 'An Old Irish homily' (1907).

75 Ibid., 3, 7–9.

76 There are many works on medieval preaching, but, for a useful survey in the context of this text, see M. Clayton, 'Homiliaries and preaching in Anglo-Saxon England' (1985).

77 Strachan, 'An Old Irish homily'.

78 A. Hamlin, '*Dignatio diei dominici*: an element in the iconography of Irish crosses?' (1982); M. D'Aughton, 'The Kells Market Cross: the Epiphany sequence reconsidered' (2004).

79 A valuable resource for Irish place-names is the Irish Place Names Commission's database www.logainm.ie. In recent years, excellent regional studies have been produced under the auspices of the Irish Place Names Commission and the Northern Ireland Place-Names Project at Queen's University Belfast.

80 Neill, *Archaeological survey of County Armagh*, pp 507-14.

81 J. Carney (ed.), 'Three Old Irish accentual poems' (1971), 23-80 at 23-9, §§1, 5 (with minor changes to Carney's translation).

82 Okasha and Forsyth, *Early Christian inscriptions of Munster*, pp 165-9.

83 M.J. Carruthers, *The book of memory: a study of memory in medieval culture* (1990; repr. 1998), p. 111.

84 D. Ó Corráin, 'The early Irish churches: some aspects of organisation' (1981); E. Breathnach, 'The genealogies of Leinster as a source for local cults' (2001).

85 A.S. MacShamhráin, *Church and polity in pre-Norman Ireland: the case of Glendalough* (1996); E. O'Brien, 'Churches of south-east County Dublin, seventh to twelfth century' (1988).

86 C. Plummer (ed.), *Irish litanies: text and translation* (1925), p. 92.

87 Charles-Edwards, '*Érlam*: the patron saint of an Irish church'.

88 Mulchrone, *Bethu Phátraic*, 89.1683-8; Stokes, *Tripartite Life*, II, pp 145-7.

89 Mulchrone, *Bethu Phátraic*, 66.1189-1204; Stokes, *Tripartite Life*, II, p. 107.

90 Meyer, *Triads of Ireland*, p. 7, §57.

91 J. White Marshall and C. Walsh, *Illaunloughan Island: an early medieval monastery in County Kerry* (2005), pp 55-66.

92 C. Doherty, 'The use of relics in early Ireland' (1984).

93 *FAIre.* (909).

94 Binchy, 'Old-Irish penitential', p. 267, §§6, 10.

95 E. FitzPatrick, 'The early church in Offaly' (1998), p. 99.

96 J. O'Sullivan, T. Ó Carragáin et al., *Inishmurray: monks and pilgrims in an Atlantic landscape* (2008), pp 295-6.

97 Ibid., pp 8, 31.

98 D.A. Binchy, 'The Old-Irish table of commutations' (1962), 281, §31.

99 E. Breathnach, 'The construction of the stone fort at Cahercommaun: a historical hypothesis' (1999).

1 White Marshall and Walsh, *Illaunloughan Island*.

2 Ibid., pp 12-16.

3 Ibid., p. 79.

4 S. Ferber, 'The pre-Constintinian shrine of St Peter: Jewish sources and Christian aftermath' (1971), 10.

5 White Marshall and Walsh, *Illaunloughan Island*, pp 61-2.

6 For details regarding burials of this period in Ireland, see www.mappingdeathdb.ie. I am grateful to my colleague Elizabeth O'Brien for sharing her valuable insights into burial practices in Ireland with me over the past two decades. The text of this section is based on a report co-authored with Dr O'Brien.

7 P. Stevens, 'Burial and ritual in late prehistory in north Wexford: excavation of a ring-ditch cemetery in Ask townland' (2007).

8 *CCH*, p. 56 (cap. 2).

9 www.excavations.ie (Durrow Demesne 1985:46 N323306).

10 www.mappingdeathdb.ie.

11 D.P. Hurl, C. Sandes and L. Buckley, 'The excavation of an early Christian cemetery at Solar, County Antrim, 1993' (2002); A. Hamlin, *The archaeology of early Christianity in the north of Ireland* (2008).

12 Y. Whitty and M. Tobin, 'Rites in transition: the story told by Holdenstown 1 and 2' (2009), 19-21. I wish to thank Yvonne Whitty and the team at Irish Archaeological Consultants Ltd. for permission to use material relating to Holdenstown.

13 O'Brien and Breathnach, 'Irish boundary *ferta*'.

14 Ó Riain, *CGSH*, §366; Ó Riain, *DIS*, pp 189-90.

Conclusion

1 MacNeill, *Celtic Ireland*.

2 Ibid., p. xv.

3 G.F. Smith et al., 'Landscape study of Great and Little Sugar Loaf Mountains, Co. Wicklow' (report prepared for Wicklow County Council, 2010) (§6: Archaeology and cultural heritage, pp 32-40).

4 E. Grogan and A. Kilfeather, *Archaeological inventory of County Wicklow* (1997): see entries for the townlands Ballyremon Commons and Glanamullen; C. Corlett, 'The prehistoric landscape of the Great Sugar

Loaf', *Wicklow Archaeology and History*, 1 (1998), pp 1–8.

5 Knott, *Togail*, passim.

6 E. MacNeill, 'Sescenn Uarbeoil of the sagas and other place-names to the south of Dublin' (1935), 9–22.

7 M. O Daly (ed.), 'A chóicid choín Chairpri crúaid' (1962–3), 190, §36.

Bibliography

PRINTED/PUBLISHED SOURCES
(*primary printed sources are indicated by an asterisk)

Adkins, Lesley and Roy A. Adkins (eds), *Dictionary of Roman religion* (Oxford, 1996).
Aldhouse-Green, Miranda J., *Dictionary of Celtic myth and legend* (London, 1997).
Aldhouse-Green, Miranda J., *The gods of the Celts* (Stroud, 1986).
Aldhouse-Green, Miranda J., *The world of the druids* (London, 1997).
Anderson, Alan O. and Marjorie O. Anderson (eds), *Adomnan's Life of Columba* (London, 1961; 2nd ed. Oxford, 1991).*
Baker, Christine, 'Occam's duck: three early medieval cemeteries or ecclesiastical sites?' in Corlett and Potterton (eds), *Death and burial in early medieval Ireland* (2010), pp 1–21.
Barber, John, 'Excavations on Iona, 1979', *PSAS*, 111 (1981), 282–380.
Beard, Mary, 'Priesthood in the Roman republic' in Mary Beard and John North (eds), *Pagan priests: religion and power in the ancient world* (London, 1990), pp 19–48.
Bell, Catherine, *Ritual: perspectives and dimensions* (Oxford and New York, 1997).
Bergin, Osborn and Richard Irvine Best (eds), 'Tochmarc Étaíne', *Ériu*, 12 (1938), 137–96.*
Bertelli, Sergio, *The king's body: sacred rituals of power in medieval and early modern Europe* (Philadelphia, PA, 2001). Trans. R. Burr Litchfield.
Best, Richard Irvine, 'Some Irish charms', *Ériu*, 16 (1952), 27–32.*
Bhreathnach, Edel, 'Abbesses, minor dynasties and kings *in clericatu*: perspectives of Ireland, 700–850' in Michelle P. Brown and Carol A. Farr (eds), *Mercia: an Anglo-Saxon kingdom in Europe* (Leicester, 2001), pp 113–25.
Bhreathnach, Edel, 'Medieval sub-kingdoms of Brega: the kingships of Calatruim, Déssi Breg, Mugdornae Breg and Uí Maic Uais Breg' in Ailbhe MacShamhráin (ed.), *The island of St Patrick: church and ruling dynasties in Fingal and Meath, 400–1148* (Dublin, 2004), pp 38–51.
Bhreathnach, Edel, 'Níell cáich úa Néill nasctar géill: the political context of *Baile Chuinn Chétchathaig*' in Bhreathnach (ed.), *Kingship and landscape* (2005), pp 49–68.
Bhreathnach, Edel, 'Perceptions of kingship in early medieval Irish vernacular literature' in Linda Doran and James Lyttleton (eds), *Lordship in medieval Ireland: image and reality* (Dublin, 2007), pp 21–46.
Bhreathnach, Edel, 'Tara and Cashel: manifestations of the centre of the cosmos in the north and the south' in J. Borsje, A. Dooley, S. Mac Mathúna and G. Toner (eds), *Celtic cosmology: perspectives from Ireland and Scotland* (Toronto, forthcoming).
Bhreathnach, Edel, 'Temoria: caput Scotorum?', *Ériu*, 47 (1996), 67–88.

Bhreathnach, Edel, 'The construction of the stone fort at Cahercommaun: a historical hypothesis' in Claire Cotter, 'Cahercommaun fort, Co. Clare: a reassessment of its cultural context', *Discovery Programme Reports*, 5 (1999), 41–95.

Bhreathnach, Edel, 'The genealogies of Leinster as a source for local cults' in John Carey, Máire Herbert and Pádraig Ó Riain (eds), *Studies in Irish hagiography: saints and scholars* (Dublin, 2001), pp 250–67.

Bhreathnach, Edel (ed.), *The kingship and landscape of Tara* (Dublin, 2005).

Bhreathnach, Edel, 'The medieval kingdom of Brega' in Bhreathnach (ed.), *Kingship and landscape* (2005), pp 410–22.

Bhreathnach, Edel, 'The *seanchas* tradition in late medieval Ireland' in Edel Bhreathnach and Bernadette Cunningham (eds), *Writing Irish history: the Four Masters and their world* (Dublin, 2007), pp 18–23.

Bhreathnach, Edel, 'The Tech Midchuarta "house of the mead circuit": feasting, the royal circuits and the king's court in early medieval Ireland', *Archaeology Ireland*, 12:4 (1998), 20–2.

Bhreathnach, Edel, 'Transforming kingship and cult: the provincial ceremonial capitals in early medieval Ireland' in Schot et al. (eds), *Cult and kingship* (2011), pp 126–48.

Bhreathnach, Edel and Conor Newman (eds), *Tara* (Dublin, 1995).

Bhreathnach, Edel and Conor Newman, *Tara, Co. Meath: a guide to the ceremonial complex*, Archaeology Ireland Heritage Guide, 41 (Dublin, 2008).

Bhreathnach, Edel and Kevin Murray (eds), '*Baile Chuinn Chétchathaig*: edition' in Bhreathnach (ed.), *Kingship and landscape* (2005), pp 73–99.

Bieler, Ludwig, *The Irish penitentials* (Dublin, 1963; repr. 1975).

Bieler, Ludwig (ed.), *The Patrician texts in the Book of Armagh* (Dublin, 1979).

Binchy, Daniel A., 'Aimser chue' in John Ryan (ed.), *Féil-sgríbhinn Eóin Mhic Néill* (Dublin, 1940; repr. 1995), pp 18–22.

Binchy, Daniel A. (ed.), '*Bretha Crólige*', *Ériu*, 12 (1938), 1–77.

Binchy, Daniel A., *Corpus iuris Hiberniae: ad fidem codicum manuscriptorum* (6 vols, Dublin, 1978).*

Binchy, Daniel A. (ed.), *Críth Gablach* (Dublin, 1970). [CG]

Binchy, Daniel A., 'The fair of Tailtiu and the feast of Tara', *Ériu*, 18 (1958), 113–38.

Binchy, Daniel A. (ed.), 'Irish law tracts re-edited: *Coibnes Uisci Thairidne*', *Ériu*, 17 (1955), 52–85.

Binchy, Daniel A. (ed.), 'The Old-Irish penitential' in Ludwig Bieler (ed.), *The Irish penitentials* (Dublin, 1975).

Binchy, Daniel A. (ed.), 'The Old-Irish table of penitential commutations', *Ériu*, 19 (1962), 47–72.

Bitel, Lisa, '"Conceived in sin, born in delights": stories of procreation from early Ireland', *Journal of the History of Sexuality*, 3:2 (1992), 181–202.

Bitel, Lisa, 'Sin, sex and celibacy in early Christian Ireland', *PHCC*, 7 (1987), 65–96.

Blair, John, 'Small towns, 600–1270' in David M. Palliser (ed.), *The Cambridge urban history of Britain*, 1 (Cambridge, 2000), pp 245–70.

Blair, John and Richard Sharpe (eds), *Pastoral care before the parish* (Leicester, London and New York, 1992).

Borsje, Jacqueline, 'Druids, deer and "words of power": coming to terms with evil in medieval Ireland' in Nelly Van Doom-Harder and Lourens Minnema (eds), *Coping with evil in religion and culture: case studies* (Amsterdam and New York, 2008), pp 25–49.

Borsje, Jacqueline, 'Monotheistic to a certain extent: the "good neighbours" of God in Ireland' in Anne-Marie Korte and Maaike De Haardt (eds), *The boundaries of monotheism: interdisciplinary explorations into the foundations of western monotheism* (Leiden, 2009), pp 53–82.

Borsje, Jacqueline, *The Celtic evil eye and related mythological motifs in medieval Ireland* (Leuven, Paris and Walpole, 2012).

Borsje, Jacqueline and Fergus Kelly, '"The evil eye" in early Irish literature and law', *Celtica*, 24 (2003), 1–39.

Bourke, Cormac, 'Antiquities from the River Blackwater IV; early medieval non-ferrous metalwork', *UJA*, 69 (2010), 24–135.

Bourke, Cormac (ed.), *Studies in the cult of Saint Columba* (Dublin, 1997).

Bourke, Cormac, 'The Blackwater shrine', *Dúiche Néill*, 6 (1991), 103–6.

Bowersock, G.W., Peter Brown and Oleg Grabar, *Late antiquity: a guide to the post-classical world* (Harvard, 1999).

Bowes, Kim, *Private worship, public values and religious change in late antiquity* (Cambridge, 2008).

Boyer, Pascal, *Religion explained: the human instincts that fashion gods, spirits and ancestors* (London, 2002).

Bozóky, Edina, *La politique des reliques de Constantin à Saint Louis* (Paris, 2006).

Bracken, Damian, 'Authority and duty: Columbanus and the primacy of Rome', *Peritia*, 16 (2002), 168–213.

Bradley, John, 'Excavations at Moynagh Lough, County Meath', *JRSAI*, 121 (1991), 5–26.

Bradley, John, 'Some reflections on the problem of Scandinavian settlement in the hinterland of Dublin during the ninth century' in John Bradley, Alan Fletcher and Anngret Simms (eds), *Dublin in the medieval world: studies in honour of Howard B. Clarke* (Dublin, 2009), pp 39–62.

Bradley, John, 'The monastic town of Clonmacnoise' in King (ed.), *Clonmacnoise Studies*, 1 (1998), pp 42–55.

Bradshaw, P.F., *The search for the origins of Christian worship: sources and methods for the study of early liturgy* (London, 2002).

Brady, Niall, 'Mills in medieval Ireland: looking beyond design' in Steven A. Walton (ed.), *Wind and water in the Middle Ages: fluid technologies from antiquity to the Renaissance* (Tempe, AZ, 2006), pp 39–68.

Breatnach, Liam, *A companion to the* Corpus Iuris Hibernici (Dublin, 2005).

Breatnach, Liam, 'Satire, praise and the early Irish poet', *Ériu*, 56 (2006), 63–84.

Breatnach, Liam (ed.), 'The caldron of poesy', *Ériu*, 32 (1981), 45–93.

Breatnach, Liam (ed.), *Uraicecht na Ríar: the poetic grades in early Irish law* (Dublin, 1987).

Breen, Aidan, 'The evidence of antique Irish exegesis in Pseudo-Cyprian, *De duodecim abusivis saeculi*', *PRIA*, 87C (1987), 71–101.

Brisch, Nicole (ed.), *Religion and power: divine kingship in the ancient world and beyond* (Chicago, 2008).

Brogiolo, Gian Pietro, Nancy Gauthier and Neil Christie (eds), *Towns and their territories between late antiquity and the early Middle Ages* (Leiden, 2000).

Brown, Peter, *The cult of the saints: its rise and function in Latin Christianity* (Chicago, 1981).

Brown, Peter, *The rise of western Christendom: triumph and diversity, AD200–1000* (Oxford, 1996; repr. 2003).

Brown, Peter, *Through the eye of a needle: wealth, the Fall of Rome, and the making of Christianity in the West, 350–550AD* (Princeton, NJ, 2012).

Bumke, Joachim (trans. Thomas Dunlap), *Courtly culture: literature and society in the High Middle Ages* (Munich, 1986; repr. Berkeley and Los Angeles, 1991).

Byrne, Francis John, *Irish kings and high-kings* (London, 1973; repr. 2001) [*IKHK*]

Byrne, Francis John, 'Senchas: the nature of Gaelic historical tradition' in J.G. Barry (ed.), *Historical Studies*, 9 (Belfast, 1974), pp 137–59.

Byrne, Paul, 'Ciannachta Breg before Síl nÁeda Sláine' in Smyth (ed.), *Seanchas* (2000), pp 121–6.

Cahill, Mary and Maeve Sikora (eds), *Breaking ground, finding graves: reports on the excavations of burials by the National Museum of Ireland, 1927–2006* (2 vols, Dublin, 2012).

Carey, John, 'From David to Labraid: sacral kingship and the emergence of monotheism in Israel and Ireland' in Ritari and Bergholm (eds), *Approaches to religion and mythology* (2008), pp 2–27.

Carey, John, 'Scél Tuáin meic Chairill', *Ériu*, 35 (1984), 93–111.*

Carey, John, 'Tara and the supernatural' in Bhreathnach (ed.), *Kingship and landscape* (2005), pp 32–48.

Carey, John, 'The Irish national origin-legend: synthetic pseudohistory', *Quiggin pamphlets on the sources of mediaeval Gaelic history*, I (Cambridge, 1994).

Carey, John, 'Time, memory and the Boyne necropolis', *PHCC*, 10 (1993), 24–30.

Carmichael Watson, J. (ed.), *Mesca Ulad* (Dublin, 1941).*

Carney, James (ed.), 'Three Old Irish accentual poems', *Ériu*, 22 (1971), 23–80.*

Carr, A.D., '*Teulu* and *Penteulu*' in Thomas M. Charles-Edwards Morfydd E. Owen and Paul Russell (eds), *The Welsh king and his court* (Cardiff, 2000), pp 63–81.

Carruthers, Mary J., *The book of memory: a study of memory in medieval culture* (Cambridge, 1990; repr. 1998).

Castellanos, Santiago and Iñaki M. Viso, 'The local articulation of central power in the north of the Iberian Peninsula (500–1000)', *Early Medieval Europe*, 13:1 (2005), 1–42.

Chapman Stacey, Robin, *Dark speech: the performance of law in early Ireland* (Philadelphia, 2007).

Charles-Edwards, Thomas M., 'A contract between king and people in early medieval Ireland? *Críth Gablach* on kingship', *Peritia*, 8 (1994), 107–19.

Charles-Edwards, Thomas M., 'Boundaries in early Irish law' in Peter Sawyer (ed.), *Medieval settlement: continuity and change* (London, 1976), pp 83–7.

Charles-Edwards, Thomas M., *Early Christian Ireland* (Cambridge, 2000). [*ECI*]

Charles-Edwards, Thomas M., *Early Irish and Welsh kinship* (Oxford, 1993). [*EIWK*]

Charles-Edwards, Thomas M., 'Early medieval kingships in the British Isles' in Steven Bassett (ed.), *The origins of Anglo-Saxon kingdoms* (Leicester, 1989), pp 28–39.

Charles-Edwards, Thomas M., '*Érlam*: the patron-saint of an Irish church' in Thacker and Sharpe (eds), *Local saints and local churches* (2002), pp 267–90.

Charles-Edwards, Thomas M., 'Irish warfare before 1100' in Thomas Bartlett and Keith Jeffrey (eds), *A military history of Ireland* (Cambridge, 1996), pp 26–51.

Charles-Edwards, Thomas, 'The Airgíalla charter poem: the legal content' in Bhreathnach (ed.), *Kingship and landscape* (2005), pp 100–23.

Charles-Edwards, Thomas M. (ed.), *The chronicle of Ireland* (Liverpool, 2006).*

Charles-Edwards, Thomas M., 'The pastoral role of the church in the early Irish laws' in Blair and Sharpe (eds), *Pastoral care before the parish* (1992), pp 62–80.

Clancy, Thomas Owen and Gilbert Márkus (eds), *Iona: the earliest poetry of a Celtic monastery* (Edinburgh, 1995).*

Clark, Gillian, *Women in late antiquity: pagan and Christian lifestyles* (Oxford, 1993).

Clarke, Howard, Máire Ní Mhaonaigh and Raghnall Ó Floinn (eds), *Ireland and Scandinavia in the early Viking Age* (Dublin, 1998).

Clayton, Mary, 'Homiliaries and preaching in Anglo-Saxon England', *Peritia*, 4 (1985), 207–42.

Clinton, Mark, *The souterrains of Ireland* (Bray, 2011).

Coffey, Brendan, 'The Stowe enigma: decoding the mystery', *Irish Theological Quarterly*, 75:1 (2010), 75–91.

Coffey, George, 'On the excavation of a tumulus near Loughrea, Co. Galway', *PRIA*, 25 (1904), 14–20.

Colgrave, Betram and R.A.B. Mynors, *Bede's Ecclesiastical history of the English people* (Oxford, 1993).*

Comber, Michelle, 'Trade and communication networks in early historic Ireland', *JIA*, 10 (2001), 73–92.

Comyn, David, Patrick S. Dinneen and David Nutt (eds), *Foras feasa ar Éirinn le Seathrún Céitinn DD: The history of Ireland by Geoffrey Keating DD* (4 vols, London, 1902–14).*

Connolly, Sean, '*Vita Prima Sanctae Brigitae*: background and historical value', *JRSAI*, 119 (1989), 5–49. [*VPrima*]

Connolly, Sean and Jean-Michel Picard (eds), 'Cogitosus's Life of Brigit: content and value', *JRSAI*, 117 (1987), 5–27.*

Connon, Anne, 'Prosopography II: a prosopography of the early queens of Tara' in Bhreathnach (ed.), *Kingship and landscape* (2005), pp 225–357.

Corlett, Christiaan, 'The prehistoric landscape of the Great Sugar Loaf', *Wicklow Archaeology and History*, 1 (1998), 1–8.

Corlett, Christiaan and Michael Potterton (eds), *Death and burial in early medieval Ireland in the light of recent archaeological excavations* (Bray, 2010).

Cotter, Claire, 'Cahercommaun fort, Co. Clare: a reassessment of its cultural context', *Discovery Programme Reports*, 5 (1999), 41–95.

Cotter, Claire, *The Western Stone Forts Project: excavations at Dún Aonghasa and Dún Eoghanachta*. 2 vols. (Dublin, 2013).

Coustant, Pierre, *Epistolae romanorum pontificum* (repr. Farnborough, 1967).

Crick, Julia and Elisabeth Van Houts (eds), *A social history of England, 900–1200* (Cambridge, 2011).

Cubitt, Catherine, 'Pastoral care and conciliar canons: the provisions of the 747 council of *Clofesho*' in Blair and Sharpe (eds), *Pastoral care before the parish* (1992), pp 193–211.

Curran, Michael, *The Antiphonary of Bangor and the early Irish monastic liturgy* (Dublin, 1984).

D'Aughton, Malgorzata, 'The Kells Market Cross: the Epiphany sequence reconsidered', *Archaeology Ireland*, 17:4 (2004), 16–19.

Dark, K.R., *Civitas to kingdom: British political continuity, 300–800* (London and New York, 1994).

De Paor, Liam, 'The high crosses of Tech Theille (Tihilly), Kinnitty, and related sculpture' in Etienne Rynne (ed.), *Figures from the past: studies on figurative art in Christian Ireland in honour of Helen M. Roe* (Dublin, 1987), pp 131–58.

De Vogüé, Adalbert, *La communauté et l'abbé dans la règle de Saint Benoit* (Paris and Brussels, 1961).*

De Vogüé, Adalbert, *Regards sur la monachisme des premiers siècles* (Rome, 2000).*

Deane, Marion, 'From sacred marriage to clientship: a mythical account of the establishment of kingship as an institution' in Schot et al. (eds), *Cult and kingship* (2011), pp 1–21.

Deevy, Mary B. and Donald Murphy (eds), *Places along the way: first findings on the M3* (Dublin, 2009).

Dillon, Myles (ed.), *Serglige Con Culainn* (Dublin, 1953).*

Dillon, Myles, *The cycles of kings* (London, 1946; repr. 1994).

Dillon, Myles, 'The Hindu act of truth in Celtic tradition', *Modern Philology*, 44 (1947), 137–40.

Dillon, Myles (ed.), 'The story of the finding of Cashel', *Ériu*, 16 (1952), 61–73.*

Dillon, Myles (trans.), 'The wasting sickness of Cú Chulainn', *Scottish Gaelic Studies*, 7 (1953), 47–88.*

Doherty, Charles, 'Érainn' in Seán Duffy (ed.), *Medieval Ireland: an encyclopedia* (New York, 2005), p. 156.

Doherty, Charles, 'Exchange and trade in early medieval Ireland', *JRSAI*, 110 (1980), 67–89.

Doherty, Charles, 'Kingship in early Ireland' in Bhreathnach (ed.), *Kingship and landscape* (2005), pp 3–31.

Doherty, Charles, 'Some aspects of hagiography as a source for Irish economic history', *Peritia*, 1 (1982), 300–28.

Doherty, Charles, 'The cult of St Patrick and the politics of Armagh in the seventh century' in Jean-Michel Picard (ed.), *Ireland and northern France, AD600–850* (Dublin, 1991), pp 53–94.

Doherty, Charles, 'The monastic town in early medieval Ireland' in Howard Clarke and Anngret Simms (eds), *The comparative history of urban origins in non-Roman Europe* (1985), I, pp 45–75.

Doherty, Charles, 'The use of relics in early Ireland' in Proinséas Ní Chatháin and Michael Richter (eds), *Irland und Europa: Die Kirche im Frühmittelalter/ Ireland and Europe: the early church*, (2 vols, Stuttgart, 1984), pp 89–101.

Doody, Martin, *The Ballyhoura Hills Project* (Dublin, 2008).

Downham, Clare, *Viking kings of Britain and Ireland: the dynasty of Ívarr to A.D. 1014* (Edinburgh, 2007).

Doyle, Ian W., 'Mediterranean and Frankish pottery imports in early medieval Ireland', *JIA*, 18 (2009), 17–62.

Doyle, Ian W., 'The early medieval activity at Dalkey Island: a reassessment', *JIA*, 9 (1998), 89–103.

Dumville, D.N., 'Mael Brigte mac Tornán, pluralist coarb (†927)', *Journal of Celtic Studies*, 4 (2004), 97–116.

Dumville, D.N., 'St Finnian of Movilla: Briton, Gael, ghost?' in L. Proudfoot (ed.), *Down, history and society* (Dublin, 1997), pp 71–84.

Dunn, Marilyn, *The emergence of monasticism* (Malden, 2000; repr. 2003).

Edmonds, Fiona and Paul Russell (eds), *Tome: studies in medieval Celtic history and law in honour of Thomas Charles-Edwards* (Woodbridge, 2011).

Edwards, Nancy, 'Celtic saints and early medieval archaeology' in Thacker and Sharpe (eds), *Local saints and local churches* (2002), pp 225–65.

Edwards, Nancy, 'The archaeology of early medieval Ireland, c.400–1169: settlement and economy', in Ó Cróinín, *NHI*, I, pp 235–300.

Eliade, Mircea, *The sacred and the profane* (San Diego, 1959).

Etchingham, Colmán, *Church organisation in Ireland, AD650 to 1000* (Maynooth, 1999).

Etchingham, Colmán, 'Pastoral provision in the first millennium: a two-tier service?' in Elizabeth FitzPatrick and Raymond Gillespie (eds), *The parish in medieval and early modern Ireland: community, territory and building* (Dublin, 2006), pp 79–90.

Fenwick, Joseph and Conor Newman, 'Geomagnetic survey on the Hill of Tara, Co. Meath, 1998–9', *Discovery Programme Reports*, 6 (2002), 1–17.

Ferber, Stanley, 'The pre-Constintinian shrine of St Peter: Jewish sources and Christian aftermath', *Gesta*, 10:2 (1971), 3–32.

Fitzgerald, Maria A., 'Insular dress in early medieval Ireland' in G.R. Owen-Crocker (ed.), *Anglo-Saxon texts and contexts* (Manchester, 1997), pp 251–61.

Fitzgerald, Maria A., 'Textile production' in George Eogan, *The archaeology of Knowth in the first and second millennia AD* (Dublin, 2012), pp 552–63.

FitzPatrick, Elizabeth, 'Raiding and warring in monastic Ireland', *History Ireland*, 1:3 (1993), 13–18.

FitzPatrick, Elizabeth, *Royal inauguration in Gaelic Ireland, c.1100–1600: a cultural landscape study* (Woodbridge, 2004).

FitzPatrick, Elizabeth, 'The early church in Offaly' in William Nolan and Timothy P. O'Neill (eds), *Offaly, history and society* (Dublin, 1998), pp 93–129.

FitzPatrick, Elizabeth, 'The landscape of Máel Sechnaill's *rígdál* at Ráith Áeda, AD859' in Tom Condit and Christiaan Corlett (eds), *Above and beyond: essays in memory of Leo Swan* (Bray, 2005), pp 267–80.

Flechner, Roy, 'Patrick's reasons for leaving Britain' in Edmonds and Russell (eds), *Tome* (2011), pp 125–33.

Fletcher, Alan J. and Raymond Gillespie (eds), *Irish preaching, 700–1700* (Dublin, 2001).

Follett, Wesley, *Céli Dé in Ireland: monastic writing and identity in the early Middle Ages* (Woodbridge, 2006).

Fomin, Maxim, 'Classifications of kings in early Ireland and India', www.celto-indica.celtologica.com.

Frandsen, Paul J., 'Aspects of kingship in ancient Egypt' in Brisch (ed.), *Religion and power* (2008), pp 47–73

Fraser, J., P. Grosjean and J.G. O'Keeffe (eds), *Irish texts*, IV (London, 1934).

Freidel, David, 'Maya divine kingship' in Brisch (ed.), *Religion and power* (2008), pp 191–206.

Gantz, Jeffrey (trans.), *Early Irish myths and sagas* (London, 1981).

Gaskell-Brown, C. and A.E.T. Harper, 'Excavations on Cathedral Hill, Armagh, 1968', *UJA*, 47 (1984), 109–60.

Gelling, Margaret and Ann Cole, *The landscape of place-names* (Donington, repr. 2003).

Geraghty, Siobhán, *Viking Dublin: botanical evidence from Fishamble Street* (Dublin, 1996), pp 57–71.

Gies, Frances and Joseph, *Marriage and the family in the Middle Ages* (New York, 1989).

Goetz, Hans-Werner, ed. Steven Rowan, *Life in the Middle Ages: from the seventh to the thirteenth century* (Notre Dame, 1993). Trans. Alfred Wimmer.

Graham-Campbell, James and Michael Ryan (eds), *Anglo-Saxon/Irish relations before the Vikings* (Oxford, 2009).

Gray Elizabeth A. (ed.), *Cath Maige Tuired. The second Battle of Mag Tuired* (London, 1982).*

Greene, D.H., 'From Germania to Europe: the evidence of language and history', *Modern Language Review*, 92 (1997), xxix–xxxviii.

Greene, David (ed.), *Fingal Rónáin and other stories* (Dublin, 1975).*

Griffiths, David, 'Sand dunes and stray finds: evidence for pre-Viking trade?' in Graham-Campbell and Ryan (eds), *Anglo-Saxon/Irish relations* (2009), pp 265–80.

Griffiths, David, 'Town and their hinterlands' in Crick and Van Houts (eds), *A social history of England* (2011), pp 152–78.

Grogan, Eoin, *The North Munster Project, 2: the prehistoric landscape of north Munster* (Dublin, 2005).

Grogan, Eoin and Annaba Kilfeather, *Archaeological inventory of County Wicklow* (Dublin, 1997).

Grogan, Eoin, Caroline Velzian and Seamus Caulfield, *The Rath of the Synods, Tara, Co. Meath: excavations by Seán P. Ó Ríordáin* (Dublin, 2008).

Gross, Thomas and Rudolf Schieffer (eds), *Hinkmar von Reims: de ordine palatii* Monumenta Germaniae Historica (Hannover, 1980).*

Gwynn, Edward J. (ed.), 'The rule of Tallaght', *Hermathena*, 44 (1927) (2nd supplement), 24–7.*

Gwynn, Edward J. and Walter J. Purton (eds), 'The monastery of Tallaght', *PRIA*, 29C (1911–12), 115–79.*

Hall, Valerie, *The making of Ireland's landscape since the Ice Age* (Cork, 2011).

Halpin, Andrew, *Weapons and warfare in Viking and medieval Dublin* (Dublin, 2008).

Hamlin, Ann, '*Dignatio diei dominici*: an element in the iconography of Irish crosses?' in Dorothy Whitelock, Rosamond McKitterick and David Dumville (eds), *Ireland in medieval Europe: studies in memory of Kathleen Hughes* (Cambridge, 1982), pp 69–75.

Hamlin, Ann, *The archaeology of early Christianity in the north of Ireland* (Oxford, 2008).

Hamlin, Ann, 'Using mills on Sunday' in B.G. Scott (ed.), *Studies on early Ireland: essays in honour of M.V. Duignan* (Belfast, 1982), p. 11.

Handley, Mark A., 'Beyond hagiography: epigraphic commemoration and the cult of the saints in late antique Trier' in R.W. Mathisen and D. Shanzer (eds), *Society and culture in late antique Gaul* (Aldershot, 2001), pp 187–200.

Harvey, Anthony, 'Problems in dating the origin of the ogham script' in John Higgitt, Katherine Forsyth and David N. Parsons (eds), *Roman, runes and ogham: medieval inscriptions in the insular world and on the Continent* (Donington, 2001), pp 37–50.

Hayes, John W., *Late Roman pottery* (London, 1972).

Heist, W.W. (ed.), *Vitae sanctorum Hiberniae ex codice olim Salmanticensi nunc Bruxellensi* (Brussels, 1965).*

Hellmann, Siegmund (ed.), *Ps.-Cyprianus. De xii abusiuis saeculi.* (Leipzig, 1909).*

Helms, Mary W., 'Before the dawn: monks and the night in late antiquity and early modern Europe', *Anthropos*, 99 (2004), 177–91.

Herbert, Máire, 'Goddess and king: the sacred marriage in early Ireland' in Louise O. Fradenburg (ed.), *Women and sovereignty* (Edinburgh, 1992), pp 264–75.

Herbert, Máire, *Iona, Kells and Derry: the history and hagiography of the monastic familia of Columba* (Oxford, 1988; repr. Dublin, 1996).

Herbert, Máire, '*Rí Éirenn, Rí Alban*: kingship and identity in the ninth and tenth centuries' in Simon Taylor (ed.), *Kings, clerics and chronicles in Scotland, 500–1297* (Dublin, 2000), pp 62–72.

Hodkinson, Brian, 'The Rock of Dunamase', *Archaeology Ireland*, 9:2 (1995), 18–21.

Hollo, Kaarina, 'Allegoresis and literary creativity in eighth-century Ireland: the case of *Echtrae Chonnlai*' in Joseph F. Eska (ed.), *Narrative in Celtic tradition: essays in honour of Edgar M. Slotkin, CSANA Yearbook*, 8–9 (2011), pp 117–28.

Hollo, Kaarina, 'Fingal Rónáin: the medieval Irish text as argumentative space' in John Carey, Máire Herbert and Kevin Murray (eds), *Cín Chille Cúile: texts, saints and places: essays in honour of Pádraig Ó Riain* (Aberystwyth, 2004), pp 141–9.

Howlett, David R. (ed.), *Liber Epistolarum Sancti Patricii Episcopi: the book of letters of Saint Patrick the Bishop* (Dublin, 1994).*

Hughes, Kathleen, *The church in early Irish society* (London, 1966).

Hull, Vernam (ed.), 'Cáin Domnaig', *Ériu*, 20 (1966), 151–77.*

Hull, Vernam (trans.), 'Conall Corc and the Corco Luigde', *PMLA*, 62 (1947), 887–909.*

Hull, Vernam (ed. and trans.), 'The exile of Conall Corc', *PMLA*, 56 (1941), 937–50.*

Hurl, Declan P., Caroline Sandes and L. Buckley, 'The excavation of an early Christian cemetery at Solar, County Antrim, 1993', *UJA*, 61(2002), 37–82.

Hurtado, Larry W., *At the origins of Christian worship: the context and character of early Christian devotion* (Carlisle, 1999).

Innes, Matthew, *State and society in the early Middle Ages: the Middle Rhine Valley, 400–1000* (Cambridge, 2000).

Jackson, Kenneth H. (trans.), *A Celtic miscellany* (London, 1951; repr. 1971).*

Jaski, Bart, *Early Irish kingship and succession* (Dublin, 2000).

Jaski, Bart, 'Marriage laws in Ireland and on the Continent in the early Middle Ages' in Christine E. Meek and Mary Katharine Simms (eds), *'The fragility of her sex'? Medieval Irish women in their European context* (Dublin, 1996), pp 16–42.

Johnson, Ruth, *Viking Age Dublin* (Dublin, 2004).

Kehnel, Annette, *Clonmacnois – the church and lands of St Ciarán: change and continuity in an Irish monastic foundation (6th to 16th century)* (Münster, 1997).

Kelleher, J.V., 'The Táin and the annals', *Ériu*, 22 (1971), 107–27.

Kelly, Amanda, 'The discovery of Phocaean Red Slip Ware (PRSW) Form 3 and Bii Ware (LR1 amphorae) on sites in Ireland: an analysis within a broader framework', *PRIA*, 110C (2010), 35–88.

Kelly, Fergus, *A guide to early Irish law* (Dublin, 1988). [*GEIL*]

Kelly, Fergus, 'An Old-Irish text on court procedure', *Peritia*, 5 (1986), 74–106.*

Kelly, Fergus (ed.), *Audacht Morainn* (Dublin, 1976).*

Kelly, Fergus, *Early Irish farming* (Dublin, 1997). [*EIF*]

Kenney, James F., *The sources for the early history of Ireland: ecclesiastical. An introduction and guide* (New York, 1929; repr. Dublin, 1995).

King, Heather A. (ed.), *Clonmacnoise Studies*, 1 (Dublin, 1998).

King, Heather A. (ed.), *Clonmacnoise Studies*, 2 (Dublin, 2003).

King, Heather A., 'New graveyard, Clonmacnoise' (1995: 240): www.excavations.ie.

Knight, Jeremy K., *The end of antiquity: archaeology, society and religion, AD235–700* (Stroud, 1999).

Knott, Eleanor (ed.), *Togail Bruidne Da Derga* (Dublin, 1975 repr.).*

Koch, John T. (ed.), *Celtic culture: a historical encyclopedia* (5 vols, Santa Barbara and Oxford, 2006).

Koch, John T., 'Celts, Britons, and Gaels: names, peoples and identities', *Transactions of the Honourable Society of Cymmrodorion*, new ser. 9 (2003), 41–56.

Koch, John T. and John Carey (eds), *The Celtic heroic age: literary sources for ancient Celtic Europe and early Ireland and Wales* (Malden, 1994).*

Lacey, Brian, *Cenél Conaill and the Donegal kingdoms, AD500–800* (Dublin, 2006).

Lapidus, Ira M., *A history of Islamic societies* (Cambridge, 2002).

Latvio, Ritta, '*Neimed*: exploring social distinctions and sacredness in early Irish legal sources' in Ritari and Bergholm, *Approaches to religion and mythology* (2008), pp 220–42.

Lawlor, Henry Cairnes, *The monastery of Saint Mochai of Nendrum* (Belfast, 1925).

Lawlor, Hugh Jackson and Richard Irvine Best (eds), 'The ancient list of the coarbs of Patrick', *PRIA*, 35C (1919), 316–62.*

Lawson, Thomas E., 'Ritual form and ritual frequency: from ethnographic reports to experimental findings' in H. Whitehouse and R.N. McCauley (eds), *Mind and religion: psychological and cognitive foundations of religiosity* (Walnut Creek, CA, 2005), pp 57–67.

Leclercq, Jean, *L'amour des letters et le désir de Dieu: initiation aux auteurs monastiques du moyen age* (3rd ed., Paris, 1990).

Lehane, John, Marta Muñiz Pérez, Jerry O'Sullivan & Brendon Wilkins, 'Three cemetery-settlement excavations in Co. Galway at Carrowkeel, Treanbaun and Owenbristy' in Corlett and Potterton (eds), *Death and burial in early medieval Ireland* (2010), pp 139–56.

Lucas, A.T., 'Washing and bathing in ancient Ireland', *JRSAI*, 95 (1965), 65–114.

Lynn, Chris, 'Excavations at 46–48 Scotch Street, Armagh, 1979–80', *UJA*, 51 (1988), 69–84.

Lynn, Chris, 'Houses in rural Ireland, AD500–1000', *UJA*, 3rd ser., 57 (1994), 81–94.

Lynn, Chris, *Navan Fort: archaeology and myth* (Bray, 2003).

Lynn, Chris, 'Recent archaeological excavations in Armagh city: an interim summary', *Seanchas Ard Mhacha*, 8 (1977), 275–80.

Lynn, Chris J. and Jacqueline A. McDowell, '*Críth Gablach* and the status of the rath occupants' in Lynn and McDowell (eds), *Deer Park Farms* (2011), pp 603–10.

Lynn, Chris J. and Jacqueline A. McDowell, *Deer Park Farms: the excavation of a raised rath in the Glenarm Valley, County Antrim* (2011).

Mac Airt, Seán (ed.), *Annals of Inisfallen* (Dublin, 1951).*

Mac Airt, Seán and Gearóid Mac Niocaill (eds), *The Annals of Ulster (to AD1131)* (Dublin, 1983).*

Macalister, R.A.S., *Corpus inscriptionum insularum Hiberniae* (2 vols, Dublin, 1945–9).*

Mac Cana, Proinsias, 'Aspects of the theme of king and goddess in Irish literature', *Études celtiques*, 7 (1955–6), 76–114, 356–413; 8 (1958–9), 59–65.

Mac Cana, Proinsias, 'On the word *láech* "warrior"', *Celtica*, 11 (1976), 125–8.

MacCotter, Paul, *Colmán of Cloyne: a study* (Dublin, 2004).

MacCotter, Paul, *Medieval Ireland: territorial, political and economic divisions* (Dublin, 2008).

MacDonald, A.D.S., 'Aspects of the monastery and monastic life in Adomnán's Life of Columba', *Peritia*, 3 (1984), 271–302.

Mac Giolla Easpaig, Dónall, 'Significance and etymology of the place-name *Temair*' in Bhreathnach (ed.), *Kingship and landscape* (2005), pp 423–48.

MacNeill, Eoin, *Celtic Ireland* (Dublin, 1921; repr. 1981).

MacNeill, John [Eoin], 'Early Irish population-groups: their nomenclature, classification and chronology', *PRIA*, 29C (1911–12), 59–114.

MacNeill, Eoin, 'Sescenn Uarbeoil of the sagas and other place-names to the south of Dublin', *JRSAI*, 65 (7th ser., 5:1) (1935), 9–22.

MacNeill, Máire, *The festival of Lughnasa* (Dublin 1962; repr. 1982).

Mac Niocaill, Gearóid, 'The "heir-designate" in early medieval Ireland', *Irish Jurist*, 3 (1968), 326–9.

MacShamhráin, Ailbhe S., *Church and polity in pre-Norman Ireland: the case of Glendalough* (Maynooth, 1996).

MacShamhráin, Ailbhe and Paul Byrne, 'Prosopography I' in Bhreathnach (ed.), *Kingship and landscape* (2005), pp 159–224.

Maloney, Aenghus, 'From east to west, crossing the bogs at Clonmacnoise' in King (ed.), *Clonmacnoise Studies*, 1 (1998), pp 7–10.

Manning, Conleth, 'Clonmacnoise Cathedral' in King (ed.), *Clonmacnoise Studies*, 1 (1998), pp 57–86.

Markus, Robert, *The end of ancient Christianity* (Cambridge, 1990).

Mayr-Harting, Henry, 'Artists and patrons' in Timothy Reuter and Rosamund McKitterick (eds), *The New Cambridge Medieval History, c.900–c.1024* (Cambridge, 1999).

Mc Carthy, Daniel P., *The Irish annals: their genesis, evolution and history* (Dublin, 2008).

McCone, Kim, '*Aided Cheltchair maic Uthechair*: hounds, heroes and hospitallers in early Irish myth and story', *Ériu*, 35 (1984), 1–30.

McCone, Kim, 'A tale of two ditties: poet and satirist in *Cath Maige Tuired*' in Ó Corráin et al. (eds), *Sages, saints and storytellers* (1989), pp 122–43.

McCone, Kim, '"King" and "Queen" in Celtic and Indo-European', *Ériu*, 49 (1998), 1–12.

McCone, Kim, *Pagan past and Christian present* (Maynooth, 1990).

McCone, Kim, 'Werewolves, cyclopes, *díberga* and *fíanna*: juvenile delinquency in early Ireland', *Cambridge Medieval Celtic Studies*, 12 (1986), 1–22.

McCormick, Finbar, 'Iona: the archaeology of the early monastery' in Bourke (ed.), *Cult of Saint Columba* (1997), pp 45–68.

McCormick, Finbar, 'The decline of the cow: agricultural and settlement change in early medieval Ireland', *Peritia*, 20 (2008), 210–25.

McCormick, Finbar and Emily V. Murray, *Excavations at Knowth 3: Knowth and the zooarchaeology of early Christian Ireland* (2007).

McCormick, Finbar, G. Cribben, M.E. Robinson, D.W. Shimwell and E. Murphy, 'A pagan-Christian transitional burial at Kiltullagh', *Emania*, 13 (1995), 89–98.

McErlean, Thomas and Norman Crothers (eds), *Harnessing the tides: the early medieval tide mills at Nendrum monastery, Strangford Lough* (Belfast, 2007).

McErlean, Thomas, Rosemary Conkey and Wes Forsythe, *Strangford Lough: an archaeological survey of the maritime cultural landscape* (Belfast, 2002).

McKay, Patrick, *A dictionary of Ulster place-names* (Belfast, 1999).

McKay, Patrick and Kay Muhr, *Lough Neagh places: their names and origins* (Belfast, 2007).

McLeod, Neil, 'Kinship', *Ériu*, 51 (2000), 1–22.

McManus, Damian, 'A chronology of Latin loan-words in early Irish', *Ériu*, 34 (1983), 21–71.

McManus, Damian, *A guide to ogam* (Maynooth, 1991).

Meens, Rob, 'Politics, mirrors of princes and the Bible: sins, kings and the well-being of the realm', *Early Medieval Europe*, 7 (1998), 345–57.

Meyer, Kuno (ed.), 'Conall Corc and the Corco Luigde', *Anecdota from Irish manuscripts*, 3 (Dublin, 1910), 57–63.*

Meyer, Kuno (ed.), *Sanas Cormaic: an Old-Irish glossary compiled by Cormac úa Cuilennáin, king-bishop of Cashel in the tenth century. Anecdota from Irish manuscripts*, 4 (Halle and Dublin, 1912; repr. 1994).*

Meyer, Kuno (ed.), 'The expulsion of the Déssi', *Ériu*, 3 (1907), 135–42.*

Meyer, Kuno (ed.), *The instructions of King Cormac mac Airt* (Dublin, 1909)*

Meyer, Kuno (ed.), *The triads of Ireland* (London, 1906).*

Monk, Michael A. and E. Kelleher, 'An assessment of the archaeological evidence for Irish corn-drying kilns in the light of the results of archaeological experiments and archaeobotanical studies', *JIA*, 14 (2005), 77–114.

Monk, Michael A. and John Sheehan (eds), *Early medieval Munster: archaeology, history and society* (Cork, 1998).

Moore, Finbar, 'Ireland's oldest bridge', *Archaeology Ireland*, 10:4 (1996), 24–7.

Moore, Finbar, 'Munster ogham stones: siting, context and function' in Monk and Sheehan (eds), *Early medieval Munster* (1998), pp 23–32.

Moore, Michael, *Archaeological inventory of County Waterford* (Dublin, 1999).

Morris, Richard, *Churches in the landscape* (London, 1989).

Mount, Charles, 'Excavation of an early medieval promonotary fort and enclosed cemetery at Knoxspark, Co. Sligo' in Corlett and Potterton (eds), *Death and burial in early medieval Ireland* (2010), pp 187–216.

Mulchrone, Kathleen (ed.), *Bethu Pátraic* (Dublin and London, 1939).*

Murdoch, Brian, 'Preaching in medieval Ireland: the Irish tradition' in Fletcher and Gillespie (eds), *Irish preaching* (2001), pp 40–55.

Murphy, Donald, 'Excavation of an early monastic enclosure at Clonmacnoise' in King (ed.), *Clonmacnoise Studies*, 2 (2003), pp 1–33.

Murphy, Margaret and Michael Potterton, *The Dublin region in the Middle Ages: settlement, land-use and economy* (Dublin, 2010).

Murray, Kevin (ed.), *Baile in Scáil 'The Phantom's Frenzy'* (Dublin, 2004).*

Nagy, Joseph F., *Conversing with angels and ancients: the literary myth of medieval Ireland* (Dublin, 1997).

Neill, Kenneth, *An archaeological survey of County Armagh* (Belfast, 2009).

Nelson, Janet, 'Kingship and royal government' in Rosamund McKitterick (ed.), *The new Cambridge medieval history*, II: *c.700–c.900* (Cambridge, 1995), pp 383–430.

Neuman de Vegvar, Carol, 'Romanitas and realpolitik in Cogitosus' description of the church of St Brigit, Kildare' in Martin Carver (ed.), *The cross goes north: processes of conversion in northern Europe, AD300–1300* (Woodbridge, 2003; repr. 2005), pp 153–70.

Newman, Conor, 'Re-composing the archaeological landscape of Tara' in Bhreathnach (ed.), *Kingship and landscape* (2005), pp 361–499.

Newman, Conor, *Tara: an archaeological survey* (Dublin, 1997).

Newman, Conor, 'The sacral landscape of Tara: a preliminary exploration' in Schot et al. (eds), *Cult and kingship* (2011), pp 22–43.

Ní Bhrolcháin, Muireann, *An introduction to early Irish literature* (Dublin, 2009). [*EIL*]

Ní Bhrolcháin, Muireann, 'Death-tales of early kings of Tara' in Schot et al. (eds), *Cult and kingship* (2011), pp 44–65.

Ní Chonaill, Bronagh, 'Child-centred law in medieval Ireland' in R. Davis and T. Dunne (eds), *The empty throne: childhood and the crisis in modernity* (www.eprints.gl.ac.uk).

Ní Chonaill, Bronagh, 'Fosterage, child-rearing in medieval Ireland', *History Ireland*, 5:1 (1997), 28–31.

Ní Dhonnchadha, Máirín (ed.), 'The guarantor list of *Cáin Adomnáin*, 697', *Peritia*, 1 (1982), 178–215.*

Ní Mhaonaigh, Máire, *Brian Boru. Ireland's greatest king?* (Stroud, 2007).

O'Brien, Elizabeth, 'Burnt magic' in M. Davies, U. MacConville and G. Cooney (eds), *A grand gallimaufry collected in honour of Nick Maxwell* (Dublin, 2010), pp 195–8.

O'Brien, Elizabeth, 'Churches of south-east County Dublin, seventh to twelfth century' in Gearóid Mac Niocaill and Patrick F. Wallace (eds), *Keimelia: studies in medieval archaeology and history in memory of Tom Delaney* (Galway, 1988), pp 504–24.

O'Brien, Elizabeth, 'Early medieval sentinel warrior burials', *Peritia*, 20 (2008), 323–30.

O'Brien, Elizabeth, 'Excavation of a multi-period burial site at Ballymacaward, Ballyshannon, Co. Donegal', *Journal of the County Donegal Historical Society*, 51 (1999), 56–61.

O'Brien, Elizabeth, *Post-Roman Britain to Anglo-Saxon England: burial practices reviewed* (Oxford, 1999).

O'Brien, Elizabeth, 'The location and context of Viking burials at Kilmainham and Island-bridge, Dublin' in Clarke et al. (eds), *Ireland and Scandinavia* (1998), pp 203–21.

O'Brien, Elizabeth and Edel Bhreathnach, 'Burial in early medieval Ireland: politics and religion' in James Kelly and Mary Ann Lyons (eds), *Death and dying in Ireland, Britain and Europe: historical perspectives* (Sallins, 2013), pp 37–58.

O'Brien, Elizabeth and Edel Bhreathnach, 'Irish boundary *ferta*, their physical manifestation and historical context' in Edmonds and Russell (eds), *Tome* (2011), pp 53–64.

O'Brien, M.A., *Corpus genealogiarum Hiberniae* (Dublin, 1962; repr. 1971).*

Ó Carragáin, Tomás, *Churches in early medieval Ireland: architecture, ritual and memory* (New Haven and London, 2010).

Ó Cathasaigh, Tomás, *The heroic biography of Cormac mac Airt* (Dublin, 1977).*

Ó Cathasaigh, Tomás, 'The threefold death in early Irish sources', *Studia Celtica Japonica*, 6 (1994), 53–76.

Ó Corráin, Donnchadh, 'Historical need and literary narrative' in D. Ellis Evans (ed.), *Proceedings of the Seventh International Congress of Celtic Studies held in Oxford, from 10th to 15th July, 1983* (Oxford, 1986), pp 141–58.

Ó Corráin, Donnchadh, 'Irish law and canon law' in Proinsias Ní Chatháin and Michael Richter (eds), *Irland und Europa Christenheit* (Stuttgart, 1987), pp 284–307.

Ó Corráin, Donnchadh, 'Irish regnal succession: a reappraisal', *Studia Hibernica*, 11 (1971), 7–39.

Ó Corráin, Donnchadh, 'Marriage in early Ireland' in Art Cosgrove (ed.), *Marriage in Ireland* (Dublin, 1985), pp 5–24.

Ó Corráin, Donnchadh, 'The early Irish churches: some aspects of organisation' in Donnchadh Ó Corráin (ed.), *Irish antiquity: essays and studies presented to Professor M.J. O'Kelly* (Cork, 1981), pp 327–41.

Ó Corráin, Donnchadh, 'Women and the law in early Ireland' in Mary O'Dowd and Sabine Wichert (eds), *Chattel, servant or citizen: women's status in church, state and society* (Belfast, 1995), pp 45–57.

Ó Corráin, Donnchadh, 'Women in early Irish society' in Margaret MacCurtain and Donnchadh Ó Corráin (eds), *Women in Irish society: the historical dimension* (Dublin, 1978), pp 1–13.

Ó Corráin, Donnchadh, Liam Breatnach and Kim McCone (eds), *Sages, saints and storytellers: Celtic studies in honour of Professor James Carney* (Maynooth, 1989).

Ó Cróinín, Dáibhí, *Early medieval Ireland, 400–1200* (London and New York, 1995).

Ó Cróinín, Dáibhí (ed.), *Prehistoric and early Ireland: a new history of Ireland*, I (Oxford, 2005). [*NHI*]

Ó Cróinín, Dáibhí, 'Who was Palladius "first bishop of the Irish"?', *Peritia*, 14 (2000), 205–37.

Ó Cuív, Brian, 'The motif of threefold death', *Éigse*, 15 (1973), 145–50.

O Daly, Máirín (ed.), 'A chóicid chóin Chairpri crúaid', *Éigse*, 10 (1962–3), 177–97.*

O Daly, Máirín (ed.), *Cath Maige Mucrama* (Dublin, 1975).*

O Daly, Máirín (ed.), 'Lánellach tigi rích ⁷ ruirech', *Ériu*, 19 (1962), 81–6.*

O'Donnell, M.G., 'Lisnacaheragh, Garranes' in I. Bennett (ed.), *Excavations 1990: summary accounts of archaeological excavations in Ireland* (Dublin, 1992).

O'Donoghue, Tadhg (ed.), 'Advice to a prince', *Ériu*, 9 (1921–3), 43–54.*

O'Donovan, John (ed.), *Annala Rioghachta Éireann. Annals of the Kingdom of Ireland by the Four Masters from the earliest period to the year 1616* (7 vols, Dublin, 1848–51; repr. Dublin, 1990).*

O'Donovan, Edmond and Jonny Geber, 'Excavations on Mount Gamble Hill, Swords, Co. Dublin' in Corlett and Potterton (eds), *Death and burial in early medieval Ireland* (2010), pp 227–38.

Ó Fiaich, Tomás, 'The church of Armagh under lay control', *Seanchas Ard Mhacha*, 5 (1969), 75–127.

Ó Floinn, Raghnall, 'Clonmacnoise: art and patronage in the early medieval period' in King (ed.), *Clonmacnoise Studies*, 1 (1998), pp 87–100.

Ó Floinn, Raghnall, 'Early Christianity in Ireland based on the most current archaeological research' in O. Heinrich-Tamáska, N. Krohn and S. Ristow (eds), *Christianierung Europas: Christianisation of Europe: archaeological evidence for its creation, development and consolidation* (Regensburg, 2012), pp 11–35.

Ó Floinn, Raghnall, 'Freestone Hill, Co. Kilkenny: a reassessment' in Smyth (ed.), *Seanchas* (2000), pp 12–29.

Ó Floinn, Raghnall, 'Patrons and politics: art, artefact and methodology' in Mark Redknap, Nancy Edwards and Susan Youngs (eds), *Pattern and purpose in insular art* (Oxford, 2001), pp 1–14.

Ó Floinn, Raghnall, 'The Anglo-Saxon connection: Irish metalwork, AD400–800' in Graham-Campbell and Ryan (eds), *Anglo-Saxon/Irish relations* (2009), pp 231–51.

Ó Floinn, Raghnall, 'The archaeology of the early Viking Age in Ireland' in Clarke et al. (eds), *Ireland and Scandinavia* (1998), pp 131–65.

O'Grady, Standish Hayes (ed. and trans.), *Silva Gadelica* (2 vols, London, 1892).*

O'Hara, Robert, 'Final report: M3 Clonee–North of Kells; Dunshaughlin–Navan. Collierstown 1, Co. Meath' (2009).

Okasha, Elizabeth and Katherine Forsyth, *Early Christian inscriptions of Munster: a corpus of inscribed stones* (Cork, 2001).

O'Keeffe, J.G. (ed.), 'The rule of Patrick', *Ériu*, 1 (1904), 216–24.*

O'Keeffe, J.G., 'Cáin Domnaig', *Ériu*, 2 (1905), 189–214.*

O'Loughlin, Thomas, 'Irish preaching before the end of the ninth century: assessing the extent of our evidence' in Flethcher and Gillespie (eds), *Irish preaching* (2001), pp 18–39.

O'Loughlin, Thomas, 'Living in the ocean' in Bourke (ed.), *Cult of Saint Columba* (1997), pp 11–23.

O'Loughlin, Thomas, 'Marriage and sexuality in the Hibernensis', *Peritia*, 11 (1997), 188–206.

O'Loughlin, Thomas, 'Reading Muirchú's Tara-event with its background as a trial of "biblical divinities"' in Jane Cartwright (ed.), *Celtic hagiography and saints' cults* (Cardiff, 2003), pp 123–35.

Olsen, Glenn, 'The idea of the *ecclesia primitiva* in the writings of the twelfth-century canonist', *Traditio*, 25 (1969), 61–86.

Ó Muraíle, Nollaig, 'Some early Connacht population-groups' in Smyth (ed.), *Seanchas* (2000), pp 161–77.

Ó Murchadha, D., 'Rubbings taken of the inscriptions on the Cross of the Scriptures, Clonmacnois', *JRSAI*, 110 (1980), 47–51.

Ó Murchadha, Diarmaid, 'Carman, site of Óenach Carmain: a proposed location', *Éigse*, 33 (2002), 57–70.

Ó Murchadha, Diarmaid, 'Early history and settlements of the Laígis' in Pádraig G. Lane and William Nolan (eds), *Laois, history and society: interdisciplinary essays on the history of an Irish county* (Dublin, 1999), 35–62.

Ó Néill, John and J. Coughlan, 'An enclosed early medieval cemetery at Cherrywood, Co. Dublin' in Corlett and Potterton (eds), *Death and burial in early medieval Ireland* (2010), pp 239–50.

O'Rahilly, Cecile (ed.), *Táin Bó Cúailnge: recension*, 1 (Dublin, 1976).*

O'Rahilly, Thomas F., 'Eachlach urláir', *Ériu*, 9 (1921/3), 15–16.

O'Rahilly, Thomas F., 'On the origin of the names Érainn and Ériu', *Ériu*, 14 (1946), 7–28.

Ó Riain, Pádraig, *Corpus genealogiarum sanctorum Hiberniae* (Dublin, 1985). [CGSH]*

Ó Riain, Pádraig, *Dictionary of Irish saints* (Dublin, 2011). [DIS]

Ó Riain, Pádraig, 'Finnio and Winniau: a return to the subject' in John Carey, John T. Koch and Pierre-Yves Lambert (eds), *Ildánach Ildírech: a Festschrift for Proinsias Mac Cana* (Andover and Aberystwyth, 1999), pp 187–202.

Ó Riain, Pádraig, 'Irish saints' cults and ecclesiastical families' in Thacker and Sharpe (eds), *Local saints and local churches* (2002), pp 291–302.

Ó Riain, Pádraig, 'The *Táin*: a clue to its origins' in J.P. Mallory and G. Stockman (eds), *Ulidia: Proceedings of the First International Conference on the Ulster Cycle of Tales, Belfast and Emain Macha, 8–12 April 1994* (Belfast, 1994), pp 31–7.

Ó Riain, Pádraig, 'Traces of Lug in early Irish hagiographical tradition', *Zeitschrift für celtische Philologie*, 36 (1977), 138–56.

Ó Riain, Pádraig, 'When and why *Cothraige* was first equated with *Patricius*?', *Zeitschrift für celtische Philologie*, 49–50 (1997), 698–711.

Ó Ríordáin, Seán P., 'The excavation of a large earthen ringfort at Garranes, Co. Cork', *Proceeding of the Royal Irish Academy*, 47 (1942), 77–150.

O'Sullivan, Aidan, *Crannogs: lake-dwellings in early Ireland* (Dublin, 2000).

O'Sullivan, Aidan (ed.), *Foragers, farmers and fishers in a coastal landscape: an intertidal archaeological survey of the Shannon Estuary* (Dublin, 2001).

O'Sullivan, Aidan, Rob Sands and Eamon P. Kelly, *Coolure Demesne crannog, Lough Derravaragh: an introduction to its archaeology and landscapes* (Bray, 2007).

O'Sullivan, Aidan and Tríona Nicholl, 'Early medieval enclosures in Ireland: dwellings, daily life and social identity', *PRIA*, 111C (2011), 59–90.

O'Sullivan, Catherine, *Hospitality in medieval Ireland, 900–1500* (Dublin, 2004).

O'Sullivan, Jerry, 'Excavations beside Sruth a'Mhuilinn ("the Mill Stream"), Iona', *PSAS*, 124 (1994), 491–508.

O'Sullivan, Jerry and Tomás Ó Carragáin, *Inishmurray: monks and pilgrims in an Atlantic landscape. Volume 1: Archaeological survey and excavations, 1997–2000* (2008).

O'Sullivan, Muiris, *Duma na nGiall: the Mound of the Hostages, Tara* (Bray, 2005).

Outler, Albert C. (ed. and trans.), *Confessions and Enchiridion*, 123–4 (www.ccel.org; www.stoa.org/hippo (original Latin text)).*

Palmer, James, 'Defining paganism in the Carolingian world', *Early Medieval Europe*, 15:4 (2007), 402–25.

Paterson, T.G.F. and Oliver Davies, 'The churches of Armagh', *UJA*, 3rd ser., 3 (1940), 82–103.

Piggott, Stuart, *The druids* (London, 1999; repr.).

Plummer, Charles (ed. and trans.), *Bethada náem nÉrenn: Lives of Irish saints* (2 vols, Oxford, 1922).*

Plummer, Charles (ed.), *Irish litanies: text and translation* (London, 1925).

Plummer, Charles (ed.), *Vitae sanctorum Hiberniae* (2 vols, Oxford, 1922).*

Power, Nancy, 'Classes of women described in the Senchas Már' in Rudolf Thurneysen et al. (eds), *Studies in early Irish law* (Dublin and London, 1936), pp 81–108.

Radner, J.N. (ed.), *Fragmentary annals of Ireland* (Dublin, 1978).*

Raftery, Barry, *Trackway excavations in the Mountdillon Bogs, Co. Longford, 1985–91* (Dublin, 1996).

Raftery, Barry, *Trackways through time: archaeological investigations on Irish bog roads, 1985–1989* (Dublin, 1990).

Randolph-Quinney, P., 'An unusual burial at Ballygarraun West', *Seanda: NRA Archaeology Magazine*, 2 (2007), 30–1.

Reynolds, Susan, *Kingdoms and communities in western Europe, 900–1300* (Oxford, 1984; repr. 1997).

Riley, F.T., 'Excavations in the townland of Pollacorragune, Tuam, Co. Galway', *Journal of the Galway Archaeological and Historical Society*, 17 (1936–7), 44–54.

Ritari, Katja and Alexandra Bergholm (eds), *Approaches to religion and mythology in Celtic studies* (Newcastle, 2008).

Ryan, John, 'Historical addendum: Uí Echach Muman' in Ó Ríordáin, 'Garranes' (1942), 145–50.

Salway, P., *The Oxford illustrated history of Roman Britain* (Frome, 1993).

Scarth, H.M., 'Recent discoveries on the site of the Old White Hart Hotel, Bath', *Archaeological Journal*, 25 (1868), 159–62.

Schot, Roseanne, Conor Newman and Edel Bhreathnach (eds), *Landscapes of cult and kingship* (Dublin, 2011).

Schulze-Thulin, Britta, 'Old Norse in Ireland' in P. Sture Ureland and Iain Clarkson (eds), *Language contact across the North Atlantic* (Tübingen, 1996), pp 103–11.

Scott, Brian G., 'An early Irish law tract on the blacksmith's forge', *JIA*, 1 (1983), 59–62.

Seaver, Matthew, 'Against the grain: early medieval settlement and burial on the Blackhill. Excavations at Raystown, Co. Meath' in Corlett and Potterton (eds), *Death and burial in early medieval Ireland* (2010), pp 261–79.

Semple, Sarah, 'A fear of the past: the place of the prehistoric burial mound in the ideology of middle and later Anglo-Saxon England', *World Archaeology*, 30:1 (1998), 109–26.

Semple, Sarah, 'Locations of assembly in early Anglo-Saxon England' in Aliki Pantos and Sarah Semple (eds), *Assembly places and practices in medieval Europe* (Dublin, 2004), pp 135–54.

Shanahan, Brian, 'Roscommon landscape: Baslick parish centre', *Discovery Programme Annual Report 2009*, 22.

Sharpe, Richard, 'Hiberno-Latin *laicus*, Irish *láech*, and the devil's men', *Ériu*, 30 (1979), 75–92.

Sharpe, Richard, *Life of S. Columba by Adomnán* (London, 1995).*

Sharpe, Richard, 'Martyrs and local saints in late antique Britain' in Thacker and Sharpe (eds), *Local saints and local churches* (2002), pp 75–154.

Sharpe, Richard, 'Paleographical considerations in the study of the Patrician documents in the Book of Armagh', *Scriptorium*, 36 (1982), 3–28.

Sharpe, Richard, 'Some problems concerning the organization of the church in early medieval Ireland', *Peritia*, 3 (1984), 230–70.

Shaw, Francis (ed.), *The dream of Óengus: Aislinge Óenguso* (Dublin, 1934).*

Sheehan, John, 'A peacock's tale: excavations at Caherlehillan, Iveragh, Ireland' in Nancy Edwards (ed.), *The archaeology of the early medieval Celtic churches* (Leeds, 2009), pp 191–206.

Sheehan, John, 'Ireland's Viking Age hoards: sources and contacts' in Anne-Christine Larsen (ed.), *The Vikings in Ireland* (Roskilde, 2001), pp 51–9.

Sheehy, Maurice P. (ed.), *Pontificia Hibernica* (2 vols, Dublin, 1962).

Sherley-Price, L. (rev. R. Latham), *Bede: a history of the English church and people* (London, 1977).

Simpson, Linzi, 'The first phase of Viking activity in Ireland: archaeological evidence from Dublin' in John Sheehan and Donnchadh Ó Corráin (eds), *The Viking Age: Ireland and the West. Proceedings of the 15th Viking Congress* (Dublin, 2010), pp 418–29.

Sindbæk, Søren M., 'Close ties and long-range relations: the emporia network in early Viking Age exchange' in Sheehan and Ó Corráin (eds), *Ireland and the West* (2010), pp 430–40.

Smith, G.F., R. Cronin, E. Delaney, A. Merkie, B. O'Connell and K. O'Hora, *Landscape study of Great and Little Sugar Loaf Mountains, Co. Wicklow*. Report prepared for Wicklow County Council (2010).

Smith, Roland M. (ed.), 'Bretha im gatta' in Fraser et al. (eds), *Irish texts*, IV (1934), pp 18–20.*

Smith, Roland M. (ed.), 'Urchuillti bretheman' in Fraser et al. (eds), *Irish texts*, IV (1934), pp 24–7.*

Smyth, Alfred P. (ed.), *Seanchas: studies in early and medieval Irish archaeology, history and literature in honour of Francis J. Byrne* (Dublin, 2000).

Smyth, Alfred P., 'Húi Néill and the Leinstermen in the Annals of Ulster, 431–516AD', *Études celtiques*, 14 (1974), 121–43.

Southall, Aidan, *The city in time and space* (Cambridge, 2000).

Sproule, David, 'Origins of the Éoganachta', *Ériu*, 35 (1984), 31–7.

Sproule, David, 'Politics and pure narrative in the stories about Corc of Cashel', *Ériu*, 36 (1985), 11–28.

Stafford, Pauline, 'Queens and queenship' in P. Stafford (ed.), *A companion to the early Middle Ages: Britain and Ireland, c.500–1100* (Chichester, 2009), pp 459–76.

Stafford, Pauline, *Queens, concubines and dowagers: the king's wife in the early Middle Ages* (London, 1983).

Stafford, Pauline, 'Sons and mothers: family politics in the early Middle Ages' in Baker (ed.), *Medieval women* (Oxford, 1978), pp 79–100.

Stalley, Roger, 'The Tower Cross at Kells' in C.E. Karkov, R.T. Farrell and M. Ryan (eds), *The insular tradition* (Albany, NY, 1997), pp 115–41.

Stancliffe, Clare, 'Columbanus's monasticism and the sources of his inspiration: from Basil to the Master?' in Edmonds and Russell (eds), *Tome* (2011), pp 17–28.

Stevens, Paul, 'Burial and ritual in late prehistory in north Wexford: excavation of a ring-ditch cemetery in Ask townland' in Jerry O'Sullivan and Michael Stanley (eds), *New routes to the past* (Dublin, 2007), pp 35–46.

Stokes, Whitley (ed.), *Lives of saints from the Book of Lismore* (Oxford, 1890).

Stokes, Whitley (ed.), 'On the deaths of some Irish heroes', *Revue celtique*, 23 (1902), 303–48, 438.

Stokes, Whitley (ed.), 'The Annals of Tigernach', *Revue celtique*, 16 (1895), 374–419; 17 (1896), 6–33, 119–263, 337–420; 18 (1897), 9–59, 150–97, 267–303, 374–91 (repr. 1993, Felinfach, 2 vols).*

Stokes, Whitley (ed.), *The martyrology of Oengus the Culdee. Félire Óengusso Céli Dé* (London, 1905).

Stokes, Whitley (ed.), *The Tripartite Life of Patrick* (2 vols, London, 1887).*

Stokes, Whitley (ed. and trans.), 'The voyage of Máel Dúin', *Revue celtique*, 10 (1889), 50–95.

Stokes, Whitley and John Strachan (eds), *Thesaurus Paleohibernicus: a collection of Old-Irish glosses, scholia, prose, and verse* (2 vols, Cambridge, 1901–3; repr. 1975).*

Stout, Matthew, *The Irish ringfort* (Dublin, 1997).

Strachan, John (ed.), 'An Old Irish homily', *Ériu*, 3 (1907), 1–10.*

Sweetman, P.D., Olive Alcock and Bernie Moran, *Archaeological inventory of County Laois* (Dublin, 1995).

Swift, Catherine, 'Early priests within their own localities' in Edmonds and Russell (eds), *Tome* (2011), 29–40.

Swift, Catherine, 'Forts and fields: a study of "monastic towns" in seventh- and eighth-century Ireland', *JIA*, 9 (1998), 105–25.

Swift, Catherine, *Ogam stones and the earliest Irish Christians* (Maynooth, 1997).

Swift, Catherine, 'Sculptors and customers: a study of Clonmacnoise grave-slabs' in King (ed.), *Clonmacnoise Studies*, 2 (2003), pp 105–23.

Swift, Catherine (with contributions by Francis John Byrne), 'The early history of Knowth' in F.J. Byrne, W. Jenkins, G. Kenny and C. Swift (eds), *Excavations at Knowth 4: historical Knowth and its hinterland* (Dublin, 2008), pp 5–87.

Thacker, Alan, 'Loca sanctorum: the significance of place in the study of the saints' in Thacker and Sharpe (eds), *Local saints and local churches* (2002), pp 1–43.

Thacker, Alan, 'Monks, preaching and pastoral care in early Anglo-Saxon England' in Blair and Sharpe (eds), *Pastoral care before the parish* (1992), pp 137–70.

Thacker, Alan and Richard Sharpe (eds), *Local saints and local churches in the early medieval West* (Oxford, 2002).

Thomas, Charles, *Christianity in Roman Britain* (London, 1981).

Thomas, Charles, 'Early medieval Munster: thoughts on its primary Christian phase' in Monk and Sheehan (eds), *Early medieval Munster* (1998), pp 9–16.

Thompson, Tok, 'Clocha geala/cloche uaisle: white quartz in Irish tradition', *Béaloideas*, 73 (2005), 111–33.

Thurneysen, Rudolf, Nancy Power and Myles Dillon (eds), *Studies in early Irish law* (Dublin, 1936).*

Tobin, Redmond and John Sunderland et al., 'Excavations and specialist reports: Corbally 1' (unpublished reports for Kilsaran Concrete Products Ltd. and Margaret Gowen and Co. Ltd).

Todd, James Henthorne and Algernon Herbert (eds), *The Irish version of the Historia Britonum of Nennius* (Dublin, 1848).*

Toner, Gregory, 'Identifying Ptolemy's Irish places and tribes' in David N. Parsons and Patrick Sims- Williams (eds), *Ptolemy: towards a linguistic atlas of the earliest Celtic place-names of Europe* (Aberystwyth, 2000), pp 73–82.

Van Hamel, Anton G. (ed.), *Compert Con Culainn and other stories* (Dublin, 1933).*

Van Hamel, Anton G. (ed.), *Immrama* (Dublin, 1941).*

Waddell, John, 'Continuity, cult and contest' in Schot et al. (eds), *Cult and kingship* (2011), pp 192–212.

Walker, G.S.M. (ed.), *Sancti Columbani Opera* (Dublin, 1957; repr. 1970).*

Wallace, Patrick F., 'Ireland's Viking towns' in Larsen (ed.), *The Vikings in Ireland* (2001), pp 37–50.

Wallace, Patrick F., 'The economy and commerce of Viking Age Dublin' in K. Düwel, H. Jankuhn, H. Siems and D. Timpe (eds), *Untersuchungen zu Handel und Verkehr derv or- und frügeschichtlichen Zeit in Mittel- und Nordeuropa* (Göttingen, 1987), pp 200–45.

Wallace, Patrick F., 'The English presence in Viking Dublin' in M.A. Blackburn (ed.), *Anglo-Saxon monetary history* (Leicester, 1986), pp 201–21.

Walsh, Maura and Dáibhí Ó Cróinín (eds and trans.), *Cummian's letter 'De controversia paschali' and the 'De ratione computandi'* (Toronto, 1988).*

Ward, Benedicta and Norman Russell, *The lives of the Desert Fathers* (London and Oxford, 1981).*

Warmind, Morten, 'Sacred kingship among the Celts', *PHCC*, 12 (1992), 196–206.

Warner, Richard, 'Clogher: an archaeological window on early medieval Tyrone and mid-Ulster' in C. Dillon and H.A. Jefferies (eds), *Tyrone, history and society* (Dublin, 2000), pp 39–54.

Warntjes, Immo, 'The alternation of the kingship of Tara between 734 and 944', *Peritia*, 17–18 (2004), 394–432.

Warren, F.E. (ed.), *The Antiphonary of Bangor: an early Irish manuscript in the Ambrosian Library at Milan* (2 vols, London, 1893).*

Wasserschleben, Hermann (ed.), *Die irische kanonensammlung* (Leipzig, 1885). [CCH]*

Watkins, Calvert, '*Is tre fhír flathemon*: marginalia to *Audacht Morainn*', *Ériu*, 30 (1979), 181–98.

Watkins, Calvert, 'Religion and belief' in Crick and Van Houts (eds), *A social history of England* (2011), pp 265–89.

White Marshall, Jenny and Claire Walsh, *Illaunloughan Island: an early medieval monastery in County Kerry* (Bray, 2005).

Whitehouse, Harvey and Robert N. McCauley (eds), *Mind and religion: psychological and cognitive foundations of religiosity* (Walnut Creek, CA, 2005).

Whitfield, Niamh, 'A suggested function for the holy well?' in Alastair Minnis and Jane Roberts (eds), *Text, images, interpretation: studies in Anglo-Saxon literature and its insular context in honour of Éamonn Ó Carragáin* (Turnhout, 2007), pp 495–513.

Whitfield, Niamh, 'Dress and accessories in the early Irish tale "The Wooing of Becfhola"' in Robert Netherton and Gale R. Owen-Crocker (eds), *Medieval Clothing and Textiles*, 2 (Woodbridge, 2006), pp 1–34.

Whitty, Yvonne and Maeve Tobin, 'Rites in transition: the story told by Holdenstown 1 and 2', *Seanda: NRA Archaeological Magazine*, 4 (2009), 19–21.

Wincott Heckett, Elizabeth, *Viking Age headcoverings from Dublin* (Dublin, 2003).

Winterbottom, Michael (ed.), *Gildas: the ruin of Britain and other works* (Chichester, 1978).

Wood, Ian, 'The audience of architecture in post-Roman Gaul' in L.A.S. Butler and Richard Morris (eds), *The Anglo-Saxon church: papers on history, architecture and archaeology in honour of Dr H.M. Taylor* (London, 1986), pp 74–9.

Wood, Ian, 'Varia: Germanus, Alban and Auxerre', *Bulletin du Centre d'études médiévales d'Auxerre (BCEMA)*, 13 (2009), 123–9.

Wooding, Jonathan M., *Communication and commerce along the western sealanes, AD400–800* (Oxford, 1996).

Woodward, Ann, *Shrines and sacrifices* (London, 1992).

Youngs, Susan (ed.), *'The work of angels': masterpieces of Celtic metalwork, 6th–9th centuries AD* (London, 1989).

ELECTRONIC RESOURCES

www.archaeology.ie	National Monuments Service Archaeological Survey Database, Department of Arts, Heritage and Gaeltacht
www.confessio.ie	St Patrick's Confessio Hypertext Stack, Royal Irish Academy
www.dil.ie	Electronic Dictionary of the Irish Language
www.emap.ie	Early Medieval Archaeology Project, School of Archaeology, University College Dublin
www.excavations.ie	Database of Irish Excavation Reports, Department of Arts, Heritage and Gaeltacht
www.heritagecouncil.ie	Heritage Council of Ireland
www.logainm.ie	Placenames Database of Ireland, The Placenames Branch, Department of Arts, Heritage and Gaeltacht
www.mappingdeathdb.ie	Mapping Death Project, UCD Mícheál Ó Cléirigh Institute, University College Dublin and The Discovery Programme, Dublin
www.monasticon.celt.dias.ie	Database of the Monasticon Hibernicum Project, School of Celtic Studies, Dublin Institute for Advanced Studies
www.nra.ie/archaeology	National Roads Authority Archaeology
www.ucc.ie/celt	Corpus of Electronic Texts, University College Cork

Index